GOUCHER COLLEGE
LIBRARY

THE GIFT OF
THE FRIENDS OF THE LIBRARY
IN MEMORY OF
MARY LOUISE FLEISCHMANN GUTMAN
CLASS OF 1940

Performing Patriotism

EARLY AMERICAN STUDIES

Daniel K. Richter and Kathleen M. Brown, Series Editors

Exploring neglected aspects of our colonial, revolutionary, and early national history and culture, Early American Studies reinterprets familiar themes and events in fresh ways. Interdisciplinary in character, and with a special emphasis on the period from about 1600 to 1850, the series is published in partnership with the McNeil Center for Early American Studies.

A complete list of books in the series is available from the publisher.

Performing Patriotism

National Identity in the Colonial and Revolutionary American Theater

JASON SHAFFER

PENN

University of Pennsylvania Press

Philadelphia

Copyright © 2007 University of Pennsylvania Press

All rights reserved. Except for brief quotations used for purposes of review or scholarly citation, none of this book may be reproduced in any form by any means without written permission from the publisher.

Published by
University of Pennsylvania Press
Philadelphia, Pennsylvania 19104-4112

Printed in the United States of America on acid-free paper

10 9 8 7 6 5 4 3 2 1

A Cataloging-in-Publication record is available from the Library of Congress

ISBN-13: 978-0-8122-4024-5
ISBN-10: 0-8122-4024-3

792.0973
S525p
2007

*To my parents, Tom and Linda Shaffer,
and in memory of my grandparents
Ray and Minnie Cook*

Sure never was picture more drawn to the life,
Or affectionate husband more fond of his wife,
Than America copies and loves Britain's sons,
Who conscious of freedom, are as bold as great guns,
Hearts of oak are we still, for we're sons of these men,
Who always are ready, steady, boys, steady,
To fight for their freedom again and again.

—*"Song for the Sons of Liberty in the Several American Provinces"*

Contents

Prologue   1

1. Theater, Nation, and State in Early America   10

2. Cato and Company: A Genealogy of Performance   30

3. Free-Born Peoples: The Politics of Professional Theater in Early America   66

4. A School for Patriots: Colonial College Theater   105

5. Bellicose Letters: Propaganda Plays of the Revolution   138

Epilogue: Post-Revolutionary Patriotism and the American Theater   166

Notes   179

Index   219

Acknowledgments   229

Prologue

Over the long July Fourth holiday weekend in 2000, *The Patriot*, one of the action movie star Mel Gibson's periodic forays into costume drama, premiered in multiplex theaters across the United States.[1] Like Gibson's earlier movie *Braveheart* (1995), which was based on the legend of the medieval Scottish rebel William Wallace, *The Patriot* features Gibson as an insurrectionist, a frontier partisan waging a guerilla war from the margins against the corrupt English imperial center. In *The Patriot*, Gibson plays an American revolutionary, Benjamin Martin, also known among the British officer corps as "The Ghost." Martin is loosely based on two American patriot officers from the southern colonies: Brigadier General Francis Marion, "The Swamp Fox," a legendarily elusive guerilla commander from South Carolina whose band of partisans was noted for its use of guerilla tactics against the British, and Brigadier General Daniel Morgan, a Virginia officer known for his physical courage, his common touch with enlisted soldiers, and his use of tactical deception in engineering the American victory at the battle of the Cowpens in 1781.[2]

The film's depiction of the American Revolution articulates a series of dramatic and cultural conventions common in eighteenth-century America while also, perhaps quite unintentionally, reflecting a number of trends in scholarship of the Revolutionary era. Although *The Patriot* is indisputably a "popcorn" movie that takes significant liberties with early American history, its melodramatic revisions of that history yield some surprising connections to the ways that the participants in that history viewed themselves, as well as the ways that those who study them today view the Revolution and the culture that gave rise to it. The film is by no means a reliable document of Revolutionary history, but it captures many important elements of the mythology of the Revolution—both as that mythology was fashioned in the eighteenth century, and as it is refashioned now by scholars and purveyors of popular historical narratives.

While both of Benjamin Martin's historical models were enthusiastic partisans, Gibson's character, a South Carolinian planter with a modest estate and a member of the provincial assembly, is at best a reluctant revolutionary. He is a widower, the audience quickly learns, an essentially private man wholly devoted to his five children and his land (which he tills himself, aided, implausibly, by free black laborers). Like both Marion and Morgan, however, Martin is a veteran of the Seven Years' War, having fought in the southern conflict of 1760–61 known as "The Cherokee War." As soldiers in this gruesome campaign, Martin and his men massacred a combined force of French and Cherokees in retaliation for their having slain a group of British colonials, including women and children. Martin's retiring ways seem to stem, in no small part, from his lingering guilt over this incident, which he conceals from his children.

The war's impact on Martin and his secrecy about his violent past are emblematized by a tomahawk, which he keeps in a small chest under his bed. The tomahawk, when considered in light of the increasing importance to early Americanist scholarship of representations of Native Americans, also symbolizes the complex identity position occupied by both the fictional Martin and the real generation of Seven Years' War veterans that led the Continental Army, including George Washington. As a trophy taken from the defeated Cherokee enemy, the tomahawk identifies Martin as one of the victorious English while imputing to him some of the traditional Anglo-American republican virtues of stoicism and courage commonly associated by Europeans with Native Americans; as a painful reminder of Martin's own capacity for bloodthirsty violence, it marks him as a colonial, subject to the constant environmental pressure to turn "savage" that caused metropolitan Britons to view colonials with suspicion; as a weapon that Martin eventually turns against the British, it mirrors the appropriation of a "native" identity carried out by patriot activists beginning in the early 1770s as they sought an autochthonous "American" nationality through which to distance themselves from the British, thereby learning to think of themselves as "colonized rather than colonizers."[3]

Despite its wealth of such symbolically powerful (yet largely incidental) historical details, *The Patriot* only rarely acknowledges the potent brew of competing allegiances and identities that its characters must balance in the performance of everyday life during a time of political crisis that yokes together the global and the local. The importance of the Seven Years' War to the origins of the Revolution is not touched upon, and non-Anglo-American peoples such as the Cherokee, the thirteen colonies' vast slave (and smaller free black) population, and even the French act chiefly as window dressing for the film's transatlantic feud between true-born Englishmen.[4] *The Patriot* opens in mid-1775, after the outbreak of hostilities between colonials and British troops at Lexington and Concord in April of that year. Martin receives a summons to attend a meeting of the colonial assembly and rides off to Charleston; there, the assembly considers a request for troops and funds from the Continental Congress, and Charleston's streets flicker at night with blazing effigies burnt in political protests.

Martin, however, speaks out against the muster. He pointedly asks an old comrade-in-arms from the Cherokee War, now an emissary from the Congress (played by the grizzled Chris Cooper), "Why should I trade one tyrant three thousand miles away for three thousand tyrants one mile away?" and vows not to serve in an insurgency. Martin's political ambivalence, as displayed by both his libertarian rhetoric and his fear of his own capacity for violence, becomes the central obstacle that the plot must overcome in both its hero and its Martin/Gibson-identifying audience in order to impose a new "American" identity on the surviving cast members at the film's conclusion. Ironically, Martin's paradoxical question to his old comrade, which betrays a radical mistrust of government, also echoes a statement famously made by the Bostonian Tory Reverend Mather Byles, while observing a massive funeral procession for victims of the Boston Massacre.[5]

In a surprising twist on the depictions of filial rebellion common to representations, both British and American, of the Revolution as a revolt of colonial "sons" against a mother country and a paternalist king, Martin's public adherence to his status as a private citizen enrages his eldest son, Gabriel (played by young heartthrob Heath Ledger).[6] Accusing his father of cowardice, Gabriel enlists in the Continental Army. When Gabriel suddenly reappears at home, and on the run from the British after a battle near Martin's estate, Benjamin Martin can no longer maintain his neutralist stance. As Martin tends to both the British and the American wounded, the brutal British Colonel Tavington (Jason Isaacs) and his dragoons enter the scene, executing American troops, impressing Martin's free black laborers, capturing Gabriel, and killing Martin's second son, Thomas (Gregory Smith), in cold blood. (Tavington is an obvious stand-in for Lieutenant Colonel Banastre Tarleton, a British dragoon infamous for offering no quarter in battle to the Continentals, and a fierce campaigner in Lord Cornwallis's assault on the Carolinas.)[7] Before leaving, Tavington sets fire to Martin's house; Martin responds by breaking out his tomahawk and attacking the troop detachment guarding Gabriel, killing them to a man.

The grieving Martin subsequently joins the Continental Army, training his troops in unconventional tactics such as the intentional targeting of officers. (Martin's personal fighting style is unconventional for a European American as well: he uses his tomahawk—though only sparingly—on the battlefield, and throughout the film he melts down Thomas's prized collection of toy British soldiers for ammunition.) Tavington, in response to Martin's asymmetrical tactics, slaughters the families of Martin's men in a series of hideous (and sometimes completely fictional) war crimes—

at one point he burns down a church filled with patriot sympathizers, including women and children—and kills Gabriel Martin, transforming the film into a proxy duel between Martin père and Tavington.[8] This duel concludes during the film's climactic battle scene, an operatic replay of the battle of the Cowpens, where Martin kills Tavington in single combat as the American troops achieve a decisive victory over the British in the southern campaign.

The Patriot touches on a number of American mythologies: the complicated interactions between European and Native Americans, the uprising of the founding generation against monarchy, and the generic demands of late twentieth-century popular cinema. It also, somewhat surprisingly, holds a mirror up to the dominant form of commercial popular entertainment of the late colonial era: the colonial theater. The film, a text that seems fueled by both an ideological impulse and the profit motive, shares important features with many of the British plays that were popular among theater audiences in British North America between the Seven Years' War and the outbreak of the Revolution. These common features include Martin's initial reluctance to sacrifice his privacy and his family to enter the political fray of the Revolution and the symbolically freighted deaths of Martin's sons, who predecease their father by sacrificing themselves for the good of the patriot cause. The cosmopolitan culture of colonial South Carolina, and particularly the fondness of Charleston audiences for the theater, ties these eighteenth-century plays to Gibson's film both aesthetically and historically. Even the film's attempt to recast the multinational, multiracial conflict of the Revolution as a showdown between white Englishmen—despite the "Indian" undertones of Benjamin Martin—mirrors the racial and gender typecasting typical of the patriotic British dramas popular in the colonial theater, where displays of martial valor by property-holding Englishmen were the order of the day.

A South Carolinian assemblyman who attended the Charleston theater as tensions were escalating between Britain and the colonies during the spring of 1774—the last professional season played in North America until the early 1780s—would have been able to witness a number of plays that share key plot elements with *The Patriot* being performed by the American Company of Comedians and its actor-manager, David Douglass.[9] The film's depiction of patriotism as the simultaneous guarding of private liberty and sacrificing of one's own flesh and blood for the public good bears a marked similarity to the political program of Joseph Addison's tragedy *Cato* (1713), the staunchly republican hero of which loses one of his sons in battle and commits suicide rather than surrender to Julius Caesar. Douglass staged this play, described as the most popular literary text in the colonies throughout the eighteenth century, in a performance specially commissioned by the Charleston Masons during the

1774 blockade of Boston in sympathy with the sufferings of the people of Massachusetts.[10]

The spirit of military volunteerism permeates both *The Patriot* and *Cato*, and also *The Recruiting Officer* (1706), one of the most popular British comedies of the eighteenth century and a military-themed farce that Douglass staged by request for an audience of South Carolinian militia in March 1774. Several plays staged by Douglass during the 1774 Charleston season also feature a climactic episode of single combat between a "patriot" character similar to Martin, who risks his life for his country's good, and a remorseless, tyrannical figure akin to Tavington. These plays include Sir William Davenant's Restoration revision of *Macbeth* (1664), Colley Cibber's revised *Richard III* (1700), and Nicholas Rowe's Williamite heroic play *Tamerlane* (1701).

The depictions of patriotic virtue and grandly wicked tyranny in these plays won them widespread popularity in the colonies during periods of war against France in the mid-eighteenth century; it is a testimony to the pliability of the theater, the plays, and the libertarian and patriotic sentiments espoused in the plays that these texts remained popular among Americans (and often among British soldiers!) even as the political ties of the British Atlantic community were beginning to sunder in 1774. The themes of liberty, tyranny, and self-sacrifice that dominate these plays, as well as the character types (or "lines") that typify them—the patriot hero, the bloodthirsty tyrant, and the lamentable victim of tyrannical violence—still influence depictions of heroism in contemporary popular culture, particularly in works that reinvent history. These powerfully allegorical figures, in such revised guises as Benjamin Martin, a Cincinnatus in breeches called from his plow to save the republic; the bloodthirsty British officer, Tavington; and Martin's bookish, adolescent son Thomas, continue to haunt contemporary dramatic representations of patriotism, illustrating the lingering power of eighteenth-century narratives both dramatic and political. This perdurant popularity also reveals a particularly American lust for origins, a desire for imaginative and emotional links to the "founding" period of the nation's history—preferably featuring the sharply defined political morality of eighteenth-century tragedies and modern action films.

The connections between *The Patriot* and eighteenth-century performance culture do not end at the playhouse door. The film also presents a cornucopia of paratheatrical performances, from the street theater of effigy burnings and torch-lit processions to the fluent oratory of Benjamin Martin and the other South Carolina assemblymen. The study of popular ritual and public speaking in the eighteenth century, especially as these media relate to the rise of United States nationalism, has undergone a renaissance in recent years thanks to the efforts of theater historians and other scholars influenced by cultural studies and performance studies.[11] In *The Patriot* occasions for public speech, such as the debate in the colonial assembly during which Martin refuses to fight, provide self-consciously theatrical moments that allow for expressions of civic idealism.

Several of the film's most arresting visual effects, meanwhile, feature staged civic processions and the use of straw and rag effigies common in the folk rituals of the transatlantic British community, such as Guy Fawkes Day and its American cousin, Pope Day. Before the debate scene, for instance, director Roland Emmerich presents a bustling nocturnal street scene, from which his camera retreats slowly to reveal a panoramic view of the colonial capital, with a crowd of torch-bearing patriot partisans in the street and burning effigies of British soldiers and politicians swinging from the city's lampposts, a tableau of political unrest. Similarly, during his military campaign Martin secures the release of American prisoners of war by constructing a group of British "captives" using a telescope, a group of scarecrows, and some captured British uniforms. This episode presents an exercise in both effective public speaking (as Martin convinces Lord Cornwallis to believe the scarecrows are British officers) and effigy making.

Moreover, the film's depictions of war resonate with Gillian Russell's exploration of the interactions between warfare and theatricality in the late eighteenth century: notably, Martin's climactic victory replays Daniel Morgan's tactical misdirection at the Cowpens, where he staged a retreat by "cowardly" colonial militia in order to draw Banastre Tarleton into a trap.[12] The film's most powerful scenes underscore the importance of popular ritual and political oratory to students of eighteenth-century culture; of "theatrical" deception to military maneuvers; and of all these forms of performance to moviemakers anxious for a somewhat long-in-the-tooth Mel Gibson to seem "foxy" in the intellectual sense.

The similarities of plot between *The Patriot* and the dramas popular with colonial Americans and the film's underlying use of such popular performance practices as effigy burning produce a modern narrative that touches on several aspects of the fashioning of early American nationalism from the political culture of Great Britain. Martin and his fellow revolutionaries do not create their revolution ex nihilo: they adapt the culture of the British Atlantic community, including its performance traditions, to the American republican cause. In the words of Benedict Anderson, the militants of the imagined revolutionary community are "creole nationalists" who hold "virtually the same relationship to . . . European culture as the metropolitans" of the homeland, thus affording them "the political, cultural and military means for asserting themselves."[13] Martin's speeches about freedom and tyranny, for instance, sound notes commonly heard in the patriotic plays of the eighteenth-century theater;

they also pay homage to the influence on colonial politics of the British Commonwealth tradition and the parliamentary "Country party" opposition's romantic vision of "British liberty."[14] As Martin wars with His Majesty's armed forces, his rhetoric echoes both the stage and the parliamentary chamber. Popular British dramas and the political ideas that influenced them proved to be equally legible and rhetorically useful to the politically opposed metropolitan Britons and colonials in their disputes over imperial policies throughout the eighteenth century.

I contend that this political literacy shared throughout much of the British Atlantic, along with the susceptibility of theatrical texts—especially those presenting political arguments—to appropriation and redeployment in nontheatrical settings, was a crucial element in the establishment of the practice of theatrical performance in the North American colonies. Eventually such appropriations of texts, both theatrical and polemical, helped to generate an American nationalism that used British culture against itself, invoking both the cultural affinity between the two nations and their irreconcilable political differences. This process of appropriation is realized physically in one of *The Patriot*'s most striking motifs: Martin's smelting of his son's miniature effigies of British soldiers into pistol balls. The complex processes of cultural interchange that still prevail around the Atlantic rim, like the surprisingly porous nature of nations and states made evident in the secession of the North American colonies from Great Britain, undergird such comparatively young academic disciplines as performance studies and Atlantic studies. These new perspectives have drawn attention to previously overlooked aspects of eighteenth-century culture that inform both past and present, exerting an influence capable of shaping even a Hollywood fable of the American Revolution in surprising ways.

The pervasiveness in both eighteenth-century theatrical productions and political rhetoric of the themes of patriotism and tyranny, along with the recurring involvement of men like George Washington with both colonial and revolutionary politics and the colonial theater, guides my attempt to place the performance culture of British North America in the broader context of the politics of the British Atlantic. Because the colonial and revolutionary periods feature rich traditions of professional and amateur theatrical performance, as well as a number of print and paratheatrical forms with attachments to the theater, the ensuing chapters have been arranged by performance media rather than by historical period. This approach, as outlined in the first chapter, allows for a consideration of multiple overlapping media and venues while tracing the overall shift in colonial performance culture from its use in fostering pro-British sentiment to the emergence of its potential for the redeployment of British culture for pro-American purposes during the Revolution.

The second chapter explains the importance to colonial and Revolutionary culture of Joseph Addison's *Cato*, which as already noted was a key part of the colonial repertoire. Addison's play, which has its roots in the War of the Spanish Succession, was greeted upon its premiere in Great Britain with universal accolades from both Whigs and Tories. This popularity translated into great commercial success both in Britain and the colonies, although in the latter venue, the play acquired a tinge of radicalism by its association with the "real Whig" writings of James Trenchard and Thomas Gordon. From *Cato*'s popularity in the colonies springs a figure that I have dubbed the Catonic effigy, a self-sacrificing patriot of great histrionic proficiency and a central figure in the rhetoric of both British and American patriotism during periods of colonial warfare with the French and colonial resistance to British policies. The second chapter tracks the pervasive presence of *Cato* in the political literature of colonial print culture, while also analyzing a group of amateur performances of the play during the Revolutionary period, its intersection with a protest ceremony (known as a "liberty funeral") enacted by colonial patriot activists during the Stamp Act Crisis, and the use of the play by a number of important political figures to mold their public personae, including the executed American spy Nathan Hale, King George III, George Washington, and the revolutionary orator Patrick Henry.

Building on the interconnections between theatrical texts, the ideology of British liberty, and paratheatrical performance, the third chapter addresses more explicitly the relationship between professional theater and the nature of political communities in the British Atlantic by analyzing the history of a number of touring companies in the North American colonies. As the professional theater expanded in the colonies it developed a repertoire of plays, such as *Cato*, *Richard III*, and *Tamerlane*, which fluctuated in popularity during periods of war and political crisis and sometimes disappeared from the stage during periods of hostility to the theater. These plays also overlapped occasionally with colonial street theater, and allusions to them appeared frequently in the colonial newspapers and pamphlets where issues such as war, taxes, and the legitimacy of the colonial theater were debated. The cultural influence of the colonial stage extended far beyond the playhouse door.

The fourth chapter focuses on the neglected tradition of theatrical productions in eighteenth-century North American colleges. Collegiate performances, which were often closely monitored by school officials and occasionally took place despite outright bans on stage plays, were common from midcentury through the Revolutionary period. These theatricals provided students with an opportunity to practice public speaking and glean, from popular works of the British stage, a mastery over accepted forms for the public display of civic virtue. Foresighted educators such as the Reverend William Smith of the College of Philadelphia used the enactment of plays and dramatic dialogues to train their students as effective public speakers and patriotic Britons. Throughout the 1760s and 1770s, young men at colonial colleges and their teachers used drama in order to grasp the sociopolitical upheaval occurring around them, testing both old and new forms of citizenship on the stage.

The didactic practice of the colonial collegiate theater strongly influences the subject of the fifth chapter: a series of propaganda plays written by pro-American partisans during the 1770s. Three such plays, John Leacock's *The Fall of British Tyranny* and Princeton graduate Hugh Henry Brackenridge's *The Death of General Montgomery* and *The Battle of Bunkers-Hill*, were staged by students at Harvard in the early 1780s. Like collegiate theatricals, the propaganda plays of the Revolutionary period have remained largely unstudied, mentioned briefly in histories of American drama but rarely given the detailed scholarly attention they deserve as literary and theatrical expressions of their historical moment. Their topical recreations of current events as propagandistic tales of tyrannical British generals and politicians, self-sacrificing patriot activists, and heroic American officers employ not only snippets of popular British dramas, but also, frequently, the iconography of British military and political martyrdom itself. These plays dress the revolutionary efforts of American colonials in decidedly British borrowed robes, using the patriotic spectacle of the British theater and the spectacular violence of British political history to promote a radical "American" patriotism.

With the achievement of American independence and the subsequent ratification of the Constitution, a new problem arose in early American culture—how to join the spirit of the Revolution with the new social realities of the established federal republic and the emerging urban commercial order. The epilogue addresses the postwar representation of heroic American patriotism in the professional theater by analyzing Royall Tyler's *The Contrast*, the first major play written by an American author for the post-Revolutionary stage. By fusing the ostentatious republican forms of public speech and behavior of the Revolutionary period with the world of postwar commerce and the British comedy of manners, Royall Tyler attempts a revision of the earlier, and somewhat outmoded, cultural forms of the Revolutionary era—themselves largely fashioned from older British traditions—by inserting them into the urban milieu of the new republic. Such repetition with revision extends into both the past and future, as evidenced both by the enthusiasm of British North Americans for the appropriation and reinterpretation of metropolitan performance traditions and theatrical texts, and by our own ongoing reconstruction of the Revolution in the era of Mel Gibson, the bestsellers of Joseph J. Ellis, and the History Channel.

Chapter 1
Theater, Nation, and State in Early America

Sources, Influences, and Methods

American theater history has become an increasingly prominent field of study in the past two decades, in no small measure because of the efforts of theater scholars working in a number of different historical periods to join in a reevaluation of the meaning of "American" identities.[1] Much of the earliest work in American theater history to develop this approach has been carried out by scholars of the nineteenth-century theater, but in recent years scholars working on the early republican and colonial eras have begun to flesh out the cultural significance of American theater during their respective periods as well.[2] This book attempts to contribute to that ongoing effort by examining the role of the theater in propagating patriotism, both British and American, in the colonial population of North America, thereby tracing an important aspect of the role of performance in the political life of Americans before and during the Revolution.

The groundwork for this investigation has been laid by a number of scholars whose work explores the circulation of performances and the changing public perception of the theater in the British Atlantic during the eighteenth century. Jeffrey Richards, for instance, has argued that early American culture is saturated with the figure of the theater. Richards maintains that the religious and political lives of even the most staunchly anti-theatrical American colonials were informed by a performative ethos—the trope of the *theatrum mundi*, or world stage—that led public men in British America, especially such prominent American revolutionaries as John Adams and George Washington, to draw on dramatic texts for political purposes in their writings and to comport themselves as actors on the public "stage" during the American Revolution. Public men thus viewed themselves as "heroes of the tragedy then playing on the Theater of Action."[3] Richards also outlines the ways in which theatrical metaphors and texts provided civic affairs in early America with "an instantly recognized symbolic language, whose proper frame, the stage, confers an imaginative power to otherwise quotidian acts" (237).

Richards is not alone in emphasizing the longstanding ties between the theater and Anglo-American intellectual history. In *Worlds Apart,*

Jean-Christophe Agnew explores the co-evolution of capitalist markets and professional theaters, institutions with the power to destabilize and rearrange individual identities and social structures, in Great Britain and the American colonies from the Renaissance to the mid-eighteenth century. Agnew's study regrettably concludes in 1750, just as the professional theater was beginning to establish roots in the North American colonies, which leads him to underplay the importance of the theater itself in the colonies. Agnew argues that the British plays produced by touring companies in North America were ill-suited to their audiences, too lacking in "local topics, local idiom, or local inflections" for the colonies, where society was "too young and colonial authority too brittle to countenance the collective public dreamwork" of a professional theater. Nonetheless the growing wealth of the North American colonies, the desire of colonials for the prestige of "British" goods such as theatrical performances, and the skilled marketing of theater managers like David Douglass led to the establishment of a vibrant professional theater in the colonies.[4] The establishment of a commercial theater, in fact, suggests that colonial theatergoers often went to the theater *not* to see "local" material but to consume a luxury commodity and to see texts that would reinforce their own sense of connection to the metropole. As Kathleen Wilson observes, "colonial as well as English theaters functioned as sites for the definition, performance and dissemination of Englishness" and as "part of the effort to transplant English culture to Britain's colonial possessions."[5]

The portability of the theater and the performativity of national identity are crucial to Joseph Roach's theory of circum-Atlantic cultural exchange. In *Cities of the Dead*, Roach argues that Atlantic societies "have invented themselves by performing their pasts for others." This process most commonly takes place as improvisation, the appropriation and revision of preexisting forms, thereby also allowing circum-Atlantic cultures to define themselves by performing "what and who they thought they were not."[6] The physical and cultural colonization of the Americas by Europeans, including the exportation of patriotic British plays to the colonial stage and other transfers of cultural goods to the creole populations of the colonies, facilitated the invention of "British America" and a panoply of liminal characters known as "British Americans." Such characters ranged from West Indian sugar planters, who moved easily in the society of metropolitan London, to the hard-bitten descendants of Interregnum republicans in New England, who sheltered three of the judges who signed the death warrant of King Charles I in a cave at West Rock in New Haven.[7] The processes of appropriation, revision, and counterperformance outlined in Roach's theories of Atlantic cultural syncretism allowed British North Americans, relegated to the margins of the British colonial system, to reinvent themselves in new hybrid identities such as the American patriot activist: a British subject and an inhabitant of North America, culturally "British" but self-consciously colonial and "American," defiantly asserting both his rights as an Englishman and his fervent desire not to be held subject to the government of Englishmen.

In the case of British North America, these performance practices, especially in the case of the theater, tended to produce texts that illustrate the importance of collective forgetting, another key component of circum-Atlantic culture.[8] The performance texts latched onto by British North Americans generally depict a "pure" British genealogy for the colonies. These texts commonly reshape the circum-Atlantic rim of Europe, Africa, and the Americas into a transatlantic line between London and the North American colonies and repress the presence of African slaves, native peoples, and non-anglophone European populations in the Americas. As if simply acknowledging the racial and ethnic mélange of the Americas threatened their British identity, the colonials seem to have attempted to perform the origins of a society that was as white and that spoke as much English as possible.[9] Because this book will focus on the cultural influence of professional and amateur theater in the colonies—a cultural practice produced chiefly by and for white, property-holding males—and the texts popular in these theaters, its analysis will necessarily be limited in large part to their effects on those individuals who possessed the cultural authority to comment on the various controversies surrounding both colonial politics and the colonial theater, and who had access to the media through which these topics were debated: the pulpit, political platforms both official and informal, and the printing press.

This overview of colonial performance, then, will follow a relatively conservative transatlantic model of cultural exchange. Such studies of colonial and Revolutionary culture have in recent years been written by a number of scholars whose works illustrate the complicated nature of the colonial ethos of performance even within a demographically limited frame of reference. Jay Fliegelman, in his history of the "elocutionary revolution" in oratory in the eighteenth century, observes that the quest of British and American teachers of rhetoric for a more "natural" form of speech led to "a new social dramaturgy" that helped to spread revolutionary republicanism in America through the charisma of public speakers, whose performances displayed "the . . . internal drama of republicanism, in which the citizen's double identity as sovereign (part of the authorizing people) and as subject (one of the governed) endlessly contend."[10] In addition, historians of parades and processions such as David Waldstreicher, Simon P. Newman, and Peter Shaw have revealed the complex means by which patriot activists reconfigured performance traditions imported from Britain and turned them into new forms of political protest that could be transmitted to radicals in other colonies via protest coverage in radical newspapers, thereby generating a circulating set of performances that established "a dynamic relationship between local street theater, print culture, and the imagined community of the Revolutionary American nation."[11]

Indeed, so pervasive has the trope of performance become that even a scholar of print culture such as Michael K. Warner, who contends that the "civic and emancipatory" nature of print communication in the British public sphere produced an American Revolution "largely undertaken by writers," has incorporated the idea of oral performance into his work, noting the remarkable degree to which many American colonials "insisted on seeing writing as a form of speaking"—a form of revolutionary performance rooted in British pamphleteering and political reportage.[12] Yet despite the increasing concern with performance in studies of colonial political culture, the theater itself has rarely been explored as a vehicle either for the propagation of British patriotism in the far-flung colonies of North America or for the dissemination of the principles of the American patriot movement. The intimate relationship between stage and state, an idea familiar to students of the British metropolitan theaters, has not yet been fully developed in the study of early American culture.[13]

American theater historians have from the start been aware of the political ramifications of the strong institutional ties between the North American theater in the eighteenth century and the systems of political, intellectual, and economic interchange operating between Britain and the Americas. The first historian of the early American theater, the theater manager and playwright William Dunlap, articulated the problem of establishing a national theater in the post-Revolutionary United States as one of overcoming the lingering influence of seventeenth-century British republicanism in the United States. The theater's champions in America, Dunlap claims, had to overcome the anti-theatrical biases of "our enlightened ancestors Hampden, Pym, Vane, Milton, and their glorious companions" in the British Commonwealth.[14] Subsequent historians have frequently discovered possible connections between theatrical performances—both professional performances and those conducted by amateurs—and local political conditions in the colonies, such as boycotts of the theater by patriot activists or patronage of the theater by colonial officials. Historians of the written American drama, for their part, have frequently attempted to situate the fledgling efforts of American dramatists, including a series of propaganda dialogues and plays related to the Revolution, within the rising nationalism among North American creoles.[15]

These studies, however, remain incomplete. While scholars have documented a number of interactions between theater and politics in North America, their studies have heretofore often focused on the history of professional theater in North America as an artistic, rather than a civic, institution. As Odai Johnson notes, this approach—influenced by the relative paucity of records other than those of the legal variety—has led scholars mistakenly to treat the theater not as a popular commercial institution subject to a vigorous public debate, but as "an unlawful and unauthorized entity struggling to gain legitimacy in the social landscape of colonial America."[16] This interpretive strategy is challenged by the evidence of "large permanent playhouses . . . built by subscriptions of sizeable audiences . . . six-nights-a-week performances" and "six-hundred-copy runs of playbills."[17] Such histories have also focused on the essential task of preserving the limited archives of documentary evidence for colonial theater. This necessary focus on preservation has left open to further study the interaction of the theatrical repertoire with the politicized print culture of the colonies, the development of patriot and loyalist propaganda plays and dialogues during the 1770s, and the popularity of theatrical performances—which often contained explicitly patriotic political messages—in colonial American colleges, the self-described incubators of British American statesmen.[18]

Ideally, a study of the early American theater would explicate the patriotic appeal of theatrical texts in both their printed and written form, from the deployment of dramatic texts in colonial political literature to the rise of revolutionary propaganda composed for both page and stage, and from performances carried out by professionals capitalizing on local political conditions to those staged by college students training for prominent roles in the theater of colonial public affairs. Such a study would document both the roots of popular British plays in the politicized London theater and the changes in meaning introduced by their reproduction in colonial theaters, marking at each stage the changing political valences of these stereotypically "British" texts.[19] Examining theatrical performance in British North America through the lenses of print culture, popular performance, and contemporary political rhetoric, the theater historian can discover nodal points in the culture of the British Atlantic where theatrical performances and dramatic texts emerge as "an instantly recognized symbolic language" legible to both colonial and Briton, or to revolutionary and loyalist.[20]

This symbolic language bridges the gap between print and oral media. As Julie Stone Peters has noted, the printing press was critical to the growth of the theater in Europe. By the eighteenth century, she observes, "Drama was understood to play itself in two arenas—on the stage and on the page"; dramatic texts increasingly provided staging details to aid the print audience in reconstructing stage performances, and playwrights increasingly began to identify the "republic of letters" to which they addressed their works with the specific national identities of their reading and theatrical audiences.[21] In 1760, as professional theater began to take a firm hold in the North American colonies, the Philadelphia printer Andrew Steuart began to print editions of popular plays for colonial consumption, a supplement to the supply of imported playbooks already available from colonial booksellers.[22] Colonial newspapers, which carried theatrical advertisements, the missives of pro- and anti-theatrical partisans, and political commentary laced with references to popular drama, contributed to this intermingling of the theatrical and the political in colonial culture. The availability of both live theatrical performances and playbooks joined with the power of newspapers (and other elements of the print culture that drew on popular theatrical texts, such as almanacs and political pamphlets) to bring the "British" institution of the theater, as well as news from London and other corners of the empire, to the colonies. This cultural transfusion helped to produce a sense of patriotic identification, however mediated, among North American colonials with Great Britain.[23]

This model of a community bound together by the theater, whether on the stage or the page, bears certain similarities to the print-based colonial public envisioned by Warner. Warner posits a depersonalized print discourse capable of creating a community even among distant, unacquainted, and potentially radically unlike readers. In this abstract community drawn together by print, individual benefit is subsumed within the public's devotion to rational argument and the common good, and the discursive limitations of individual speakers' communal standings are overcome by anonymity and the printed page's potentially infinite number of unknowable readers. Warner supposes that the same principles "could doubtless be translated to oral settings, as long as people agreed to behave as though they were being supervised by an indefinite number of others, any one of whom might occupy their own position irrespective of status."[24]

For anyone familiar with the experience of being an audience member in a theater (or even at a political rally), Warner's sense of a print community should resonate. Tensions between individual and collective response, and between spectatorship and participation, underlie the interchangeable positions upon which his model of the reading public depends. In much the same way, an audience member at a performance is caught between his own individual reactions and the collective reaction of the group, and between his sense of spectatorial distance from the actions onstage and the constant invitations issued by both performer and script to identify with those actions. (Hence the inexhaustible supply of theatrical anecdotes about neophyte theatergoers—almost always male—rushing the stage to save the hero or the damsel in distress.) The communities formed by actors and audience members for a performance, like communities based in print, construct themselves around a distinction between those who can identify with the action of the performance and grasp its meaning—for whom the text is legible—and those who cannot—for whom the performance is alien and therefore, at best, only partly legible. Warner argues that gaining admission to the self-abnegating republic of print, with its devotion to pure reason and the public good, implied—since white male citizens dominated the consumption of printed matter—a privileged standing within the colonial community of readers, who in theory could be of any age, race, or gender, disguised under the cover of print. So too could the colonial theater, and the related fields of folk performance and oratory, give rise to any number of communities based on knowledge of the relevant texts: the theatrical public, the participants and spectators of civic rituals such as Pope Day processions, the audiences for popular political orators, or even those capable of deciphering theatrical allusions in the print culture.

Oral performance, it should be noted, precludes its audiences from indulging in the same negation of personal qualities that Warner argues was available to colonial print audiences at least in theory, if not in practice. Early American audience members, theatrical or otherwise, surely could not have avoided noticing their own relative position in the socioeconomic hierarchy of theater seating, their personal history with the speechifying local politician, the identities and reputations of the men burning a hated colonial official in effigy, or even the fact that a theater in Williamsburg or Philadelphia was not ancient Rome or a London drawing room. It is a particular quality of successful performances, however, to draw audience members together into a collective identity that somehow negates, if only partially and temporarily, the obvious differences between them. The imagined communities of both the British Atlantic and the patriotic union of rebellious American colonies, in a very real sense, were created both within, and according to the logic of, the playhouse.

Stage and State: The Patriot Theater

The colonial theater helped to form first a colonial British, and later a revolutionary American, imagined community. Beyond the general principle of "patriotism," which as Kathleen Wilson notes could be used as a mask for a number of party positions in the eighteenth century, what sort of principles did these communities share?[25] Based on the current scholarly consensus about the politics of colonial and Revolutionary America, the answer would seem to be "republicanism," a term that embraces both seventeenth-century Commonwealth political theorists and eighteenth-century "Country" party proponents of the mixed British constitution. As Annabel Patterson observes, quoting John Adams, "there is not a more unintelligible word in the English language," and "republicanism" has become "a grab-bag for ideas of civic virtue and disinterestedness."[26] The earliest observers of American theater culture, however, do display a concern for the connection between American theaters, American independence, and republicanism. William Dunlap, who frequently comes off in his *History* as an aging Federalist adrift in populist Jacksonian America, longs for a theater "induced by our republican institutions" but retains a claim to "the works of the dramatists before the Restoration of Charles the Second," which "are ours, as *much ours*, being the descendants of Englishmen, as if our fathers had never left the country in which they were written. We may say the same of the philosophy of Milton, and Locke, and Newton."[27]

Alexis de Tocqueville maintains in *Democracy in America*, "The Puritan founders of the American republics were not only hostile to all pleasures but professed a special abhorrence for the stage. They thought it an abominable amusement, and so long as their principles prevailed without question, the drama was wholly unknown among them."[28] Dunlap holds that an American theater should be an aesthetic extension of an unbroken line of bona fide English republicanism stretching back to Milton, whom Dunlap incidentally hails as a great playwright. For Dunlap, the suppression of English theater during the Interregnum illustrates how far short of the republican ideal the parliamentary forces in the English civil war actually fell.[29] (Moreover, Dunlap's vision of republicanism flirts with the inclusion of the individualist liberal John Locke.) For de Tocqueville, who unhelpfully uses New England as a synecdoche for the entire country, the evolution of nineteenth-century theater seems to suggest a move away from the crude (and coincidentally anti-theatrical) tastes of the founding period toward a more cosmopolitan form of republicanism.

In both cases, Dunlap and de Tocqueville find themselves struggling to resolve the apparent contradiction between the anti-theatricality of the classical republican tradition as practiced in England—and, as de Tocqueville implies, in at least some of the American colonies—and their own belief in the importance of theater to a free society. De Tocqueville even suggests that the theater is an artistic barometer for widespread political change: "If you want advance knowledge of the literature of a people which is turning toward democracy, pay attention to the theater," he writes, since there "the crowd can enjoy sights on the stage more easily than any other form of literature."[30] Moreover, de Tocqueville sees in the American theater something akin to the patriotic republican stage envisioned by Dunlap, noting that democratic audiences with "little reverence" for classical learning "want the talk [on stage] to be about themselves and to see the present world mirrored" (490). Dunlap's vision of republicanism is muddied by his enthusiasm for Locke, whom proponents of the republican thesis have excommunicated from colonial American culture; de Tocqueville's vision appears to be blurred by his historical position as an observer of populist Jacksonian democracy and by a French heritage of stylized academic drama that died in England with the Stuart court masque and never really reached colonial America.[31] Georgian Englishmen, in London or in New York, always went to the theater precisely to see something with which they identified.

But the question remains unanswered. Did the ideas presented in the theater, through which colonials could identify themselves as patriotic British subjects, qualify as "republican" ones? Certainly the dominant political language of the stage, as well as the political culture, of the colonies stressed civic idealism and service to one's country. Yet as Annabel Patterson observes, many colonial patriots, such as John Adams, read widely in the classical republican, Commonwealth, and liberal traditions. Joyce Appleby argues that "republican" rhetoric of civic idealism was used by the British Country party to unite its sometimes disagreeing factions, and she notes that colonial citizens had access to a political vocabulary of rights-based, individualist liberalism as well as the vocabulary of republican sacrifice. Isaac Kramnick identifies four forms of political discourse at play in eighteenth-century America: republicanism, liberalism, Protestant theology rooted in the "work ethic," and theories of sovereignty centered on state power.[32] The political allegiances of the playwrights whose work was displayed in the colonial theater show a similar diversity.

In the 1774 Charleston season alone, for instance, Douglass's American Company displayed plays by the Stuart-apologist Tory John Dryden, the Williamite-apologist Whig Nicholas Rowe, the pro-Walpole Court Whig Colley Cibber, and the anti-Walpole Tory John Gay. A profusion of political positions, often decades out of date in relation to current affairs, were on display in the colonial theater as well as in the broader political discussions taking place in the colonies. Consequently, I will continue to describe the mixed ideology that dominates the political discourse of the colonial and Revolutionary theater as "patriotism," and its adherents across the metropolitan and colonial political spectrum as "patriots." In addition to providing refuge for scoundrels, the term is capacious enough to contain a broad range of party positions and philosophical traditions, as well as both the British and Revolutionary identities of North Americans.

Certainly the anti-theatrical rhetoric of the colonial era was tinged with republican concerns for the moral health of the body politic, concerns that Ann Fairfax Withington traces to the anxieties expressed about the influence of public theaters during the Roman republic.[33] Yet by the late seventeenth century such "republican" arguments about the theater's moral influence on the viewing public could be made by even the Reverend

Jeremy Collier, an arch-royalist minister who complained that the scurrility of contemporary plays did not fulfill the essential function of the theater: "to recommend Virtue, and discountenance Vice; To shew the Uncertainty of human Greatness, the suddain Turns of Fate, and the Unhappy Conclusions of Violence and Injustice."[34] And although he urges strict censorial control over the moral content of plays, lest impressionable audience members fall prey to bad examples, Collier acknowledges the theater's potential as an institution for civic improvement.

The champions of the eighteenth-century British theater, meanwhile, adumbrated a model of the theater that would spread the tenets of civic virtue and British patriotism among playgoers. The playwright George Farquhar, author of *The Recruiting Officer*, presages de Tocqueville in his "Essay on Comedy" by arguing that the British playwright's business "is not to hold forth to ancient Greece, nor to moralize upon the Vices and Defaults of the Roman Commonwealth: No, no—An English Play is intended for the Use and Instruction of an English Audience, a People not only separated from the rest of the World by Situation, but different also from other Nations in the Complexion and Temperament of the Natural Body, as in the Body Politick."[35] Farquhar's case for a didactic theater suited to the "constitution" of English audiences prefigures the argument of his contemporary Sir Richard Steele, founder of the London periodical *The Tatler* and co-founder with Joseph Addison of *The Spectator*. Steele muses in *The Tatler*, while meditating on the funeral of the great Restoration actor Thomas Betterton, that "[t]here is no Human Invention so aptly calculated for the forming [of] a Free-born people as that of a Theatre . . . Hence it is, that I extremely lament the little Relish the Gentry of this Nation have at present for the just and noble Representations in some of our Tragedies," from which spectators might learn "to speak justly, and move gracefully."[36]

In the colonies, opponents of the theater not only railed against plays' supposed tendencies to "debauch the Minds and corrupt the Morals" of its audiences but also against the possible fiscal threat posed by the theater to local governments and to denizens of the lower social orders easily charmed out of their cash. During 1761, one anti-theatrical partisan in New York referred to the professional theater as "laying a heavy tax on the City, to maintain a Set of Vagrants that are of no use to Society," while during the economic downturn of 1768 another New Yorker lamented the sight of tradesmen and the poor, who might well have received charitable donations from their fellow citizens, "throw[ing] their money away on Play-tickets!"[37] As Kramnick observes, the virtue of frugality certainly belonged to the republican tradition, but it could also be found in the writings of liberal economists and the champions of Protestant work ethic theology, suggesting that the debate over the theater's role in colonial society, though heavily influenced by republicanism, extended beyond the republican conception of society.[38]

Pro-theater partisans such as the actor-manager David Douglass, meanwhile, advocated the theater's power to improve its spectators in language echoing a Whiggish concern with the refinement of manners, the paternalistic concern with public virtue of colonial republicanism, and the deference accorded to English literature in the colonies. Douglass, advertising subscriptions to build a new theater in Annapolis in 1770, opined, "A well-regulated Theatre has been allowed by men of liberal sentiments, in all ages, and in all countries . . . to be a noble institution: calculated, according to Addison, for the improvement and refinement of human society; to be the most rational entertainment an enlarged mind can enjoy; and of the utmost utility to the Commonwealth, by polishing the manners, and forming the taste of the people."[39]

Douglass invokes the name of a prominent English social critic and the author of a popular tragedy, a man with a reputation for Whiggish patriotism and scrupulous morality who had also been dead for decades, in order to impress his colonial subscribers. He might well have invoked Addison's collaborator Steele in turn, reminding his subscribers that the patriotic spectacle of the British theater could not only form "the taste of the people" but also serve as the basis for the formation of a "Free-born people," a performance not unlike the act of collective improvisation that would shortly give rise to the United States.

Civic Violence: Bloodshed on the Atlantic Stage

One of the most important elements of the eighteenth-century theater's power to reinforce political bonds is its capacity to represent ritual political violence. Writing to Colonel William Stephens Smith, son-in-law to John Adams, with regard to Shays' Rebellion, Thomas Jefferson inquires, "What country can preserve its liberties if their rulers are not warned from time to time that their people preserve the spirit of resistance? . . . What signify a few lives lost in a century or two?"[40] Jefferson seeks a solution to two fundamental challenges of his era: how to preserve a revolutionary spirit while establishing a post-revolutionary government, and how to defend a political ideal—liberty—that seems to be in perpetual retreat from the inevitable onset of corruption and the machinations of encroaching statesmen.[41] Jefferson finds his answer in periodic shows of force and flourishes of bloodshed. The expenditure of human life in defense of liberty, Jefferson posits, braces the will of the people to defend their rights while warning off the ambitions of their leaders, allowing for a renewal of civic purity, the status quo ante bellum, before decay inevitably returns. Always ready with an earthy metaphor, Jefferson famously concludes, "The tree of liberty must be refreshed from time to time with the blood of patriots and tyrants. It is its natural manure."

The theater as a medium was uniquely qualified to reproduce such symbolic incidents of bloodshed. Because individual performances cannot be repeated, a violent death depicted onstage is as unique as our own death; yet theatrical deaths, despite the uniqueness of each performance, are infinitely reproducible and can be repeated as often and in as many different locales as actors and audiences can be found for them. (The contingencies of live theater and other rituals also provide a richer meaning to the experience than, say, an annual viewing of *The Patriot*, which is regularly re-aired on Memorial Day and the Fourth of July, since, once recorded, the filmed text of the actors' performances never changes.) Theatrical violence is also more readily choreographed to convey a specific political message than the violence that occurs during the chaos of a political uprising. The path to martyrdom on the stage is (usually) less fraught with contingencies than death on a battlefield or after a political show trial, although the cathartic effect of such theatrical displays, as in the death of Gabriel Martin or Colonel Tavington in *The Patriot*, follows the same guidelines.

The destruction of tyrants and patriots, whether in a Jeffersonian political upheaval or on the stage of David Douglass's American Company, presents a ritual of civic renewal that follows Rene Girard's theory of sacrificial violence, in which a community ritually sacrifices one member, often drawn from the social margins of the group, as a surrogate for the whole community. In Girard's model, "The surrogate victim dies so that the entire community, threatened by the same fate, can be reborn in a new or renewed cultural order . . . [T]he god, ancestor, or mythic hero . . . dies himself or selects a victim to die in his stead. In doing so he bestows a new life on men."[42] The "death" of an actor onstage, like that of Girard's sacrificial victim—a figure at once in the center of the audience's collective imagination and on the margins of its collective identity—offers a spectacle from which sentiments of patriotic fellow-feeling can spring. The portability of the theater allows these same spectacles to be recreated, and these patriotic feelings to be engendered, across distances as vast as those between Great Britain and North America, or between Boston and Charleston.

Jefferson's observation that the "tree of liberty" must be fertilized with the blood of both patriots and tyrants touches upon an important point in the relationship between the politics of the British Atlantic and its professional theaters, and an essential aspect of the drama's power as a tool both for the propagation of British patriotism in North America and for the growth of colonial opposition to British policies. Tyrants and patriots do not exist in isolation, either in politics or in the theater, but in a much broader cast of characters. In studying the interactions of politics and performance in colonial North America this book will address with particular interest a trio of characters common in British polemical and dramatic literature during the long eighteenth century: the tyrant, the sacrificial victim, and the patriot. The interlocking nature of these three figures yields what might be called a drama of patriotism, whether that term is defined at a given moment as loyalty to the status quo or as a desire to overturn it. When these figures spring from the page to the stage, either inside or outside a playhouse, the theatrical violence generated by their interrelationships emerges as what Roach refers to as an effigy, "a set of actions that hold open a place in memory into which many different people may step according to circumstances and occasions."[43]

These characters have genealogies as complex as those of the communities they sustain, lineages rendered ambiguous by the tendency of these figures to blend with one another or to exchange positions, sometimes in surprising ways. The tyrant figure, for instance, was a bugbear of the English stage long before the first Anglophone colony existed in North America, but in the theater as in politics the definition of a "tyrant" tends to shift with prevailing political winds.[44] After the execution of Charles I, for instance, English Royalists began an extensive recuperation of his image as that of a royal martyr; John Barrell, meanwhile, notes in his study of depictions of regicide in late eighteenth-century Britain that even Britons who supported the French Revolution as a justified uprising against a tyrannical monarchy were "almost as susceptible to the pathos" of the execution of Louis XVI as their anti-Jacobin opponents.[45]

The grisly public spectacles of royal executions, in conjunction with the royalist reinvention of Charles I as the Beloved Martyr that preceded the American Revolution and the sentimental recuperation of the French monarchy by British conservatives that followed it, afford a decidedly ambiguous lesson in the "uncertainty of human greatness," Jeremy Collier's formula for theatrical morality. The fungible, malleable nature of the royal image—the utility of depictions of monarchy in distress for stirring both radical and reactionary sentiments—along with the liberties both Whigs and Tories took in bandying the term about in eighteenth-century political writings and the perennial temptations of political power toward arbitrariness, threaten at times to rob the word "tyrant" of any specific meaning. As Girard observes of the Greek tragedies, "Tyranny . . . is essentially unstable. A newcomer can ascend unexpectedly to the very summit of power, only to plummet, while one of his opponents assumes his lost position. In short, there is always a tyrant and an oppressed, but the roles alternate."[46]

The exact definition of "tyranny" at any given point in the eighteenth century, then, except as the defining Other of patriotic partisan rhetoric, can be lost in the intricacies of political maneuvering that form the melodrama of conspiracy and statecraft. The equally slippery definition of Anglo-American "liberty," especially as it is to be defined according to the political syncretism practiced by the colonial American radical community, renders decoding the meanings of "tyranny" and "liberty" in early American texts particularly difficult. The different motivations that frequently drew various interest groups in colonial communities, from merchants to sailors and artisans, into conflict with the policies of the crown further confuse any attempt to define these terms in context. During the Stamp Act Crisis, one cynical (or perhaps simply exasperated) member of the Board of Trade, the government organ charged with administering the North American colonies, declared, "The Liberty of an Englishman is a Phrase so various a [sic] Signification, having within these Years been used as a synonymous Term for Blasphemy, Bawdy, Treason, Libels, Strong Beer, and Cyder, that I shall not . . . presume to define its meaning."[47]

The figure of the tyrant on the English stage, as various in its eighteenth-century permutations as the concepts of tyranny and liberty, is, like the concept of the effigy, best defined as a series of actions, a pre-scripted role but one still open to revision in performance. Rebecca Bushnell notes in her study of the tyrant figure in English drama that following the struggles between Parliament and King Charles I, the label of tyrant (on- or offstage) was commonly applied by British political thinkers to any ruler who deprived his people of liberty and property, and it is this idea of tyranny that predominantly concerns the popular playwrights of the transatlantic theater.[48] The tyrant's identity may vary from sitting monarch to aspiring usurper to demagogue according to local political conditions, but the character exhibits a standard litany of flaws: boundless ambition, hypocrisy (which renders the tyrant a virtuoso performer), a love of faction, bloodthirstiness, and an unwillingness to forswear personal desires for the benefit of the commonweal. The tyrant, claiming to be the sole voice of the state, thereby becomes the personification of arbitrary power, which must be resisted; this resistance ideally (and frequently) results in the tyrant's death, or at the very least his defeat and capture, which symbolically concentrates the social renewal promised by revolution in the undoing of his person.[49] Bushnell observes that "not only is the tyrant explicitly depicted as committing bloody acts of [presumably arbitrary] punishment . . . but the tyrant sovereign himself is the public victim of a 'public' execution, perversely continuing [Michel] Foucault's observation that 'in the darkest region of the political field the condemned man represents the symmetrical inverted figure of the king.'"[50]

The tyrant's power to order (or in some cases, to commit!) executions and assassinations gives rise to the second character in my dramatic taxonomy: the sacrificial victim. The theater, like a revolution, loves martyrs. The sacrificial victim, who either dies resisting the tyrant or is put to death on the tyrant's orders, provides a rallying point for the political opposition. These victims may be opposition leaders, or they may be political bystanders—usually women or children. As in determining the identity of the tyrant, local conditions dictate the political status of sacrificial victims, but the role operates within a clear set of parameters.

The manner of the sacrificial victim's death represents a mode of behavior that encompasses both the stage and the scaffold, the British tragic repertoire—in which Addison's Cato and Shakespeare's Brutus and Cassius, who kill themselves rather than surrender to their enemies, remain the martyrs nonpareil—and the Anglo-American canon of political saints drawn from Roman, British, and eventually American political history. Accounts of the trial and execution of the English republican Algernon Sidney, for example, were popular in both Britain and the North American colonies, and as the American Revolution approached, Sidney's death at the behest of the Stuarts also became, as Annabel Patterson notes, "part of the *American* national myth."[51] Sidney's appeal to American revolutionaries stemmed in particular from "the manner of his death," since "by his martyrdom he graphically illustrated the evils of unchecked power."[52] In the theater and on the scaffold, the tyrant's martyred opponents gain a place in the gallery of oppression's enemies where their examples will inspire others to emulate their performances. Like Foucault's body of the condemned man, the body of the sacrificial victim bears witness to the ruler's power, although it confirms the perfidy, rather than the legitimacy, of the tyrant's rule.

The transformation of politically active men into sacrificial victims seems to be an accepted part of the struggle against tyranny on the eighteenth-century stage and, at least rhetorically, in eighteenth-century politics as well. When such deaths befall women and children, however, other dramaturgical rules apply. As Roach argues, women and children, as persons outside the official realms of power who serve as the media through which the legal procedures of its transmission flow, occupy prominent positions in the eighteenth century's economy of sacrificial expenditure.[53] Roach views the lavish depictions of women and children in eighteenth-century art and literature as an illustration of the fear of material superabundance in the circum-Atlantic British economy; I would add that the deaths of women and children in plays focusing on tyranny and rebellion also indicate an attendant possessive individualist concern with the autonomy of the domestic "private" sphere. Since women and children in these texts are excluded from the public sphere occupied by white men of legal age and subject to their spousal and paternal rule, violence committed against these vulnerable figures (usually in scenes written to be as gory and emotive as possible) represent the tyrant's violation of the individual subject's sovereign authority over his own household.

Whereas violence against male citizens is public, and subject to partisan debate, violence against women and children admits of no such debate. Both categories are "out of bounds" as targets of politically motivated violence. While public virtue is, as Ruth Bloch argues, overwhelmingly depicted as masculine in the eighteenth century, Appleby points out that in an "ideological division of labor" liberal discourse reaffirmed this masculine model by making women into vessels of "dependency" and "exemplifiers of the personal and intimate, maintainers of family cohesion, and repositories of romantic fantasies about the past."[54] Both women and children (including boys) are deficient in the masculine force needed to compete in the public arena and are, in some sense, property. Violence against them thus becomes doubly a crime, and the sacrificial spilling of the blood of women and children instantaneously converts all "right-thinking" citizens into members of the resistance.

Such horrifying moments often prove climactic in English tragedies, drawing support en masse to the tyrant's political opponents and sparking popular uprisings. Public opinion openly begins to turn against Shakespeare's Richard III, for instance, after the assassination of his young nephews in the Tower of London, and Shakespeare chooses the murder of women and children—the slaughter of the MacDuff family—for his ultimate display of Macbeth's descent into tyranny before the English invasion of Scotland. During the course of the Revolutionary period in America, the theatrical rhetoric surrounding such sacrificial victims became a particularly useful counter-argument for revolutionaries in disarming the familial analogies between paternal king and filial subject, as well as mother country and dutiful, child-like colony, used to justify British rule in North America.[55]

Last among this trio of characters is the patriot, the staunch leader of the chosen party of liberty and justice. As in the case of the tyrant, the exact nature of this character, whether a republican insurgent, a dispossessed heir apparent, or a sitting head of state, varies, usually in relation to the nature of the tyrant depicted. Whatever the patriot's social standing, however, the character invariably displays both rugged individualism and a complete devotion to the rule of law and liberty in their local manifestations. The patriot thus encompasses virtues common to the devoted republican and the impartial, constitutional monarch advocated by the Tory (and recuperated Jacobite) Henry St. John, Viscount Bolingbroke in his 1749 essay *The Idea of a Patriot King* (a text that played a prominent role in the education of the future George III).[56] The patriot inspires his supporters with powerful speeches and his own flawless behavior while working to restore the integrity of the state and, if necessary, assuming control of the government himself and filling the power vacuum created by tyrannicide. In keeping with Girard's observations about the mobility of tyranny, the patriot is the tyrant's mirror image, offering an inspirational performance of everyday life in place of the tyrant's hypocrisy and stepping forward as a Brutus to receive the crown for Caesar's better parts. Should the patriot be martyred either in resistance or while holding power, moreover, his corpse, like that of the tyrant Julius Caesar in Shakespeare's play, becomes a powerful symbol for further revolutionary action; a body "which signified public heroism when whole" demands in death both "a language that will interpret or gloss its gashes" and revenge for its unfortunate fate.[57] As Sandra Gustafson observes, in the act of commemorating such patriotic self-sacrifice, the aura surrounding the dead can be transferred to the survivors who commemorate their sacrifice, so that "the image of the national body condenses with peculiar force" in the doubled forms of commemorated and commemorator.[58]

As noted before, these roles are by no means distinct. They are in fact remarkably protean and tend to blur and shift with each appearance in the intertwined spheres of theatrical and political representations. Figuratively, one man's tyrant is another man's patriot. This reversibility appears in classic episodes of the English theatrical canon such as Marc Antony's post mortem display of Caesar's wounds in *Julius Caesar*, which turns the Roman mob against the republicans. It is likewise applicable to politicians, especially those with a flare for theatrical self-presentation. As Gustafson observes of the colonial Whig and Tory perspectives on the patriot pamphleteer and politician James Otis, "Turned one way . . . Otis embodied the patriot orator; turned another, the demagogue."[59] This reversibility also influences the political observations of educated transatlantic Britons such as John Adams, who praised George III's 1760 accession as the advent of a "friend of Liberty" and a "Patriot King," an opinion that would change markedly over the ensuing decades, although Americans would persist in employing this image of George III, at least in their public utterances, until the very outbreak of the Revolution.[60] As Simon P. Newman observes, the waning American enthusiasm for monarchy did not dispel "the popular faith in popular leaders."[61]

The patriot's charismatic appeal, then, is not purely insurrectionary, although it is closely bound up with the patriot's potential death. The patriot who undergoes execution, like the American spy Nathan Hale or Algernon Sidney, or who chooses suicide over surrender, like Cato at Utica or Brutus and Cassius falling on their swords at Philippi, elevates himself to mythical status.[62] The sacrificial expenditure of blood by the patriot gives rise to a new mythology of blood based not on regal birthright but on a performative willingness to suffer and bleed for the good old cause, a literal and rhetorical grafting of one's life, fortune, and sacred honor onto the figure of the imperiled nation. Yet the patriot's professed impersonal loyalty to national liberty also allows him to lead the restored state, both in politics and on the stage, providing a moment when the revolution ossifies into an institution. This is the transitional moment that so troubles the imagination of Thomas Jefferson, among others, and at this moment representations must be found that, as Cathy N. Davidson observes of post-Revolutionary American literature, "articulate a carefully limited and defined concept of progress."[63] The intrinsically theatrical figure of the patriot is ideally suited to provide a defining center for the public imagination in such moments of crisis; its capacity to fuse revolutionary ardor with reassuring, paternal stability is perhaps nowhere better displayed than in Revolutionary American culture's elevation of the inveterate playgoer George Washington into a figure of heroic proportions.[64]

Along with the interlocking trio of the tyrant, the sacrificial victim, and the patriot, the figure of Washington provides a link between the various dramatic and print media of early American culture that will be discussed in the ensuing chapters. Washington had been an active playgoer for over twenty years when the Revolutionary War began in 1775, having first attended the theater on a trip to Barbados with his brother in 1752.[65] Between the 1750s and the outbreak of the Revolution he figures prominently as a subject in both patriot and loyalist propaganda employing dramatic texts and tropes; as a regular attendee of professional theatrical productions; and, during the Revolutionary and early national periods, as a privileged audience for a number of politically symbolic performances by American soldiers, college students, and professional actors.

At such moments Washington became a focal point for the actors and audience, as important for his visible presence in the theater as the performance itself, a combination of Jonathan Goldberg's always-already-onstage vision of King James I and the embodiment of a republican government that its citizens were obliged "to monitor, ogle, and canvass."[66] This immersion in dramatic spectacle seems to reflect the very lessons that Washington drew from the theater, including the formation of his placid public demeanor; Paul K. Longmore claims that, owing in part to the theater's influence, "as his career advanced, Washington became an increasingly skillful public actor."[67] As Gustafson observes, Washington's grasp of theatricality did not make him more than an average orator when reading, as was his custom, from a prepared text, but Washington's grasp of the essential theatricality of the role of the patriot—including his physical carriage and his capacity for improvisation during prepared speeches—suggests a talented performer who became markedly more comfortable when working "off book," without the burdensome prop of a written script.⁶⁸ Washington's public persona, even at moments when his performance in the role seems less than self-assured, remains the very embodiment of the self-dramatized patriot in American history.

Partly through his own efforts and partly through the efforts of others who glorified him, Washington emerged as the public face of the Revolution, a figure surrounded by the major theatrical and political tropes of the eighteenth century. This transfer of social energies in North America during the American Revolution shifted the spectacular center of colonial society from a British "tyrant" formerly regarded as a "Patriot king" to an insurrectionist creole general who served the role of a surrogate king. Washington's public image as a patriot republican leader supplemented the "decadent" British monarchy in the American public imagination. During the Continental Congress's 1775 meeting in Philadelphia, a rumor circulated among the delegates that Washington had declared that "he wished to God! The Liberties of America were to be determined by a single combat between himself" and King George.⁶⁹

This improvised legend, springing up in a revolutionary assembly, neatly illustrates the need for such episodes of single combat; they are the stuff of myth, and in particular of the myths that dominate the British and colonial stages of the eighteenth century (as well as the Hollywood action adventure). Among popular tragedies on the Anglo-American stage, for instance, *Macbeth*, *Tamerlane*, and *Richard III*—the pro-American London newspaper *The Crisis* compared George III to Richard III twice in 1776—all feature decisive single combat between the patriot and the tyrant figure.⁷⁰ The regicidal impulse implicit in the story of Washington's yearning for single combat, even when coupled with the nomination of Washington to fill the gap caused by the tyrant's downfall, does not entirely banish the specter of monarchy from Revolutionary culture, however. Examining the lingering tinges of monarchy in Revolutionary depictions of Washington, Simon P. Newman refers to the general as "America's new 'patriot king.'"⁷¹

Both the lingering American cultural dependence on Britain and the radicalism of Revolutionary culture's appropriations of British symbols can be seen in this "coronation." In October 1775, the revolutionary Dr. Benjamin Rush declared, "There is not a king in Europe that would not look like a *valet de chambre* by [Washington's] side."⁷² Public readings of the Declaration of Independence resulted in celebratory riots throughout the country that featured the demolition of any and all available representations of the crown, including the beheading of an equestrian statue of King George III in New York. Washington's image partially filled the gap left by this symbolic regicide.⁷³ American revelers redeployed traditional honors accorded to Hanoverian monarchs in Washington's honor, drinking to "the Illustrious George Washington" rather than the King's health, reassigning to Washington the title of "Father of his Country" formerly accorded to George III, and holding feasts in honor of Washington's birthday. Perhaps most tellingly, in 1779 patriot wits in New Jersey altered the chorus of "God Save the King" to "God save great Washington, God damn the King."[74] Washington, in effect, replaced George III as a ceremonial monarch residing, as Rene Girard would have it, at "the very heart of the community" of the former British colonies in North America. (In an uncanny echo of Thomas Jefferson's thoughts on blood and the tree of liberty, Girard compares such ruler/performers to chemical plants that produce fertilizer from waste, "convert[ing] sterile, infectious violence into positive cultural values.")[75] The patriot ruler's performance in the theater of public action, like the heroic performance of an actor onstage, binds his audience together, molding them as a "free-born" community and, in Washington's case, validating the patriotic bona fides of the Revolution.

Chapter 2
Cato and Company: A Genealogy of Performance

On 22 September 1776, Captain Nathan Hale, an officer in the Continental Army of the United States and a prisoner of war, was executed for espionage by the British in Manhattan after being captured near Huntington, a town on Long Island.¹ Hale, a 1773 graduate of Yale College, had volunteered for the reconnaissance mission that cost him his life, an errand stemming from the Continental Army's exposure to attack after the disastrous American loss at the Battle of Brooklyn in August 1776 and subsequent retreat to Manhattan. With his troops demoralized and vulnerable, General George Washington had asked for a volunteer from his officer corps to cross enemy lines and gather intelligence on British troop maneuvers. According to the memoirs of General William Hull, a schoolmate of Hale's, Hale accepted the mission even though the first man that had been approached had declined it. Hale also disregarded Hull's objections that his friend Hale's "nature was too frank and open for deceit and disguise," and that "he was incapable of acting a part equally foreign to his feelings and habits."²

Hale traveled from Washington's encampment on Harlem Heights to Norwalk, Connecticut, before sailing to Huntington, where he was captured while gathering intelligence (he had posed as a Dutch schoolmaster). Hull reports Hale's story as it was related to the American forces by the British officer Captain John Montresor. According to Hull, Montresor stated that at the execution "Captain Hale . . . was calm, and bore himself with gentle dignity, in the consciousness of rectitude and high intentions."³ Montresor also noted that after Hale's execution the British had burned two letters written by the American spy in his cell, one intended for his brother and one for a fellow American officer, so that "the rebels should not know that they had a man in their army who could die with so much firmness."⁴ Compounding the sense of erasure caused by the obliteration of his final written testaments, Hale's body was never recovered. Nathan Hale, having been denied the final, material testimony provided by a jailhouse letter or even a forensic toe tag, instead exists primarily in American history as a disembodied performance. His death has generated a character type, a line of business composed of the calm demeanor and measured actions of a revolutionary facing the gallows. The contours of this character are exemplified in Hale's famous last words, related to posterity by his counterpart Montresor: "I only regret that I have but one life to lose for my country."[5]

The intermingling of legal ritual, revolutionary politics, and bloodshed in the tale of Hale's death invite a Foucauldian reading of this public, martial display of state power as a gruesome theatrical spectacle.[6] Nathan Hale's death, featuring both the hideous spectacle of the scaffold and the executed man's combination of studied indifference and defiance, illustrates the rich raw materials available to theater historians, and particularly scholars of performance studies, in the history of eighteenth-century British North America. Hale's execution features a potboiler historical plot, a spectacular ending, and a sympathetic lead—to say nothing of the uneasy tensions between the corporeal (Hale's death on the gallows) and the incorporeal (his vanished corpse) that commonly inform performance theory. Hale himself invited a performative reading for his death, selecting as his last words an allusion to a popular eighteenth-century tragedy, Joseph Addison's *Cato* (1713). Hale's dying words, "I only regret that I have but one life to lose for my country," are either a reference to, or a misreported direct quotation of, Cato's line "What pity is it / That we can die but once to serve our country!"[7]

That Hale, a young revolutionary with a college education and a literary bent, should frame the public reception of his death by making his last utterance a reference to a popular tragedy seems to demand an explication. While Sarah J. Purcell in her history of commemorative culture during the Revolutionary era maintains that the meaning of political martyrdom is always a postscript to the martyrdom itself, something "made by the community of the living," the sense of purpose suggested by Hale's stoic demeanor and his theatrical last words—his apparent staging of his last moments—suggests that he saw himself as performing a scripted role, and one with a predetermined meaning, at the gibbet.[8] Unpacking this stirring episode offers a reminder of the closely interrelated nature of theater and politics in the eighteenth century, and also of the dominance of theatrical forms in the culture of the British Atlantic.

An account of Hale's execution written by a British officer states that after hanging Hale, British troops "got, out of a rebel gentleman's garden, a painted soldier on a board, and hung it along with the Rebel [Hale]; and wrote upon it–General Washington."[9] The British troops' conversion of Hale and the painted soldier into effigies of Washington, along with the inverted presence of George III's regal image reflected in Hale's suspended corpse, illustrate the confluence of the characters of the tyrant, the sacrificial victim, and the patriot in rich Revolutionary performance texts such as Hale's execution and the play from which he drew his last words. It is a telling if not surprising coincidence to discover that both Washington and George III were also familiar with *Cato*, and, like Hale, capable of using the play in displays of political symbolism. Although George Washington and George III were not "onstage" during the final act of Nathan Hale's political drama, both of them could read between his lines.

Hale's theatrical flourish is not unusual in the context of the American Revolution, nor is the analysis of it out of place in a study of the eighteenth-century American theater, given the established bloodline for the study of the influence of British literature on the formation of early American culture. The American reputation of *Cato*, in particular, has attracted impressive scholarship, most notably Fredric M. Litto's seminal history of the play's popularity in the North American colonies, Garry Wills's analysis of *Cato*'s importance to the crafting of George Washington's public persona, and Julie K. Ellison's noteworthy examination of the plot's colonialist and liberal, homosocial implications.[10] Each of these important studies, however, lays bare only a part of *Cato*'s role in the history of the British Atlantic.

Litto's account of the contemporary cultural valences of *Cato*, either onstage or in allusive performances such as Hale's, is limited by his historiographical methods, which predate the advent of performance studies. Wills's focus on the figure of Washington limits the scope of his analysis, obscuring the complexities of the text's literary and theatrical history in North America. Ellison's analysis of *Cato* in the colonies is only one small part of a much larger study of sentiment and sensibility in Anglo-American culture. Fully to grasp the cultural power that *Cato* possessed in the eighteenth-century theater, as well as its influence on the culture of colonial and Revolutionary British North America, requires a supplemental reading of the text and its history that considers Addison's play as a both a print and a performance text. Also, rather than treating the play's widespread popularity as a function of British political and intellectual hegemony over the colonies, the play should be considered as a contested text, as it was even before being exported to North America. *Cato* served as a touchstone in the pitched rhetorical (and military) battles marking the evolution of the British Atlantic in the eighteenth century, a script available to interpreters ranging from princes to day laborers, whose stages extended from the seat of the British monarchy to the crowded streets of North American cities and an unmarked grave in Manhattan.

Addison's Uncanny Romans

The political and literary reputation of Joseph Addison as both a dependable Whig and a public moralist no doubt enhanced the status of his tragedy *Cato* in British North America. Dramatic texts were popular in the North American colonies for self-improvement as well as entertainment, even in the generally theater-averse New England provinces. In 1732, for instance, *The New England Weekly Journal* published installments of George Lillo's moralistic tragedy *George Barnwell*, the tale of a London apprentice undone by profligacy, only a year after the play premiered in London.[11] Nathan Hale probably discovered *Cato* while studying at Yale. Both the college's library and that of the Linonian Society, Hale's fraternity, possessed copies of dramatic works by Addison and a number of other prominent playwrights, along with classical authors and religious tracts, for the students' pleasure and edification.[12]

Cato's Roman republican subject matter, in particular, would have attracted contemporary audiences for whom narratives of "Classical Republican Rome, like some South Sea tribes for twentieth-century anthropologists, became the means by which enlightened eighteenth-century Englishmen could distance themselves from their own society and achieve the perspective from which to criticize it."[13] *Cato*, an exemplary narrative endorsing courage in the face of adversity, traces the declining fortunes of Cato Uticensis, a Roman senator who opposed Julius Caesar's rise to the dictatorship of Rome. The play takes place in Utica, a northern African outpost of Rome, after Caesar's triumphant victory over the republican forces at the battle of Pharsalia. Cato, along with his sons Marcus and Portius, his daughter Marcia, and his few surviving allies from the Senate, have taken refuge with their troops in the Roman garrison at Utica, accompanied by a small allied force of Numidian troops commanded by Prince Juba, a young man much enamored of both Cato's stoic virtue and Marcia's beauty. As Caesar's troops advance, the garrison determines to endure a siege until forced to surrender. However, two separate mutinies—one of Roman soldiers encouraged by the traitorous senator Sempronius and the other of Numidian troops led by Juba's Rome-hating adjutant Syphax, which leads to the death of Cato's son Marcus—sap Cato's endurance. Having secured the means of escape for those among his allies who prefer exile to submission, Cato commits suicide rather than surrender to the approaching Caesar. As the play closes, his corpse is borne off stage to Caesar, a white flag pleading for clemency toward the remaining republicans.

After its premiere in 1713 *Cato* became a smash hit, due in no small part to Addison's precisely *not* seeking a partisan purchase from which to criticize contemporary society but rather offering a broad treatment of the struggle between the political abstractions of "tyranny" and "liberty," the controlling terms of eighteenth-century British political debate. The pyrotechnic libertarian rhetoric of Addison's script stubbornly resists interpretation as a partisan allegory. Addison instead uses the play to promote "service to country" and "patriotic virtue," which, as Lisa A. Freeman notes, "were practically the only principles," whether political or dramaturgical, "upon which contemporary critics agreed." Also, the play demands "the necessary transmission of . . . [the] love of freedom to the coming generation" and stresses the obligation of such coming generations to deserve the inheritance of their political rights and privileges, whether these liberties are Roman or British.[14]

Addison's political prudence suited the temper of the times: *Cato* premiered during the waning days of the War of the Spanish Succession, amid intense partisan sniping by the anti-war Tory majority and the pro-war Whig minority. Linda Colley observes that one key factor in forging a "British" national identity in the eighteenth century was repeated conflict with "a hostile Other" through war, but Addison's patriotic play, written for a self-consciously nationalist professional theater, largely withdraws from the ongoing conflict and seeks instead to confront the creeping threat of tyranny at home.[15] Withdrawing into the bipartisan rhetoric of patriotism and sacrifice, the Whig Addison judiciously offered the composition of the play's prologue to the Tory satirist Alexander Pope and allowed the Tory ministers Bolingbroke and Oxford to examine the script before the play went into production.[16] Samuel Johnson's life of Addison observes that the playwright's resistance to political pressure to fashion a topically allegorical "party play" resulted in universal accolades on opening night, although, as Johnson notes, the applause was by no means bipartisan in intent: the Whigs applauded at every utterance of the word "liberty," in order "to satirize the Tories," and "the Tories echoed every clap to show that the satire was unfelt."[17]

Although *Cato* is not an à clef "party play," it is not politically inert. As the example of Nathan Hale suggests, for instance, Addison's storyline captured the imaginations of many colonials inclined toward a break with Great Britain. Bernard Bailyn argues that Americans "found their ideal selves" in the inherently theatrical process of trying on classical identities such as Brutus, Cassius, and Cicero.[18] Nowhere is this process more in evidence throughout colonial and Revolutionary American culture than in the case of Cato, a figure that suffuses the print and performance culture of the colonies decades before the Revolution. Even in a pre-Revolutionary context, however, references to *Cato* in the colonies generally suggest reformist sentiments, often couched in the terms of republican-tinged patriotism.

This whiff of opposition politics stems in part from the play's intersection, in the figure of Cato, with the writings of the radical Whigs James Trenchard and Thomas Gordon, who during the South Sea Bubble scandal of 1720–23 published a series of anti-Walpole essays known as *Cato's Letters*. Trenchard and Gordon's polemics proved to be quite popular not only in England but also in the North American colonies. In 1722, for instance, the Boston printer James Franklin published a radical pamphlet, *English Advice to the Freeholders, &c of the Province of Massachusetts Bay*, which was signed by "Brutus and Cato" and reminded New Englanders that "Liberty is a Jewel of inestimable Value, which when once lost, is seldom recovered again." (When James had earlier been jailed for offending the provincial government with his newspaper, *The New England Courant*, his brother Benjamin protested by reprinting excerpts from Trenchard and Gordon in the paper during James's confinement.)[19] A letter to John Peter Zenger's *New York Weekly Journal* in 1733, moreover, joined the ongoing power struggle between former Chief Justice Lewis Morris and Governor Cosby (who was allied with Walpole) by invoking Trenchard and Gordon as well as Addison. Echoing Trenchard and Gordon's even-handed repudiation of both parties in Parliament—since each adapts the others' methods when in or out of power—the author declares his mistrust for Cosby: "A Tory out of Power adopts the Principles ascribed to a Whigg [*sic*], and a Whigg in Power falls into the worst measures of those that are attributed to Tories." Simultaneously, he encourages his fellow citizens with two hopeful lines from Portius: "'Tis not in mortals to command success, / But we'll do more, Sempronius, we'll deserve it."[20]

Julie K. Ellison suggests that as the eighteenth century progressed, the journalistic voice of Cato became "the muse of antigovernment politics" for those, such as the author of the *English Advice*, seeking to project a disinterested patriotism, even as the dramatic character remained the epitome of self-sacrifice for the good of the state.[21] Bernard Bailyn, meanwhile, sees a fusion of dramatic and nondramatic representations of Cato, arguing that the popularity of these divergent depictions created an amalgamate figure that he calls "the Catonic image," a synthesis of Trenchard's and Gordon's jealous attachment to individual (and especially property) rights and the professed willingness to die for the res publica associated with Addison's tragic hero. The Catonic image embodies a vision of British patriotism (albeit in toga-party costume) stressing fidelity to the "Revolution principles" affirmed in 1689, along with zealous cultural and political nationalism and a vociferously expressed willingness to die in order to preserve the state from the encroachments of arbitrary power.

These ideals were shared by radicals and conservatives, and by advocates of republican government and supporters of constitutional monarchy, in both the British home islands and the North American colonies.[22] As Gordon S. Wood observes, George III, at least publicly, "celebrated liberty as proudly as the humblest plebeian," professing the wholehearted devotion to constitutional liberties and abiding faith in English political exceptionalism implied in the construction of Cato as an "*exemplum virtutis*" of patriotism.²³ Indeed, the future king had portrayed Cato's son Portius in an amateur performance of *Cato* that was given at Leicester House, the main residence of his father, Frederick Louis, Prince of Wales, and thus the unofficial headquarters of the opposition politicians grouped around the prince. (The performance also featured a number of George's siblings.) According to an occasional prologue composed for the young George, the Catonic conception of patriotic, libertarian "Britishness" was

... the first great lesson I was taught.
What, though a boy, it may with pride be said,
A boy, in England born, in England bred:
Where freedom well becomes the earliest state,
For there the love of liberty's innate.²⁴

The performance of the young prince as Cato's dutiful son implies, through the complex relationship between character, actor, and audience, that the "necessary transmission" of the heritage of liberty central to the English construction of national identity has taken place within the House of Hanover and that the future king, like a dutiful Englishman and son of liberty, will strive to emulate the Catonic ideal and preserve from tyranny the freedoms secured by the throne he stands to inherit. A poem published in the next issue of *The London Magazine* in praise of George's performance hails the young prince as both a future patriot leader and a promising actor, "A buskin'd hero of the Brunswick race."²⁵

The uncanny resemblance between the performances of George III at Leicester House and Nathan Hale at the gallows, with each man claiming a niche for himself within the prestigious edifice of Addison's text, illustrates both the inspirational power of the play and its capacity to support politically allegorical readings that seem mutually exclusive. The text's ambiguity stems not only from Addison's political vacillations but also from the status of the theatrical character Cato, the rugged individualist and self-sacrificing republican, as an effigy, and the essentially performative model of political behavior followed by Addison's dramatic personae. Concentrating on themes of tyranny and patriotism, *Cato* demonstrates the theatricality of political character and the importance of sacrifice in the rhetoric of transatlantic British patriotism in two important ways. First, the text depicts Cato, Caesar, and Sempronius alike as self-consciously histrionic characters, men accomplished in self-presentation. Second, as the play progresses, Cato transforms himself from an unflappable patriot devoted to the preservation of republican Rome into a sacrificial suicide, an oddly Caesarean personification of the fallen republic.

Cato opens with a dialogue between Cato's two sons, the stoic Portius and the passionate Marcus. Portius assesses Cato's potential value as a symbolic sacrifice in the theater of Roman politics thus: "Our Father's

Death / Would fill up all the guilt of Civil war, / And close the scene of blood."[26] Portius also contrasts Caesar's distinguishing faults, his "Ambition" and his possession of autocratic power, which lead men to behold him "in a false glaring light" (1.1.11; 2.2.49), with the exemplary force of Cato's virtues, which reveal, rather than obscure, Cato's true character: "[Cato's] sufferings shine, and spread a glory round him; / Greatly unfortunate, he fights the cause / Of honour, liberty, virtue, and Rome" (1.1.30–32). Cato's luminous exemplarity, however, bears an uncomfortable resemblance to the false "light" that envelops Caesar. Echoing his brother, Marcus describes Cato as "[a] poor epitome of Roman greatness" (1.1.140), another identification of man and state eerily reminiscent of Caesar's own executive embodiment of the state. Cato is marked from the very beginning for theatrical slaughter as a blood sacrifice to the patriotic spirit of Roman republicanism.

The actions of Sempronius, the treacherous senator who serves as the offstage Caesar's alter ego—the visible, local representative of tyranny in Utica—further underscore the symbolic reversibility of the tyrant and the patriot, as well as their mutual dependence on public performance for the maintenance of authority. Sempronius uses bold patriotic rhetoric to mask his plan to overthrow Cato and surrender Utica to Caesar. Plotting with Syphax, Sempronius, like Richard III and other traditional dramatic "vice" characters, gives away his hypocritical gambit to the audience: "I'll conceal / My thoughts in passion ('tis the surest way;) / I'll bellow out for Rome and for my country, / And mouth at Caesar 'til I shake the Senate" (1.4.36–39). As the exiled senators debate their course of action, Sempronius delivers a rousing speech calling for a suicidal battle with Caesar, an outburst composed of equal parts elegy and rant, laden with professions of loyalty to the martyred dead of the Roman republic:

My voice is still for war.
Gods, can a Roman Senate long debate
Which of the two to chuse, slavery or death!
. . . Attack the foe, break through the thick array
Of his throng'd legions, and charge home upon him.
Perhaps some arm, more lucky than the rest,
May reach his heart, and free the world from bondage.
. . . Rouse up for shame[,] our brothers of Pharsalia
Point at their wounds, and cry aloud—to battle!
Great Pompey's shade complains that we are slow,
And Scipio's ghost walks unavenged amongst us! (2.1.23–42)

Cato gently rebukes Sempronius for this inflammatory speech, urging a protracted resistance followed by eventual surrender and cautioning Sempronius against "immoderate valour" (2.1.81). The criticism seems equally applicable to Sempronius's self-destructive advice and to his hectoring manner of delivery. Sempronius's performance, however, illustrates both the theatrical power of the tyrannical hypocrite and the ease with which the rhetoric of the patriot's devotion to liberty—defiant speeches that privilege death over servitude, demonizing descriptions of the tyrant as the personification of all political oppression, and reverent invocations of the genealogy of patriot martyrdom—can be appropriated in performance for decidedly unpatriotic ends.

Cato's own professions of self-identification with the republic echo Sempronius's histrionics. Offered carte blanche terms of surrender in the Senate by Caesar's envoy, the turncoat senator Decius, Cato declines to endorse Caesar's dictatorship, instead subsuming himself entirely within the republican state. He protests that his "life is grafted on the fate of Rome: / Would [Caesar] save Cato? Bid him spare his country. / Tell your dictator this: and tell him, Cato / Disdains a life, which he has power to offer" (2.2.7–10). This stinging rebuke both denies Cato's self-interest and reiterates Cato's embodiment of republican Rome, his uncanny doubling of Caesar's dictatorial self-identification with the state. Cato's defiance eliminates the possibility of surrender, however, and consequently his declaration of the patriot's fundamentally dichotomous worldview—"It is not now a time to talk of aught / But chains, or conquest; liberty, or death" (2.4.78–79)—mirrors Sempronius's hypocritical call for martial self-immolation, illustrating Cato's similarities to Sempronius as well as to Caesar.[27]

Cato also confirms his status as a virtuoso performer in the aftermath of the Roman and Numidian mutinies. Confronting the Roman mutineers, Cato metaphorically shows his wounds, reminding the rebels of the hardships that the republican forces have endured together—an account that does not stint on recounting his own personal sufferings—and concluding: "hence! And complain to Caesar / You could not undergo the toils of war, / Nor bear the hardships that your leader bore" (3.5.41–43). This pronouncement reduces the rebellious soldiers to tears. Having outfaced this rebellion and sentenced the offenders to death, Cato utters another paean to liberty, urging his allies to pass on "[t]he gen'rous plan of power deliver'd down, / From age to age, by your renown'd forefathers" to their children and imploring, "Do thou, great Liberty, inspire our souls, / And make our lives in thy possession happy, / Or our deaths glorious in thy just defense" (3.5.74–75, 79–81). In like manner, when Cato's son Marcus dies while suppressing the Numidian mutiny, Cato greets the arrival of his son's corpse (an iconic forerunner of Cato in sacrificial death) not with the grief of a private man but with meditations on death, glory, and the citizen's overwhelming obligations to the republic:

How beautiful is death, when earn'd by virtue!
Who would not be that youth? What pity is it
That we can die but once to serve our country!

... Portius, behold thy brother, and remember
Thy life is not thy own, when Rome demands it. (4.4.80–87)

Cato, wedded to the res publica, laments not Marcus's death but the Numidians' betrayal of Roman idealism and the collapse of Rome's public spirit in the face of advancing tyranny, crying tearfully: "O liberty! O virtue! O my country!" (4.4.95). These ejaculations mark the culmination of Cato's choice between bondage and death, and in the fifth act he stabs himself in the privacy of his own chamber, ironically just as a messenger arrives to announce that reinforcements for the garrison have arrived. Without Cato, the pillar of the endangered state, resistance to Caesar is futile. As Ellison observes, "With Cato's suicide, the Roman republic ceases to exist as a political entity."[28] By sacrificing his life, however, Cato transcends the law of Caesar, transforming both himself and the overthrown republic into the stuff of legend. By refusing to become part of the spectacle of Caesar's triumph over his own country, Cato becomes instead an always already lost spiritual patriarch for Anglo-American devotees of resistance to arbitrary power, a surrogate for the politically purer Rome that constitutes a point of mythological origin for Britain's Atlantic expansion.

Page and Stage: Colonial Catos

Commercial and intellectual exchange between Britain and North America brought the Catonic effigy to the colonies. The power that the effigy conferred on its subsequent occupants in the "new world" is evident in the closing stanza of a Revolutionary ballad commemorating Nathan Hale's death:

The faith of a martyr the tragedy shewed
As he trod the last stage, as he trod the last stage;
And Britons will shudder at gallant Hale's blood,
As his words do presage, as his words do presage:
"Thou pale king of terrors, thou life's gloomy foe,
Go frighten the slave, go frighten the slave.
Tell tyrants, to you their allegiance they owe,
No fears for the brave, no fears for the brave."[29]

The ballad employs the conceit of the execution as a tragedy, the dramatic death of a sacrificial victim. It also illustrates, as does Hale's life itself, the uneasy relationship between artifice and nature, between the *theatrum mundi* trope of "playing a role" in the "theater of action" and genuine theatrical behavior. Hale's friend Hull, so concerned that Hale would be unable to "act" the role assigned to him, explicitly equates deceit with the-atrical performance. Yet Captain Montresor's account of Hale's disciplined demeanor and defiant last words, which would no doubt have allayed Hull's fears about Hale's thespian skills, suggests a more constructive view of the relationship between personality and performance.

While Hale was a student at Yale he participated in public debates and acted in Linonian Society theatricals, for which he penned and spoke occasional epilogues. Perhaps due in part to those formative histrionic experiences, he seems to have approached the moment of his own death with the self-observant eye of an actor, striving to convey both stoicism and passion.[30] Hale's final allusion to *Cato*, moreover, suggests that the stoic persona Hale displayed at his execution was not necessarily part of his ontological essence—the "open" and "frank" nature described by his friend Hull—but a studied role, much as Hale's last words reveal themselves not as original speech but as an intentional, albeit impromptu, reference to a popular play. Hale's last act was to claim kinship with a chain of political and theatrical martyrs including antique Romans and British tragic heroes. Choosing for his last words Cato's exhortations to courage delivered over Marcus's body, Hale layered his performance, casting himself as "both the self-sacrificing son who emulates, *avant la lettre*, his father's principled suicide and the appreciative paternal commentator on such a death," both a good son of Liberty, the "innate" passion of every Englishman and American, and a citizen of a new nation attempting to prove that it had reached its political majority.[31]

Hale has been interred in the national memory of the United States as one of a chain of Revolutionary martyrs who serve as "symbols of a new kind of national political commitment that their very deaths made possible."[32] Although his symbolic connection to Washington is rarely noted, his story has become, like Washington's, a part of the mythology of the American Revolution. His life and death remain an instructive tale of "manly" republican virtue inserted as a human interest sidebar into documentary accounts of the Revolution and collections of Americana such as *Our Sacred Honor*, a devotional collection of quotations from and stories about the Founding Fathers edited by the conservative pundit and former Secretary of Education William J. Bennett. As Babcock, Hale's first biographer, claims, "Such sacrifices [as Hale's] have ever been rare, and they who made them, have, in all ages, been looked upon as among the exalted models of human kind." Nathan Hale died "not for ambition, not for power or a throne, but for [his] country—for all mankind."[33]

Although Hale lacks the shrine that Babcock's rather Christ-like description implies that he deserves, Hale has achieved an iconographic fame in the form of a statue representing him with his hands tied behind his back, ready for the scaffold, which adorns the campus of Yale University. Absent any known representation of Hale, the sculptor Bela Lyon Pratt modeled the statue on an anonymous Yale student. The statue bears an inscription of Hale's famous last words on its base.[34] Full-sized copies of

Pratt's statue stand at the CIA headquarters in Langley, Virginia; in front of the Tribune Tower in Chicago; on the campus of the Phillips Academy in Andover, Massachusetts; and in the Federal Triangle of Washington, D.C., near the Department of Justice. The Federal Triangle statue originally stood at the Hale homestead in Coventry, Connecticut, where two smaller copies of the statue still stand.[35] (Statues of Hale by other sculptors also stand at the west edge of Central Park in New York City; in New London, Connecticut; in the Connecticut state capitol building in Hartford; and in the Wadsworth Athenaeum museum in Hartford.)

The Hale statue, an improvised form holding the place of an absent original and inscribed with the physical and linguistic trace of that original's past actions, provides an excellent metaphor for the effigy that Hale's death has become and the performance tradition in which it participated. The enduring claim of Hale's story in popular legend, disregarding the unsavory connotations of espionage, presents a pattern of behavior marked by controlled yet defiant courage in the face of death, a Stanislavskian "beat" of Catonic action captured in the media of bronze and legend, and invites (or challenges) the spectator to occupy this position, if only temporarily and under drastically altered circumstances. The Hale story presents a challenge of narrative emulation—the replication of Hale's self-sacrificing patriotism within the different circumstances of one's own life, as well as the kinesthetic challenge of physically representing Hale, as the unknown undergraduate placeholder who modeled his statue did.

Notably, during a brief period in 1969 when the statue was removed for cleaning, according to one former university official, "New Haven schoolboys attending summer programs on campus amused themselves by climbing upon the pedestal and posing for passing photographers."[36] Contemporary visitors to Yale's Old Campus quadrangle continue this curious form of mimetic play by mimicking Hale's gallows posture while posing for snapshots next to the statue.[37] The lingering appeal of the story transmutes the blood sacrifice of Hale's execution for military espionage into a prearranged sequence of actions suitable and scripted for later reenactment. Hale's death remains a theatrical role, a situational set of instructions awaiting its material embodiment by a new actor in a performance necessarily requiring alteration. Likewise, his own performance was an iteration of the Catonic effigy, an extemporized performance suited to the circumstances of the American Revolution but echoing the long history of republican political discourse and the repertoire of the British theater.

Like the Hale incident, the broader phenomenon of *Cato*'s influence in America provides a lens through which the student of performance can examine the roles of theatricality, the British drama, and the early

United States theater in the politics of the American Revolution. *Cato* appealed to American colonists no doubt in part because of its setting in a colonial outpost of liberty surrounded by hostile forces. While records of the play's earliest North American performances suggest that its first colonial spectators understood the play as an expression of British patriotism, a notable episode from Boston in 1730 suggests that, at least in New England, the tinge of political opposition colored the British patriotism of Catonic rhetoric almost from the moment of the play's introduction to the colonies. Governor Belcher of Massachusetts, formerly the colony's agent in Britain, had been sent to London on a mission to ensure that the colonial assembly retained the power of the purse over the royally appointed colonial governor, a power commonly used by legislators to press for the nullification of unpopular executive policies by not appropriating a salary for the governor until he acquiesced to the assembly's demands. While in London, however, Belcher was appointed as governor.

Having been elevated to office, the Massachusetts native Belcher's opinion on the gubernatorial salary changed markedly, and upon his return he presented the assembly with a demand for a fixed annual salary that did not require legislative action. As part of his justification for his conversion to the crown's position on this issue, Belcher fell back on *Cato* to explain the importance of compromise with the crown and Parliament: "The fate of Cato's Wisdom reflected honour on old Rome, while he made so brave a stand for the Liberty of his Country, but when Caesar had shut him up in his little Utica, and offer'd him Terms of Honour, his Murdering himself rather than submit to a power he could no longer rationally Resist, has left a lasting brand of Infamy on that great Patriot. This, Gentlemen, I mention as some illustration of the Dispute lately subsisting between his Majesty and his People of this Province."[38] The equations are quite clear: Massachusetts is Utica, Britain is Rome, Belcher and the people of Massachusetts are so many Catos, and resistance to royal authority is political suicide. Belcher's reference to *Cato* undercuts itself somewhat, however, by equating King George II with Julius Caesar, hardly flattering to a monarch whose title ostensibly rested on the consent of the governed.

Some of Belcher's enemies responded to their former emissary's political maneuverings in 1730–31 by circulating manuscript copies of a three-act satirical play, *Belcher Apostate*, which documents the battle over the gubernatorial salary. In the play, Belcher sets forth from Boston as a steadfast patriot and steward of colonial liberty but returns a ministerial toady.[39] The script takes as its prologue a lampoon that one Boston wit nailed to the door of the General Court. The lampoon rebuts Belcher's depiction of Cato as an emblem of colonial intransigence, reframing the stubbornness of the assembly as proof that the colonials, like Cato's little

Utican senate, honored their heritage. After reciting a genealogy of freedom stretching from Rome and (strangely) Sparta to Britain (which "by her Parliaments, hath shown / That She'll keep Kings, to what they've Justly Sworn"), the pasquinade continues:

Our Fathers crost the wide Atlantick Sea
And blest themselves when in the Desart Free,
And shall their Sons, thro' Treachery, or Fear,
Give up that Freedom that has Cost so dear?
What-e'er Pretence Our Enemies may frame,
The Man is alter'd, but the cause the same.
From Caesar's court should Cato fawning come,
Be sure that Cato is no friend to Rome.[40]

The prologue's concern for the paternal bequest of liberty and its depiction of Cato, when placed in the transatlantic context of the Puritan emigration, expresses a concern for British liberties that characterizes Massachusetts's status as a "free" English outpost as almost atavistic. Massachusetts, and by extension perhaps all the New England colonies, are vital bastions of rights and privileges that have fallen into desuetude in Britain itself, which has been reduced by the poet to "Caesar's court."[41] The poet's ironic retention of Belcher's application of the Catonic analogy to himself as well as the assembly echoes the second act of *Cato*, wherein Decius, the former republican turned tool of Caesar and foil for Cato, enters the Senate at Utica and attempts to win Cato's endorsement of Caesar. Whereas Cato refuses the terms offered by Decius, the satire implies that Belcher, who in his speech sought to position himself as a more prudent Cato and the assembly as a group of suicidal die-hards, has debased himself by accepting Caesarean royal patronage. Belcher/Cato is thus left an "alter'd" shadow of his former self, a turncoat like the sunshine patriot Decius.

The poem's "cause," moreover—the liberty that the "Fathers" of New England carried across the Atlantic to the North American "Desart"—remains unchanged by Belcher's shift in allegiance. The burden of this inheritance descends upon the "sons," the current generation of Massachusetts politicians, who must continue to resist "treachery," "fear," and Caesarism. Cato owes his allegiance not to Rome as a geographical entity but to the vision of Rome established by the republic, which stands so long as he does despite his being "shut up" in Utica. The Boston lampoon suggests that New Englanders owe their primary allegiance not to the nation-state of Great Britain but to the liberties granted them as Britons. As the text's reappearance outside New England (including a reprinting in the *New York Gazette*) reveals, such a view of the duties of colonials was not regionally exclusive to Boston.

The enthusiasm of one New York printer for the Boston satire, however, does not confirm that this radical construction of the Catonic image dominated colonial discourse. Early appearances of *Cato* in the southern colonies suggest that the play was open to equally passionate interpretations of liberty that focused on the intellectual and cultural affinities between Britain and America rather than on the vision of perfect (and perpetually endangered) freedom posited by such radical texts as Trenchard's and Gordon's essays and the Boston satirist's squibs. The earliest records for the play's performance in North America point to a production in New York (though it is unclear whether this was professional or amateur) in 1732, a staging by students at the College of William and Mary coincidental with the meeting of the general courts in Williamsburg during 1736 (the first of many student performances in America of this play), and three performances during 1736 in Charleston as part of that city's amateur theater season.[42]

The New York staging, given the ongoing conflict between Van Dam and Cosby, might well have had radical overtones. The performance took place in a building owned by Morris ally Rip Van Dam, and a number of letters from "Cato" were published in Zenger's *Weekly Journal* during 1733–34, assailing Governor Cosby and later defending Zenger during his trial for libeling the governor.[43] Governor William Gooch of Virginia, however, was far more popular than Cosby was in New York; it seems unlikely that this staging implied anything more than a general admonishment toward public virtue during the court term.[44] As a 1735 Charleston prologue written for Otway's *The Orphan* suggests, meanwhile, in a climate devoid of serious clashes between the colonials and their governors, such amateur performances provided pleasure rather than political instruction, specifically the pleasure of consuming British culture in colonial locations: "From the old World in minature [*sic*] we shew / Her choicest pleasures to regale the new."[45] Yet an epilogue to *Cato* written after the Charleston performances indicates that an appreciation of the play's ideological program seems to have been one of the pleasures conveyed by its staging.

The epilogue's anonymous author laments Cato's suicide, preferring instead that Cato should have lived and "by superior Virtue awed the Throne." Such resistance, argues the epilogue, might have effected a "Restoration," which the author compares to the Restoration of Charles II ("The Rump's deposed, to raise her lawful King"). Under a similar set of happy circumstances in Rome, posits the author,

So, vice versa Rome's old Genius might
Have humbled Caesar, and usurp'd her Right:
But oh! Her Generals and her Consuls were no more
And Caesar triumphed with a Conqueror's Power:
Hence was the Patriot's Breast with Glory fired,
And Liberty, and he at once expired.[46]

The author's equation of the Restoration and a hypothetical deposition of Caesar strains the limits of the analogy, particularly since the epilogue was written some seventy-five years after Charles II ascended the throne. Yet even a response to a staging of *Cato* that was ostensibly dedicated to "pleasure" exhibits the familiar Catonic interplay between tyranny, resistance, and sacrificial violence. The Boston satire and the Charleston epilogue mark the extremes of a political spectrum upon which the various colonial print citations and enactments of *Cato* fall during the early eighteenth century, all of them finding common ground for their disparate views in the ideological program of Addison's play. Each "Catonic" American text shares Addison's focus on self-sacrificing patriotism and disinterested devotion to the mutable ideal of "liberty," the same vague but widely endorsed principles that drew universal applause for *Cato* at London in 1713.

The Orature of the Stamp Act

The earliest interactions of *Cato* with colonial culture illustrate that the play and its hero presented both an emblem of British cultural affiliation and an icon of colonial political pugnacity. It is particularly important here to point out once again that the intertwined media cultures of print and performance that the play influenced were not geographically segregated in the colonies, despite the general hostility of the New England colonies to theater. Perhaps nowhere do Catonic allusions in print and performance, whether professing loyalty or opposition to Britain, intermingle so freely and fruitfully as in colonial New England, and especially in Massachusetts. Although theatrical performances in the regional metropolis of Boston were frowned upon, New England's traditions of oratory and street theater lent a decidedly performative air to its urban culture. Moreover, private dramatic reading seems to have been tolerated, and public performances of plays were not unknown in New England during the mid-eighteenth century. Records exist for a controversial amateur performance (of Thomas Otway's *The Orphan*) in Boston in 1750, half a dozen recorded performances of *Cato* and George Farquhar's military comedy *The Recruiting Officer* by Harvard students during the Sevens Years' War, and controversial abortive attempts by the London Company of Comedians to play at Newport, Portsmouth, and Providence during 1761–62. The almanac publisher Nathaniel Ames, who participated in the wartime Harvard productions as a student, notes in his diary that when the London Company played their brief season in Rhode Island during 1761, "Boston people flock[ed] up to Newport to see the English Actors." (Notably, one of the plays the London Company staged during their abbreviated campaign at Providence in 1762 was *Cato*.)[47]

Ames's fellow Harvard alumnus John Adams, who was already an apprentice attorney by the time of the stagings in which Ames participated, had also participated in a club whose (unrecorded) college performances predated those in which Ames took part: "[The members'] plan was to spend their Evenings together, in reading any new publications, or any Poetry or Dramatic compositions, that might fall in their Way. I was as often requested to read as any other, especially Tragedies, and it was whispered to me and circulated among others that I had some faculty for public speaking and that I should make a better Lawyer than Divine."[48] Whatever controversy public theatrical performance aroused in New England, the private enactment or recital of plays apparently held value for the privileged young men of the region. In the case of Adams, the results of this early experience are telling. Adams's writings demonstrate both a fondness for theatrical metaphor and an impressive familiarity with the drama, particularly the works of Shakespeare. Addison, however, clearly captured his imagination as well, as witnessed by Adams's 1765 pamphlet protesting the Stamp Act, *A Dissertation on the Canon and Feudal Law*.[49]

First published in four installments in the *Boston Gazette* during August and September 1765, the *Dissertation* was republished at the behest of the English philanthropist Thomas Hollis in the *London Chronicle* later that year and issued in London as a pamphlet during the Townshend Duties Crisis in 1768.[50] The essay's forceful prose artfully employs English revolutionary history and the Catonic rhetoric of liberty, arguing both for Warner's emancipatory vision of print culture and the pamphlet's own status as a performance, an example of "restored behavior." Adams places a particular emphasis on the rejection of power and the Catonic injunction to preserve the inheritance of liberty. This inheritance, says Adams, echoing an earlier generation of Massachusetts controversialists, derives from "our fathers," who "have earned and bought it for us, at the expense of their ease, their estates, their pleasure and their blood."[51]

In particular, Adams praises the radical *Boston Gazette* and its publishers, Benjamin Edes and James Gill, for "publishing and pointing out . . . avarice and ambition." Such vices are attributed to Caesar in *Cato* and to tyrants in theatrical and political discourse more generally, as well as in the government of the colonies by Parliament and its proxies, and Adams condemns them in spite of whatever virtues those men and institutions might possess by quoting Addison's text: "Curse on such virtues, they've undone their country." The line quoted is Cato's, dismissing the possibility of submission to Caesar, possessor of "the virtues of humanity," in order to preserve his own life. While Adams never assigns a particular target to this barbed allusion, his criticism might well have been meant to apply to Massachusetts Lieutenant Governor Thomas Hutchinson, a native of the colony and an ally of the crown. Readers might also imagine that the criticism applied to the first minister, George Grenville, a former ally of William Pitt, under whose leadership the Stamp Act had been enacted.[52] Adams's citation of *Cato* reflects the broader preference expressed in both his text and Addison's, as well as in the anonymous 1730 satire on Belcher, for the hardscrabble freedom of the desert, a hazardous liberty. Adams sees this "spirit of freedom" as the common inheritance of Britons in both the home islands and the American colonies, and he argues that this shared patriotic attachment should unite, rather than divide, the colonies and Britain.

In a rhetorical move that should by now seem familiar to the reader, Adams constructs a genealogy of resistance to tyranny in order to justify this argument:

> Let us take it for granted that the same great spirit which once gave Caesar so warm a reception, which denounced hostilities against John till Magna Charta was signed, which severed the head of Charles the First from his Body and drove James the Second from his kingdom, the same great spirit (may heaven preserve it till the earth shall be no more) which first seated the great grandfather of his present most gracious majesty on the throne of Britain—is still alive and warm in England; and that the same spirit in America, instead of provoking the inhabitants of that country, will endear us to them forever and secure their good-will.[53]

Just below the surface of Adams's argument rests the possibility of violence: ministerial encroachments on colonial liberties, he implies, risk violent resistance. Adams's rhetoric, as the subsequent history of opposition to the Stamp Act makes clear, captured the spirit of 1765, and his quotation of *Cato* would not be an isolated reference during the Stamp Act Crisis.

Adams's essay, which originally appeared in a provincial newspaper, appears for all its rhetorical force to be an unlikely text upon which to center a reconsideration of colonial political identity. The timing of this publication, however, could have potentially allowed Adams to reach a much broader North American audience. One of the *Gazette*'s publishers, Benjamin Edes, was a member of the Loyal Nine, a group that constituted the nucleus of the Boston chapter of the Sons of Liberty, whose various chapters had begun an impressive intercolonial correspondence by late 1765. As Pauline Maier has shown, newspapers run by the Sons of Liberty or their sympathizers, which could easily be sent between colonies via the post, played a major role in passing news and ideas within the radical communities of the far-flung colonies.[54] Publishing in an avowedly radical newspaper with links to this colonial network allowed Adams the freedom to address not only a Bostonian but also possibly an intercolonial audience including men in less theater-averse colonies who would be at least as familiar with *Cato* and the English drama as he. Likewise, the philanthropy of Thomas Hollis afforded Adams the opportunity to address a metropolitan audience, making the colonials' case for patriotic opposition to the Stamp Act in the London press.

Catonic texts produced during the 1760s were usually brief, consisting of short allusions such as Adams's or the use of the pseudonym "Cato," as it was adopted, for instance, by a Yale professor of divinity, Napthali Daggett, in a series of 1765 newspaper essays attacking Connecticut's stamp agent Jared Ingersoll. Despite the frequent brevity of these texts, however, the Stamp Act triggered a profusion of them. The *New Hampshire Gazette*, for instance, during the Stamp Act Crisis featured not only at least one reprinted excerpt from *Cato's Letters* but also an extended dramatic monologue in the editorial voice of the newspaper itself, as it prepared, Cato-like, to commit suicide in order to evade the tyranny of the Act. The monologue, which begins with an allusion to Portius's somber opening lines from *Cato*, noting the arrival of "Th' great, th' important day, big with the fate / Of Cato and of Rome," declares that the paper "chuse[s] Death, in hopes of escaping this Servitude."[55]

A number of other Stamp Act texts engaged Addison's text in the lengthier form of the monologue.[56] In its 30 December 1765 issue, for instance, the *Boston Gazette* ran a parody of the famous soliloquy from *Cato* 5.1, in which Cato contemplates suicide. In this scene, Cato enters carrying a dagger in one hand and a copy of *Phaedo*—identified by Addison only as "Plato's book on the immortality of the Soul"—in the other. Concluding that "[i]t must be so—Plato thou reason'st well!" (5.1.1), Cato determines that his self-slaughter will constitute not defeat, but victory, since while the plunge of his dagger "in a moment brings me to an end," Plato's argument "informs me I shall never die" (23, 24). Envisioning his immortality as a moral victory—an escape from political capitulation into an eternal, disembodied exile—Cato addresses his soul in the second person:

The stars shall fade away, the sun himself
Grow dim with age, and nature sink in years,
But thou shalt flourish in immortal youth,
Unhurt amidst the war of elements,
The wrecks of matter, and the crush of worlds. (27–32)

The reappearance of this soliloquy in the *Boston Gazette* parody indicates that Addison's Cato correctly predicts the endurance of, if not his "soul," then at least the theatrical actions that constitute his being. In the *Gazette* parody, Cato is replaced with "America," the dagger with "The Stamp Act," and the volume of Plato with the Resolves passed by the Stamp Act Congress in October 1765, which declared the opposition of the colonies to British taxation.[57] "It must be so—my Sons ye reason well!" declares America; the parodist's decision to substitute "America," rather than simply "Liberty," for Cato in the soliloquy seems particularly telling. While using "America" sidesteps the explicit naming of the Sons of Liberty, the filial metaphor clearly implies the involvement of this group in opposition to the Stamp Act. The sympathetic potential sacrificial victim offered up by the parody is, moreover "America," the real "mother country" of the Congress's nine individual colonial delegations.

The parody follows Addison's text faithfully, including the second-person address to the soul, which America names "Liberty," an equation which, like the depiction of "America" as a mother country, appears to be a more radical, separatist statement of principle than Adams's invocation of a "spirit of freedom" common throughout the transatlantic British community. The Stamp Act, says America to Liberty, with an emphatic gesture included in a stage direction, "in a Moment stabs Thee to the heart," but the list of Resolves adopted by the fractious Americans

Assures me thou shalt still survive:
. . . .
Kingdoms shall fade away, proud France herself
Decline with Age, and B[ritain] sink in Years
But thou shalt flourish in these Western Climes,
Unhurt, nor heed the Jars of Eastern Realms,
The shock of Emp[ir]es and the Crush of Th[an]es.

Like Adams's essay, the anonymous parody asserts a specifically Catonic identity for an intercolonial American opposition, a vision of liberty embodied in the self-sacrificing actions of patriots opposing tyranny.[58] Such acts, like theatrical roles and Cato's effigy, survive in a miasma of past narratives that encompass human life in the present tense, enduring history's vicissitudes while awaiting redeployment. Meanwhile, the specific treatment afforded by these authors to Addison's tragic hero strongly implies a shift in the colonial perspective on the political relationship between Britain and the North American colonies.

The protorevolutionary Catonic texts of the Stamp Act Crisis, like the play they allude to, illustrate both the potential for revolutionary violence inherent in the resistance to arbitrary power and a strong belief in the eternal verity of human freedom. As the parodic soliloquy illustrates, these tropes found a literary voice in Cato's act of self-sacrifice. Such Catonic ideals also shape the street theater of protest sparked by the Stamp Act, another style of performance spread throughout the colonies by the widespread availability of accounts of the events in colonial newspapers. "Sitting at home or in a coffee house," says Simon P. Newman, "a colonist could read about the similarity of rites of protest from far and near," and Ann Fairfax Withington observes that such circulated accounts began to establish the "rules" for such rituals, acting as, in effect, scripts for readers wishing to stage a protest of their own.[59] The Stamp Act, scheduled to take effect on 1 November 1765, provoked major protests in communities from Massachusetts to Georgia to St. Kitt's and St. Nevis. These protests largely took the form of parades involving the destruction of wooden or stuffed dummies ("effigies") after funeral parades—mock tyrannicides clearly reminiscent of public executions, of the Guy Fawkes and American "Pope Day" ceremonies commonly held on 5 November, and of the preferred fate of tyrants in the British theater.[60] Stamp Act protests throughout the colonies were reported by newspapers from the *Boston Gazette* to the *Georgia Gazette*. The literature of the public sphere made it possible for these improvised performances to spread rapidly up and down the Atlantic Coast, producing new performance practices in North America simultaneously rooted in British traditions and directed against the actions of the British ministry.

Among the new performance practices that evolved out of the Stamp Act Crisis was the "liberty funeral," a mock interment for an effigy, generally either the Catonic figure of an old man or the vulnerable figure of a young woman, designed to illustrate the fatally deleterious effects of the stamp duty on American liberty. Such a ceremony was originally planned for 31 October 1765 in New York but never materialized. A Boston "funeral" that would otherwise have interfered with the ongoing efforts of Bostonians to practice austerity in funeral celebrations was scheduled to be performed at night on 1 November, and although no liberty funeral took place in Philadelphia, muffled bells, in the style of New England funerals, rang throughout the city on 1 and 2 November. (It is unclear if the Boston funeral actually took place.)[61] Meanwhile, confirmed liberty funerals took place throughout October and November in Portsmouth, New Hampshire (where the obituary for Liberty listed its age as 145, making it coeval with the founding of the Plymouth colony); Newport, Rhode Island; Baltimore, Maryland; Wilmington, North Carolina; and Charleston, South Carolina.[62]

The rhetorical connections between this ceremony and the parody of Cato's fifth-act soliloquy in the *Boston Gazette* become clear in that paper's account of the Newport protest, reprinted from the *Newport Mercury*. The article begins with an Addisonian allusion, citing Portius's opening declaration that the sun rising in Utica betokens "the great, th' important day, big with the fate / Of Cato and of Rome."[63] "[T]he Day appointed," intones the account's narrator, "for the Stamp Act's taking effect in America was similar to a description in Addison's Cato: – ' The Dawn was overcast, and heavily in Clouds brought on the Day[,] the great, the important Day! Big with Fate of ruin'd Trade, and loss of Liberty!' "[64] The Addisonian allusion establishes a familiar line of interpretation, with the ministry and its representatives serving as Caesar and the colonies as beleaguered Utica; indeed the public invitation for the Newport ceremony specifically invited the "true sons" of the old man "Freedom" to attend, another incursion of the role of the loyal Portius onto the identity of the Sons of Liberty and other colonial patriots.[65]

According to the newspaper account:

> Summon'd by Death's clanking Knell, the Funeral began to move at 12 O'Clock, from the Crown Coffee-House, toward the Burying Ground.—The Concourse of the Mourners and Spectators was prodigious, consisting of Persons of all ranks, from the highest even down to the Blacks, who seem'd from a Sense of their Masters' Sufferings, to join the Mourning Course. The Proclamation was solemn, and with sullen Tread, and heavy Hearts, at length arrived at the Place of Interment, where the Mourners were about taking their LAST FAREWELL of their old Friend LIBERTY.—"Oh LIBERTY!—Oh! FREEDOM!—Oh, where art Thou going?—My ruin'd Country!"— The mournful Aspiration was scarcely utter'd, when a Son of Liberty, emerging from the horrid Gloom of Despair, addressed himself thus: "Oh liberty! The Darling of my Soul!—GLORIOUS LIBERTY! admir'd, ador'd, by all true Britons!—LIBERTY dead! It cannot be!"—A Groan was then heard, as if coming from the Coffin; and upon closer Attention, it proved to be a trance, for old FREEDOM was not dead.

Instead, Freedom emerges from the coffin transformed into a young woman, "Liberty Revived," thereby uniting the sacrificial figures of the opposition leader and the innocent (usually female) bystander as Liberty breaks out of Old Freedom's Catonic chrysalis and prompts a festival celebration.

The figure of a resurrection, common to the liberty funeral ceremonies, asserts the durability of British liberty as a political ideal by allowing for the resuscitation of victims of tyranny. The quotation from Addison in the account of the Newport funeral and the procession's intimations of immortality, reminiscent of Cato's soliloquy in both its original and parodied forms, suggest the presence of key elements of Addison's text in the ceremonial aspects of the liberty funeral itself, which reproduces the national dynamics of *Cato* in its own cast. Britain represents the advancing, offstage Caesar; Freedom stands in for Cato, the sacrificial symbol of patriotism; the marching colonials double as the Roman republicans, political exiles left to mourn the passing of the Catonic figure and bear the corpse; and the slaves are refigured as voluntary sympathizers bearing the mantle of the Numidians, the admiring, although imperially subject, "allies" of the republican stalwarts. The ceremonial resurrection of liberty, like several of the Catonic texts printed in 1765, revises Addison's narrative, emphasizing Cato's moral victory as an immortal one and signaling a major shift in the rhetoric of North American patriotism away from the unified purpose of warfare against France and toward political fractiousness.

The association of the Catonic effigy with anti-tax sentiment became commonplace among American patriot activists in the wake of the Stamp

Act Crisis. This "Americanization" of Cato proved to be a self-consciously colonial rebuttal to the stress placed by British officials and American loyalists upon the common interests and heritage of Britain and the American colonies. New England activists remained the masters of deploying the theatrical discourse of Catonic rhetoric, continually stressing the political differences between Britain and the colonies and the threat that these differences posed to the "English" freedoms of America. Cato's fifth-act soliloquy became such a commonplace that the *Massachusetts Spy* printed a parody in which a hungry Cato meditates his impending consumption of a joint of "beef! Most glorious beef!"[66]

On a more serious note, Nathaniel Ames, who, as noted above, had acted in *Cato* while a student at Harvard during the Seven Years' War, included in his 1772 *Almanack* an engraving of the Pennsylvania activist John Dickinson, "with his elbow resting on 'Magna Carta' and holding a scroll inscribed 'Farmer's Letters,'" a reference to Dickinson's influential 1767 anti-tax pamphlet *Letters from a Farmer in Pennsylvania*, under which were written the lines:

'Tis nobly done to stem Taxation's Rage,
And raise the Thoughts of a degenerate Age,
For Happiness and Joy, from Freedom spring;
But Life in Bondage is a worthless Thing.

The verse derives from Lawrence Eusden's prefatory poem to *Cato*:

'Tis nobly done thus to enrich the stage,
And raise the thoughts of a degenerate age,
To show how endless joys from freedom spring,
How life in bondage is a worthless thing.[67]

Ames's alteration replaces the British stage with the specifically American theater of political action—colonial resistance to British taxation. The depiction of Dickinson leaning upon Magna Carta, like the appropriation of Eusden's verses, argues that the roots of this American opposition spring from fundamental British political principles. Ames's sweeping assertion of authority over both Magna Carta and *Cato* also, inadvertently, establishes Addison's play as a foundational text of American patriotic sentiment. By linking the play to the common law, ironically, Ames also transforms *Cato*'s advocacy of unstinting resistance to power into an injunction to be followed by each of his readers in their role as subjects of the crown.

The legalistic emphasis of Ames's image conceals a new element that had entered into political relations between Britain and America two years earlier with the Boston Massacre, however: the use of deadly force by colonials and British soldiers against one another. The Catonic dichotomy of liberty or death, as previously noted, renders sacrificial bloodshed necessary for the maintenance of freedom. Ames's elevation of John Dickinson, a relative moderate who would later oppose the Declaration of Independence, to iconic status misdiagnoses the increasing tensions in the American colonies and the escalating violence of radical rhetoric. In the wake of the Boston Massacre, a commemorative practice sprang up marking the fifth of March in Boston with a ceremony that combined passionate political orations with "tolling bells, . . . orations, and gory transparencies" and readings of occasional poems, "reminding citizens of the 'Theatre of Blood,'" as Silverman notes, that had played in their streets.[68] The colonial patriot press also increasingly stressed the threat posed by British tyranny to individual citizens, suggesting that at any moment citizens might be forced to don the toga of the Catonic effigy and play not only the patriot stoically withstanding an imperial siege but also the patriot martyr.[69] From 22 November 1771 to 6 April 1775 the *Massachusetts Spy* printed in its masthead Cato's prayer to liberty after condemning Sempronius's mutineers to death: "Do thou Great Liberty inspire our souls—, / and make our Lives in thy Possession happy, / Or, our deaths glorious in thy Defence."[70]

This fear of future events also took a firm hold in allusions to *Cato* made by two of the most famous women of the Revolutionary generation. Mercy Otis Warren's propaganda play *The Adulateur*, first published in the *Spy* in 1772 and reprinted in 1773 as a pamphlet, includes both thinly veiled allegorical scenes recounting the Massacre and an epigraph taken from a speech that Cato makes to the Utican Senate after rejecting Caesar's overtures:

Then let us rise, my friends, and strive to fill
This little interval, this pause of life,
(While yet our liberty and fates are doubtful)
With resolution, friendship, Roman bravery,
And all the virtues we can crowd into it;
That Heaven may say, it aught [*sic*] to be prolong'd.[71]

A letter from Abigail Adams to Mercy Warren after the pamphlet printing of *The Adulateur* in 1773 shows that these published implications of the potential for spectacular violence reflected actual tensions in the street: commenting on the controversy caused by the presence of the tea ship *Dartmouth*, the object of the Boston Tea Party's raid, in Boston Harbor, the astute Mrs. Adams observes: "Such is the present Spirit that prevails that if once they are made desperate many, very Many of our Heroes will spread their lives in the cause, with the Speech of Cato in their mouths, 'What a pitty is it, that we can dye but once to save our Country.'"[72] Three years later, of course, Nathan Hale would fulfill her prophecy.

Janus: Patrick Henry as Orator

Deployments of *Cato* by patriot partisans were not restricted to New England, however. The *Pennsylvania Evening Post*, for instance, in September 1775 reprinted the prologue to *Cato* spoken by the then Prince George in 1749, specifying the occasion and the speaker's role as the good son Portius without explicitly naming the king. Given the prologue's celebration of "those heroes . . . / Whom the great William brought to bless [Britain]" and its identification of William of Orange's ancestors as the speaker's "GOOD FOREFATHERS," the speaker's identity could not have been in doubt, nor could the editor's implication that the king's refusal to address colonial grievances had betrayed his constitutional principles, his American subjects, and his very "British" patrimony.[73] In the southern colonies, the *Georgia Gazette* published a long, angry letter from "An American" that deplores British tyranny and quotes from Cato's speech invoking "the gen'rous plan of power deliver'd down, / From age to age, by your renown'd forefathers" and seeking inspiration from "great Liberty."[74]

Addison's play also resonated in Virginia, where the pervasive oratorical culture had "weakened the role of the written word itself" in favor of the power of public speaking, and where, as elsewhere in the colonies, the political system had experienced the development of a new form of popular oratory in the wake of the Great Awakening and the birth of the patriot movement.[75] One of the most famous Catonic performances in Revolutionary history is associated with Virginia's greatest patriot orator, the attorney Patrick Henry, in his famous "St. John's Day" speech, delivered on 23 March 1775 before the Virginia House of Burgesses. As the House debated the muster of a militia in the wake of the outbreak of hostilities in Massachusetts at Lexington and Concord, Henry, rising in favor of the muster, made explicit the implicit violence of the patriots' pro-war rhetoric, declaring, "The war is inevitable—and let it come! I repeat it sir, let it come!" Echoes of Addison resound in the speech's famous peroration, which invokes *Cato*'s familiar dichotomy: "Is life so dear, or peace so sweet, as to be purchased at the price of chains and slavery? Forbid it, Almighty God!—I know not what course others may take; but as for me, give me liberty, or give me death."[76] Edmund Randolph, on hand for this debate, noted the balance between Henry's stoic gaze and the intense theatricality of this performance, which included "slavelike gestures of submission and bondage, the shattering of chains, and the plunging of an invisible dagger into his breast," suggesting that in this moment Henry appeared to be literally enacting the Catonic text's conflicts between stoicism and passion, and between freedom, slavery, and death.[77]

At least one observer noticed the Catonic allusion embedded in Henry's histrionic performance and committed it to writing. The Virginia jurist St. George Tucker compares Henry's delivery of this speech to "the calm dignity of Cato, of Utica," and the audience of Virginia delegates to "the Roman Senate."[78] Henry's allusion, however, is more complex than Tucker's observation suggests. While Henry alludes to Cato's trademark line, "It is not now time to talk of aught / But chains, or conquest; liberty, or death," Cato does not utter these lines in the Senate but in a private conversation with Prince Juba after the Senate resolves to defy Caesar.[79] Henry's speech, including its endorsement of inevitable war, also echoes the speech delivered by Sempronius to the Senate: "My voice is still for war. / Gods, can a Roman Senate long debate / Which of the two to chuse, slavery or death!".[80] Sempronius, in order to disguise his treachery with patriotic zeal, appropriates Cato's characteristic rhetoric as part of a very different performance indeed, underscoring once again the essentially theatrical nature of the personae of both the tyrant and the patriot.

Julie K. Ellison, observing Henry's debt to both of these speeches, suggests that Henry's oration "sanitized the implications of the traitorous Sempronius's speech."[81] Henry's fiery rhetoric and simultaneous references to both Cato and Sempronius, however, also address a profound anxiety over the performance practice of political oratory during the Revolutionary period. The "elocutionary revolution" of the mid-eighteenth century had democratized (relatively speaking) oratory by making the tools of successful speechmaking available to an ever-wider audience. Public speaking, particularly when marked by Catonic rhetoric subsuming the individual self within the state, also affords those with less-than-benign designs on power the opportunity for "a Machiavellian concealment of real motives and opinions."[82] Consequently, a number of contemporary observers express reservations that fervent patriotic rhetoric—the "rage . . . fire . . . [and] fury" unleashed by Sempronius and by Henry—provides an ample disguise, thanks to the theatricality displayed by such exemplary figures as Cato himself, for those whose politics lean toward tyranny.[83]

Such concern over the authenticity of the political motives of orators was an issue for loyalist and patriot alike during the Revolutionary period. As early as 1761, John Adams privately expressed his fear of the potential dangers to the health of the body politic posed by inflammatory speech: "Eloquence that may be employed wisely to persuade, is often employed wickedly to seduce, from the Eloquence of Greece and Rome down to the rude speeches of our American Town Meeting . . . [T]he most refined Patriotism to which human Nature can be wrought, has in it an alloy of Ambition, of Pride and Avarice that debases the Composition."[84] In an oration delivered at Braintree, Massachusetts, on 2 March

1772, Adams once again reveals this concern with the reversibility of the tyrant and the patriot, interrogating not only the putative devotion of George III to the liberty of his subjects but also the fiery rhetoric of patriotism itself, a language swirling in the New England air around him at the time: "In England, the common Rout to Power has been by making clamorous Professions of Patriotism, in early life, to secure a great Popularity, and to ride upon that Popularity, into the Highest Offices of State, and after they have arrived there, [such men] have generally been found, as little zealous to preserve the Constitution, as their Predecessors whom they have hunted down."[85]

Adams's observation echoes Trenchard's and Gordon's exasperated conclusion in *Cato's Letters* that "[a] Tory under Oppression, or out of Place, is a Whig; a Whig with Power to oppress, is a Tory."[86] American loyalists, going further than Adams, commonly displayed open disdain for the republican rhetoric and heated oratorical performances of American radicals, beginning with the pioneering patriot activist James Otis, by characterizing them as demagogic tyrants in waiting.[87] These sharp critiques focus not only on the status of the republican identity as a persona, a mask beneath which to hide aspirations toward factional dominance, but also on the radicals' oratory as bad acting. In 1772, the *Maryland Gazette* parodied this radical practice in both form and content by running a quotation from Shakespeare's Jack Cade, the aspiring demagogue from *Henry VI, Part 2*: "I have thought upon it, it shall be so. Away, burn all the records of the Realm; my mouth shall be the parliament of the land. And henceforth all things shall be common."[88]

In a 1773 sermon, the Reverend Jonathan Boucher, a patron of the Annapolis theater and unabashed loyalist, elaborated upon the argument suggested by the Cade quotation: "[A]s though there were some irresistible charm in all extraneous speaking, however rude, the orators of our committees, and sub-committees, like those in higher spheres, *prevail with their voices*. To public speakers alone is the government of our country now completely committed . . . An empire is thus completely established within an empire; and a new system of great power erected, before the old one is formally abolished."[89] Boucher's text and the *Gazette* quotation establish the self-contradictory conservative critique of revolutionary orature, of which Henry's peroration would become the most famous example: the radicals' speech is both rude and uncivilized on the one hand, and over-refined and hypocritical, a mere mask for tyrannical aspirations, on the other.

Both of these strains sounded louder after the outbreak of the Revolution. One loyalist broadside proclaimed:

Behold yon Patriot bellowing loud
For Liberty—that darling Theme.

Pull off the Mask—'tis private Grudge
Or Party Rage that forms the Scene.[90]

This rejection of both radical oratory and radical politics subtly suggests that all American patriots were, in fact, mere Semproniuses at heart, and thus traitors to Rome/Britain. In 1775, the Reverend Myles Cooper, rector of King's College (now Columbia) in New York, published a satire, "The Patriots of North America," in which Cooper, who had written a prologue in 1773 for a charity performance by David Douglass's London (by then renamed "American") Company in New York, compared American patriot orators to "mere Punchinellos," puppets for a cabal of republican conspirators and participants in a decidedly lowbrow theater:

Like Punch, who struts, and swears, and roars,
. . . .
Like Punch, who speak their Prompter's Sense,
Like his, their pow'rful Eloquence,
Like his, their wond'ring Audience.

Ironically, Cooper's life would be saved by just such a feat of oratory. In 1775, a mob accusing Cooper of being connected to the outbreak of hostilities in Massachusetts surrounded his home; only a lengthy harangue delivered to the crowd by Cooper's former student Alexander Hamilton allowed Cooper time to escape from his would-be attackers.[91]

Patrick Henry's mixed allusion to Cato and Sempronius, then, plays off a charge made throughout the colonies against public speakers who favored American independence. Rather than sanitizing the implications of Sempronius's speech, Henry's performance evokes both Cato and Sempronius and demands that the audience judge which speech, Cato's temperate statement of resolve or Sempronius's overzealous, hypocritical rant, best represents both the speaker and his words in this very theatrical public moment. Henry's other famous rhetorical performance during the House of Burgess's 1765 debate over passage of Henry's resolves against the Stamp Act displays a similar concern to avoid, as Cato cautions Sempronius, "Immoderate valour" that "swells into a fault."[92] During this debate, relates Henry's biographer, William Wirt:

[Henry] exclaimed in a voice of thunder, and with the look of a god: "Caesar had his Brutus—Charles the First, his Cromwell—And George the Third—("Treason!" cried the Speaker—"Treason, treason!" echoed from every part of the house. It was one of those trying moments which is decisive of character. Henry faltered not for an instant; but rising to a loftier attitude . . . he finished his sentence with the firmest emphasis)—*may profit by their example*. If this be treason, make the most of it."[93]

Henry's performance flirts with, but does not embrace, the revolutionary nihilism of Sempronius's speech urging suicidal combat with Caesar in hopes that "some arm, more lucky than the rest, / May reach [Caesar's] heart, and free the world from bondage."[94] The audience, however, is once again drawn into his performance and forced to make interpretive choices as to the relative status of both Henry and King George as tyrants or patriots before Henry steps back across the line, having ironically forced those audience members who shout "treason!" to describe the king as a tyrant. In a different rendition of the speech recorded in the journal of a French traveler in the audience, Henry says, "'he had read that in former times tarquin and Julius had their brutus, Charles had his Cromwell, and he Did not Doubt but some good American would stand up, in favour of his Country,'" and when condemned for treason apologizes if he has "'affronted the speaker, or the house, he was ready to ask pardon, and he would show his loyalty to his majesty King G. the third, at the Expence of the last Drop of his blood,'" while excusing himself for having spoken in the "'heat of passion'" and out of concern for "'his Countrys Dying liberty.'"[95] While engaging in the formal ritual of asking for a pardon, Henry nonetheless engages in a performative utterance that cannot entirely be unsaid. The audience, like a jury, can never wholly disregard the comment that has been withdrawn from the official record.

Henry, famous for his "natural" and undisciplined oratory, in both versions of the story figures the act of the Revolution as a "vocal assertion" structured around a climactic moment of improvisation.[96] Even in the less melodramatic French version, the apology that he has been moved by "passion" suggests that, by playing off his reputation as an orator, Henry is both disavowing his words and acknowledging the veracity of his sentiments. The audience must decide for themselves whether to believe Henry's speech, his apology, or both. Ten years later, grounding his speech in the conflicting characters of republicanism presented in *Cato*, he fashioned another legendary early American performance by blurring the lines between the tyrant and the patriot in his advocacy of independence. That speech demanded that his audience judge which character Patrick Henry embodied and, by extension, the nature of their own personal relationship to the ideals that Henry espoused. The image of Henry in 1775 declaring his preference for death over slavery encompasses a number of powerful abstractions: the political watchwords of the British Atlantic, "liberty" and "tyranny"; the ghosts of the Roman republic, the English Civil War, and the Glorious Revolution; and the unstable dichotomies of sovereign and subject, tyrant and patriot, traitor and martyr. Like the figure of Nathan Hale facing execution three years later, the image of Henry that history presents in these brief moments embodies the effigy of the self-sacrificing patriot so critical to the collective improvisation of the Revolution.

Washington: Valley Forge and Beyond

Despite the persuasive force of Patrick Henry's orations and the equally puissant sympathetic stage moment engineered by Nathan Hale, another figure familiar with the theater, and with Addison's text in particular, emerged during the Revolution as the living embodiment of the American Revolution and its Catonic idealism. As Simon Newman observes, "The American Revolution created any number of credible heroes, but it was Washington who held the limelight."[97] Washington's emergence as the public face of the Revolution—a figure surrounded by the major theatrical and political tropes of the eighteenth century—demonstrates both his own remarkable skill as a performer and the tremendous transfer of social energies during the American Revolution that shifted the spectacular center of American society from a "tyrant" British king to a "patriot" insurrectionist general. Washington fashioned a public image based on personal and rhetorical modesty, a quiet dedication to the ideal of liberty, and a Catonic stoicism that followed "the Whig model of leadership" displayed in Addison's play.[98]

Washington's public representation of the Catonic ideal, given his occasional awkwardness in public speaking and his generally reserved attitude, seems to reflect the calm stoicism of Cato, but not the character's loudly declaimed devotion to liberty and country.[99] His "act" was more Portius than Marcus. In print, however, *Cato* served Washington the commander well as a literary vehicle for delivering praise and silencing debate, often in rather Olympian tones. Faced with complaints from New England's congressional representatives that their region was underrepresented among the officer corps of the new army, Washington wrote in July 1775, only a month after his commissioning, "I should hope every Post would be deemed honourable which gave a man opportunity to serve his Country," a paraphrase of Cato's dying advice to Portius, "When vice and impious men bear sway, / the post of Honour is a private station," and a tart reply intimating undue factionalism on the part of the objecting representatives.[100] Washington repeated this line in a letter to the newly commissioned Benedict Arnold in September 1775. Then in December 1775, praising his subordinate's early military successes, Washington informed Arnold, "It is not in the power of mortals to command success, but you have done more, you have deserved it," paraphrasing, ironically, Portius's line to the traitorous Sempronius: "'Tis not in mortals to command success, / But we'll do more, Sempronius; we'll deserve it."[101]

Washington did not single-handedly fashion himself as the Cato of the Revolution. During 1777 and 1778, he had plenty of help. In November 1777, General William Howe led an attack on Washington's forces in

Pennsylvania, soundly defeating the Continental Army at Brandywine and Germantown and taking possession of Philadelphia, where the wintering British army celebrated their victories with an elaborate theatrical season.[102] Washington was forced to retreat to nearby Valley Forge, where his undersupplied troops passed a miserable winter. In an address to the Massachusetts militia delivered during this crisis in the Revolution, the Reverend Peter Thacher underscored the tremendous danger posed by these recent British victories, both to the American cause and to its figurehead, in a sermon clearly influenced by the gallows theater of martial and political martyrdom: "Why doth [imagination] transport me to the field of blood, the place of execution for the friends of American liberty! Who doth it there call me to view led to the scaffold, with the dignity of a Cato, the firmness of a Brutus, and the gentleness of a Cicero in his countenance? It is the gallant Washington deserted by his countrymen and sacrificed because he loved his country and fought in its defense!"[103] Thacher constructs an image of Washington as a patriot sacrifice in the tradition of Roman republican martyrs that heightens the drama of his battlefield leadership. As Gutafson observes, Washington serves as both Moses and Christ, "at once a leader of the nation and a sacrificial offering on its behalf."[104]

The risk of death, and subsequent conversion to martyrdom, is key to the role of the patriot, as evidenced by the symbolic connection established between Hale and his fellow *Cato* fan George Washington—the Revolution's most famous martyr and its commander in chief—by the British troops who suspended an improvised "portrait" of Washington next to Hale's corpse. Thacher's sermon follows the same symbolic logic as the mockery of Hale's executioners, inviting the listener to meditate upon the potential death of Washington. The general serves in Thacher's text as a metaphorical embodiment of American liberty, mirroring, like his placeholder Hale, the Roman martyr's figurative embodiment of the republic. Thacher's *Cato* comparison also, like Patrick Henry's self-dramatizing oratorical performances, demands a renewed political commitment from both the individual auditor and collective audience in order to interpret the text properly.

Washington's soldiers interpreted the general's Catonic status in a surprisingly optimistic fashion at the end of their encampment in Valley Forge. On 11 May 1778, Washington's troops staged a performance of *Cato*, in open defiance of the congressional ban on stage plays, in order to celebrate the news of a military alliance with France, which had reached the camp on 6 May.[105] William Bradford, a young colonel in Washington's army, reported in a letter to his sister in Philadelphia that "last Monday Cato was performed before a very splendid and numerous audience" including "His Excellency" General Washington and his wife, Martha, and

General William Alexander. "If the Enemy does not retire from Philadelphia soon," continues Bradford, "our Theatrical Amusement will continue . . . The 'Recruiting Officer' is also on foot. I hope, however, that we shall be disappointed in these by the more agreeable Entertainment of taking possession of Philadelphia."[106]

Washington's tacit approval of this performance, signified by his attendance at the celebration, attests not only to his fondness for the theater in general and *Cato* in particular but also to his skilled manipulation of his own image. If *Cato*'s setting in the last desert bastion of Roman liberty appealed to American colonists during wars with the French, so much the more must the analogy have obtained in the minds of Washington's troops after enduring battle with their former countrymen and a winter of short rations and harsh weather, a frigid equivalent of the Addisonian desert's "burning wastes, / Its barren rocks, parched earth, and hills of sand, / Its tainted air, and all its broods of poison."[107] Furthermore, the metatheatrical resurrection of Utica on American soil in this performance clearly designates Washington, by virtue of his command, as Cato, risking his life (as noted in Thacher's sermon) for the American cause and sharing the miseries of his troops. As Juba says of Cato:

Renouncing sleep, and rest, and food, and ease,
He strives with thrift and hunger, toil and heat;
And when his fortune sets before him all
The pomps and pleasures that his soul can wish,
His rigid virtue will accept of none.[108]

Washington's attendance at the Valley Forge *Cato* thus affirmed both his concern for the welfare of his men and his command over them, meanwhile acknowledging the stoic "republican" virtue demanded of the army at Valley Forge. The potential production of *The Recruiting Officer*, a play that both satirizes and celebrates military life, and especially the military practice of impressment, would have been a demonstration of the capacity of a suffering army (and one that faced major difficulties with reenlistment throughout the war) to laugh at military life itself through the vehicle of a patriotic romp.[109] The Valley Forge *Cato*, likewise, renewed the vows of loyalty between Washington and the Continental Army and confirmed the revolutionary commitment of the entire army to the Revolution, a collective stripping of the sleeve to display wounds earned in their new nation's service and a proclamation of willingness to shed further blood in its defense.

The question of sacrificial bloodshed also distinguishes the pessimistic conclusion of Cato's life from the circumstances attendant upon the Valley Forge performance. The forlorn Cato commits suicide just as fresh reinforcements headed by other enemies of Caesar arrive at Utica. As the obligatorily late messenger announces during Addison's final tableau:

Pompey's son . . . through the realms of Spain
Calls out for vengeance on his father's death,
And rouses the whole nation up to arms.
Were Cato at their head, once more might Rome
Assert her rights, and claim her liberty.[110]

Only Cato's too hasty self-slaughter precludes Rome's salvation. Washington and his troops, however, had survived their ordeal at Valley Forge to hear the news of the alliance with France, rendering such star-crossed suicide unthinkable. The performance's celebration of the French alliance rendered Valley Forge both Utica and not Utica, and Washington both Cato and not Cato, claiming identification with the Roman republicans for their valor and stoic endurance while holding out the tantalizing possibility that the Continental Army might be able to embrace both liberty and life—a critical, improvisational revision of political and theatrical history.

With the American and British armies stationed so close to each other, moreover, that "scouts and spies were in constant traffic between the armies and both sides were fully aware of what the other was doing," the production of *Cato* was doubtless also aimed at Howe's thespian troops in their comfortable Philadelphia billets. This counter-performance transmitted the image of a distressed but unbroken army still capable of staging a play of its own. The Continental Army's Valley Forge *Cato* announced the stern resolve of the army and the justice of its cause—not to mention the arrival of its French allies—in literary and aesthetic terms shared with the British enemy. On 23 May, orders were issued to General Sir Henry Clinton, who had replaced Howe as commander of the British forces at Philadelphia, to evacuate to New York in light of France's entry into the war. The Continental Army retook the city in June 1778, and William Bradford never got his chance to see *The Recruiting Officer*.[111]

The Valley Forge *Cato* was not an isolated performance during the winter of 1778: *Cato* was also performed at the Bow Street Theatre in Portsmouth, New Hampshire, at this time.[112] While no firm date can be established for the performance, the occasional epilogue written by Portsmouth resident Jonathan Mitchell Sewall, which criticizes France's delaying aid to the American forces, suggests that the Portsmouth performance predates the Valley Forge staging. Sewall's epilogue conducts an extended allegorical reading of the play, making explicit the familiar analogies between Britain and Rome, as well as Washington and Cato, implied in the Valley Forge performance. Sewall inquires:

Did Caesar, drunk with power and madly brave
Insatiate burn, his country to enslave?
Did he for this, lead forth a servile host,
And spill the choicest blood that Rome could boast?
Our British Caesar too has done the same,
And damn'd this age to everlasting fame.[113]

Sewall then nominates Washington as the patriot figure to oppose the British tyrant:

Did Rome's brave senate nobly strive t'oppose
The mighty torrent of the domestic foe?
. . . .
Our senate too, the same bold deed has done,
And for a Cato, arm'd a Washington!
A chief in all the ways of battle skill'd,
Great in the council, and glorious in the field!
Thy scourge, O Britain! And Columbia's boast,
The dread, and admiration, of each host!

Sewall's epilogue, which was quickly reprinted in a handful of New England newspapers and then reproduced in editions of *Cato* printed in Portsmouth in 1778 and Providence in 1779, typifies the literary reconstruction of *Cato* as an "American" text. The analogies raised by this revolutionary appropriation also participated in the formation of the postwar self-image of the United States as a bastion of republican liberty. The epilogue was even included in postwar editions of *Cato* printed in Worcester, Massachusetts, in 1782 and Boston in 1793.[114] Sewall's final exhortation to his audience, however, also signals, albeit unintentionally, that a republican revolution would not, in itself, be adequate to shed the self-imposed shackles of empire:

Rise then, my countrymen! For fight prepare,
Gird on your swords, and fearless rush to war!
For your griev'd country nobly dare to die,
And empty all your veins for Liberty.
No pent-up Utica contracts your pow'rs,
But the whole boundless continent is yours![115]

Sewall's urging Roman valor upon his audience shifts, in the closing couplet, from an exhortation to resistance into an endorsement of territorial expansion, the cultural desideratum that drew Roman forces to North Africa and British colonists to North America, and which had helped to sow dissension between land-hungry colonists and colonial administrators after the Royal Proclamation of 1763. Sewall sweeps aside the limitations imposed on American expansion by both "Caesarian" Britain through legal decree and by Americans themselves through their self-characterization as "pent-up" republicans, claiming for the United States a "boundless" transcontinental domain.

This wartime shift of revolutionary rhetoric away from a purely oppositional vision of republican patriotism is further underscored by an additional 1778 performance in Portsmouth, this time of *Coriolanus*. It is unclear whether this performance staged Shakespeare's version or the adaptation written by James Thomson in 1747, although the only known colonial performance of the play, in June 1767 at Philadelphia, was Thomson's version.[116] Never one of Shakespeare's most popular plays, *Coriolanus* chronicles the downfall of Caius Marcius Coriolanus, a patrician Roman exiled for his anti-republican sentiments, and his subsequent attempt to conquer the city with the aid of an opposing nation, the Volscians. When Coriolanus agrees to a truce with the Romans, however, he is assassinated by a group of Volscian conspirators. Thomson's revisions excise several displays of Coriolanus's condescension toward the plebeians of Rome and add a number of lectures delivered both to and by Coriolanus on the importance of submitting personal interests to the good of the state, thus rendering its flawed hero as both the glory of the republic and its potential destroyer.[117]

Just as Sewall's epilogue to *Cato* mixes republicanism with territorial expansionism, his epilogue to *Coriolanus* takes up the cause of Coriolanus, who declares war against his own republican country, as its own. Hearkening back to the earlier production of *Cato* in Portsmouth, Sewall declares that rather than displaying a "martyr bleeding in his country's right," *Coriolanus* depicts "a majestic Roman, great and good, / Driv'n by his country's base ingratitude, / From parent, wife, and offspring, whelm'd in woe."[118] Sewall, having previously exalted the Catonic sacrifices of Washington and his patriot army, here equates Britain not with Caesarian Rome but with the moribund and faction-ridden Roman republic, a polity in need of reinvigoration by a strong, charismatic leader—an executive role that could be filled by either a patriot or a tyrant. Sewall's derisive equation of the Hanoverian monarchy with the same Roman republic that he praised in his epilogue to *Cato*, and which offered an inspirational political analogue for the American revolutionaries, presents decidedly ominous implications for the future of the United States, as does his implicit equation of Washington and the imperious Coriolanus, which effaces the Roman's objectionable authoritarianism while lauding his heroic individualism.

In 1776, Nathan Hale gave the American uprising a martyr, one whose sacrificial death signified the United States' attainment of their political majority. Sewall's epilogues, like the elevation of Washington to the status of a patriot effigy in which they participated, illustrate that the United

States, even in the midst of rebellion, had begun to seek out new figures on the public stage capable of both embodying the Revolution itself and providing a symbolic, personal identity for the nascent state that the Continental Congress had erected to replace the British monarchy of its former patriot king, George III. The introduction of the Caesarian themes of territorial expansion and the rule of charisma to these Catonic strains indicates not only the latent ideological sympathies between the American revolutionaries and the political traditions (both idealistic and pragmatic) of Great Britain. This uncomfortable intertwining of the republican and the imperial visions of patriotism also, in retrospect, illustrates the uncanny similarities between the role of the tyrant and the patriot in the politicized theaters and theatrical politics of the eighteenth century.

Chapter 3
Free-Born Peoples: The Politics of Professional Theater in Early America

On 15 September 1752, a major event in the theatrical history of British North America took place: the London Company of Comedians, a troupe of English professional actors led by Lewis Hallam Sr. and one of the pioneering companies of the early American theater, opened at Williamsburg, Virginia, by staging *The Merchant of Venice*. This performance featured an occasional prologue championing the theater's promulgation of private and public morality, arguing that "on Athen's [*sic*] infant Stage":

The Tragic Muse did Honour to the State,
And in a Mirrour taught them to be great;
The Comick too, by gentle Means reprov'd;
Lash'd every Vice, and every Vice remov'd:
. . . .
Thus was the Grecian Stage, the Romans too;
When e'er they wrote, had Virtue in their View:
In this politer age, on British ground,
The sprightly Scenes, with Wit and Sense abound.

For the virtue as well as the pleasure of the British people, the prologue explains, the London Company's players have hastened to the "unknown Climes" of "Virginia's plains," an outpost of their state and people, confident of a reception from a British (albeit colonial) audience, "sensible, polite, and kind."[1]

This inaugural speech deploys the figure of theatrical performance as a mirror—a commonplace at least since Hamlet first offered his instructions to the players—to establish the British (or British American) theater as a space for instruction in both civic and private virtue. The explicit connections that the prologue makes between theatrical performance and nation building, the growth of Athens and the establishment of the British colonies, carry special significance in the transatlantic venue of the Williamsburg theater. The North American locale and the liminal political status of the audience members as creole colonials, English Americans, afford a special intensity to the quintessentially "British" experience of theatergoing. The transplanted body and voice of an actor from the British homeland both generate and demystify the "Britishness" of the colonial locale.[2] The poet's deployment of the mirror image, as well as the implicit genealogy that he fashions with Athens, Rome, and Britain itself as precedents, also affords a view of the place of professional theater in the public life of the colonies at midcentury.

It is no coincidence that the Williamsburg prologue's display of the theater's value in terms of British cultural capital also asserts the theater's power to sway an audience. This text implies that many colonials did indeed welcome the theater, both as a link to British culture and as an institution for the improvement of civic life. The battle over the legitimacy of the theater in North America was generally fought in such civic terms during the eighteenth century. In both Britain and the colonies, opponents of the theater decried the iniquitous behavior of playgoers and the moral (and sometimes political) content of the popular drama as dangerous to the virtue of the viewing public.[3] Frequently the theater's opponents countered the argument that theater improved its audience and produced a sense of common identity among its audience members by invoking the disdain displayed in the Puritan and republican intellectual traditions for the theater as a symbol of courtly corruption. This argument remained current well into the eighteenth century and had particular relevance for colonial debates over the legitimacy of the theater.

The author of *A Sure Guide to Hell, by Belzebub* (1750), a moral tract first published in London that became a bestseller in the colonies, notably ignores the question of theatrical "falsehood" entirely while still presenting arguments about the danger of the theater to society that are redolent of the doctrines of the Country party opposition, if not of the Interregnum commonwealth. Ostensibly an advice manual for sinners written by a proto-Screwtape, the *Sure Guide* advises young rakes to frequent "Taverns . . . Operas and Masquerades, all which are Nurseries of Vice and Folly," and suggests that ministers of state who encourage the luxury and indolence fostered by the playhouse "may easily surprise [the People] out of their Privileges, Rights, and Properties, and every Thing else that is dear to them."[4]

The political ramifications of the debate over the role of the theater in British society on both the mainland and the colonial periphery have prompted a reconsideration of the received accounts of the professional theater's establishment in North America and its role in the sociopolitical development of the colonies. A theater enmeshed in public controversy and alternately exalted as an edifying patriotic spectacle or damned as a tool for tyrannical luxury, for instance, allows for the refinement of traditional hypotheses such as David D. Mays's argument that acting company managers overcame colonial hostility to the professional theater by selecting anodyne plays that "confirmed the middle-class feelings of [the] developing audience."⁵ The colonial popularity of Addison's decidedly political *Cato*, even among the generally theater-averse residents of the New England colonies, suggests that although middle-class North Americans may have preferred to have their political opinions affirmed rather than challenged by the drama, they were prepared to stomach controversial, political theater.

Meanwhile, in the print public sphere of Britain, where most colonial anti-theatrical arguments originated, not even *Cato* was immune from political criticism. Despite Addison's attempts to write a patriotic tragedy centered on principles rather than party loyalties, his tragic tale became fodder for the argument that the stage fostered civic disorder. As a critic writing in the *Universal Spectator, and Weekly Journal* argued in 1731, no doubt looking backward to the efforts of Trenchard and Gordon in *Cato's Letters*,

> But Cato itself has increased the Evils of the present Time, [*sic*] how many Poetasters have since then infested the World with wild notions of Liberty and Patriotism! What strange romantic Whims have they had of Freedom, and independency from Power! As if, as Mr. Dryden says,
>
> "They led their wild Desires to Rocks and Caves,
> And thought that all, but Savages, were Slaves."⁶

This critique of *Cato* (by an author who nonetheless lavishes praise on both Addison and his script) echoes both Dryden's ridicule of seventeenth-century Whig politics in *Absalom and Achitophel* and Hobbes's chilling political quietism in *Leviathan*. It also illustrates that not even Addison's reputation as a moralist could preserve his play from the political fray. Even *Cato*, written to appeal to a broad spectrum of patriotic opinion encompassing both Whig and Tory, could be made to reveal a (perhaps unintentional) bias toward radicalism under the critical microscope. The conservatism implicit in this comment and its origin in the metropole rather than the colonies, moreover, suggest that the colonial popularity of *Cato*, both on stage and in frequent allusions to the text by colonial patriots (some of whom were likely also staunch opponents of the theater) rested in no small part on these undertones of political controversy, a tinge of radical histrionics that marked the text as available for appropriation.

The complexities of the relationship between colonial politics and colonial playhouses also require a revision of the binary relationship between metropole and colonial periphery posited in the early work of Peter A. Davis, in which he argues that the theater served as a symbol of political and economic hegemony, a focal point for colonial resentment. More recently Davis has acknowledged the catholicity of colonial opinion regarding the theater evidenced by the Williamsburg prologue, although he still argues that the colonial theater was enmeshed in the civil broils of the transatlantic British community.[7] Even such revisionary arguments, however, more often than not take place within histories of American theater and drama that emphasize mainly the post-Revolutionary growth of the theater and the evolution of the "national" American drama in the nineteenth century. In such cases, the overwhelming cultural "Britishness" of the early American theater serves to complicate, rather than enrich, the argument. When read from an Atlanticist rather than a nationalist perspective, however, the intertwining developments in colonial theater history and politics illustrate the centrality of the patriotism promoted by British plays and theatrical criticism to the evolution of the North American professional theater and the North American patriot community.

Theater managers and political activists in North America, operating in a cultural climate where fierce passions attached themselves to the theater, deployed both British theatrical texts and the image of the British theater itself in response to local, contemporary political conditions. As in the case of *Cato* in the colonies, the dramaturgical trio of the tyrant, the sacrificial victim, and the patriot played leading roles in the history of the theatrical repertoire, appearing in a variety of British plays, both as theatrical performances chosen by professional managers to capitalize on local political conditions and as fodder for allusions in colonial political literature. The genealogy of these figures in the colonial theater dovetails with the efforts made by theater managers to use the theater's power to disseminate the doctrine of British (or American) liberty—to serve the interests of "patriots" as opposed to those of "tyrants"— in order to promote their medium in the colonies. The printed drama and the theater also, periodically, intersect (as in the case of *Cato*) with the colonial street theater of political protest, including one occasion where a theater fell victim to a group of self-appointed American patriots opposed to both the Stamp Act and the staging of plays.

Brief Chronicles of the Time: An Introduction to the Players

Understanding the rich interactions between the professional theater and colonial politics requires a basic familiarity with the history of the touring companies. The Hallams' London Company was not the first professional acting company to tour in British North America. Among documented theater troupes, the Hallams were preceded by professional or amateur companies playing in Williamsburg, Philadelphia, New York City, Charleston, and Jamaica between 1710 and the 1740s.[8] They were most closely preceded by a company originating in Philadelphia, headed by Walter Murray and Thomas Kean (whose personal origins have not been satisfactorily explained), and also by Robert Upton, who contracted to be the Hallams' advance man but unsuccessfully attempted to establish himself in New York ahead of his employers' arrival. The Murray-Kean company's first performance came in 1749, a staging of *Cato* in Philadelphia that at least one prominent theater historian has deemed the point of origin for the North American theater, professional or otherwise. The Murray-Kean troupe then went on to tour New York, Williamsburg, Norfolk, and Annapolis before apparently dissolving in December 1752, shortly after the arrival of the Hallams.[9] Upton played a brief season from January to March 1752.[10] The London Company, run first by the Hallams and then (after Mrs. Hallam's remarriage to David Douglass) by Mr. and Mrs. Douglass, however, is the preeminent touring company of the pre-Revolutionary American theater.[11]

While the records of their opening season display some significant gaps, the Hallams appear to have played in Williamsburg until early 1753 and spent the spring of that year following the trail through Virginia and Maryland first blazed by the Murray-Kean Company. The London Company then toured the three other major venues for colonial theater: New York (July 1753–March 1754), Philadelphia (April–June 1754), and Charleston (October 1754–January 1755). The Hallams' repertoire prominently featured three patriotic texts also popularized by the Murray-Kean Company: *Cato*, Farquhar's *The Recruiting Officer*, and Colley Cibber's revision of *Richard III*; the Hallams also introduced Nicholas Rowe's Williamite paean *Tamerlane* to the colonial stage. After concluding their run in Charleston, the London Company sailed for Jamaica, where Lewis Hallam Sr. died in 1756. Thereafter the widowed Mrs. Hallam married David Douglass, the manager of a theater company based in Jamaica, and the merged company returned to North America in 1758.[12]

Arriving in North America in the midst of the Seven Years' War, David Douglass and the London Company embarked on two major circuits of the colonies between 1758 and 1764, during which time, it appears, he and the rest of the company proved themselves to be adept at promoting the theater as a patriotic spectacle by resurrecting the Hallam-era repertoire of popular patriotic plays and employing prologues that praised the plays themselves and the war effort they were intended to glorify. The company's first tour began in New York (December 1758–February 1759), and then proceeded to Philadelphia (June–December 1759), Annapolis (March–May 1760), Upper Marlborough, Maryland (May–July 1760), and Williamsburg (October 1760–March 1761) before finishing with a stint in Newport, Rhode Island (August–October 1761). The company's second circuit began with a return to New York (November 1761–May 1762), followed by a second, mostly unsuccessful attempt to play in New England—specifically, Providence, Rhode Island, and Portsmouth, New Hampshire—during the summer (June–August) of 1762, and concluding with seasons in Williamsburg (November 1762–May 1763) and Charleston (November

1763–May 1764). After completing their run in Charleston, during which Douglass had renamed the troupe the American Company, the players left North America for Barbados until late 1765.[13]

The American Company played in Barbados throughout 1764–65, during which time Douglass also sailed to London to recruit new actors. In 1765 the North American colonies began to undergo the upheavals of the Stamp Act Crisis, a potential political dilemma for British actors that Douglass seems to have done his best to avoid after returning to Charleston with part of the company in November 1765. Douglass's partial company played there apparently without incident until May 1766, although a hybrid professional/amateur company headed by one "Mr. Tomlinson," formerly of the American Company, that played in New York during April–May 1766 was caught up in the public furor over the Stamp Act. As the Stamp Act Crisis ebbed, Douglass and the American Company traveled to Philadelphia, where they christened a new theater, the Southwark, enjoying enormously successful runs from November 1766 to July 1767 and September to November 1767 that were also marked by Douglass's renewed efforts at public relations, including the introduction of *Macbeth*—a touchstone for the British and colonial opposition—to the Company's repertoire.[14]

At the conclusion of the American Company's supplementary season at the Southwark, the troupe relocated to New York and opened another new facility, the John Street Theatre, playing there from December 1767 to June 1768. (Meanwhile, a new company billed as the "Virginia" or "New American" Company, headed by a former Douglass associate, William Verling, had begun a lengthy tour through Virginia and Maryland that lasted from January 1768 into the spring of 1769, before the troupe vanished and then reappeared in the Leeward Islands during 1770.)[15] After the conclusion of the John Street Theatre's somewhat controversial and financially disappointing opening season, however, the American Company's receipts for their next two runs in Philadelphia (September 1768–January 1769) and New York (January–June 1769) appear to have taken a downturn.[16] This reversal of fortune was due no doubt in part to growing anti-British, pro-boycott sentiments in these cities fueled by the Townshend Duties, a phenomenon already evident during the American Company's initial run at the John Street. Douglass seems to have responded during the company's next season in Philadelphia (September 1769–June 1770) by altering the repertoire, adding new plays that reflected a more conservative, though still "patriotic," point of view while gradually removing such potentially radical texts as *Cato* and *Tamerlane*; these were replaced with plays such as *King John* and Dryden's Tory version of *The Tempest*. Douglass also took the company on an extended tour of Virginia and Maryland, from whence his actors had been absent for several years and where anti-British sentiments did not necessarily translate into opposition to the theater, from June 1770 to October 1772.[17]

Having concluded their extended tour of Virginia and Maryland, the American Company returned to Philadelphia and played there from November 1772 until March 1773. During this period Douglass seems to have begun making conciliatory gestures to the patriot community in Philadelphia, such as staging *Julius Caesar*, while still actively currying favor with the city's more politically conservative elements and the British military stationed in the local garrison. This effort involved both maintaining the quietist repertoire adopted before the company's southern tour and staging plays that emphasized the glory of His Majesty's armed forces, most notably a production of the history play *The Conquest of Canada*. The company would follow a similar pattern during its final pre-Revolutionary engagement in New York (April–August 1773), where General Thomas Gage, supreme commander of all British troops in the colonies, still maintained his headquarters. After brief engagements in Annapolis (September–October 1773) and Philadelphia once again (November 1773), the Company sailed to Charleston in December 1773, where their season stretched until May 1774, overlapping with both the Boston Tea Party and Parliament's retaliatory passage of the Intolerable Acts. The Continental Congress's 1774 ban on theater forced the American Company to sail once again for Jamaica after the conclusion of the Charleston season. The schedule for their final pre-Revolutionary season, however, illustrates that David Douglass and the American Company once again bent with the prevailing political winds as 1774 progressed, playing to the increasingly anti-British patriotic sympathies of a public ready to consume such politically charged spectacles as the American Company's productions of *Cato*, *The Recruiting Officer*, and *Julius Caesar*.[18]

Strange Bedfellows: *Cato* and *The Recruiting Officer*

The brief vogue for amateur theatricals in New York, Williamsburg, and Charleston during the 1730s suggests that colonial theater was always already enmeshed in public affairs.[19] The amateur companies that staged these productions, which introduced both *Cato* and *The Recruiting Officer*, two of the most popular plays of the colonial era, to the North American stage, commonly featured close ties to prominent local politicians. Both of these plays were produced during New York's 1732 season by a company run by Thomas Heady, the professional or amateur status of which remains unknown. The productions of this company appear, as previously noted, to have ties to the ongoing conflict between Governor (and Walpole crony) William Cosby and his opponents, led by Lewis Morris and Rip Van Dam. The company's performances took place in a building belonging to city council president and former governor Rip Van Dam, and Heady was Van Dam's wigmaker.[20]

Politicians were also involved with the theater in Virginia and South Carolina. The 1736 *Cato* performed by students at the College of William and Mary, which coincided with the annual meeting of the House of Burgesses, would inevitably have been colored by the reputation for political ambition of the college's president, the Scottish clergyman James Blair, who was also a member of the Virginia Governor's Council. An amateur production of *The Recruiting Officer* staged during this season, moreover, featured performances by the sister and son of Governor William Gooch. (Both productions, moreover, might have been influenced by Gooch's concern, dating from the beginning of his tenure in 1727, with improving the colony's military readiness.)[21] In Charleston, where both *Cato* and *The Recruiting Officer* were produced between 1735 and 1737, the development of the amateur theater was strongly influenced by Dr. Thomas Dale, a prominent English émigré then serving as an associate justice of the colony, who later served in the colonial legislature.[22]

The production of plays by amateurs (or aspiring professionals) with ties to the various colonial governments suggests that these productions endorsed civic volunteerism and theatrical displays of public virtue that mirror Sir Richard Steele's vision for a national theater that would teach its audience to bear their patriotic responsibilities as free-born Englishmen. This civic emphasis gives a special significance to the regular recurrence of *The Recruiting Officer* and its tendency to appear in tandem with *Cato*. Like *Cato*, *The Recruiting Officer* was written during the War of the Spanish Succession: in its background loom the victory of Marlborough (with whom many Whigs would identify Addison's Cato in 1713) at Blenheim in 1703 and the 1704 Act for Raising Recruits, which provided for the impressment into the British armed forces of convicts and those without visible means of support.[23] It was also one of the most popular plays of the eighteenth century: between its 1706 premiere and 1776, *The Recruiting Officer* never missed a London season, and it proved to be popular on the professional and amateur stage wherever British troops were stationed.[24]

Farquhar's somewhat rakish comedy, which follows the antics of the recruiting officer, Captain Plume, and his subordinate, Sergeant Kite, as they attempt to raise a fresh regiment of troops in the town of Shrewsbury during a winter lull in hostilities on the Continent, seems at first like an unusual text to bookend Addison's tragedy, with its ponderous displays of Roman virtue. Yet *The Recruiting Officer* exhibits a concern with the relationship between private liberty, public service, and patriotism much like Addison's preoccupation with this theme in *Cato*. In *Cato*, Addison envisions a world where all private gain must be subordinated to the good of the republic, the guarantor of liberty both public and private. Farquhar, himself a recruiting officer, depicts the state's intrusion into the comic private sphere, demanding of Shrewsbury's citizens that they supply the public good with a complement of able bodies for the war effort. Farquhar, an advocate of a national (and nationalist) theater, championed plays suited to the "Constitution of our [i.e., the British] Body Politick," but he seems equally concerned with the state's disposal of individual subjects' bodies.[25] In *The Recruiting Officer*, Farquhar campaigns vigorously for a medicinal bleeding of the civic body through the wartime sacrifice of soldiers, asserting the importance of voluntary military service as the bulwark of national and individual freedom by praising the symbolic figure of the self-sacrificing patriot. In 1721 Trenchard and Gordon argued against standing armies, observing, "In attacks upon a free state, every man will fight to defend it, because every man has something to defend in it. He is in love with his condition, his ease, and property, and will venture his life rather than lose them."[26] Fifteen years earlier, Farquhar had enshrined this principle of volunteerism, through the example of his comic hero Captain Plume, as a principle "humour" of his self-consciously British audiences—albeit in a play that also features the second most famous scene of military impressment in English literature.[27]

Farquhar's text satirizes unscrupulous recruiting practices while promoting, as Eric Rothstein notes, national service and "the honor of [Farquhar's] army."[28] *The Recruiting Officer* treats military service, as does *Cato*, as an opportunity to acquire the prestige of the patriot (and possibly the sacrificial victim), to the appeal of which Farquhar adds the material gains of plunder and social advancement. Farquhar democratizes (at least relatively speaking) the acquisition of patriotic glory, extending it from the high command to the rank and file. The song "Over the Hills and Far Away," which features prominently in the play, includes verses declaring, "He that is forced to go and fight, / will never get true honour by it, / While volunteers shall win the day" and promising soldiers that "if we go 'tis one to ten, / But we return all gentlemen."[29] The play's glorification of patriotic sacrifice, which treats warfare as a public spectacle, begins with Marlborough's offstage presence and trickles down to Plume. When Balance, a local justice of the peace and the father of Silvia, Plume's love interest, asks Plume for his account of the victory at Blenheim (displaying his affection for military pomp and circumstance and the spectacle of sacrificial bloodshed), Plume modestly refuses this request. Plume's demurral recalls the theatrical displays of stoicism that characterize Addison's Cato, both in his (partial) reticence to speak too freely of his own exploits and in the plainspoken character that his account gives of both himself and Marlborough, his exemplary patriot commander: "[A]ll that I know of the matter is, our general commanded us to beat the French, and we did so, and if he pleases to say the word, we'll do 't again."[30]

Plume's modesty, along with the forthright style of command that he attributes to Marlborough, accentuates the spectacular dramatic sacrifices of human life demanded by both military logistics and public opinion during times of war. As Julie K. Ellison observes, displays of stoicism such as Cato's refusal to weep over the body of his son Marcus or Plume's refusal to play the *miles gloriosus* are transactions that generate a surplus of sentiment, in this case patriotic sentiment, among the spectators.[31] These combinations of self-display and self-effacement, the quiet charisma of a veteran reluctant to speak of battle, provide a ground of "natural" patriotic behavior that converts eighteenth-century warfare's odd mix of chaos and rigid battlefield maneuvers into a simple exemplary tale for civilians like Balance, who explains to Plume that the taxpayers of England want "but blood for our money" and swears that if the army could repeat Marlborough's capture of the French field marshal Tallard at Blenheim, "I'd go myself for a soldier."[32]

The glories of volunteerism and battlefield service against French absolutism allow Balance to rationalize the many criminal infractions committed by Plume (and, by extension, Kite) throughout the play. When a fellow justice complains to Balance of recruiting officers' free ways with local maidenheads, Balance retorts sharply that "were it not for the bravery of those officers we should have French dragoons among us, that would leave us neither liberty, property, wife, nor daughter" (99). Moreover, Plume's and Kite's recruiting tactics, in spite of the inherent class biases of legalized impressment, emphasize the putative meritocracy of honor and patriotism afforded by military self-sacrifice. The play opens with Kite's arrival in Shrewsbury's public square, where he announces: "If any gentlemen soldiers, or others, have a mind to serve Her Majesty, and pull down the French king; if any prentices have severe masters, any children have undutiful parents; if any servants have too little wages, or any husband too much wife . . . [the cap of the Royal Grenadiers] is the cap of honour, it dubs a man a gentleman in the drawing of a tricker; and he that has had the good fortune to be born six feet high was born to be a great man" (11).

This appeal is not entirely successful, however, and Kite is forced to fall back on less reputable means of recruiting, such as planting an enlistment bonus (known as "the queen's shilling") on two unsuspecting country boys. When the marks discover the trick, however, Plume relieves them in order to avoid criminal repercussions, only to convince them to enlist voluntarily. Like Kite, Plume seasons his call to duty with the potential for advancement and material gain, declaring "Volunteers are the Men I want, those are the Men fit to make Soldiers, Captains, Generals," and inquiring of the new recruits, "What think you now of a Purse of French

Gold out of a French Monsieur's Pocket, after you have dash'd out his Brains with the But[t]-end of your Firelock?" (19, 22).

Plume and Kite use a variety of other controversial or unethical methods, both farcical and tragicomic, to enlist local men, including impressment and disguising Kite as a fortune-teller who promises riches and advancement to those who enlist under Plume. Yet as Rothstein notes, Farquhar uses Plume as a "surrogate" who takes upon himself the misdeeds of the government, from the potential dishonor of which Plume's status as a volunteer and a veteran of the front immunizes him to a certain extent.[33] The country boys that Plume recruits agree to enlist, as do the tradesmen that Kite seduces with prophecies of rapid advancement. Indeed, the true tyrants of the play, especially in the matter of impressment, seem to be Balance and his fellow justices of the peace, who in a farcical courtroom scene conscript a local pauper with five children on the shire's poor rolls and a habit of poaching game, thereby sending the community's unwanted members over the hills and far away.[34]

Through a combination of civic virtue (enlistment) and civil statute (impressment), Plume assembles a miniature of British society built on the notion of the sacrificial expenditure of blood in defense of the constitutional monarchy. Like *Cato*'s polyglot Utican garrison, Plume's regiment is a martial microcosm of British society on both sides of the Atlantic: Plume tells Justice Balance that his company is "a perfect representative of the whole commons of England" and while going over the enlistment roll with Kite notes that his men include "[a] baker, a tailor, a smith, and a butcher—I believe the first colony planted in Virginia had not more trades in their company than I have in mine."[35] As in *Cato*, moreover, the patriot identifies his household with the good of the state when Plume resigns his commission to marry Silvia in the fifth act. Like Cato's suicide, this act removes Plume from the stage of action, but his final speech makes a key distinction between post-1689 Britain and Caesarean Rome. Over the body of the slain Marcus, Cato enjoins Portius to retire from the corrupted public realm to the family homestead and till its ancestral fields: "When vice prevails and impious men bear sway, / The post of honour is a private station."[36] Plume's closing speech likewise stresses the debts of posterity (and prosperity) to service, but Plume's fate is a comic inversion of Cato's. By giving up the "liberty" of the bachelor officer's life, Plume also escapes death on the battlefield. Yet Plume, even as he removes himself from the war effort and enters private life, echoes the patriot's identification with the state, emphasizing the legitimacy of the demands placed on private citizens by Queen Anne's War. Plume declares that he will take up a form of service that combines warfare and husbandry by "rais[ing] recruits the matrimonial way," fathering, perhaps, future volunteer officers for the Royal Grenadiers.[37]

As in the case of *Cato*, there are obviously patriotic implications for the North American popularity of *The Recruiting Officer*, a play with a plot predicated on war with France. Colonial troops, including volunteer officers drawn from the ranks of the merchant and landowning classes, commonly served alongside British regulars in their clashes with the French throughout the Americas, including the War of Jenkins' Ear (1740), King George's War (1744–48), and the Seven Years' War (1754–63). (Among those veterans of the Seven Years' War who would go on to serve in the Continental Army were the revolutionary general Israel Putnam and George Washington, who began his service in the 1750s as a lanky, inexperienced lieutenant colonel in the Virginia militia.) The play's satirical treatment of impressment, however, also resonates with the complicated history of the relationship between the British military and colonial property, including the bodies of colonial subjects and their servants, in the eighteenth century.

By the time of *The Recruiting Officer*'s 1732 North American premier in New York, for instance, the colonies had already clashed with the armed forces over widespread colonial resistance to the White Pine Acts of 1722 and 1729, which effectively reserved all white pine trees in North America, even those on private property, to the use of the Royal Navy for shipbuilding material, and which had led to more than one assault on an officer of the crown.[38] During the period between 1737, the last known dates for amateur performances in Charleston, and the initial performance of the Murray-Kean troupe in 1749, moreover, questions over impressment and other methods of raising troops in the colonies also sparked serious debate between the colonial legislatures and the British military. During the War of Jenkins' Ear in 1740, faced with a pacifist Pennsylvania Assembly that refused to contribute troops to the war effort, British recruiting officers, in a stroke worthy of Captain Plume and eerily echoing Sergeant Kite's initial appeal to the young men of Shrewsbury, offered amnesty and anonymity to indentured servants and apprentices who left their masters to join the military. (The legislature appropriated money to compensate the runaways' masters.) Further anger over impressment, which many colonials claimed was illegal in North America because of an exemption granted to the colonies by Parliament in 1708, also led to assaults committed by angry citizens against military officers in Philadelphia as early as 1743.[39] During King George's War, in which New England provided the bulk of the colonial forces, an attempt by Commodore Charles Knowles to impress able-bodied seamen in Boston led to two days of widespread rioting.[40] *The Recruiting Officer*, much like *Cato*, seems to have intersected with both the overarching patriotic sentiments of British colonials in North America and their disputes with the British government over the administration of the colonies.

The Recruiting Officer was not on the bill when the theater returned to North America in August 1749 in the form of the Murray-Kean troupe's Philadelphia performance of *Cato*. Although the company would later perform *The Recruiting Officer* regularly, their avoidance of the play in Philadelphia is not surprising: even Addison's sober Roman tragedy met with resistance from the Quaker and Presbyterian communities, who expressed concern to the city council over the theater's "encouraging of Idleness and drawing great sums of money from Weak and inconsiderate People."[41] Local hostility toward the military, both because of wartime impressments and the lingering hostility over the 1740 enlistment of servants, which continued to draw protests from Philadelphians about this violation of their rights to human "property" as late as 1760, may also have led Murray and Kean to avoid staging *The Recruiting Officer*.[42] The resurrection of Addison's text does, however, suggest a certain patriotic afterglow from the recent victory over the French in King George's War among those Philadelphians who sanctioned, and could afford, the entertainment.

Kean's actors were encouraged enough by their prospects to go on the road, where they staged both *Cato* and *The Recruiting Officer* in New York during 1750–51 (acting each play three times). They acted *Cato* once and *The Recruiting Officer* twice in Annapolis in 1752 during the racing season—a gathering that drew prominent citizens from throughout Maryland and Virginia, and around which theater companies would learn to schedule their seasons whenever possible.[43] In New York, in particular, *Cato* seems to have redeemed the company in the eyes of the self-appointed guardians of the public interest: after staging *The Recruiting Officer* and *Cato* in the wake of a production of Congreve's *Love for Love*, Murray and Kean received a newspaper review suggesting that the large crowd in attendance for *Cato* "may serve to prove, that the Taste of this place is not so much vitiated, or lost to a Sense of Liberty, but that they can prefer a Representation of Virtue, to those of a loose Character."[44] The Hallams' London Company, although bringing neither of these plays to the colonies in 1752 as part of their original repertoire, added *Cato* and *The Recruiting Officer*, popularized elsewhere by their predecessors Murray and Kean, for the final stop on their tour in Charleston during 1754, a season which coincided with the escalation of preparations for war with France throughout the colonies during the autumn of that year.[45]

Global War and the Atlantic Repertoire

Cato and *The Recruiting Officer* share a remarkably similar historical background in North America, each with a production history beginning in the amateur theaters of the 1730s and each focusing on the figure of the patriot. The first touring companies also introduced two other enduringly popular plays to the American stage that provided much greater exposure for those bugbears of colonial Whig politics, French and Stuart tyranny: *Richard III* and *Tamerlane*. Murray and Kean opened their 1750 season in New York with *Richard III*, repeating it twice during that season before playing it once in Williamsburg and twice in Annapolis during 1751–52.[46] Upton's undistinguished company played *Richard III* twice in New York, and the Hallam Company also played it during in their 1753 debut in New York.[47] Meanwhile the Hallams, by introducing *Tamerlane*, Nicholas Rowe's anti-French exercise in political theater, on 12 November 1754 in Philadelphia, provided Pennsylvanians with a dramatic spectacle perfectly suited to the saber-rattling over the settlement of the territory known as "the Ohio Country" in the wake of George Washington's failed mission against Fort Duquesne and the ongoing British and French military escalations in the region.[48]

Both *Richard III* and *Tamerlane* clearly bear the imprint of the Glorious Revolution of 1689 and William III's reign. Even without Cibber's alterations of Shakespeare's script, Richard III—bloodthirsty, hypocritical, and remorseless—stands out as the very model of a stage tyrant. The character also holds a special place in the canon of literary liberalism: John Milton compared Charles I to Richard in *Eikonoklastes* as part of his attempt to strangle in its crib the Royalist recuperation of Charles as a pious, private man and national martyr. Milton notes that Shakespeare was Charles's "closest companion" during his imprisonment, and that Shakespeare "put never more pious words in the mouth of any person than that of a tyrant."[49] After climbing to the throne via trickery and assassination, assembling a pile of sacrificial victims including two of his brothers, his young nephews (one of them the heir apparent), and a brace of political opponents, Richard dies in single combat with the untested Earl of Richmond, leader of an invasion from Brittany and founder of the Tudor dynasty, who assumes the throne in the final scene.

Colley Cibber was for decades a reliable Whig who in his memoirs laments Britain's history under the Stuarts as a steady decline into tyranny from Elizabeth I's death until the Glorious Revolution. Cibber removed much of the moral ambiguity from Shakespeare's play by deleting many of the script's depictions of Yorkist infighting and playing up Richard's callousness, removing much of the tyrant's seductive theatrical appeal while converting the play into an allegory for the Glorious Revolution.[50] After killing Richard, Richmond, a cipher in Shakespeare's play but converted by Cibber into an embodiment of revolutionary principles, a surrogate William III, declares, "Farewell, Richard, and from thy dreadful end / May future Kings from Tyranny be warn'd."[51] The play closes with the presentation of the crown to Richmond by Lord Stanley, who says of the

English throne, "'Tis doubly [Richmond's] by Conquest, and by Choice," reiterating the Richmond-William III allegory and endorsing the principle of popular sovereignty that also supported William's Hanoverian descendants.[52] Constitutional monarchy, as endorsed by Cibber's reworked Shakespeare, stands in marked contrast to both Stuart "Tyranny" and the absolutist rule passed down from Louis XIV of France, William III's absolutist nemesis, to his great-grandson Louis XV, against whom the British and the colonials fought two wars at midcentury.

Rowe's *Tamerlane*, another story of tyranny defeated, was written during the waning days of William III's reign and also features a battle between a tyrant, the Turkish emperor Bajazet, and a constitutional "patriot" monarch, the Scythian Tamerlane. Rowe, a partisan Whig, composed the play during the opening months of the War of the Spanish Succession, just before William III's death, and his allegory, as John Loftis observes, is virtually transparent: Bajazet represents Louis XIV, and Tamerlane represents William III.[53] Bajazet, who needs no spur to govern but "Ambition," which "[l]ike the Food of Gods, makes [a king] Immortal," is captured and deposed by Tamerlane, a somewhat colorless good steward of a king, and the defender of the lands held by the Grecian princess and fainting virgin Arpasia, who spends much of the play in peril of becoming a sacrificial victim to Bajazet's lust for power.[54] The victorious Tamerlane vows to have Bajazet

Clos'd in a Cage, like some destructive Beast,
. . . borne about, in publick View,
A great example of that righteous Vengeance,
That waits on Cruelty and Pride like thine.[55]

Rowe's play, which was performed by a group of students at the College of New Jersey in Princeton in 1754 as well as by the London Company, provided the perfect anti-French vehicle for the early American stage, one featuring a performance effigy stretching across performance media and the Atlantic Ocean.[56]

Throughout most of the eighteenth century, the London theaters performed *Tamerlane* on 4 November to commemorate William III's birthday. Coincidentally, these celebrations occurred on the day before Guy Fawkes Day, the anniversary of a foiled plot by English Catholics to blow up Parliament in 1605.[57] The 5 November holiday, traditionally featuring fireworks and the burning of small wooden dolls called "guys," had become an increasingly Whig affair after the Restoration, when the Stuart throne was perceived to be drifting closer to the Church of Rome. Simon P. Newman notes that during this period "many Englishmen and women . . . deliberately mounted larger and more extensive celebrations" to illustrate that "November 5 was a holiday that belonged to the people, in which they could articulate [a] clear warning to the restored Stuart monarch."[58] The anti-Catholic populism of Whig 5 November celebrations spread to the North American colonies, where it inspired the "Pope Day" festivals of Boston, New York, and other northeastern cities, during which crowds paraded and burnt large wooden images of the Pope, the Devil, the Stuart Pretender, and other tyrannical scapegoats.[59]

The Hallams' production of *Tamerlane* in Philadelphia appealed directly to similar anti-Catholic and patriotic sentiments among the citizens of Pennsylvania, many of whom were of course militant Protestants. Such deployments of *Tamerlane* were common in the London theaters. As Kathleen Wilson observes, the play was used to great effect as theatrical propaganda by the Whigs after the 1715 Jacobite uprising.[60] The Hallams even went so far as to conclude their *Tamerlane* with an occasional epilogue written by local resident (and future signer of the Declaration of Independence) Francis Hopkinson, delivered by Mrs. Hallam in the character of Arpasia. The epilogue inquires:

Whilst sullen Tyranny no more to rise,
Low in the dust, debas'd and vanquish'd lies,
Who but abhors a Bajazet to see?
Who would not wish a Tamerlane to be?[61]

The expected answer is, of course: any man in the audience. The epilogue concludes by implicitly comparing George II to Tamerlane and Louis XV to Bajazet—thus extending the genealogies of these theatrical characters both on and off the stage to the descendants of their original models:

Hail, happy people! Thus with freedom blest,
By no insulting Bajazet opprest!
Here polish'd learning shall fix her radiant throne,
And ignorance and vice in fetters grone
. . . .
Whilst British liberty—celestial sound,
Bids every heart be gay, and nature smile around.[62]

Thus, declares Hopkinson in the person of Mrs. Hallam, any good patriotic Englishman in the audience should strive to emulate both Tamerlane and George II.

Fierce local opposition to the London Company's Philadelphia performances in 1754, meanwhile, included the issuance of a translation of an anti-theatrical tract written by "Armand de Bourbon, the prince of Conti," a seventeenth-century French nobleman, which presented anti-theatrical selections from the patristic literature of the early Christian church. Hoisting their opponents with their own petard, the Hallams used the publication of this pamphlet in their own defense by attacking from the stage both the Catholic Church and the French monarchy, institutions much in the news in a colony on the brink of war with France. An epilogue written for the season's opening performance says of the stage's opponents, "With red hot zeal, in dreadful pomp they come, / And bring their flaming tenets warm from Rome."[63] In London the annual onstage humiliation of Bajazet, a stand-in for the French kings whose court sheltered the exiled Stuarts, combined with the fireworks and guy-burnings to infuse Gunpowder Treason Day's celebration of liberty with a distinctly anti-French nationalism. Through the machinations of Whig politics, British and French colonial maneuvers, and street theater on both sides of the Atlantic, Rowe's tragedy premiered in a similarly receptive environment in North America. *Tamerlane* became a regular presence in the pre-Revolutionary theatrical repertoire, tying the professional theater to the aggressively Protestant nationalism of radical street politics in both London and the northeastern colonies. Along with Addison's, Farquhar's, and Cibber's plays, Rowe's text provided another medium, composed of the flesh of actors instead of sticks and rags, for the ritual battle between "liberty" and "tyranny" in North America.

The opening phase of the Seven Years' War took place without theatrical accompaniment. By the end of 1753 the Kean troupe had disbanded, and the Hallams' London Company spent the years 1755–58 in the West Indies before returning under the new leadership of David Douglass. Upon the London Company's return to North America, however, the troupe's repertoire promptly began to beat the same patriotic drums as it had during the company's first tours in the early 1750s. The revival of these patriotic plays suggests the lingering appetite of wartime audiences for plays praising the glories of all things British, and also the rapprochement between the ministry and the fractious colonies that followed William Pitt's administrative reforms of 1758, which gave more authority to colonial legislatures and officers.[64] The London Company's return engagement in New York (January–February 1759) featured regular performances of *The Recruiting Officer*, *Richard III*, and *Tamerlane*, as did their ensuing season in Philadelphia (June–December 1759), which Douglass chose to open with *Tamerlane* and *Richard III*.[65] The company's run in Annapolis and Upper Marlborough (March–October 1760) also featured *The Recruiting Officer* and two performances of *Richard III*, although *Tamerlane* was omitted, possibly due to the sensitivities of Roman Catholic Marylanders.[66]

Cato is noticeably absent during these wartime seasons and would not reappear until well after the French surrender of Canada in 1760, during the company's contested 1761–62 run in New York, when the play rejoined the rest of the patriotic wartime repertoire on the stage, and during Douglass's failed experiments in Portsmouth and Providence during the summer of 1762. The play seems to have fallen out of repertory during the company's stay in the Caribbean, possibly due to the death of

Lewis Hallam Sr., a likely candidate for the role of Cato. (Douglass, the most notable addition to the company during its Caribbean sojourn, took over the role in 1762.)[67] Douglass may well have resurrected the play both to capitalize on colonials' lingering enthusiasm for war and as a rejoinder to his critics. The New Hampshire and Rhode Island legislatures responded to Douglass's attempts to play in New England by banning stage plays in 1762; in 1761 a New York critic had attacked the theater's "instilling a strong Relish for a voluptuous and indolent life" among audience members and its "laying a heavy tax on the City, to maintain a set of vagrants," arguments likely fueled by the postwar depression then gripping the colonies.[68] Addison's paean to patriotic virtue and republican simplicity seems in retrospect a likely rejoinder to the fastidious complaints of the theater's opponents.

Even before its stage revival, however, Addison's text exerted a powerful wartime influence through amateur productions and Douglass's attempts to underscore the theater's utility for the reinforcement of patriotic sentiment in the American colonies. Stationed with the Virginia militia at Fort Cumberland, a bulwark against French and Indian incursions on Virginia's western frontier where the soldiers also appear to have formed an amateur acting company, George Washington wrote to the object of his affection, Sally Fairfax, "I should think our time more agreeably spent believe me, in playing a part in Cato, with the company you mention, and myself doubly happy in being the Juba to such a Marcia, as you must make"—ironically filling an otiose interval by musing on the fall of Utica while himself deployed, like Juba, in a war being fought by both European and colonial forces in the wilderness. (That the slave-owning Washington explicitly compared himself to the African Juba remains virtually inexplicable, although it provides a faint, suggestive echo of the common belief in the seventeenth century that the climate of Virginia would turn the bodies of its settlers black.)[69] Away from the front lines, Harvard students acted *Cato* four times over the course of 1758–59, and *The Recruiting Officer* twice in June 1759.[70]

For his part, Douglass signaled the importance of *Cato* as a symbol of the theater's power to foster patriotism from the very beginning of the company's wartime tour. Douglass published the inaugural prologue from the London Company's 1759 New York season, a revised version of the anti-Catholic prologue given five years earlier in Philadelphia, in the *New York Mercury*. Douglass reminded readers that Addison had defended plays "for the accomplishment and refining of human nature" and offered the poetic argument that

When Cato bleeds he spends his latest breath,
To teach the love of country strong in death.

With such examples and a thousand more,
Of godlike men who lived in times before,
The tragic Muse renewing every age,
Makes the dead heroes trod the living stage.[71]

The prologue's endorsement of patriotic didacticism, with its emphasis on the theatrical resurrection of the honored dead and patriotic blood sacrifice, offers a model for the generation of performance effigies, especially the Catonic effigy.

In much the same fashion, *Cato* clearly haunts the 1760 Annapolis season's opening prologue, which declares the Douglass Company's intent to "make each eye dissolve in virtuous tears" and admonishes the audience to "[b]e what we act, the heroes of our parts, / And feel that Britons here have Roman hearts." There is a certain irony in Douglass's making such a bold patriotic appeal to the residents of a colony that provided no troops for the Seven Years' War as the colonial legislature and the proprietor fought over measures to raise revenue.[72] Nonetheless, the prologue expresses a desire to draw tears and stir "Roman" valor in the hearts of British Americans that clearly alludes to Pope's prologue to *Cato*, in which Pope declares that Addison's tragedy summons "[s]uch tears as Patriots shed for dying laws" and "calls forth Roman drops from British eyes."[73]

The Annapolis prologue also nominates a surrogate Cato suited to the events in British North America during the French and Indian War by raising General James Wolfe, the British general who died in the climactic 1759 Battle of Quebec, to the status of an exemplary patriotic sacrifice:

Here as we speak each heart-struck patriot glows
With real rage to crush Britannia's foes!
To quell bold tyrants, and support the laws,
Or, like brave Wolfe, bleed in his country's cause!

Wolfe's Catonic commemoration in the prologue perfectly illustrates the ready applicability of the colonial theater to contemporary events and provides an example of the sort of patriotic promotions that Douglass used to underscore the theater's legitimacy. Popular plays outlining the conflicts of patriotism and tyranny could readily be marketed, sometimes by repackaging them with a new epilogue, to comment on current events—in this case war with France—under the new circumstances occasioned by the colonial theater of action. This intersection of performance and politics appears to have guided both the selection of the wartime repertoire of the London Company and Douglass's responses to his critics.

Street Theater and the Stamp Act: An Interlude

The postwar economic downturn that reignited opposition to the theater in the northeastern colonies was only the first in a series of events that would strain colonial relations with not only Douglass's actors but also Great Britain. At the conclusion of the Seven Years' War, George Grenville, Pitt's replacement as first minister, implemented a series of measures that were designed both to facilitate the administration of the colonies and to raise the revenue needed to address the tremendous debt incurred by the crown during the course of the war. Among these provisions were the Royal Proclamation of 1763, which restricted colonial settlement to territory east of the Appalachian mountains; the 1763 introduction of a standing military presence in the colonies, which was intended to assure the continued subjection of the defeated French and Indians and to be maintained at colonial expense; the 1764 Sugar Act, which attempted to rationalize the imposition of duties on sugar and molasses, which had declined due to wartime smuggling; the 1765 Quartering Act, which codified the billeting of troops in empty buildings and public houses; and the best-known of these measures, the Stamp Act of 1765.[74] These measures, and the ensuing chill in British-American relations, initiated changes in the political and economic relationship between Britain and the colonies that would also affect those celebrated purveyors of "British" aesthetic experience, Douglass's acting company.

Taking into account the renewed opposition to the theater expressed in some colonies at the war's end, it is difficult to gauge the immediate effects of Grenville's imperial reforms on David Douglass's bottom line. The records for his company's tour through Virginia, for instance, where the depression had also taken hold in 1763, are exceptionally poor, and listings of plays actually performed are unavailable for these dates, let alone box office records. Only after the beginning of the company's 1763–64 season in Charleston, where the local economy remained robust throughout the early 1760s, can theater historians ascertain which plays the actors staged during this southern tour. Records indicate that in addition to changing the company's name to "The American Company," possibly to avoid the stigma of British luxuriance during an economic slump, Douglass dropped all "political" plays from the repertoire during the Charleston season, featuring instead popular sentimental tragedies such as Rowe's *Jane Shore* and the Reverend John Home's *Douglas*.[75] Given Douglass's reliance on patriotic plays as a counterargument to moral and economic opposition to the theater in New York, South Carolina's continuing postwar prosperity, and the absence of a play-list for the Virginia tour against which to compare the New York and Charleston seasons, however, it seems likely that these changes in the company's repertoire resulted from a shift in consumer appetites after the conclusion of the Peace of Paris in 1763 rather than Douglass's sudden desire to avoid association with the iconography of British politics, patriotic or otherwise.

The departure of Douglass and his actors for Barbados from the conclusion of the Charleston season until November 1765 prevents us from exploring how the growing colonial opposition to British policies brought on by the Stamp Act Crisis might have affected the role of the colonial theater during a period of political upheaval in North America.[76] As the changing fortunes and shifting signification of *Cato* in the colonies discussed in the previous chapter illustrate, during the years 1765–66 the ways in which British North Americans interpreted such fundamental terms in their political vocabulary as "liberty" and "tyranny" began to change, as did many colonials' interpretations of their status as British citizens. These changes in political attitudes registered in colonial appropriations and interpretations of certain popular British dramatic texts. The absence of the American Company from its North American venues throughout the summer and early autumn of 1765, then, is an unfortunate loss.

The Stamp Act Crisis did provide a rich assortment of performances from the tradition of political protest, or "street theater," however. As Jeffrey Richards observes, such politicized ritual processions through public streets, of which the Stamp Act protests were the first concerted outburst, would eventually result in "a theater larger than that of the play house . . . a self-proclaimed revolution with serious, real-world consequences."[77] The previous chapter noted the evolution of a performance tradition known as the "liberty funeral," a new ceremony with marked similarities to the textual dynamics of Addison's *Cato*. A number of other street performances took the form of triumphal parades ending in the destruction of wooden or stuffed dummies ("effigies"), mock tyannicides reminiscent of public executions, of Guy Fawkes Day and Pope Day ceremonies, and of the preferred fate of tyrants in the British theater.[78]

On 14 August 1765, rioters in Boston beheaded and burnt effigies, including one representing a stamp revenue collector. Similar mock executions occurred throughout the colonies between August and November. All across the colonies, effigies of "stampmen" were hung or burnt after ritual parades, including in Lebanon, Norwich, New London, and Windham, Connecticut, and a number of other small towns in New England; Brunswick, New Jersey; Annapolis, Maryland; Wilmington, North Carolina; Charleston, South Carolina; and Savannah, Georgia. A figure of the devil paraded during the Norwich protest, it should be noted, sported a placard bearing Cato's injunction to Portius urging him to retire from public life: "When vice prevails, and impious men bear sway, the post of honor is a private station."[79] A funeral procession in Frederick, Maryland, featured the mock interment of both the Stamp Act and an effigy of Zachariah Hood, the local stamp collector. In Dumfries, Virginia, a stampman was tied to a horse and whipped out of town; in New York, on 1 November, an effigy of Governor Colden—who was rumored to have participated in the 1715 Jacobite uprising as a drummer boy—was burnt, as was Colden's personal coach. Despite the general lack of opposition to the Stamp Act in the Caribbean, the ceremonies reached as far as St. Kitt's and St. Nevis, where effigy burnings were held on 31 October and 5 November.[80]

Perhaps the most striking of these Stamp Act protests took place in Boston. On 4 November a crowd lynched effigies of Grenville and John Huske, a member of parliament who had been raised in New Hampshire. After hanging the effigies, the crowd tore them to pieces in a ceremony reminiscent of drawing and quartering, the traditional common law punishment for treason. On Pope Day, the traditional North End and South End gangs made peace in a public ceremony during their traditional procession, after which they held a joint celebration at which "the Pope, Devil, and several other Effigies signifying Tyranny, Oppression, Slavery, &c." were burnt.[81] Even in the absence of a politically engaged professional theater, street mobs throughout the colonies adapted their ritualized folk performances, theatrical exercises with marked symbolic (and occasionally textual) connections to popular dramatic texts, in order to express their disdain for the Stamp Act and the British ministry.

If political activists in North America embraced certain dramatic texts such as *Cato*, as well as the general theatricality of street performance, during the Stamp Act Crisis, the Stamp Act also resulted in an escalation of hostility to the professional theater in the colonies. During this period, what Davis contends were longstanding colonial desires for "economic and manufacturing independence" intensified as a result of Anglo-American disputes over tariffs and taxes.[82] This hostility flared into mob action in New York during the Chapel Street Theatre riot of 1766. When Douglass and the American Company sailed for Barbados, two former members of the company, Mr. and Mrs. Tomlinson, remained behind in North America, where, apparently with the assistance of a small company of amateur actors, they attempted to conduct a short season at the Chapel Street Theatre in May 1766. Although Douglass, who had returned to North America, was himself conducting a limited season in Charleston at the time with no apparent ill will toward his actors, the Tomlinson troupe's engagement of the theater in April 1766 aroused the wrath of the Sons of Liberty. In New York, this group had been forged by an alliance between the politically powerful DeLancey family and middle- and lower-class tradesmen and artisans, suggesting that the revival of New York theater in the wake of the Stamp Act may have stoked not only anti-British sentiment but also class resentment among the members of that group.[83]

According to the journal of John Montresor, the future chronicler of Nathan Hale's execution, on 4 April, "A Grand Meeting of the Sons of Liberty to settle matters of the Moment" was held, including "whether they shall admit the strollers, arrived here to act." Montresor's journal suggests that hostility to the actors had ties to anti-Stamp Act sentiment, since at the meeting "[s]ome Stamps . . . were publickly burnt . . . together with some Play bills."[84] Even after word of the March 1765 repeal of the Stamp Act by Parliament had reached the colonies, the Tomlinsons appear to have taken the hostility of the radical community quite seriously: their advertisement for a 5 May performance of Farquhar's *The Twin Rivals*, an innocuous comedy, includes "A Song in Praise of Liberty" on the bill and expresses the hope that "[a]s the Packet is arrived, and has been the Messenger of good news relative to the Repeal . . . the Public has no objections to the above Performance."[85]

The Sons of Liberty made good on their threatening implications by attacking the theater, however, chasing away both audience and actors while shouting, "Liberty! Liberty!" Afterward the trappings of the theater, "Both Inside and Outside," according to the *New York Gazette*, were "torn to Pieces and burnt by Persons unknown about Ten and Eleven a Clock at night, to the satisfaction of many at this distressed Time, and to the great Grievance of those less inclined to the Publick Good."[86] Rankin refers to this episode as the "funeral pyre of the Chapel Street Theatre," and the similarities between this event and the theatrical protests of 1765, from its roots in hostility to the Stamp Act to its fiery conclusion, are as unmistakable as they are ironic.[87] In New York the professional theater, championed by its practitioners for its ability to inspire patriotism, underwent a ritual demolition inspired by a very different sort of "patriot" performance: the street theater of transatlantic politics.

Scots and Scapegoats: Theater after the Stamp Act

The increasing political and economic tensions between the colonies and Britain presented a clear challenge for Douglass, who had, as noted above, already changed the name of his company from the "London Company" to the "American Company" in 1763, shifting the emphasis of the troupe's advertising from the cosmopolitanism of London to a more homespun appeal. After the Chapel Street Theatre riot, Douglass replenished the American Company with his new recruits and the Tomlinsons. Prudently avoiding New York, the company then opened their new, permanent theater, the Southwark, in Philadelphia in November 1766.[88] The play list for the new theater marked the reappearance of theatrical battles between patriots and tyrants, including performances of *Richard III* (played on 17 March 1767 to mark the anniversary of the repeal of the Stamp Act), *Tamerlane*, and *Cato*, the last of which Douglass had also staged in Charleston during April 1766, shortly before the Tomlinsons were assailed by the Sons of Liberty. (Douglass may have hoped that the favorite play of American radicals would help to mollify any lingering opposition to the theater in Charleston.)[89]

In Philadelphia, proponents of the theater used *Cato* and *Tamerlane* to court public opinion: after the American Company had staged both *Tamerlane* (2 January 1767) and *Cato* (2 February 1767), an anonymous letter appeared in the *Pennsylvania Journal*, citing Pope's prologue to *Cato*, which endorses the drama as a way "'[t]o make Mankind in conscious Virtue bold, / Live o'er each Scene and be what they behold'" and appealing to "the hearts of those who have frequented the Theatre." "Can the virtues of patriotism be more effectually cultivated," inquires the author, "than by the glorious example of the Roman Stoic? . . . Could the genius of Rowe or Addison have been employed to a more worthy purpose, than that of alluring a giddy world to the practice of virtue, and diverting them from vice?"[90] The following week, Douglass submitted to the *Journal* a suspiciously similar, though previously unpublished, essay purportedly written during the company's 1761 season in New York. Douglass pleads his case for the theater as a school for public morals, repeating the earlier letter's quotation from Pope's prologue to *Cato* and citing Cato's pre-suicidal soliloquy and Addison's endorsement in *Spectator* 446 (1 August 1712) of a well-regulated theater that recommended "the Religion, the Government, and the Publick Worship of its Country" as proof of the moral wholesomeness of the theater. Douglass singles out as particularly wholesome his own American Company, whose actors, he claims, are "taken particular notice of, and caress'd by the best families in America," apparently a reference to Governor Thomas Penn's patronage of the theater.[91]

In addition to using Addison to position his company in the respectable center of the public sphere while playing at the Southwark, Douglass introduced a new tyrannicidal tragedy to the repertoire: *Macbeth*. Eighteenth-century readers evinced great concern over the play's thematic treatment of tyranny and rebellion; one pro-theater partisan praised the "Savageness" of Macbeth along with that of Richard III, calling their ferocity "a dissuasive from tyranny and boundless ambition."[92] Although Douglass's previous staging of the play in 1759 had flopped, the play had since become a political touchstone. In his *A Dissertation on the Canon and Feudal Law*, for instance, John Adams had accused American and British Tories who advocated filial loyalty to the mother country of defending a Britain that, like Lady Macbeth, would have for the sake of power "dash'd the brains out" of her nursing infant.[93] *Macbeth* had also become associated with a Scottish nobleman and opposition scapegoat loathed by the patriot opposition in both Britain and the colonies: George III's former tutor and first minister John Stuart, the Third Earl of Bute.

Shortly after his elevation to the role of first minister in 1762, a series of cartoons appeared in the British opposition press lampooning the earl as "McBoot," a would-be tyrant of vaulting ambition, and colonials blamed him for every perceived affront to their liberties from the Royal Proclamation to the Stamp Act. Arthur Lee, a Virginian living in London who facilitated the transatlantic correspondence of the radical community, mocked Bute in a doggerel poem entitled "Oppression," inquiring:

Shall I subscribe to every dunce's nod,
Call P[itt] a villain, or L[ord] B[ute] a god?
Or yet ascribe all virtues to the THANE,
And to his wretched conduct, say, Amen?

Lee pointedly employs the archaic title of "thane" commonly used in Shakespeare's tragedy. Bute was also regularly represented as a scapegoat figure in the mock executions that took place during the Stamp Act Riots, either as a straw effigy or, occasionally, simply as a boot suspended by a noose from liberty trees and poles.[94] Given Douglass's eagerness to promote the theater in the colonies, the introduction to his company's repertoire of a text so clearly resonant with current popular prejudices as *Macbeth* hardly seems accidental.

Douglass's promotional efforts were further complicated by the enactment of the Townshend Duties in June 1767.[95] After completing their Philadelphia run in July 1767, the company began their opening run (December 1767–May 1768) at the John Street Theatre. The schedule, as one might expect, contains most of the patriotic plays acted at the Southwark: *Macbeth*, *Richard III*, and *Cato*, the last of which was staged by Douglass on the anniversary of the Stamp Act's repeal to "unbalance his critics."[96] The New York season also saw the reappearance of *The Recruiting Officer* in North America for the first time since the end of the Seven Years' War, a performance that might have produced very different readings on the part of British troops stationed in New York and some New Yorkers. (The city had experienced major anti-impressment riots during 1764–65 in addition to the Stamp Act disturbances, and the years 1766–67 were marked by a struggle between the New York assembly and Parliament over New York's refusal fully to fund the colony's military garrisons.)[97] Despite Douglass's appeals to the patriot community, however, the controversy over the Townshend Duties led many of what one contemporary anti-theatrical writer called "[New York's] most wealthy, most respectable and patriotic citizens" to avoid the theater; as Seilhamer relates, "As far as possible, the detested play-house was boycotted."[98] Although the actors were apparently welcomed to New York by Governor Henry Moore, whose tenure as lieutenant governor of Jamaica from 1755 to 1759 overlapped with the company's residence on that island, the theater seems to have become the object of scorn for those New Yorkers still angered by British tax policy.[99]

Douglass's difficulties in drawing audiences worsened as 1768 progressed and colonial merchants' associations began to plan and implement a round of non-importation boycotts, a development that caused major revisions in the American Company's repertoire. Strictures on luxury consumption, including play tickets, during these boycotts became a kind of political counterperformance, a demonstration of patriot bona fides that kept many colonial opponents of the Townshend Duties out of the theaters during 1768–70.[100] Douglass promptly made major alterations in his repertoire to reflect the changing composition of his audience, who qua their continued theater attendance must have been a less radical lot. During the American Company's remaining seasons in Philadelphia (October 1768–January 1769 and November 1769–May 1770) and New York (October 1768–January 1769) throughout the Second Non-Importation boycott, plays with connotations of political radicalism dropped out of the repertoire.

Cato's association with the Sons of Liberty, for instance, was so strong that a December 1768 issue of the *Boston Weekly News-Letter* mocked the connection in a poem entitled "Liberty":

Quoth the Rabble make Way for great Cato's Descendants!
Lo! These are the Men aptly call'd Independents!
Quaint Patriots indeed! Of Old Noll's Institution,
So Free—they'd demolish the whole Constitution.[101]

The American Company did not perform *Cato* between 1768 and 1774. Likewise, after the *Liberty* riot, which was partly directed against British impressment policies (and to which the above poem may be a reference), broke out in Boston during June 1768, *The Recruiting Officer*, still popular in Britain and profitable enough among Douglass's customers to merit a performance in New York during February 1768, promptly vanished from the repertoire until 1771.[102] While *Tamerlane* and *Macbeth* survived the first purge and continued to be performed into December 1768 and April 1769, respectively, they too fell out of production until 1773 and 1774.

In place of these "radical" texts, Douglass introduced a new collection of Shakespearean plays: *King John*, *Cymbeline*, and John Dryden's Restoration revision of *The Tempest*.[103] While no written records demonstrate a clear political intent in Douglass's play selections during this period, these plays share a more conservative stance on questions of liberty and tyranny, emphasizing social hierarchy and the rule of authoritative, patriotic kings and frowning on popular revolt. King John's claim to the British throne is questionable, based largely on the absence of his brother Richard Coeur de Lion during the Crusades, and the suicide of John's nephew Arthur, the heir apparent, is blamed on John's perfidy. The play centers, however, on Britain's longstanding enmity with France, and Shakespeare recuperates

John as a patriot and martyr in the fifth act, when John is assassinated by a French monk. In *Cymbeline*, the plot's struggle between rebellious, colonial Britain and imperial Rome resolves itself peacefully, with the British king Cymbeline deciding to submit once again to imperial rule and resume payment of England's annual tribute to Rome—a situation that might possibly have presented analogies with contemporary debates over colonial taxation. Dryden's reworking of *The Tempest* features a major expansion of the "low plot" involving the pretensions to power of Caliban and the drunken clowns Trinculo and Stephano, a satire on the English commonwealth that resonates with the *Boston News-Letter*'s parody of the Sons of Liberty as a rabble of roundheads. Several of the new plays introduced by Douglass during the Second Non-Importation Movement, then, suggest a profound respect for the innate authority of the crown (*King John* and *The Tempest*) and the fiscal authority of the imperial government (*Cymbeline*).

While Douglass had been struggling in Philadelphia and New York, another troupe styling itself "The New American Company" had been playing in Virginia and Maryland in 1768–69. Their apparent dissolution, along with the political and economic difficulties attendant upon playing in the northeastern colonies, may have helped to lure Douglass southward. While playing in Williamsburg and Annapolis during their 1770–72 southern tour, it should be noted, the American Company's actors were welcomed in these capital cities during the general sessions of both states' assemblies and during the racing season in Annapolis.[104] In Williamsburg the audience swelled with prominent citizens, including the Virginia burgesses Thomas Jefferson and George Washington. Washington in particular was a regular playgoer who frequented the theater on trips to Williamsburg for state business and Annapolis or other locales for pleasure. These visits even included, appropriately enough for a Seven Years' War veteran and the future commander of a citizen army, attending a performance of *The Recruiting Officer* in Dumfries, Virginia, on 23 January 1771.[105]

The fertility of Annapolis as a theatrical venue likewise depended on an audience of prominent men, including two young immigrants, the colonial official William Eddis and the Anglican rector Jonathan Boucher. (According to Eddis, Governor Robert Eden himself, who held "a strong conviction that the stage under proper regulations may be rendered of general utility and made subservient to the great interests of religion and virtue," also patronized the theater.)[106] Given the political and economic ramifications of theatrical production at the time, it is not surprising to discover that these men were also vocally loyal to imperial policy. Boucher, who published a paean to Nancy Hallam's performance in *Cymbeline* in 1770 and later became enmeshed in a public argument with patriot leader

William Paca over fees for the clergy that included arguments about the proper interpretation of Gay's *The Beggar's Opera* and David Garrick's farce, *Lethe*, also became well known for his sermons against the pro-independence movement. In a 1774 sermon on the story of Absalom and Achitophel, Boucher declares that "[n]o rebel . . . however naturally brave, and when engaged in a good cause, can be so undaunted as those who are enlisted in the honourable service of their king and country" and then, apparently without irony, cites as an authority in a footnote one of Richard III's battlefield speeches: "The king's name is a tower of strength, / Which they upon the adverse faction want."[107] In a similar vein, Eddis composed the opening prologue for the American Company's 1772 Annapolis season, intoning,

Long may blest Concord here maintain her Sway,
And radiant Science gild each rising Day;
Whilst Patriots plead, without one private View,
And glorious Liberty alone pursue!
So shall the Mother Isles with Joy approve,
And aid their Offspring with parental Love![108]

Eddis's prologue, like Boucher's sermon, attempts to recapture the image of the patriot wholly devoted to the public realm for those who profess unswerving loyalty to the crown during a period of relative comity between Britain and the colonies.

Print Radicalism: *Hamlet* and *Julius Caesar*

Although non-importation increased hostility to the professional theater in the late 1760s, apparently directing David Douglass toward the south and away from potentially controversial productions, the radical community's taste for the deployment of theatrical texts as symbolic shorthand in the service of liberty did not diminish during this period. *Cato* persisted as a popular school theatrical, for instance, when professional players were unavailable or out of favor. Rankin records scholastic performances of the play in 1767 in Williamsburg and 1771 in Philadelphia; according to the joking prologue of the Williamsburg performance, such performances were attempts to train "brats who pant to serve the common weal."[109] An American edition of *Cato*, meanwhile, was printed in Boston in 1767, the year of the Townshend Duties' passage. In addition to *Cato*, however, radicals on both sides of the Atlantic also began to appropriate other dramatic texts during the late 1760s, particularly *Hamlet* and *Julius Caesar*.

As in the case of radical deployments of *Macbeth*, the Earl of Bute proved to be a popular butt of satirical allusion to *Hamlet* and *Julius Caesar*, proving that these fusillades from the Shakespearean canon were based on more than mere anti-Scottish prejudice. In 1763, for instance, John Wilkes drew a comparison between his nemesis Bute and Claudius, Hamlet's usurping uncle who claims the throne by assassinating his brother the king, in his commissioned reprinting of an anti-Walpole play called *The Fall of Mortimer*, in which Edward III throws off his corrupt royal favorite under the influence of a "patriot" band of gentry. In an introductory essay to the play, Wilkes inserts a digression praising the earl's skills as an amateur actor, especially in "the famous scene in *Hamlet*, where you pour fatal poison into the ear of a good, unsuspecting king," thus imputing to him not only the tyrannical tendencies of the first minister in *Mortimer* but also Claudius's aspirations toward the throne. In 1769, the *Oxford Magazine* ran a cartoon depicting this assassination scene and featuring George III's mother the Princess Dowager, whose lover Bute was rumored to be, as a complicit Gertrude.[110] Not only Claudius but also Hamlet himself, faced with the burden of avenging his murdered father and reclaiming the throne, entered into the discourse surrounding both politics and the theater in the late 1760s. A 1768 anti-theatrical pamphlet criticizes the Danish prince for choosing to avenge his father's death, "Contrary to the dictates of religion"; a pro-theatrical rejoinder praised the play for "teach[ing] us that the judgement of heaven can reach even those who are placed above the controul of human laws," an endorsement that seems to make a glancing reference to tyrannicide.[111]

The debate between passive obedience and resistance to authority also marks the emergence in North America of *Hamlet* as an overtly politicized text. The tragedy had been an uncontroversial part of the theatrical repertoire in North America since 1759, but in the late 1760s it suddenly took on a political tinge in the newspapers affiliated with the Sons of Liberty. Josiah Quincy Jr., a young Harvard-educated patriot activist, wrote an essay in the *Boston Gazette* in October 1767 decrying both the Townshend Duties and the decay of British libertarianism in New England, which concludes with an adaptation of one of Hamlet's soliloquies mulling over his inability to avenge his father by killing Claudius: "It cannot be / But we are pigeon-livered, and lack gall / To make oppression bitter."[112] In 1769 an anonymous poet sounded a similar note by appropriating Hamlet's more famous "To be or not to be" soliloquy.[113] This parody appeared in the *Georgia Gazette* on 11 March 1769 and the *South Carolina Gazette* on 14 March 1769 and was then reprinted in the *Massachusetts Spy* on 14 August 1770:

Be taxt, or not be taxt, that is the question.
Whether 'tis nobler in our minds to suffer
The flights and cunning of deceitful statesmen,
Or to petition 'gainst illegal taxes,
And by opposing end 'em?[114]

The mock soliloquy replaces Hamlet's familiar "slings and arrows of outrageous fortune" with political machinations of the powerful, and his "sea of troubles" with troubling taxes levied on the American colonies from across the Atlantic. Although the author of this parody seems to attempt to elide the fifth-act slaughter that closes the Shakespearean source text by replacing tyrannicide with the colonials' petitions for the redress of grievances, the potential for catastrophic violence marks nearly all political references to the play in colonial literature.

Much as *Hamlet* did, *Julius Caesar* emerged in both Britain and America as a useful source of allusions during the 1760s. In Britain, an older satirical comparison of Robert Walpole to the Colossus of Rhodes, using Cassius's description of Caesar from *Julius Caesar*, "Why man he doth bestride this narrow world / like a Colossus, and we petty men / Walk under his huge legs, and peep about / To find ourselves dishonourable graves," was resurrected in the *Political Register* of 1767 as a critique of Bute.[115] (The myth of the earl's tyrannical control of the ministry, even long after he had left power, continued to dominate the imagination of Wilkites in England and the Sons of Liberty in America throughout the pre-Revolutionary era.) *Julius Caesar* first appeared the North American radical press in the *Connecticut Gazette* during the Stamp Act Crisis, in the form of a paraphrased quotation from Brutus urging engagement with the forces of Antony at Philippi: "There is a Tide, in the affairs of men, / Which, taken at the Flood, leads on to FREEDOM! / Omitted, all the voyage of their Life / Is bound in shallows and in Slavery," substituting "FREEDOM!" for the original "fortune" and "Slavery" for "misery."[116]

This allusion was not an isolated occurrence. In Massachusetts in 1767, John Adams published a series of essays in the *Boston Gazette* critical of royal prerogative; in a fragmentary addition to one of these "Governor Winthrop to Governor Bradford" essays, Adams offered as a valediction to his readers a line from *Julius Caesar*: "Cassius from bondage will deliver Cassius," a declaration made by one of Shakespeare's leading republican conspirators while brandishing a dagger and promising either to kill Caesar or himself—a powerful instance of the familiar Catonic "liberty or death" rhetoric so popular in New England.[117] In 1770 the New York Sons of Liberty, not long after their clash with British troops at the Battle of Golden Hill and just two weeks before the Boston Massacre, likewise published an essay in the *Boston Gazette*, signed "Brutus."[118] And although Parliament repealed all of the Townshend Duties except the tax on tea during April 1770, one month after the Massacre, events in Boston captured the public's imagination and may have influenced the first production of *Julius Caesar* in the North American colonies. (The play's meaning remained open to political dispute even after it became associated with the patriot movement: during Maryland's Tobacco Fee controversy in 1773, a Church of England clergyman blasted the greed and political power of colonial lawyers in the *Maryland Gazette* by resurrecting the "Colossus" speech, declaring that attorneys "do bestride our little province / Like Colossuses.")[119]

At the end of the American Company's 1769–70 season in Philadelphia, during which time Douglass's most successful production had been the premiere of Dryden's Tory *Tempest*, the company closed its season with a performance of *Julius Caesar* on 1 June.[120] Alexander Mackrabie, a young Scot of pro-British leanings living in Philadelphia, describes the city in a letter to his brother-in-law as full of "Speechifying" against taxation and the military in the wake of the Boston Massacre, noting sarcastically that in this politicized climate "the spirit of Liberty breathes on every Act and on every Occasion. Our Play-bills promise to exhibit to us the Noble Struggle for Liberty of those renowned Romans, Brutus and Cassius." Mackrabie thus classifies the American Company's production as a counterperformance to the tragic show of force that had taken place in Boston months earlier, a specifically republican exhibition of tyrannicide.[121] Mackrabie's reading accords nicely with the liberty-or-death, tyrannicide-or-suicide spirit in which American patriots were deploying *Julius Caesar*, although the overwhelming shadow cast by Caesar across the second half of the play and the eventual failure of Brutus's revolt remain ambiguous enough to suggest that Douglass, like Mackrabie, was listening to the fierce rhetoric swirling around him with bemusement. Whether Douglass read *Julius Caesar* as endorsing republicanism or Caesarism, however, the play's presentation and the continued deployment of dramatic texts by colonial partisans indicate a growing sense among some colonials that the achievement of their goals, like those of Cato, Hamlet, and Brutus and Cassius, might require an essential element of tragedy: the sacrificial shedding of blood, quite possibly their own.

Patriot Pleadings: Theater and Politics in the Early 1770s

Political conflict had encouraged Douglass and the American Company to depart for Maryland and Virginia, but it revisited them in Philadelphia in 1772. After a general easing of tensions following the bloodshed in Boston and the repeal of the Townshend Duties, British and colonial resentments flared anew after residents of Rhode Island looted and burnt the *HMS Gaspee*, a British customs ship known for its captain's abuses of customs law, which had run aground near Warwick, Rhode Island, in June 1772.[122] The American Company's schedule for 1772–73 appears to reflect Douglass's attempts to avoid controversy by courting the favor of Philadelphia loyalists and the local military garrison while also reaching out to the patriot community. Controversy, however, seems to have dogged the American Company's heels: the opening play for the season, staged on 28 October 1772, was Hugh Kelly's *A Word to the Wise*, a romantic comedy forgettable in every respect except its author's controversial defense of the use of force against supporters of John Wilkes in the St. George's Fields massacre of 1770. At Kelly's benefit night performance in London during 1770, the author's opponents hissed the players from the stage, and although Douglass had staged the play successfully in Williamsburg and Annapolis, the gallery gods of Philadelphia disrupted the performance, "commit[ting] repeated outrages on that part of the audience, who go there really to see the play."[123]

Among the other plays that Douglass produced were a revival of the patriot-oriented *Tamerlane* and *The Recruiting Officer*, a play likely selected to appeal to the military garrison. Douglass may also have been appealing to a sense of imperial unity when he produced, on two consecutive nights, George Cockings's *The Conquest of Canada* (1766). Cockings's play, a patriotic spectacle depicting General Wolfe's victory at Quebec, characterizes Wolfe as a classic patriot, a mixture of Tamerlane's military leadership and Cato's willingness to sacrifice himself for the freedom of the state. Mortally wounded, Wolfe dies just as news of his troops' rout of the French reaches him, crying: "My glory's race is run!—my country's serv'd! / Quebec is conquer'd!—Great George is victor! / I wish no more, and am completely satisfied."[124] *The Conquest of Canada*, however, also featured an onstage display of the local garrison's puissance: advertisements for the production announce that the stage "will be much crowded with the ARTILLERY, BOATS, &c., necessary for the Representation of the Piece, and with the men from both Corps, whose assistance the Commanding Officers are good enough to indulge us with."[125] While reviving in didactic fashion the past glories of the British military, resurrecting the heroic martyr Wolfe, and recalling a period of history antedating the Anglo-American tensions that emerged during the Stamp Act Crisis, the production of *The Conquest of Canada* also constituted a show of military force, a spectacle that seemed to carry an implicit warning against civil disturbances.

The American Company's season suggests that Douglass was attempting during the early 1770s to draw anti- and pro-British sympathizers, in addition to British soldiers, to the theater. The ideological jumbling of the Philadelphia season continued into the company's subsequent run in New York (April–August 1773), during which *Tamerlane* and *Richard III* played alongside *King John* and *The Tempest*—an equilibrium perhaps best exemplified by the company's performance of *Hamlet* on 28 May, which George Washington and General Gage attended together.[126] This uneasy tension in the repertoire oddly mirrors the colonial debate following the 1773 passage of the Tea Act. Colonial Tories in this period of heightened political tension had begun to endorse the perpetual union of Britain and the American colonies not according to a doctrine of passive obedience but out of what they perceived as a mutual appreciation of British constitutional freedom; this view diverged sharply from the position of colonial patriots, who increasingly characterized America as the last bastion of English liberties.

In illustrating how this debate intersected with the theater's role in the colonies during the early 1770s, it is helpful to juxtapose two texts written by the Maryland Tory and colonial official William Eddis. In 1772 Eddis published a poem in the *Maryland Gazette* praising "Sea-girt Britannia! Mistress of the isles! / Where Faith, and Liberty, united reign" and railing against "Dissension" as a "dire infection" running "from breast to breast" against which "Statesmen plan—and patriots plead in vain!"[127] Eddis continues to assert that Britain and the colonies form a single polity uniformly blessed with so-called British liberty, rather than constructing the colonies, as did colonial Whigs, as a Utican outpost of freedom threatened by the tyranny of the imperial center. (Eddis, indeed, later described advocates of independence as "petty tyrannies" and "despots.")[128] As Anglo-American relations deteriorated throughout 1773, however, Eddis penned a prologue that was used by the American Company during an 8 November 1773 staging of *Hamlet*, part of their brief final run in Philadelphia.[129]

Playing to both sides in the debate, much like Douglass himself in 1773, the prologue recalls both the colonial status of North Americans and the familiar figures of American settlement as a diaspora of free-born Englishmen:

When stern Oppression rear'd her baleful head,
To this blest clime our free-born fathers fled:
Secure from lawless sway, they chearful toil'd,
And soon the grateful glebe with plenty smil'd;
Cities arose, while Commerce pour'd her store,
And wealth flow'd in from every distant shore.
Now polish'd ease, and manners shine confest,
While ardent Freedom warms each generous breast.[130]

While Eddis accepts the "free born" status of Americans and the ideological primacy of "Freedom" in both Britain and the colonies, he dismisses the idea of contemporary British encroachments on American liberty. Whatever "stern Oppression" may have threatened Americans' English forefathers in the past, Eddis's epideictic "Now," a present in which the text, intended for performance, ensnares the British-American audience watching a British play, admits of only the freedom and prosperity fostered by transatlantic union.

Through the vehicle of the theater, where David Douglass's shifting repertoire continued to offer representations of "patriotism" and "liberty," whatever those terms meant to a given North American audience at a given moment, Eddis uses the diaspora motif long favored by fractious colonials to argue for a decidedly Tory liberty that celebrates unfettered commerce and the aesthetic pleasures of British "manners" and "ease" no less than the civil and religious liberties central to the patriot tradition. It is no coincidence, one imagines, that Eddis chose to make this plea for transatlantic, pro-union patriotism—a tempering of the radicalism of colonial patriotic politics with an appreciation of prosperity and the niceties of British culture—in a prologue written for a group of actors whose own livelihoods depended not only on the goodwill of the colonial population but also on a ready supply of hard currency and the continuing appeal of such recognizably British cultural exports as plays—the unfettered exchange of cultural as well as financial capital between homeland and periphery.

Curtain Call: Charleston, 1774

While Douglass's careful ideological tacking allowed him to negotiate the dangerous shoals of politics throughout most of 1773, during the American Company's final prewar engagement in Charleston (December 1773–May 1774) the colonial situation reached a point where such neutrality was neither profitable nor tenable. The Charleston season opened during the month of the Boston Tea Party, and several performances from this season suggest that Douglass was appealing to a growing body of patriot sympathizers in Charleston by staging productions with symbolic connections to the strained state of Anglo-American relations. Local political conditions, indeed, may have required Douglass to do so. For the first time in the company's history, Douglass faced anti-theatrical opposition in Charleston, including an unsuccessful attempt in the legislature to ban the players from the city due to South Carolina's "great want of Money" for its inhabitants "to procure the Conveniences and even the Necessaries of Life."[131]

The controversy was a familiar one for Douglass, even if the venue was new. One local proponent of the theater attempted to address these concerns by commending the theater's importance for nourishing patriotism, arguing that in ancient Greece, "The brave Hero, who had toiled in the Field of Honour and lavished his Blood on his Country's Cause, came to enjoy Amusements, which . . . elevated his Soul, and reanimated him in his glorious Career."[132] The vexed colonial interpretations of who such a "Hero" might be and in which "Country's Cause" he might fight appears to have wrought considerable changes in Douglass's use of politicized texts during the Charleston season. During January and February the American Company's play-list, which featured the warhorse *Richard III* as well as the Charleston premieres of *Cymbeline* and *The Tempest*, continues the political balancing act Douglass established in the company's just-completed runs in New York and Philadelphia. From March until the close of the season in May, however, the schedule features a number of performances with connections to colonial patriot activism.[133]

While Charleston was not a hotbed of radicalism on the order of Boston or Philadelphia, the controversy over the tea duty, perhaps coupled with the lingering effects of a visit by Josiah Quincy Jr. to Charleston in 1773, during which he acted as an emissary from the Boston Sons of Liberty to the Charleston chapter, seems to have had a marked effect on both local politics and Douglass's theatrical schedule.[134] On 17 March 1774, for instance, the American Company performed *The Recruiting Officer* at the particular request of the Charleston militia as part of their annual festivities celebrating the anniversary of the repeal of the Stamp Act. Before attending the performance, the groups performed a series of military exercises, in which "the Charles-Town Regiment of Foot Militia and the late-formed Light Infantry Company all under arms, made a very handsome appearance; they looked like what it is hoped they will be."[135]

The militia's commissioning of *The Recruiting Officer* to mark the anniversary of the Stamp Act's repeal, pairing a text equally popular in London and North America with a politicized colonial celebration, suggests that the spirit of patriotic volunteerism in South Carolina had begun to display bellicosity toward the presence of British regulars in North America. Such attitudes were already common in Massachusetts, of course, where a 1773 pamphlet written the previous year asserted, "Where his Majesty has one soldier, who art in general the refuse of the earth, America can produce fifty, free men, and all volunteers, and raise a more potent army of men in three weeks, than England can in three years."[136] Moreover, a mere two weeks before the Charleston performance John Hancock had delivered a commemorative oration for the victims of the Boston Massacre stressing the ability of the American colonies to defend themselves militarily without assistance from the army. Hancock compared colonial militias to a long series of famous military forces, proclaiming, "We want not courage; it is discipline alone in which we are exceeded by the most formidable troops that ever trod the earth. Surely our hearts flutter no more at the sound of war, than did those of . . . the Macedonian phalanx, the invincible Roman legions, . . . or the *well known Grenadiers of Britain.*"[137] Grenadiers from the British Twenty-Ninth Regiment of Foot had been conspicuous among the British troops who perpetrated the Massacre; the challenge to their reputation implicit in Hancock's rhetoric is obvious.[138] Purely by coincidence, *The Recruiting Officer*'s Captain Plume and Sergeant Kite were Grenadiers. The Charles-Town Regiment's appropriation of Farquhar's patriotic comedy represents a challenge to British military authority that oddly mirrors the gauntlet thrown down by Hancock in his masterful piece of New England street theater.[139]

In April 1774, as news of Parliament's reprisals against Massachusetts and the blockade of Boston Harbor spread throughout the colonies, Douglass staged a number of plays that had once been dropped from the repertoire in order to avoid political controversy, including the recently revived *Tamerlane*, which had never before been acted in Charleston, and *Macbeth*, which had not been acted anywhere in the colonies since 1769. The April play-list also includes a second American performance of *Julius Caesar*, unstaged in the colonies since it premiered in the wake of the Boston Massacre but prominent in the public imagination during 1774.[140] A pamphlet written by the Reverend Myles Cooper, avowed Tory and patron of the American Company, during this year warned Americans that the colonies were drifting toward a repetition of Shakespeare's tyrannicidal plotline, a rebellion that would ultimately be detrimental, he claimed, to American liberty, since it would be met with the same vengeance by George III's armies that Antony promises to Caesar's corpse: "HAVOC will be the cry; and the dogs of war will be let loose to tear out your vitals." Meanwhile Josiah Quincy, who had attended two performances by the American Company in New York on his way home from Charleston, asked in his "Observations on the Boston Port Bill," "Is not Britain to America, what Caesar was to Rome?"[141]

Perhaps no other performance illustrates Douglass's catering to the tastes of South Carolina's patriot faction as clearly as the playbill for 10 May 1774: on this date the American Company gave their first performance in Charleston of *Cato*, and their first performance of the play anywhere since 1768, as a benefit show for the Charleston Masons. (Ironically, during its absence from the American stage *Cato* had regained currency as an important text for the British radical community.)[142] Douglass, himself a Mason and surely staging a program specifically requested by the members of the Charleston lodge, followed *Cato* with Tobias Smollett's farce, *The Reprisal, or the Tars of Old England*, (1757) in which a group of heroic Jack Tars rescue a British pleasure craft illegally seized by the French during the Seven Years' War, and what we can only assume was a somewhat sarcastic singing of the Whig poet James Thomson's "Rule, Britannia," a patriotic ballad that praises the global power of the British navy and features the refrain "Britons ne'er will be slaves."[143] The entire program suggests an assertion of colonial defiance, with the familiar patriot radicalism of *Cato* being supplemented by topical commentary on British customs policy and the blockade of Boston.

Such an interpretation is consistent with the significant levels of support for the patriot community of Boston displayed in Charleston during the blockade: many South Carolinian "Gentlemen of Property" contributed food and financial aid to Bostonians. Some even took to the stage for the cause: two months after the American Company finished its run in Charleston, a number of the city's "younger Gentlemen" staged a charitable performance of *Busiris, King of Egypt,* a play featuring "an injured gallant People struggling against Oppression, resigning their All to Fortune, and wading thro' a dangerous bloody Field in Search of Freedom." Proceeds from the performance, even contributions of rice, according to the advertisement, were donated to Boston's blockade victims, fulfilling the duty of South Carolinians "*towards alleviating the Distresses of their Suffering Countrymen.*"[144] Two student productions of *Cato* that were produced during June and August 1774, after the American Company's departure, reportedly drew audiences numbering "several hundreds."[145] The American Company's run in Charleston seems not only to have "reanimated" the ardor of Charleston's patriot community for the emerging "Cause" of colonial resistance but also to have inspired some Charlestonians to apply the powers of the theater to that cause using their own talents. These Charlestonians became both emulators and disseminators of theatrical representations of patriotic virtue in an overtly politicized performance climate. Their efforts yielded a brief efflorescence of Steele's theater for a free-born people and Farquhar's nationalist, topical drama, gesturing toward the formation of a nation that neither author could have imagined.

As the outbreak of the American Revolution drew near, the professional theater in North America, the show and mirror of its times, began to reflect the changing political identities that the inhabitants of British North America were improvising from an unstable compound of creole consciousness and the mutable principles of "British liberty." Improvising identities was an activity particularly suited to the theater, where the disembodied tyrants, sacrificial victims, and patriots featured in the American Company's repertoire of popular favorites from the London stage could be reproduced and subjected to the revised interpretive strategies of the strange new breed of patriots in the audience. The composition of the repertoire of the colonial professional theater, and especially of Douglass's company, illustrates a number of important points about cultural identity and the role of theatrical forms in colonial politics. An audience for theatrical performances, even performances deeply enmeshed in the political turmoil of the British Atlantic community, clearly existed in British North America. The susceptibility of theatrical texts to competing interpretations—like the competing applause of Whigs and Tories that greeted Addison's *Cato* in 1713—in the context of the North American theater also reveals both the contingency of the concept of "Britishness" itself and the fundamental ambiguity of the terms (such as tyranny, sacrifice, and patriotism) that dominated the politics of Great Britain's Atlantic sphere. Plays like *Cato*, *The Recruiting Officer*, and *Tamerlane*—among many other popular theatrical texts featuring the protean trio of the tyrant, sacrificial victim, and patriot—that enjoyed widespread popularity during the Seven Years' War found new life and acquired new meanings during the 1760s and 1770s.

The political significance of theater and drama were not limited exclusively to periods of war with France, moreover. Colonial resistance to British policies fostered a recrudescent politics based on the assertion of "British" liberties and, eventually, secessionism—a specifically American outcropping of the opposition tradition of British politics that also radicalized such Shakespearean classics as *Macbeth*, *Hamlet*, and *Julius Caesar* in the print and theater culture of the eighteenth century. David Douglass, whose business model from 1758 to 1774 steadily plumped the appeal of theater to local and contemporary definitions of patriotism, staged the same plays in rousing colonial enthusiasm for war with the French and playing protest theater commissioned by colonial patriots—omitting such pieces from his company's repertoire, it should be added, only when those colonials boycotted the theater, disavowing the theatrical emissaries of British culture in order to prove their patriotic fidelity to "British" political principles.

Exit, Chased by a Congressman: A Postscript

The American Company's 1773–74 Charleston season, like Douglass's success in previous seasons that had been influenced by crises of colonial politics, had demonstrated that Douglass could market the performance of British plays to what were sometimes fractious American audiences. The increasingly anti-British tone of American politics in 1774 does not appear to have disturbed Douglass, who upon leaving South Carolina to recruit new actors in London announced the company's plans to play extended seasons in New York and Philadelphia for two years before returning to Charleston "with a Theatrical Force hitherto unknown in America."[146] On 20 October 1774, however, the Continental Congress intervened by passing a broad "non-importation, non-consumption, and non-exportation agreement" that contained a measure discouraging hard-currency expenditures on such (supposedly) nonessential goods as "horse-racing, and all kinds of gaming, cock-fighting, exhibitions of shows, plays, and other expensive diversions and entertainments."[147] Upon his return from London, David Douglass was greeted with a printed appeal from the pseudonymous "Pro Patria" in the *New York Journal*, imploring him to respect the wishes of the congress and the patriot community of New York and leave town for "the good people of this city, whose favour he has formerly experienced, and who may hereafter render him more essential service."[148]

Douglass, having experienced not only the favor but also the rather pointed *disfavor* of New Yorkers in the form of boycotts, to say nothing of the 1766 destruction of the Chapel Street Theatre, complied with the disembodied voice of American patriotism. On 2 February 1775 the American Company sailed for Jamaica, returning to Douglass's own theatrical roots in the Caribbean, and to a venue where the economic and military dependence of the colonies engendered by the sugar monoculture and lingering military presence of the French had prevented the evolution of a creole nationalism akin to the disposition of the North American colonies.[149] An announcement printed after the company sailed, and sounding suspiciously like a Douglass-authored press release, announced that the actors planned to exert "their justly applauded talents for the entertainment of the ladies and gentlemen of that polite and opulent island, until the unhappy differences that subsist between the mother country and her colonies in America subside."[150]

Appropriately enough, the company prefaced the opening performance of what would be a decade-long sojourn in Jamaica, a staging of *Romeo and Juliet* on 1 July 1775, with a prologue written by Benjamin Moseley, the colony's surgeon general, which echoes the promises of civic improvement through theater made by the Hallams upon their debut at Williamsburg. After gesturing toward the political struggles that led to the company's removal from North America, "When hostile strife invades the world's great stage, / ... / The Muse alarm'd at the loud tempest's roar, / Seeks an asylum on this peaceful shore," the prologue promises that

Our faithful mirror shall reflect to view,
Those blooming virtues which reside in you;—
Long may they flourish, long in vigour bloom,
Till fair JAMAICA rival Greece and Rome![151]

Faced once again with economic opposition fueled by the political intractability of North Americans, the American Company relocated to a less revolutionary corner of the British Americas, bringing with them a set of cultural practices not to be eliminated in the Atlantic world by any boycott, and a variety of imperial fictions. Not the least of these fictions was the British diaspora myth of an unbroken westward expansion of human freedom from classical antiquity to the Americas, a narrative commonly endorsed by the eighteenth-century theater and its champions in Britain and America.

Chapter 4
A School for Patriots: Colonial College Theater

Toward the end of his life, Royall Tyler, Harvard graduate and author of *The Contrast*, the first American-authored hit of the early national stage, composed *The Bay Boy*, a semi-autobiographical novel based on his youth in pre-Revolutionary Boston. Purportedly a memoir by Doctor Updike Underhill, *The Bay Boy* features a scene that, given its setting, is particularly noteworthy for its narration of a theatrical production. Since the original settlers of Massachusetts held that "[t]he players during the licentious reign of Charles the Second were the particular protégées [*sic*] of his libidinous court," Doctor Underhill observes, it should come as no surprise that some of the anti-theatrical bias of the opponents of the Stuarts "should have been transmitted to their descendants" in North America.[1] As a result of this anti-theatrical bias, the residents of Boston (and, as already demonstrated, many residents of Philadelphia, New York, and other colonial communities as well) "represented the playhouse as a receptacle of all uncleanness" in their private conversation.[2]

Having enrolled in medical school at Harvard, however, the young Underhill finds himself drawn into the cast of an "underground" amateur theatrical production being undertaken by a group of his fellow students and some Boston apprentices at night in the back room of a store. The text selected by Tyler's young men for the stage should seem familiar to the reader by now:

> Amidst this general abhorrence of dramatic writings there was one play suffered to be read, and those austere men who would rather have had a pack of cards in their house than a volume of Shakespeare still suffered their children to read Addison's Cato. This is a Whig play and though better adapted to the closet than scenic representation it contains so many fine passages about liberty and evinces such a hatred to despotism that it was a great favorite notwithstanding Cato was but a droll kind of republican, [and] killed himself like a very pagan with Plato's Phaedon in his hand, written expressly against suicide. But it was a Whig play, and those were liberty times, and every little boy who could mouth a passage of blank verse was inquiring
>
> > Whether there was not some hidden curse
> > Some chosen thunder midst the stores of heaven,

> Red with uncommon wrath to blast the man
> Who owes his greatness to his country's ruin?

meaning the Earl of Bute or Lord North as repeated at different eras.³

The staging in which the young Underhill takes part ends both comically and disastrously when the performance is broken up by the night watch and several of the actors are arrested. Not even Addison, it seems, can legitimize theatrical performances.

Tyler's amused recollection of colonial anti-theatricality and his satirical exposure of the inconsistencies in Addison's play, which did not hinder its popularity among even the sternest colonials, are doubly instructive due to the intersection of college students and the dramatis personae of *Cato*. First, the staging of *Cato* in this episode inserts the grand figures of the tyrant, the patriot, and the sacrificial victim into Tyler's burlesque of an amateur performance, offering even this motley crew of students and apprentices a certain dignity. Second, Underhill and his fellow amateurs, by producing a play approved of by the citizens of Boston (however ironically) for its educational value as a political allegory during the heady "liberty times" that Tyler records, offer a rare literary glimpse behind the curtain at one of the most underappreciated aspects of colonial and Revolutionary American culture: the performance traditions of American colleges.

Many of the earliest colonial college theatricals—productions of *Cato* and *The Recruiting Officer* at William and Mary in 1736 and Harvard between 1758 and 1760 and a performance of *Tamerlane* at the College of New Jersey in 1754—reproduced popular texts from the early American theatrical repertoire that reflected the tensions between Britain and France both in Europe and North America.⁴ The patriotic context of these collegiate productions, the culturally privileged academic settings in which they occurred, and the secondary evidence of Tyler's look back in amusement at his colonial youth also suggest that collegiate performances followed the didactic, patriotic model of the theater promoted by Addison and Steele, as well as (at least in theory) Lewis Hallam and David Douglass. Such didactic intent seems appropriate to the venues: Steele considered theater especially important for the moral and civic education of "Young Men, who are too unattentive to receive Lectures, [but] are irresistibly taken with Performances."⁵ Steele's theatrical model uses performance to instill a sense of national unity in members of the audience while providing a rich source of "strips" of proper behavior readily available for replication in the performance of their own lives.

This paradigm for performance has special resonance in academic as well as colonial performance settings, particularly given the intimate connections between public service and collegiate education in the colonies—

a relationship between the university and the state modeled on that of the homeland.[6] As one historian of the colonial college system explains, between the end of the Seven Years' War and the Revolution, American "college communities altered their relationship to the politics of the day. They went from vague proclamations and superficial implementations of an education for state service to a consciously shaped and vigorously advocated inculcation of republican political principles."[7] Both of these educational models were intertwined with the practices of public speaking and theatrical productions current on college campuses throughout the colonies. In the microcosm of the college campus, Sir Richard Steele's ideal of the theater as a vehicle for "the formation of a Free-born People" among the British nation survived, albeit that the colleges were located in a group of sometimes rebellious colonies. As were so many popular plays in colonial print culture, moreover, Steele's plan for the theater seems to have been appropriated by American students and (in some cases) educators in the college system and redirected against the country whence it came.

In addition to being among the first theatrical productions in North America, collegiate theatricals were a longstanding tradition. Beginning with a putative performance at Harvard in 1690 of a play (*Gustavus Vasa*) written by a student, Benjamin Colman, and an oratorical recitation at William and Mary in 1702, such amateur productions persisted throughout the eighteenth century. Moreover, as interest in oratory grew in American colleges, schools such as the College of New Jersey and the College of Philadelphia also began to incorporate occasional dramatic orations into such public rituals as commencement exercises.[8] As Gary A. Richardson observes, despite their artistic limitations, these exercises "provided American students with the opportunities to see and participate in dramatic productions and thereby not only encouraged would-be dramatists and prospective audiences by providing an aesthetic training ground, but also gave intellectual credibility and social acceptability to dramatic endeavors."[9] Unfortunately, the only comprehensive study of early American college theatricals and commencement orations, John L. Clark's impressive history of the genres, generally does not provide political context for the productions that it chronicles, leaving unexplained the historical resonances of many surprisingly complex performances.[10]

This lack of interpretation is especially disappointing in the case of the commencement orations of American colleges, which have too often been passed over by historians of the early American theater as "uninspired recitations" that are only "significant historically for showing the part which colleges and universities have played in the development of American drama."[11] Yet close study of the products of the collegiate theatrical and oratorical traditions of eighteenth-century America reveals the importance of colonial campuses as incubators of both early American performance culture and Revolutionary political sentiments. Intriguingly, many of the performances produced by college students reveal a predilection for depictions of tyrants, patriots, and sacrificial victims that mirrors the central political themes of the colonial professional theater and the political rhetoric of the British Atlantic community. In the semiotic laboratories of colonial colleges, the sons of the literate classes presented plays and orations that reflected the changing political and cultural landscape of British North America, communicating intimations of the future to a rising generation of public men as the colonies moved toward revolution.

William Smith: Academic Impresario

While William and Mary, Harvard, Yale, and the College of New Jersey all developed impressive theatrical traditions during the eighteenth century, perhaps nowhere was the interconnection between the college system, the theater, and the politics of patriotism in the British Atlantic as evident as in Philadelphia, owing in large part to the provost of the College of Philadelphia, the Reverend William Smith. A Scot by birth and an Anglican minister as well as a teacher, Smith was both an early patron of the theater in British North America and a controversial figure in Pennsylvania politics. After arriving at Philadelphia with a letter of recommendation from Benjamin Franklin in his possession, Smith served as the head of the Philadelphia Academy during 1753–54 and became the first provost of the newly founded college in March 1755. He seems to have acquired these positions by currying favor with both Governor Thomas Penn and Penn's chief antagonist, Franklin.[12]

Both political intrigue and patronage of the arts characterize Smith's career. A steadfast opponent of the Pennsylvania assembly's Quaker and Presbyterian factions and a staunch ally of the proprietary Penn family, Smith instituted Church of England services for the college's public ceremonies and published scabrous anonymous attacks on the Penn family's political opponents, including a 1755 pamphlet accusing Pennsylvania's Quakers and German immigrants of harboring republican sympathies.[13] Smith also became one of the theater's most vocal advocates in Philadelphia. When the London Company played their first short season in Philadelphia in 1754, Smith arranged a benefit for the academy's charity students and graced the performance with his presence—a significant display of public support; he also lobbied for the readmission of the company to Philadelphia in 1759 over the opposition of local Quakers and Presbyterians.[14] Nor was his influence over the development of the colonial theater limited to Philadelphia.

In 1757 and 1758 Smith published *The American Magazine, or Monthly Chronicle for the British Colonies,* an influential journal with a circulation base of eight hundred and fifty subscribers extending from New England to the West Indies.[15] Along with updates from the various fronts of the Seven Years' War, *The American Magazine* published extensive coverage of the controversy in Smith's native Scotland over the production of *Douglas,* a play written by the Presbyterian minister John Home. *Douglas,* a sentimental tragedy with a medieval Scottish setting, premiered in Edinburgh in 1756 and London in 1757 and met with considerable success, although controversies over Home's clerical profession, and the propriety of his fellow clergymen attending performances at Edinburgh, ultimately led Home to resign his pulpit and accept a patronage position from the Earl of Bute. *The American Magazine* published official condemnations of Home and *Douglas* by Presbyterian synods, favorable reviews of the play from London and Edinburgh newspapers, and David Hume's dedication of his *Four Essays* (1757) to Home along with its usual war correspondence, transforming the affairs of the Edinburgh stage into a debate over the relationships between theater, church, and state throughout the British Americas.[16]

Although *The American Magazine* carried both pro- and anti-theatrical pieces, Smith himself expressed no doubts about the benefits that the stage offered to civil society. In 1767, during the American Company's opening season at the Southwark Theatre in Philadelphia, Smith published a pamphlet noting that in Britain "[o]ur places of education almost universally perform [plays]—; and three times a year, the grand school of Westminster, which has afforded the most politic statesmen, the firmest patriots and the worthiest ecclesiastics for these many centuries—; encourages her sons to appear before an audience of the Nobility of Great Britain and the Ambassadors of foreign nations, in the characters of Terence."[17] Westminster was especially famous for producing patriot statesmen with histrionic skills, and the heavily publicized performances of its students included contemporary repertory pieces as well as an annual Roman comedy.[18] Smith clearly entertained hopes that his own College of Philadelphia would also produce such politic, well-spoken statesmen and patriots. In the winter of 1756–57, Smith began to promote both the drama specifically and oral performance in general as tools for molding his students in the image of the public men trained at Westminster. Among those of Smith's students with connections to either the colonial theater or colonial politics were William Paca, patriot activist, member of the Continental Congress, and governor of Maryland; Jacob Duché, who became a prominent Anglican cleric and chaplain to the Continental Congress; Thomas Godfrey, later a commissioned officer in the Seven Years' War and the author of *The Prince of Parthia,* a tragedy performed by David Douglass's American Company on 24 April 1767 at the Southwark, making it the first play written by an American-born colonial to be produced on the North American stage; and Francis Hopkinson, author of occasional prologues and epilogues for Douglass's company, who became first a colonial customs official and later a signer of the Declaration of Independence.[19]

According to Smith's own account of the college's early history, oratory was "considered an essential Branch" of his students' education from the college's inception. The progress of his students in this area of study led to the college's first official production during the Christmas holiday of 1756–57, a performance of *The Masque of Alfred*. The students repeated this performance during January 1757 to honor a visit to Philadelphia by several colonial governors and John Campbell, the Earl of Loudoun, who had been appointed commander of the British forces in North America during 1756.[20] The performance of this piece (written originally in 1740 by James Thomson and David Mallett and revised by Mallett in 1751) as a wartime entertainment for George II's new representative in the North American colonies clearly demonstrates a desire in the colonies for heroic representations of patriotism. It also shows the particular susceptibility of the patriot role, particularly in its monarchical avatar, to political appropriations that sometimes read against the grain of the text.

Alfred was originally written as a puff for the parliamentary opposition during the closing years of the Walpole regime, and at the time of its first production the text was interpreted as criticizing George II and praising his son, Frederick Louis, the Prince of Wales, around whom such key opposition figures as Bolingbroke, George Lyttelton, and William Pitt the Elder clustered during the 1730s.[21] On 6 September 1735, while George II was visiting Hanover, Bolingbroke's *Craftsman*, among other journals, reported that Frederick Louis, whom the opposition nominated during the 1730s as a regal standard-bearer for Country party principles, had commissioned a statue of King Alfred with an inscription describing the Saxon ruler as "the Founder of the Liberties and Commonwealth of England."[22] Thomson and Mallett, both recipients of the Prince of Wales's patronage, revived this symbolic connection for *Alfred*, the London production of which in 1740 participated in a major public relations campaign in the nation's theaters by playwrights associated with the opposition between 1738 and 1742.

The play's public debut was preceded by a private staging at the Prince of Wales's private country retreat, Cliveden House, to commemorate the accession of George I, a celebration that seems implicitly critical of George II.[23] However, Walpole's fall from power in 1742, the 1751 death of Frederick Louis, the incorporation of opposition politicians such as Lyttelton and Pitt into the ministry, and the immediate danger to Britons on both sides of the Atlantic from France had by 1756 thrust the superannuated George II into the role of Patriot King of British North America. Ironically, George II had resisted the initial deployments of British troops in the North American theater during 1755 for fear of weakening his grasp on his German holdings, and he remained obsessed with news from the European front throughout the war. Thus the king was conscripted to play a role that his loyal opposition had scripted for a different actor—his estranged son Frederick Louis—almost two decades earlier, and in a threatened colony to whose fate he seems to have been largely indifferent.[24]

The partisan history (and contemporary political ironies) of the play aside, *Alfred* fitted the bill as both an exercise in the civic education of Smith's students and an occasional patriotic performance in the midst of the Seven Years' War.[25] The masque's plot, which is reminiscent of Rowe's *Tamerlane*, chronicles the efforts of Alfred the Great, dethroned by the Danish tyrant Ivar's invasion of England, to regain his kingdom. Alfred wanders incognito through the forests of Somersetshire accompanied by his adjutant, the Earl of Devon, until he comes upon a religious hermit, a friendly peasant named Corin, and a surviving band of his loyal retainers. With the help of all of them he captures Ivar and his Danish war party, restoring himself to the throne and saving the kingdom from bloodthirsty foreign tyranny. "There is," writes Smith in the first of four lengthy essays detailing the College of Philadelphia production in the *Pennsylvania Gazette* (and which were later reprinted in the *New Hampshire Gazette*), expressed "through the Whole, a Sublimity of Sentiment, a Love of Liberty, and a Concern for the Commerce and Glory of Great Britain, scarce equalled by any Thing in our Language."[26] Moreover, Smith continues, the play's focus on a war between the forces of freedom and tyranny set in a British wilderness, "is most peculiarly adapted to our present Circumstances, and tends directly to inspire . . . true Heroism and public Spirit."[27]

Smith adapted *Alfred* for his students, writing out the part of Alfred's queen to suit his all-male company and accentuating, as indicated by his profuse chronicling of the event in the *Gazette*, the play's heroic elements and its analogies to the North American conflict. His adaptation focuses almost exclusively on the figure of Alfred and expands considerably the number of lines that encourage Britain's development as a global military power. (The masque expresses not only the patriotic exceptionalism common among opposition writers but also an expansionist strain: Thomson wrote the lyrics to his famous ode "Rule, Britannia" for this piece in 1740.) Smith's occasional prologue asserts that the play addresses "the noblest subject on the stage; / A Hero rising in lost Freedom's Cause, / What KINGS should be, and Godlike ALFRED was."[28] According to Smith, not only do dramatic representations in general train superior orators for "the Pulpit, the Bar, or the Senate" but in particular "this single representation of *Alfred* will contribute . . . to the forming a true Englishman, and promoting Principles both of public and private Virtue." The beneficial effects of the play are primarily due to Alfred's status as "a finished Pattern of True Heroism and diffusive Virtue . . . nobly uniting in himself two of the most exalted Characters on Earth—that of a PATRIOT KING, and of a GOOD MAN!"[29]

Smith also took great pains to translate *Alfred*'s exemplarity into a North American context. After the play's scripted closing number, a chorus of sailors singing "Rule, Britannia," Smith inserted a prophetic speech delivered by the hermit that emphasizes a comparatively egalitarian vision of patriotism (a virtue available even to common sailors, or the sons of Philadelphian commerce dressed as sailors) and "the Extension of Freedom and the British Name, to the remoter Parts of the Earth":

. . . These are the Men,
Who, ages hence, shall Britain's thunder bear
From Pole to Pole, around a trembling World!
Lo! Where, beyond the wild Atlantic Surge,
In Realms yet unexplor'd, they spread her Fame!
. . . Beneath their hand,
With Freedom Crown'd, and rich with golden Stores,
I see gay COLONIES, and future Empires,
In Glory rise.[30]

These themes of patriot leadership and the global expansion of British freedom were also fused expertly in the play's epilogue, written and spoken by the future clergyman Jacob Duché, who portrayed Alfred. Declaring that under the onslaught of the French and their Indian allies, "more than Danish Rage, with bloody Hand, / Spreads Death and Slaughter o'er this prostrate Land," the epilogue spoken by the surrogate monarch plays on the implicit connections between Alfred the Great and King George II, and between both of them and Lord Loudoun, the new military leader of the North American colonies.

In the epilogue, Duché/Alfred exhorts the spectators to perform a series of reconciliations: between past and present, the roles of audience and army of patriots, and the body natural of the ruler and the body politic of the nation. This process is to be performed by emulating the examples set forth by both the scripted play and the students' performance:

Be brave! Be one—and HEAVEN shall do the Rest!
Glad o'er the Atlantic comes our gallant Chief;
Before whose Arm our Foes have often fled,
And black Rebellion hides her gory Head.
Be you but BRITONS, as an ALFRED he;
And War and Rapine soon shall cease to be.[31]

Smith and his students, in reviving and adapting *Alfred*, provided a patriotic spectacle tailor-made for the colonial front of a global war. The epilogue merely gives an explicit, local meaning to the play's already implicitly relevant emphases on sacrifice and patriotic resistance to tyranny.

The College of Philadelphia *Alfred* is particularly useful in considering the role of college theater in the colonies for a number of reasons. First, Smith's explicit political allegorization of the text and his endorsement of theater's potential for civic instruction provide, like the politically topical prologues used by professional touring companies, clear evidence of the theater's role in public affairs. Just as importantly, Smith's allegiance to the more conservative wing of Pennsylvania politics in the form of the Anglican church and the Penn family, as well as the performance of his version of *Alfred* well before the colonial political upheavals of the 1760s and 1770s, illustrates that the theatrical practice of amateur student performances chronicled in Tyler's *The Bay Boy* extended across the colonial political spectrum and could promote British as well as American patriotism. By revising Thomson and Mallett's masque to suit the local conditions of wartime Pennsylvania, moreover, Smith engaged in the same sort of appropriation later commonly practiced by American patriot partisans, a self-consciously colonial deployment of a British text. The College of Philadelphia *Alfred* thus not only used the theater to promote British patriotism but also interrogated the transatlantic extension of "Britishness" and the theatrical figures that embodied it. Smith, attempting to train up a new generation of patriot orators, produced a performance text that examined the relationship of political and theatrical identities to both legends of the heroic past upon which they are built and the shifting winds of current politics. This experiment also tested the communicability of public and private virtue through the display of theatrical action, an issue of great importance to the expansion of the colonial theater in all its forms.

Boston in Wartime: Harvard's Patriotic Spectacles

Smith's staging of *Alfred* demonstrates the principal features of American college productions during the Seven Years' War: their focus on the figure of the patriot and the rhetoric of martial sacrifice in the fight against tyranny, their analogical applicability to the transatlantic struggle between Britain and France, and their didacticism ("Be you but BRITONS, as an ALFRED he"). The same features appear in the 1754 production of *Tamerlane* at the College of New Jersey, which like the Hallams' production of this play in Philadelphia was ideally suited to political conditions at the beginning of the Seven Years' War and extended the theatrical genealogies of William III (Tamerlane), conquering hero of the Glorious

Revolution and "restorer" of Britain's constitutional monarchy, and Louis XIV (Bajazet), the progenitor of the absolutist French monarchy, to include their sitting successors on the British and French thrones.[32]

In a similar fashion, during 1758–60 the students of Harvard College acted over a dozen performances of various plays, many of which revolved around themes of war, patriotism, or civic virtue. Two of the plays that received more than one performance dated from the War of the Spanish Succession, and, as already noted, they resonated strongly with early American political culture: Addison's *Cato* and Farquhar's *The Recruiting Officer*. *Cato* appeared on 2, 6, and 14 July 1758, and again on 7 September 1759.[33] *The Recruiting Officer* was staged twice on 20 June 1759, both as a private performance, like the *Cato* showings, and as a performance open to the public, although it is unclear where this "public" staging took place. One 1759 production (of Edward Young's *The Revenge*) by Harvard students took place in a private residence, although coffeehouses and taverns (which were also popular locations for the productions staged by Yale students in the 1750s) hosted a number of amateur productions. If the performance took place in one of the latter locations, especially, then this public performance expanded the reach of Farquhar's comedy, with its wartime setting and endorsement of volunteerism, beyond the range of private amusement and into the realm of the colonial public sphere—the same space occupied by Smith's production of *Alfred*, during a period of heavy military enlistment in New England.[34]

Intriguingly, the Boston authorities also suppressed a proposed amateur production of *Cato* in 1760, despite both the moral reputation of Addison's play and the patriotic intent of the players, for what one of the anonymous would-be participants in the play identified as the theater's putative "Vice, impiety, immorality, &c." The suppression is especially puzzling given that one actor was to have spoken Pope's prologue "in the Character of an Officer of the Army." The modified prologue for this production, after lauding Cato's stoic virtues, transfers his glory to a set of British heroes, including General Wolfe, the sacrificial victim of Quebec, and King George II:

Britons attend, virtues like these approve,
If found at home, they merit more your love;
Marcus of Rome, with martial virtue fir'd,
But faintly shows how Britain's Wolfe expir'd;
The sword of vengeance, he with justice drew,
Conquering he fell, for liberty and you;
. . . .
But peace my heart; Great George triumphant lives,
In him, kind heav'n a conquering Cato gives,
Not pent by foes within a narrow bound,
But spreading conquests all the world around.[35]

This abortive staging may well have been another attempted performance by a group of Harvard students, who apparently had access to at least one set of British regimentals.

In spite of the satirical gibes that Farquhar directs at the army in *The Recruiting Officer* and the republican tinge of *Cato*, these plays share *Alfred*'s patriotic tone and concern with the global battle between "liberty" and "tyranny"—the very materials that Provost Smith singled out in Thomson and Mallett's masque as useful for the formation of patriotic young statesmen. Such productions are of particular interest when they are made available, either in the flesh or through the proxy of newsprint, to the general public. It is worth noting that patriotic wartime theatricals took place in cities generally resistant to the authority of the crown's armed forces: whenever possible, the Pennsylvania assembly in Philadelphia blocked attempts to raise troops in the colony during the Seven Years' War, and tensions between the city of Boston and His Majesty's armed forces over the military's methods of procuring servicemen dated back at least to the Knowles riots of 1747, which broke out after a brutal (and possibly illegal) sweep of Boston Harbor by the Royal Navy's press gangs.[36] The Harvard staging of *The Recruiting Officer*, then, overlaps with a period of open war that pitted British and colonial troops against the French; it also follows a period of strained relations between the British armed forces and North American civilians that had been overcome chiefly by the popularity of Pitt's war policies, rather than a closing of the metropolitan-colonial cultural divide. A similar public production of a play, which contained both endorsements of unity under patriotic monarchical leadership and a cautionary tale of the narrow boundary between patriotism and tyranny in the conduct of kings, occurred at Harvard in 1760. On 8 April 1760, a group of students privately staged James Thomson's *Tancred and Sigismunda*, which they repeated in a public performance on 13 June that year.[37]

Tancred and Sigismunda (1745), perhaps Thomson's most artistically successful play, promotes, like *Alfred*, the ideal of the "patriot" king devoted wholly to the rule of law and the welfare of his people rather than of his ministers. This play, however, rather than endorsing the factionalism associated with the shadow court ruled by the Prince of Wales in the late 1730s, promotes political harmony—due in no small part, one imagines, to Thomson's patrons Lyttelton and Pitt having left the opposition to join the ministry during the early 1740s.[38] Set in the twelfth century, the play opens shortly after the death of King William of Sicily. The hero Tancred, raised in the household of Matteo Siffredi, Sicily's lord high chancellor, learns from Siffredi that he is the descendant of Sicily's ancient, dispossessed royal line. Although Tancred loves Siffredi's daughter,

Sigismunda, Siffredi encourages Tancred to marry the late king's sister Constantia, the rival claimant to the throne, in order to unite the nation.

When Tancred refuses to obey Siffredi, however, Siffredi forges a marriage contract between Tancred and Constantia; Tancred, for the good of the state, honors the contract as genuine. Siffredi then quietly marries Sigismunda to the Duke of Osmond, Constantia's leading supporter. After assuming the throne, however, Tancred resorts to arbitrary rule in the service of his private passions. He jails the Duke of Osmond and annuls his marriage to Sigismunda. Osmond, released from jail by a sympathetic officer, returns home to find Tancred alone with Sigismunda, where he has been attempting to persuade her to renounce her marriage. Osmond draws his sword on Tancred, but Tancred wounds him fatally. In his dying act Osmond stabs Sigismunda, even as she professes her spousal devotion to him. The play closes with Tancred disgraced and Siffredi lamenting the deceit that he employed for the public good at the expense of his own private interests.[39]

Although the plays share an abiding concern with the nature of patriotism, the unabashedly celebratory *Alfred*, at least in Smith's Philadelphia staging, bestows the opposition's idealized mantle of the patriot king upon an object of its creator's animus, George II. *Tancred and Sigismunda*, however, both as a 1745 endorsement of Lyttelton's and Pitt's defection to the ministry and as a 1760 spectacle for His Majesty's fractious subjects in Massachusetts, emphasizes the need for compromise in the name of patriotism during such emergencies as a succession crisis or a war, while also stressing the dangers posed to a commonwealth by human fallibility. Tancred, initially the hope of the nation for the easing of civil discord, cannot overcome his private passions and degenerates into an arbitrary prince once invested with his office—a warning perhaps intended especially by the youthful patriots of Harvard for the pacification of their own romantic ardor. Siffredi sacrifices his private interest (Sigismunda's happiness and his family's advancement) to the public good with a devotion approaching Catonic idealism, but his subversion of the rule of law in the name of political stability leads to catastrophe. The play's most effective example of the patriot figure, at least up until he kills his wife, is Osmond, who practices both selfless devotion to the state in public matters and a jealous defense of his prerogative in private affairs.

Osmond's simultaneous devotion to the public good and his private prerogative are both on display in a speech blessing the union of Tancred and Constantia (and recalling Lyttelton's and Pitt's transitions between factions). Osmond declares:

We meet today, with open Hearts and Looks,
Not gloom'd by Party, scowling on each other,

But all the Children of one happy Isle,
The social Sons of Liberty.⁴⁰

The coincidental appearance of the name "Sons of Liberty" hints at the applicability of Osmond's dramatic example for colonials during the Seven Years' War, who, like Osmond, jealously (and sometimes violently) guarded their liberties against any perceived encroachment by government officials. Osmond's behavior argues that the rights of the citizenry trump loyalty to the sovereign.⁴¹ As David Sambrook notes, when Osmond draws his sword on Tancred he acts not only as an aggrieved husband but also as a rebel justified by Whig principles in resisting a tyrant's invasion of his home.⁴² Not for the last time in the culture of colonial college theater, Harvard's amateur thespians showed the figure of the patriot king falling prey to the temptations of power, only to be met with a similar but opposed patriotic devotion to property and principle practiced by his subjects.

Dialogue and Dissent: College Commencement Orations

Both the principles endorsed by *Tancred and Sigismunda* and its concern with the transition between generations of royal leadership would be addressed repeatedly in the years following George II's death and George III's accession in 1760. Moments of institutional change such as the succession of kings require public rituals of renewal, and the transition between the reigns of George II and George III involved not only the investment of a new king with his office but also, at least in William Smith's Philadelphia, the public transmission of the mantle of "patriot king" to the House of Hanover's new ruler. The influence of Bolingbroke's ideas on Smith's thought, evident in both his choice of *Alfred* for a student production and his emphatic citation of the phrase "PATRIOT KING" in the play's printed extracts, also colors the College of Philadelphia's first published commencement orations. Commemorating the death of George II and the accession of George III, the scripts of these occasional performance pieces were also printed as pamphlets. In the 1761 exercise commemorating George II, Smith wrote the dialogue himself, while his student Francis Hopkinson contributed a commemorative ode.⁴³

The dialogue between the speakers Eugenio and Amyntor, which opens with Amyntor's lamentation, "All things, Eugenio, are but dust and earth! / Even kings themselves—those demi-gods enthron'd," heaps upon the deceased George II all the laurels of the "patriot king," defender of the Constitution and common father to his people: "The Godlike GEORGE / The Friend of Freedom, and the Scourge of Tyrants / The Father of his Country—Sleeps in Dust!"⁴⁴ Amyntor's praises for George II resonate strongly not only with the image of the constitutional monarch as the champion of liberty endorsed by Smith's Bolingbrokean *Alfred* but also with the wartime popularity of plays, such as Rowe's *Tamerlane,* featuring similar heroes. Eugenio's reply declares that George's reputation shall surpass those of such "patriot" kings as William III, Henry V, and even Alfred. Moreover, Eugenio recalls that beneath George II's "equal sway / Oppression was not, JUSTICE poiz'd her Scale; / No LAW was trampled and no Right denied— / The peasant flourish'd, and the Merchant smil'd."[45]

This passage is strongly reminiscent of Bolingbroke's declarations that a patriot king in his dedication to the constitution would have to "refuse . . . to be an absolute monarch, when every circumstance invites him to it." The resultant conditions of such a king's good governance would be, according to Bolingbroke: "[B]rooding peace and prosperity on the happy land; joy sitting in every face, content in every heart; a people unoppressed, unalarmed; busy to improve their private property and the public stock; fleets covering the ocean, bringing home wealth by the returns of industry, carrying assistance or terror abroad."[46] The dialogue, revisiting the idealized image of George II projected in both public and private stagings of plays by colonial students during the war-troubled final years of his reign, raises the departed monarch to the status of a national hero and sets the stage for the transmission of the role of liberty's champion to George III. This transfer occurs in Hopkinson's ode, which characterizes the role of the patriot king and all its attendant charisma as the rightful inheritance of the Hanoverian successor. Hopkinson treats the title not as a simple trapping of the office but as an essential part of the young Prince of Wales's regal patrimony, an immortal residue of kingship's mysteries that has survived the imposition of constitutional limits on the monarchy, "For GEORGE the Second in the Third still lives." The (patriot) king is dead; long live the (patriot) king.[47]

The commencement exercise for 1762, written by Hopkinson with the aid of his fellow student thespian Jacob Duché, reiterates the 1761 dialogue's elevation of George III to the status of patriot king, thus fulfilling a national longing for royal leadership. Resurrecting the speakers Amyntor and Eugenio and introducing a third, Lorenzo, Duché's dialogue declares that the previous year's exercises provided the requisite ceremony of mourning for "Majesty entomb'd" and implores the audience to "[s]hout then, ye favor'd Race, ye Sons of Freedom! / . . . / For o'er the Realms of Britain reigns supreme / The Darling of his People, George the Good."[48] Duché's rhetoric in the dialogue, like that of his teacher Smith, shows a preference for gushing epithets influenced by Bolingbroke. Duché's George III is a "[t]hrice happy Monarch! skill'd in every Art / To win a Nation's smile and fix their Love," much like Bolingbroke's ideal king, for whom "[n]othing less than the hearts of his people will content such a prince; nor will he think his throne established, till it is established there."[49] Hopkinson and Duché express similar hopes for the reign of George III, who has been raised, like his father Prince Frederick Louis, the figurehead of 1730s opposition, as a British instead of a continental prince—an education that has freed him from the ironies attendant upon the characterization of the Europhile George II as a patriot king by North American colonials.

This optimistic spirit also infuses a dialogue, *The Military Glory of Great Britain*, recited at the College of New Jersey's commencement in 1762, as well as the dialogue recited at the 1763 commencement exercise of the College of Philadelphia, which celebrates the conclusion of the Seven Years' War. Both texts combine specifically North American content with expressions of desire for global British glory under the new king. *The Military Glory of Great Britain* praises the war efforts of generals Wolfe, Amherst, and Monkton before articulating its aspirations for George III's reign:

Long may George the Regal Sceptre sway;
And scatter Blessings with a liberal Hand
Around the peaceful Globe, but dire Dismay
On all who dare his injur'd Arms withstand.[50]

In a similar fashion, the 1763 exercise at the College of Philadelphia celebrates the victorious George III as "a Sovereign . . . / Who deems in kings a virtuous name the best; / Guardian of Right and Sacred Liberty" and eagerly anticipates the material benefits that transatlantic peace under a Bolingbrokean leader will bring to both "the Old world and the New": "COMMERCE shall then expand without Controul, / Where Coasts expand or farthest Oceans swell; / These spacious Realms their Treasures shall unfold."[51] George III's reign, as forecast in these colonial performance texts, augurs not only the martial glory and individual heroism attributed to the Hanoverian line by the theater of the Seven Years' War and the selfless devotion to the state of the patriot effigy but also the renewal of the commerce upon which the British Atlantic community depended. George III is rendered as both a champion of constitutional liberty against domestic enemies and a defender of trade and property throughout his realms from foreign attack.

The transatlantic emphasis of the 1762–63 dialogues and their confirmation of George III as a patriot king extend into later orations as well, although subtle distinctions in the rhetoric of these dialogues began to emerge as rifts reappeared in the relationship between Britain and the colonies.[52] On 20 May 1766, the College of Philadelphia's commencement celebrated the repeal of the Stamp Act, an occasion that generated a variety of public celebrations throughout the colonies. Two days after that event, for instance, the Sons of Liberty in Massachusetts erected "a magnificent Pyramid" illumined with 280 lamps and set off fireworks to celebrate the Act's repeal.[53] Meanwhile Josiah Quincy, whose early writings showed a theatrical flair that was "captive to the genius of Shakespeare," upon taking his M.A. at Harvard in 1766, "pronounced the English oration, at that time a new thing in the exercises of the University," and an opportunity considered at the time to be Harvard's highest honor.

Quincy's subject was "'patriotism,'" a topic of crucial importance in 1765–66. During this time the Stamp Act Crisis forced American colonials to determine whether "patriotism" meant allegiance to the laws of Great Britain, to the person of King George III, or to the "patriot" principle of liberty that, in the opinion of many colonials, the Stamp Act violated.[54] Quincy's participation in a new performance practice, one that elevated speech in the more democratic vernacular above a traditional Latin oration in the conservative ritual of the commencement ceremony, is particularly interesting. Quincy's chosen topic is timely, and the institution of this oration at Harvard shows the progress of vernacular performance culture at the college after the days of John Adams's private dramatic readings in the mid-1750s and the students' staging of plays during the Seven Years' War. At this high-profile moment, orations in English had become an accepted part of the institutional identity of Harvard and its conservative classical curriculum, just as they were in the more liberalized curricula of the College of New Jersey and the College of Philadelphia and those schools' annual public commencement celebrations.[55]

Quincy's oration, fleeting as a pyrotechnic display, has not survived, but the College of Philadelphia's 1766 commencement exercise, like its wartime predecessors, was reprinted in pamphlet form for the consumption of the general public. The dialogue equates patriotism with obedience to the king, who is characterized in the text as the selfless, devoted guarantor of national liberty. George III in this dialogue is a sensitive, sensible servant of his people, akin to a monarchical stage patriot like Alfred, or like Bolingbroke's patriot king, who utterly rejects the temptations of absolutism:

His placid Brow no Terror sheds around,
No vengeance nerves his Arm to strike
The Blow, and triumph o'er a prostrate Land.
Mercy in Him her wildest Beams unites
To claim a People's Love. And tho', between,
The broad Atlantic rolls its azure Wave,
Our tongues shall still confess the generous Hand,
That gives us Peace, and fosters Liberty.[56]

The dialogue, while flattering in its portrayal of George III, nonetheless leaves open the possibility that during the Stamp Act Crisis the colonies were indeed a "prostrate land," even if the king did not choose to strike a blow that would have been fatal to them. George III's defense of the colonies is not that of a champion of freedom entering the lists but that of a cartoon Roman emperor turning the upward thumb to a gladiator, benevolently employing the autocrat's power over life and death. If this figure guarantees the liberties of British patriots in America, then that liberty's condition is precarious indeed.

The dialogue does, however, provide more vigorous patriot champions in the persons of those members of the Rockingham ministry who pressed for the Stamp Act's repeal: the dialogue praises Rockingham himself, as well as Lords Grafton, Shelburne, Camden, and William Pitt the Elder. Pitt, whose speech against the Stamp Act in Parliament helped to ensure its repeal, is singled out for particular attention, and his characterization as a patriot in the dialogue establishes a textual presence that rivals George III's, presenting him as a more strenuous advocate of liberty than the figure of the king. Pitt, in this depiction, bears a striking similarity to the doomed heroes of the Roman republic admired by Britons on both sides of the Atlantic throughout the eighteenth century.[57] "A Cato's firmness," declares the oration, "and a Tully's zeal, / And every worth that grac'd the Roman sires / . . . In PITT, behold them all collected shine," as "With all the PATRIOT flashing in his Eye, / The Cause of sinking Liberty he Pleads."[58] Whereas George III's relationship with the American colonies is remote and godlike, Pitt engages in a histrionic, public apologia for American liberty. Pitt's image in the dialogue savors of the principled resistance to tyranny of Addison's tragic Cato, an example of devotion to liberty and country that stands ready for emulation by the oration's audience and the reading public of Philadelphia.

The college's 1767 commencement oration echoes this subtle shift away from the equation of loyalty to crown and love of country and toward expressions of loyalty to Britain as the homeland of the cherished ideal of liberty, a change that marks the theatrically inflected discourse of patriotism in North America during and after the Stamp Act Crisis.[59] Gone is the awe-inspiring image of George III, British colossus and champion of his subjects' freedom, and in its place has emerged a vision of political idealism and patriotic sacrifice strongly suggestive of the universal "spirit of liberty" endorsed by John Adams in *A Dissertation Upon the Canon and Feudal Law*.[60] While the name of Great Britain still conjures up "filial awe," in this dialogue the loyalty of the North American lies not with regal paternalism, but with Britain's status as

The Queen of Justice, Liberty and Law;
Britain, whose Blood thro' antient Worthies runs,
Her Charter seal'd by Heroes and their Sons;

Britain, whose name strikes Terror all around,
The Sons of Freedom glory in the sound.[61]

While North American "Sons of Freedom" retain their allegiance to the crown, this loyalty is subsumed within a broader ideal of patriotism: "Be this great truth upon our Hearts imprest," declares one of the dialogue's representatives of Philadelphia's best and brightest, "He loves his *King*, who serves his *Country* best."

Likewise, the 1770 dialogue, which laments the fresh crisis in British relations with the colonies caused by the Boston Massacre, acknowledges the misfortune of the "mutual Trust and Love" between mother country and colonial children yet focuses not on allegiance to the king but the liberties of the populace:

Attend, ye patriot throng! Ye noble sons
Of Freedom, who, to save your Country's rights
With rigid self-denial, sacrifice
Your private gain—O! be your worth approv'd
Attend! Be firm![62]

The College of Philadelphia's exercises in dramatic oratory, instituted by Provost Smith for the training up of young patriots capable of serving their country on the great stage of public affairs, had begun to reflect the changing ways in which the residents of British North America perceived liberty, tyranny, and the theatrical representation of politics.

It is worth noting here, out of historical sequence, that these commencement dialogues of the 1760s were resurrected in Philadelphia during the Revolution. In May 1775, after the outbreak of the Revolution, Smith, who opposed British colonial policies but did not initially endorse independence, stitched together fragments of these earlier dialogues in a commemoration of the proprietor of Pennsylvania (and Smith's political patron), Thomas Penn, who had recently died. Commemorating Penn, like George II, as the "Father of his country," and celebrating American allies in Parliament such as Pitt and Edmund Burke, the dialogue also bemoans those "causes [that] damp this festal day":

When *peace* is fled—when sacred *freedom* mourns,
And her fair sister *commerce*, by her side
Sits bound in fetters—when untwisted lies
The golden chord of mutual trust and love
That should unite the *parent* and the *child*,
And slaughter'd brethren strew th' ensanguin'd plain.[63]

Smith converts the college's earlier paeans to the glory of British patriotism into a meditation on the tragic nature of the newly erupted conflict between Britons and Americans. Smith, whose political trimmings during the Revolution did not prevent his legislative enemies from stripping him of control over the college in 1779, also revived a modified version of the 1763 dialogue celebrating peace in the Seven Years' War at the conclusion of the Revolution in 1783 at the first commencement ceremony of his new school, Washington College in Maryland.[64] This reframing of the 1763 dialogue as a pro-independence text mirrored not only Smith's own apparent conversion to full-throated American patriotism after losing control of the College of Philadelphia but also a broader trend in the versions of patriotism displayed in commencement dialogues throughout the 1760s.

Debate and Drama at Yale and Princeton

As the students at the College of Philadelphia employed dramatic oratory to mark major public events during the 1760s, theatrical presentations—both play performances and public speaking—became important parts of the collegiate experience for students at both Yale and the College of New Jersey during the late 1760s. Yale's disciplinary records indicate plays were being performed there as early as 1755, and the records of the Linonian Society, the fraternity of which Nathan Hale became a member in 1770, indicate that as early as December 1768 dramatic performances and debates were common recreations for the Linonians. The fraternity members determined that "for one Wensday eve in every month there is to be a Commedy Acted. Every other Wensday Eve there is to be Disputes and other Exercises." The society's minutes for meetings between 1768 and 1770 regularly list "Narrations," "Dialogues," and "Orations" spoken by members, for both edification and amusement. At least one documented staging of a play took place, on 15 February 1770, before Nathan Hale joined the society in November of that year—an induction that coincided with a blossoming of theatrical performance among the young men of Linonia at Yale.[65]

While the Linonians were experimenting with amateur theatricals and dramatic dialogues as complements to debates, the College of New Jersey welcomed in 1768 a new teacher with his own connections to both the theater and the eighteenth century's preoccupation with effective public speaking: the college's new president, the Reverend John Witherspoon. While serving in the Presbyterian Church in Scotland in 1757, Witherspoon had taken part in the *Douglas* controversy covered so extensively by Smith's *American Magazine*, publishing an anti-theatrical pamphlet entitled *A Serious Enquiry Into The Nature and Effects of the Stage*. In this pamphlet Witherspoon rejects the claims of those who champion the theater as a school for public virtue, scorning popular English dramas for their moral content, arguing that "Pride, under the name of greatness of mind, ambition and revenge, under those of valour and heroism, have been . . . constant themes" and claiming that such displays have potentially ill effects on audience members.[66]

Witherspoon's disdain for the stage, however, did not lead him to reject the ideal of virtuoso performance entirely. At Princeton, Witherspoon began in 1769 to deliver an annual series of "Lectures on Eloquence," the first official course in public speaking documented at an American college. In the first of these lectures, Witherspoon notes approvingly that "[t]he grace of elocution and the power of action might not only acquire a man fame in speaking, but keep up his influence in public assemblies," citing as his examples the revivalist preacher George Whitefield and William Pitt.[67] Such a tacit endorsement of rhetorical manipulation suggests that Witherspoon, like Jeremy Collier, objected not to theatricality per se, but to what he perceived as the scurrility of the contemporary drama.

This interpretation is supported by Witherspoon's citation of what he perceived to be a less objectionable scene from the theater as a model for good public speaking:

One talent of great moment towards raising the passions is a strong and clear imagination and a descriptive manner of speaking to paint scenes and objects and set them strongly before the eyes of the hearers. To select such circumstances as will have the most powerful effect and dwell upon only these, we have not anywhere in English a finer example of the pathetic, and the choice and use of circumstances, than the speech which Shakespeare has made for Anthony in the tragedy of Caesar. It appears from the history that Anthony did successfully raise the fury of the Romans against those who killed Caesar, and I think he could hardly select better images than those we have in the English poet.[68]

Witherspoon's citation of Marc Antony turning the Roman tide of public opinion against the republicans and in favor of the assassinated autocrat, while an ironic choice for a man who would later sign the Declaration of Independence, endorses theatrically embellished patriotic speech as means of moral persuasion for the public good.[69] This attitude toward both education and public speaking was not far removed from that of Witherspoon's theater-loving Anglican counterpart in Philadelphia, William Smith. Indeed, Witherspoon seems as sensitive as Smith to the peculiar power associated with performances that employ the rhetoric of liberty, tyranny, and patriotic sacrifice.

Among the students at Princeton who would have heard Witherspoon's lectures in the late 1760s were three founding members of the College of New Jersey's answer to Yale's Linonia, the American Whig Society: the future president James Madison, the Revolutionary poet Philip Freneau, and the aspiring playwright and novelist Hugh Henry Brackenridge. If Madison is to be believed, Witherspoon's students (most likely members of the Whig Society) were, like their counterparts at other colleges, dabbling in the drama, either by reading plays individually or in groups. Writing in 1772 to William Bradford, son of a patriot Philadelphia printer, future witness to the Valley Forge *Cato*, and a fellow founding member of the Whig Society, the recently graduated Madison observes that while he was a student, "plays," along with a variety of other belletristic forms, "captivated me much." Unfortunately, he continues, the various crises of Anglo-American relations have recently led him to focus his reading on history and political philosophy, reserving for the arts "but a moderate portion" of his time.[70]

Freneau and Brackenridge also developed a taste for the drama, as well as a deeper understanding than Madison of the utility of theatrical texts in political crises. Discussions of Brackenridge's two propaganda plays written during the Revolution will follow in the ensuing chapter. Freneau, for his part, also adapted the forms of dramatic speech to the patriot cause during the war. Between 1778 and 1779, the two men published *The United States Magazine*, a short-lived literary review sprinkled with propaganda pieces. Among Freneau's contributions were poems written in dramatic forms, such as "George The Third's Soliloquy" and "A Dialogue Between His Britannic Majesty and Mr. Fox," that depicted George III as either a tyrant (in the "Soliloquy") or a dupe of his tyrannical ministers (in the "Dialogue").[71]

Their literary collaboration, however, began under Witherspoon's tutelage, when the two composed a 1771 commencement dialogue titled *The Rising Glory of America*. This dramatic oration manifested three key features of Revolutionary collegiate theater and oratory: the soaring rhetoric endorsed by Witherspoon, the characterization of North America as a refuge for British liberty, and, as Gary Richardson notes, images of "the supplanting of English authority" through the growth and political maturation of the North American colonies.[72] The dialogue recalls in exhaustive fashion the colonial development of British North America, embracing that favorite settlement narrative of patriot activists, the transatlantic flight from Stuart tyranny. One speaker, Leander, declares:

By persecution wrong'd
And popish cruelty, our fathers came
From Europe's shores to find this blest abode
Secure from tyranny and hateful man,

and then praises these forefathers of the North American colonies as men "warm in liberty and freedom's cause."[73]

Composing this piece during the year following the Boston Massacre, moreover, Freneau and Brackenridge appointed the slain of Massachusetts as the new guardians of American liberty. They incorporated these sacrificial victims, who stand in for all the patriotic citizens of the disjointed colonies, into a genealogy extending from the classical world to North America and forward into eternity:

And here fair freedom shall forever reign.
I see a train, a glorious train appear,
Of patriots placed in equal fame with those
Who nobly fell for Athens or for Rome.
The sons of Boston resolute and brave,
The firm supporters of our injur'd rights,
Shall lose their splendors in the brighter beams
Of patriots fam'd and heroes yet unborn.[74]

Through the exertions of those who join the procession of martyrs, enthuse the young orators, America will transcend its status as a mere collection of colonies and become "[t]he seat of empire," "the abode of kings," and—perhaps most tellingly among the dialogue's epithets—"[t]he final stage" for the development of human freedom.[75] Freneau and Brackenridge employ Witherspoon's lessons in raising the passions through dramatic oratory, invoking the topos of *translatio imperii* and the vivid example of the most recent Americans to occupy the effigy of the sacrificial victim as an idealized teleology and genealogy for human freedom. They plant a family tree fertilized at regular intervals with the blood of tyrants and patriots, of Julius Caesar and the citizens of the Boston mob.

Circum-Atlantic New Haven

While Freneau and Brackenridge were composing their dramatic oration at Princeton in 1771, the development of amateur theater continued apace among the members of Yale's Linonian Society. Beginning in 1771, the society's annual celebration of its founding became an occasion for the staging of a play, a practice that continued, except for a possible interruption in 1772 and another in 1775 "on account of the publick difficulties arising from the controversy between Great Britain and the Colonies," until the temporary suspension of these festivities in 1777. The Linonian repertoire is notable for the general absence of tragedies. All of its performances between 1771 and 1776 were comedies, of which two particular plays, Sir Richard Steele's *The Conscious Lovers* (1722) and Richard Cumberland's *The West Indian* (1771), are particularly significant, given the American connections of their plots in the years approaching and during the Revolution.[76]

The plots of *The Conscious Lovers* and *The West Indian* turn on the circum-Atlantic exchange of goods (and human beings) between Britain, Africa, and the Americas, as well as the growing centrality of merchant capitalism to British, and eventually American, society. This geographic coverage, combined with the colonial circulation of plays that involve the interaction of Britons from the metropole and the colonial fringe, allows these plays to serve as a gauge for the sociopolitical impact that free trade, as well as the colonial system built to take advantage of it, had on the transatlantic British community's understanding of patriotism and its relationship to individual liberties and civic authority. In *The Spectator*, Steele and Addison attempt to domesticate global trade, as they do the theater, turning both of these potentially destructive forces into pillars of civil society and national identity. In the issue for 2 March 1711 (No. 2), Steele introduces Mr. Spectator's fellow club member Sir Andrew Freeport, the Whig merchant, noting that Sir Andrew "will tell you that it is a stupid and barbarous way to extend Domain by Arms; for the Power is to be got by Arts and Industry."[77] The Spectatorial merchant, however, is essentially patriotic and civic-minded: Addison, meditating on the spectacle of London's Royal Exchange in the 19 May 1711 issue (No. 69), declares his delight in witnessing traders at work, "Men thriving in their own private Fortunes, and at the same time promoting the Publick Stock," and concludes that "there are not more useful Members in a Commonwealth than Merchants" (294, 296). (In 1755, the Cambridge don Benjamin Newton would elaborate on Steele's point, claiming that the citizens of trading nations "exert more courage and more strenuously defend their country" than those of other countries.)[78]

Yet if Freeport's Whiggish conception of trade is essentially patriotic, the patriot effigy's devoted antagonism to arbitrary rule also often characterizes the relationship between the merchant and the state in the eighteenth century. Trenchard and Gordon, rather more radical Whigs than Addison and Steele, portray trade as a nubile sacrificial victim who must be protected by virtuous men from arbitrary government. Trade is "a coy and humorous dame," who "always flies force and power," and "her contexture is so nice and delicate, that she cannot breathe in a tyrannical air; will and pleasure are so opposite to her nature, that but touch her with the sword, and she dies."[79] The patriotism of merchants, moreover, according to Trenchard and Gordon's "Cato," is not merely the selfless devotion of a civil servant but a zealous libertarianism prepared to take advantage of the ever-increasing global mobility of capital and the relative fixity of the state: "True merchants are citizens of the world, and that is their country where they can live best and most secure; and whatever they can pick up and gather together in tyrannical governments they remove to free ones" (445–46).[80]

Trenchard and Gordon, like the colonial radicals who defined patriotism as adherence to their liberties, disavow—in tones as blunt as the bluster of a Stamp Act protest—the politics of unswerving allegiance to the state. The form of patriotism specific to the merchant class resists the ideals of social hierarchy and public service traditionally espoused by the landed aristocracy, as well as any impositions placed upon trade by arbitrary governments, whether they be in the form of "Monopolies" and "exclusive companies" (such as the East India Company) or the impressment of merchant sailors and "new impositions . . . on trade."[81] The mobile civic allegiance and commitment to trade and property rights associated with merchants by radical definitions of patriotism, along with economic self-interest, led to active lobbying by British merchant associations on behalf of the North American colonies with which they traded extensively during the Stamp Act Crisis, and also during later disputes over the Townshend Duties and the Tea Act.[82] Unsurprisingly, given the economic ties between homeland merchants and colonials and the influence of opposition writers on colonial politics, Trenchard and Gordon foresee in their letters the major complaints of North American colonials (and the merchants who traded with them) against the ministry a half-century later. Their voices, as well as Addison's, echo in the Newport liberty funeral of 1765 when merchants and colonials felt themselves equally threatened by "ruin'd Trade . . . and loss of liberty!"[83]

Benedict Anderson describes colonial creoles as a liminal group, "essential to the stability of . . . empire" and ascertains "a certain parallelism between the position of creole magnates and of feudal barons, crucial to the sovereign's power, but also a menace to it."[84] Anderson's analogy is equally applicable to colonial creoles and metropolitan merchants. As liminal figures in an Atlantic British society that still supported a landed aristocracy in Britain and government by metropolitan royal officials in the colonies, these groups were tied together not only by national allegiance but also by a very different mutual interest: the wealth produced through colonial trade. The relative openness of colonial society also provided both groups with opportunities for self-invention that deepened the division of loyalties between liberty and state among merchants identified by Trenchard and Gordon, thus adding to the tension observed by Anderson between the colonials' metropolitan and creole identities.

Trenchard and Gordon's libertarian merchant patriots and the rebellious colonists who shared these merchants' politics—crucial figures in the expansion of circum-Atlantic British society—find a theatrical voice in the colonial merchants and creoles of Steele and Cumberland's plays. These men with experience in far-flung locales are jealous of their private liberties and social positions, skeptical of traditional hierarchies, and prepared to take full advantage of the difficulties of the nation-state in governing those far-flung corners of the globe being increasingly domesticated by trade and economic development. In short, they represent a new breed of the patriot figure. The extended geography of the colonial system, like the mobility of capital, loosens the bonds between state and citizen, a potential hazard to governance even when hostility to government is commonly considered a stereotypical component of the national temperament, as in the case of the English in the eighteenth century. Edmund Burke noted in his 1775 "Speech on Conciliation with America" that the fabled British political disposition, "This fierce spirit of liberty," was "stronger in the English colonies, probably, than in any other people on earth" and also reminded his fellow MP's that the three thousand miles between London and the east coast of North America weakened the reins of compulsory obedience. "Nothing worse happens to you than does to all nations who have extensive empire," explains Burke, "and it happens in all the forms into which empire can be thrown. In large bodies, the circulation of power must be less vigorous at the extremities."[85] The circulation of capital, of radical political opinions, and of theatrical performances in the colonies all served to demonstrate the accuracy of his observations.

On the British margins in New Haven, the young creole gentlemen of the Linonian Society had originally planned to play *The Conscious Lovers* for their fraternity's 1771 anniversary, but the society's records do not indicate its performance that year. A subsequent staging did occur, however, on 9 April 1776. Steele's comedy, which revolves around a double marriage plot, depicts the role of global trade in the rise of the merchant class at the expense of the political power of the landed aristocracy during the early eighteenth century.[86] The aristocratic Bevil Junior, the son of Sir John Bevil, is engaged to Lucinda Sealand, the daughter of an aptly named and prosperous merchant who made his fortune as a trader in the West Indies. Lucinda is, however, the beloved of Bevil Junior's friend Myrtle, while Bevil Junior himself dotes on Indiana, the orphaned ward of a French privateer captain who rescued her during one of his raids on British shipping, presumably during the War of the Spanish Succession. Lucinda's dotty aristocratic mother, Mrs. Sealand, meanwhile, schemes to marry Lucinda to her cousin Cimberton, while Bevil Junior supports Indiana financially and refrains from making romantic overtures until he can escape his engagement to Lucinda. When Bevil Junior's connection to Indiana arouses Mr. Sealand's suspicions, he visits Indiana only to discover that she is, in fact, his long-lost daughter, shipwrecked and presumed drowned years before on her way to the West Indies to live with her father.[87]

The play proved to be quite popular in the British Americas, forming part of the London Company's original repertoire under the Hallams and remaining in repertory production under David Douglass's direction of the company until 1773.[88] The play was also performed in the West Indies: John Paul Jones, who would later become the "father" of the United States Navy, having resigned his position as second mate on a slave ship in 1768, sought temporary employment as an actor in Kingston, Jamaica, until he could find a billet on a return voyage to Scotland. He made his debut as Bevil Junior.[89] The play's family dynamics coincide with the familial analogies commonly used to describe the relationship between Britain and the colonies: Bevil Junior, by sheer (and almost Catonic) stoicism, shames his father into breaking off his engagement to Lucinda, a passive victory over paternal authority that proved impossible for the colonies in their "filial" relationship with George III.[90] The marriage of Bevil Junior and Indiana, moreover, unites mother country and colony, and landed and commercial capital, in a fantastical reunification of the global British family that became increasingly improbable in real life as the 1770s progressed.

In the wake of the various crises over trade and taxation between the 1760s and 1770s that fanned the flames of the Revolutionary War, the most interesting political subtext of Steele's play lies in the strained relationship between its aristocrats, Mrs. Sealand and Sir John Bevil, and the wealthy merchant commoner Mr. Sealand. Mrs. Sealand's scheme to marry Lucinda to the odious Cimberton is designed to remove the supposed taint of commercial activity from the family; she decries as déclassé and un-English her husband's trading "with all parts of the world," his participation in the circum-Atlantic merchant economy that supported both Britain's expansion into a global commercial and military power and the development of its American colonies.[91] Mr. Sealand, meanwhile, measures himself against Sir John in a theatrical incarnation of *The Spectator*'s debates between Sir Andrew Freeport and the landed Tory Sir Roger de Coverley. As the two hold a spirited discussion of Bevil Junior's obligations to Lucinda and Indiana, Mr. Sealand seems to speak for the political and economic power of not only the increasingly powerful merchant class of Great Britain but also for that of the vast commons of North America, particularly the northern colonies that sent their young men to colleges like Yale—men dangerous, but necessary, to the stability of Britain's global power.

Mr. Sealand speaks with the authority of a member of a rising class. He mocks Sir John's aristocratic beliefs in noble birth and martial valor by cataloguing the noble names of his late father's fighting cocks: "Earl Richard, the father of Henry the marquis, the father of Duke John . . . Duke John won him many battles, and never lost one." Mr. Sealand then informs Sir John "We merchants are a species of gentry, that have grown into the world this last century, and are as honourable, and almost as useful, as you landed folks, that have always thought yourselves so much above us."[92] John Loftis sees this scene as an articulation of Steele's court Whig principles, but Mr. Sealand seems more akin to Trenchard's and Gordon's "Country Whig" model of the merchant than to Mister Spectator's.[93] Mr. Sealand, like a Son of Liberty defending "British" freedom in America, underlines the centrality of his own liminal social role to the health of the nation. The truth of his assertion shows in Sir John's acceptance of Sealand's mockery, which he bears out of consideration for his own role as "a father, who knows how useful wealth is, and how necessary even to those who despise it."[94]

The assertive, blunt speech of the upwardly mobile commoner Mr. Sealand also bears a considerable resemblance to the (supposedly) artless, forthright manner of patriot characters from Shakespeare's Brutus to Addison's Cato to contemporary action movies. This rhetorical style is likewise displayed by the leading man in Cumberland's *The West Indian*, which was staged at Yale by the Linonians during their anniversary celebration on 13 April 1773. The play follows the romantic misadventures in London of Charles Belcour, a young Jamaican planter with an estate producing "rum and sugar enough . . . to make all the water in Thames into punch."[95] Belcour, unbeknown to himself, is the son of the English lawyer Stockwell, who during a period of employment in Jamaica married the daughter of a prominent planter and then arranged for the reception of their offspring as a foundling, a fact not revealed until the climactic fifth act of the play.

This revelation coincides with the resolution of the play's main marriage plot, which chronicles Belcour's pursuit of Louisa Dudley, the daughter of an impoverished, decommissioned army captain and the sister of an aspiring young ensign. The play ends with a family reunion emblematic of transatlantic harmony between British parent and colonial son, British soldier and colonial citizen. The marriage also disavows British complicity for the tyrannical, Afro-Caribbean component of the circum-Atlantic economy from which Belcour derives his wealth. During his pursuit of Louisa, Belcour offers Captain Dudley the funds to secure a colonial post in Senegambia—a valuable slave-trading region ceded to Britain by France in 1763—that Dudley resigns in the closing scene, once his family's future has been secured, in favor of a peaceful retirement. Like so many of the patriots in both the British home islands and colonies who railed against the "slavery" of governmental corruption and imperial taxation during the long eighteenth century, Belcour the wealthy creole and Captain Dudley the brave old soldier will continue to reap the benefits of an economy fueled in large part by the enslavement of Africans.[96]

Belcour's status as a colonial slaveholder is, however, crucial to his identity as a comic version of the patriot figure, and also to the play's depiction of the political relationship between Britain and the American colonies. Burke observes that in the slaveholding colonies of the Americas: "those who are free are by far the most proud and jealous of their freedom. Freedom is to them not only an enjoyment, but a kind of rank and privilege. Not seeing there that freedom, as in countries where it is a common blessing as broad and general as the air, may be united with much abject toil, with great misery, with all the exterior of servitude, liberty looks amongst them like something that is more liberal and noble."[97] Belcour's very arrival in England educates him in both the aristocratic and egalitarian implications of British liberty. Cumberland as well as Burke attributes this independence of spirit not only to the landed and merchant classes but also to the laboring subjects of George III. Belcour's first visit to Stockwell is delayed during his disembarkation at the London docks, where, as he explains, "accustomed to a land of slaves, and out of patience with the whole tribe of custom-house extortioners, boatmen, tidewaiters, and water-bailiffs, that beset me on all sides, worse than a swarm of musqetoes, I proceeded a little too roughly to brush them away with my rattan; the sturdy rogues took this in dudgeon, and beginning to rebel, the mob chose different sides, and a furious scuffle ensued."[98] While Stockwell disdains the actions of the mob that Belcour describes, Belcour responds with delight to this mass outburst of self-assertion: "as a fellow subject, and a sharer in their freedom, I applaud their spirit, though I feel the effects of it in every bone of my skin."[99]

Of this passage Maaja A. Stewart observes, "The ever-available fiction of the 'free-born Englishman' distinguishes the metropolitan workers from the colonial slaves."[100] In light of Burke's observations on the slaveholder's conception of liberty, both Belcour's attitude toward the dockworkers and his comment about feeling their freedom in his skin are more chilling than merry, yet Belcour's egalitarian sympathies stem from his twin roles as patriotic colonial subject and tyrannical slave-owner. Only when the laborers strike back and start a riot can Belcour appreciate them as fellow free (and thus white and English) men. This bruising revelation stirs in Belcour an affection for the laborers that contrasts with the reaction of Stockwell, who seems to mask his own inferior class origins and his youthful plantation experience in this exchange by criticizing the dockworkers as mere ruffians.

Belcour's appreciation for the liberties of the mob, as well as his willingness to assert his liminal political and cultural status as a colonial subject —at one point he tells a prim young metropolitan lady, "I am a West-Indian; and you must try me according to the charter of my colony, not by a jury of English spinsters"—no doubt helped to promote the widespread popularity of Cumberland's play in North America.[101] David Douglass opened *The West Indian* in Williamsburg in October 1771, shortly after its London premiere, and it proved popular on the colonial stage from New York to Charleston from its premiere until the American Company departed for Jamaica in 1774.[102] Cumberland's comedy shares the moral thrust and circum-Atlantic subplotting of *The Conscious Lovers*, to which Cumberland adds an appreciation of urban street life and colonial self-assertion that seems to echo the patriotic street theater of the colonies. The play also attracted the young men of Yale College, whose staging included features that seem to aspire toward professional production values, such as "the Officers appearing dress'd in Regimentals" and an occasional epilogue written and spoken by Nathan Hale.[103]

Although the play ends with the bonds of transatlantic community renewed by the wedding of Belcour and Louisa and the revelation of Belcour's paternity, Belcour's jealous concern for his liberties, his fellow-feeling with the laborers of the London docks (marred by his comedic but brutal relationship to the slave economy), and his willingness to exploit the ambiguities of colonial identity—markers of the emerging type of the American patriot—are the play's most original features. George Washington, veteran, slaveholder, and future leader of the Continental Army, and Nathan Hale, the martyr of the American Revolution, both witnessed (and in Hale's case, acted in) performances of *The West Indian* in the early 1770s. This coincidence serves as a reminder of the complicated political and economic relationships between Great Britain and the Americas that were generated by the colonial system in the eighteenth century. These relationships found expression in the importance of the theater as symbolic capital in early American culture, the major role played by theatrical manipulation in the generation of Revolutionary imagery, and at times, as in Steele's and Cumberland's scripts, in the very texts of popular plays.[104]

"A News Athens Rising": Revolutionary Collegiate Theater

Although the Revolution put a damper on both the amateur and professional theaters, American college students proved tenacious in their desire to continue acting plays. In 1781, for instance, students at Harvard produced several propaganda plays recounting important events of the Revolution. Yet these so-called pamphlet plays account for only part of a series of performances tied to the American collegiate system that occurred during the Revolution, particularly in its waning years. On 16 November 1781, the Harvard faculty authorized a group of students to perform a selection of scenes from Benjamin Young's *Busiris, King of Egypt*, which had been performed in 1774 by a group of young men in Charleston, South Carolina, as a benefit for the relief of victims of the Royal Navy's blockade of Boston.[105]

Elsewhere in New England, Professor John Smith composed two dialogues during the Revolution for recitation by students at Dartmouth College, where the evidence for dramatic performances as early as 1769 includes records for a 1773 performance of *Cato*, in which the primitive, treacherous Syphax dressed like an Indian chief. One of Smith's dialogues,

"A Dialogue Between An Englishman and An Indian," is a short piece in which the Indian, equal parts noble savage and white colonial in greasepaint, convinces the Englishman that his people are no more "barbarous" than the English themselves, and no less deserving of freedom. Partly because, as Laura M. Stevens has pointed out, by 1771 Dartmouth had already begun to move away from its original goal of educating Native Americans, the performative appropriations of native identity in these performances is striking. The Indian is, alternatively, a treacherous colonial savage like Syphax or a patriot alternative to the tyrannical identity of Englishman. Professor Smith noted in a letter that the Indian dialogue was "pretty naturally acted," since the part of the Indian was played by "a real Aboriginal," thus presumably leaving a white student to portray the Englishman, mixing the identities of patriot creole actor and tyrannical white European in seemingly inextricable ways and further confusing the masquerade-like quality of colonial "Indian" identity.[106]

Experimentation at Yale and the College of New Jersey also continued apace. In 1776 a group of Yale students delivered two dialogues in a ceremony marking a quarter day, including one that idealized American officers as reincarnation of the Roman republican generals Scipio Africanus the Elder and Younger (the conquerors of Hannibal and of Carthage, respectively), "Heroic warriors . . . like to those whom ancient Rome named 'Thunderbolts of War.'"[107] During 1779, moreover, Yale students put on an impressive patriotic spectacle for both their own amusement and that of a wider audience including residents of New Haven. Ezra Stiles's diary for 17 March notes: "After Dinner in the Hall, assembled in the Chapel, where were exhibited the following exercises a number of Gentlemen and Ladies present, viz. a Latin Oration; then a Dialogue; an Anthem; a second Dialogue or dramatic representation of the invasion of the Tories and Indians upon Susquehanna, led on by Col. Butler . . . and [an] English Oration; an Anthem concluded."[108] The Linonian Society, meanwhile, appears to have kept up an interest in the drama as a literary form, if not as a documented performance practice, during the Revolution's years of active fighting. The society's records note a considerable "tax" of eighteen dollars assessed on each brother in November 1779 to buy a series of twenty quarto volumes listed as "British Theatre," no doubt the popular series of drama anthologies printed in Philadelphia for Robert Bell.[109]

By 1782, even the College of New Jersey had embraced the stage: a group of students staged three plays that year, among them John Home's *Douglas*, the very play that President Witherspoon had denounced when it premiered in Scotland decades earlier.[110] Witherspoon's interest in oratory also led to a special addition to the college's commencement ceremonies in 1783, which were attended by George Washington: Witherspoon's students publicly debated the question "Was Brutus justified in killing Caesar?" The question implicitly elevates Washington to the status of Brutus, while also replaying an important debate previously staged in print by Trenchard and Gordon in *Cato's Letters*, which the college's library had acquired in 1760.[111]

Such officially sanctioned public spectacles became more common as the war drew to a close, and some of the earliest collegiate dramatists lent their talents to diplomatic exchanges of performances that occurred between representatives of the United States and France during the closing years of the war. These spectacles, much like the collegiate performances in which their authors honed their skills, revise the dominant, British-inflected symbols of early American culture by dressing them in homespun attire. Francis Hopkinson, the College of Philadelphia alumnus who had written prologues for the American Company, commencement odes for the college, and his name on the Declaration of Independence, composed a musical entertainment, *The Temple of Minerva*, that was performed four times in Philadelphia during 1781: twice for the French ambassador to the United States, Luzerne; once for General Washington, and once in a performance jointly honoring both men.[112]

Hopkinson's libretto, featuring the Genius of France, the Genius of America, the goddess Minerva, and her High Priest, celebrates the achievement of American independence and the success of the Franco-American alliance. Hopkinson's final two verses partake in the wartime rush to elevate Washington to the status of an effigy, a patriot king for the emergent republic:

Now the dreadful conflict's o'er,
Now the cannons cease to roar,
Spread the joyful tidings round,
He comes, he comes, with conquest crown'd,
Hail Columbia's god-like son!
Hail the glorious WASHINGTON!

Fill the golden trump of Fame,
Through the world his worth proclaim;
Let rocks, and hills, and vales resound,
He comes, he comes, with conquest crown'd,
Hail Columbia's godlike son!
Hail the Glorious WASHINGTON![113]

On 2 January 1782, Washington and Luzerne again met as part of an assembly to watch the French comedy *Eugenie* by Beaumarchais and the English *The Lying Valet*, a farce by Garrick that was popular as an afterpiece in the colonies. The program concluded with "a brilliant illumination, consisting of thirteen pyramidal pillars, representing the thirteen States,— on the middle column was seen a cupid, supporting a laurel crown over the motto, 'WASHINGTON, the pride of his Country and terror of Britain.'"[114] The play had begun, moreover, with a prologue on the prospects for peace composed by Philip Freneau in honor of Washington. The prologue, like Freneau's earlier dialogue *The Rising Glory of America*, envisions America supplanting Britain as a global power. To this end Freneau addresses Washington as the central figure of the public's collective imagination, the font from which all civic blessings flow:

You made us first our future greatness see,
Inspired by you, we languished to be free;
Even here where Freedom lately sat distrest,
See a new Athens rising in the West!
Fair science blooms, where tyrants reigned before,
Red war, reluctant, leaves our ravaged shore—
Illustrious hero, may you live to see
These new Republics powerful, great, and free.[115]

Pace Freneau's apparent poetic intentions, his prologue, like the central inscription in the afterpiece of this performance, reveals that in the public consciousness the reign of "tyrants" had not only been replaced by the "fair science" that Freneau had acquired while a student at the College of New Jersey. The "tyrant" had also been replaced by the figure of the patriot commander of the Revolution—himself a master of patriotic self-representation.

I am strongly tempted to end this chapter with the theatrical beatification of George Washington, an intersection of performance and politics that extended beyond the Revolutionary era to influence the forms of public display in the early national period. One anecdote from the history of Yale's Linonian Society, however, remains unmentioned. This episode underscores the importance of both dramatic performance and the college system to early United States culture, and particularly the important part that the rituals of both institutions played in the civic life of a society in the midst of a war. Although the Linonians had suspended their anniversary celebrations in 1776, in 1781 the society "conven'd to celebrate the Anniversary Solemnity, which tho omitted for several years past on account of the precarious and unhappy situation of the affairs of this country," was revived since by that time "the affairs of things of this country [wore] a more favourable aspect."[116] The program for the anniversary celebration of 20 March 1781 consisted of a double bill by Colley Cibber, the tragedy *Ximena; or, The Heroick Daughter* (1712), a revised translation of Corneille's *Le Cid*, in which the Spanish Christian hero attempts to fend off a Moorish (read: Scottish) invasion, and the sentimental comedy *Love Makes a Man* (1701). On 12 April 1782, the Linonians presented that traditional favorite of transatlantic Whigs and

American patriots, *Tamerlane*, followed by Susanna Centlivre's comedy *A Bold Stroke for a Wife*.

Of greater interest than the plays enacted by the Linonians, however, is the spectacle of the anniversary celebration itself. The Linonian Society's records, after noting the improved circumstances of the United States in 1781, state that the society's anniversary was "thought proper to be celebrated with usual pomp and solemnity and in a public manner, wherefore the members of this meeting walk'd in procession, from the Chapel Doors to the State House where we were met by a large and Respectable Audience." This procession was repeated in 1782. The walk from the chapel to the state house would have followed a path across the New Haven Green, the very heart of the community. Two years earlier, the Green had been the central encampment for the British during their abortive occupation and sacking of New Haven, which had been resisted by many Yale students.[117]

The act of marching across the Green during these two processions suggests a powerful gesture of reclamation that underscores the very public nature of the theatrical performances that follow each procession. The entire episode, from the public nature of the procession, its conclusion with a play acted by the Linonians before the respectable citizens of New Haven, and even the use of the state house for theatrical performances, has the air of a civic ritual. This ceremony, like the commencement exercises and public stage plays performed by students before the Revolution, had ramifications for the community beyond the college. For not only the Linonians but also for the communities of Yale College and New Haven, the resumption of the society's annual theatrical exercises symbolized both a return to the status quo ante of peacetime in a New England college town and the success of the Revolution. The patriots had reasserted control over a contested performance space, the Green, as well as the government of the American colonies, emblematized in this anecdote by the capitol. Marking this occasion as well as their own anniversary by making their private theatricals into a public event, the Linonians engaged in both a performative reassertion of quotidian routine and a public demonstration that the citizens of the United States had achieved an unprecedented political innovation.

Chapter 5
Bellicose Letters: Propaganda Plays of the Revolution

In 1781 Abbé Claude Robin, a chaplain with the French army, paid a visit to Harvard College. Robin observed that American students enjoyed acting plays in their leisure time:

> Their pupils often acted tragedies, the subject of which is generally taken from their national events, such as the battle of Bunker's Hill, the burning of Charlestown, the Death of General Montgomery, the capture of Burgoyne, the treason of Arnold, and the Fall of British tyranny. You must easily conclude that in such a new nation as this, these pieces must fall infinitely short of that perfection to which our European literary productions are wrought up; but still, they have a greater effect upon the mind than the best of ours would have among them because these manners and customs are delineated, which are such as interest them above all others. The drama is here reduced to its true and ancient origin.[1]

Robin's observations, made during the same year in which combined American and French forces won the decisive victory of the American Revolution by forcing Cornwallis's surrender at Yorktown, reveal his grasp of the complex relationships between dramatic literature, politics, and performance in early American culture. His remarks prefigure de Tocqueville's observation that the theater, as the "most democratic" of literary forms, is also the most intimately tied to current events, especially among democratic societies where the audience "want the talk to be about themselves, and to see the present world mirrored."[2]

The scenes that Robin observed at Harvard also attest to the stubborn roots that the drama had developed in the former colonies. The students' fondness for performing tragedies serves as a reminder that the Continental Congress's 1774 ban on stage performances and the subsequent departure from North America of David Douglass's American Company did not extinguish theatrical performance as a cultural practice in North America during the Revolution. Nor did the Congress achieve this end when in 1778 they passed two more strongly worded measures (no doubt brought on in part by the staging of *Cato* at Valley Forge) that specifically banned military theatricals and declared once again the inimical nature of theater to republican virtue: "Whereas true religion and good morals are the only solid foundations of public liberty and happiness: . . . it is hereby earnestly recommended to the several states, to take the most effectual measures for the encouragement thereof, and for the suppressing of theatrical entertainments, horse racing, gaming and other such diversions as are productive of idleness, depravity, and a general dissipation of principles and manners."[3] Defying multiple congressional resolutions, Massachusetts' 1750 strictures against performing stage plays, and Harvard's own proscription of theatricals dating from the mid-1760s, the students observed by Robin sought amusement in patriotic plays, recreating the recent history of the Revolution in private, improvised theaters in Cambridge.[4]

The students' theatrical recreations of major events from the ongoing war demonstrate once again the political topicality of the early American theater. Early American political activity was heavily freighted with both the cultural capital of the English theater and its own essential performativity. The early American theater, meanwhile, often addressed the issues facing its audience with current events, either through indirect connections between text and the audience's political concerns, such as Douglass's tailoring the American Company's repertoire to suit the colonial political climate, or through more explicit performances, such as the Valley Forge *Cato*, that engaged in more direct forms of theatrical self-definition. The confluence of politics and the drama also inspired the development of a significant performance tradition in colonial colleges. Abbé Robin's careful notation of the subject matter enacted by the Harvard students illustrates that American theater, especially on college campuses, had become even more explicitly politicized by the Revolution.

Rather than producing English plays requiring analogical application to the hostilities between the United States and Great Britain, Harvard's amateur thespians had begun to stage forthrightly nationalist propaganda. While Robin's notes indicate a certain clumsiness in the dramatic texts, these performances indicated the desire of these students, among other Americans, to find performances suited to the new political realities of the Revolution, their "evolving manners and customs"—hence Robin's judgment of the college theatricals as a radical rebirth of the ancient drama, a revival of "the true and ancient" form of the classical theater. In such a theater the performance serves as a cohesive rite of civic religion, and the public stage as a liminal space in which the boundaries between the individual and the group, the citizen and the state, can be explored. As in the case of the ancient Greek tragedies, the founding myths are reenacted for an audience that already knows how the story ends. In the case of the Revolutionary propaganda plays, the difference in the context of these "true and ancient" dramas from that of such classical works as the *Oresteia* is that in the American case the foundational events are being mythologized almost as they happen. While professional and amateur theatrical productions staged before and during the Revolution often brought onstage dramas depicting tyrants, patriots, and sacrificial victims from the distant past or wholly imaginary realms, the propaganda plays of the Revolution incorporated these symbolic characters into stories drawn from the ongoing events of the war.

This sense of immediacy is especially crucial when the composition, rather than the performance, dates of these plays are taken into account. Robin's notes contain an important clue on this score. Three of the topics that Robin cites as subjects of Harvard productions are also the titles of propaganda plays written and published as pamphlets during the Revolution, shortly after the events they depict: Hugh Henry Brackenridge's *The Battle of Bunkers-Hill* (1776) and *The Death of General Montgomery, in Storming the City of Quebec* (1777), and John Leacock's *The Fall of British Tyranny* (1776).[5] (The plays connected to Robin's remaining topics have not been positively identified.)[6] Robin's letter indicates that these plays were actually performed by Harvard students, the only known performances of such plays to have taken place during the Revolution

In Defense of Propaganda

Eighteenth-century collegiate performances have historically received scant critical attention, and the propagandistic "pamphlet plays" of the Revolution have fared little better. Even in an anthology devoted to these propaganda writings, Norman Philbrick argues that "[t]he uneven writing and the lack of polish of the pamphlet plays precludes an evaluation of them as works of literature."[7] These texts, although their existence has been well documented in histories of the American drama, have largely been ignored as serious texts worthy of careful reading.[8] There are some signs of an ongoing revival of interest among early Americanists in Revolutionary drama, however, especially in the works of the playwright and historian Mercy Otis Warren.[9]

Understanding the interaction of transatlantic politics and performance demands a study of the dramatic works produced by educated, politically active amateurs before and during the Revolution that reads these texts not only topically but also tropically. Such a reading must document the complex interactions of contemporary politics and eighteenth-century aesthetics in these texts while treating their limited historical scope as an opportunity to study the mutually reinforcing effects of politics and literature during the American Revolution.[10] Both Philbrick and Richardson argue, for instance, that the pamphlet plays share their limited historical scope with such overtly politicized plays of the late seventeenth and early eighteenth centuries as Addison's *Cato*—the very plays that the pamphlet plays' authors would likely have been reading or observing in professional or amateur productions.[11] Richardson hypothesizes about both the propaganda plays and their dramatic precursors, that a "comprehensible understanding" of such nakedly political texts "may depend as much on the ability to recover Whig ideology as on a refined dramatic aesthetic."[12] This chapter will take up Richardson's gauntlet by exploring the attempts made by the authors of Revolutionary propaganda plays, particularly Brackenridge and Leacock, to create a politically aware, self-consciously "American" drama that acknowledges both the political rift between Britain and the United States and the still prevalent cultural affinities between the two nations by restaging the battle of liberty and tyranny using current events.

Despite their relatively poor critical reputation, the pamphlet plays, in the composition of which Americans literally took events into their own hands by composing dramatic texts that mingle the history of the Revolutionary period with contemporary theatrical and ideological tropes, are surprisingly rich and varied. The plays range in generic scope from Mercy Otis Warren's series of tyrannicidal tragedies—*The Adulateur* (1773), *The Defeat* (1773), and *The Group* (1775)—to farces such as the Tory *The Battle of Brooklyn* (1776) and the Whig *Blockheads* (1776), the latter a mock reenactment of the Battle of Bunker Hill and the subsequent British evacuation of Boston sometimes attributed to Mercy Warren.[13] Of greatest importance for the purposes of this study, however, are three plays reported by Abbé Robin to have been acted by the students of Harvard during the Revolution: John Leacock's chronicle play *The Fall of British Tyranny; or, American Liberty Triumphant* (1776) and Hugh Henry Brackenridge's two heroic tragedies, *The Battle of Bunkers-Hill* (1776) and *The Death of General Montgomery, in Storming the City of Quebec* (1777).

These three plays represent the conflict of liberty and tyranny undergirding both contemporary patriot and loyalist rhetoric, a commonplace feature of the other propaganda dialogues and plays of the period. As Ginger Strand comments on the relationship between pamphlet plays and their political environment, even the act of reading such texts in their printed form contains a performative element, since "[r]eversing the figure by which printed texts are normally said to represent the voice of the people, audience members are not letting the pamphlet speak for them; rather, they are speaking themselves in unison with it."[14] The status of these three plays as actual performance texts, however, adds to their ideological relevance an immediacy as theatrical texts that cannot be attributed even to the fine, yet unstaged, plays of Mercy Otis Warren, much less the dramatic dialogues of the period. The favor of the Harvard actors identifies these plays as privileged texts among the potentially stage-worthy propagandistic dramas of the period, particularly strong representations of the "manners and customs" of the American Revolution.

New Wine, Old Bottles: The Fall of British Tyranny

The first of these plays, and the text with perhaps the broadest generic and geographical range, is *The Fall of British Tyranny*, apparently written between January and March 1776 by a Philadelphia goldsmith named John Leacock.[15] The scope of this drama is unusually ambitious, defying the Aristotelian unities and combining, as Jeffrey Richards notes, both "farce" and "patriot tragedy," generic forms popular, as we have seen, on both the professional and the collegiate stage in the North American colonies—a reflection of the public's mixed appetite for both exemplarity (in heroic characters) and scurrility (in attacks on the British enemy.)[16] The result is, as Gary Richardson observes, a text that combines disparate perspectives on the Revolution, deploying onstage many key tropes of Revolutionary-era culture.[17] Prominent among these tropes is the interlocking trio of the tyrant, patriot, and sacrificial victim.

The play's printed text, ironically, refers to the anti-theatrical rhetoric of colonials opposed to the stage, a group whose numbers were, as already demonstrated, plentiful in Philadelphia, the site of the play's first printing. Ostensibly written by the blunt, plainspoken "Dick Rifle," the play's introduction is dedicated to "Lord Boston, and the Remnant of the Actors, Merry Andrews, and Strolling Players, in Boston," a reference to General John Burgoyne, one of the commanding officers of the British troops that occupied Boston during 1775–76. Burgoyne was himself a published playwright who produced a series of amateur theatricals in Boston's Faneuil Hall, much to the dismay of the city's inhabitants, before being forced to evacuate in March 1776 as Washington's army advanced on Boston.[18] "Dick Rifle" dedicates the play to the British, "as the most of you have already acted your particular parts of it, both comic and tragic" on the battlefield, characterizing the script's chronicling of the Revolution as a counterperformance to the theatricals of the British troops. "Rifle" pushes even further, intimating performances yet to come that echo both the street theater of colonial protest and the professional stage with a decidedly tyrannicidal flair: "may our gallows-hills and liberty poles be honour'd and adorn'd with some of your heads," he declares, also vowing that if he should get within "three hundred yards" (that is, rifle range) of the British commanders, he should "receive the clap of the whole house, and pass for a second Garrick" (iii).[19]

The assertive "Dick Rifle" presents a culturally distinct "American" patriot personality in the play. Ironically, this character possesses a surprising knowledge of theatrical convention given the amount of criticism that he levels at the British for their theatrical frivolity. Both the voice and the inherent theatricality of Dick Rifle, this potential "second Garrick," echo throughout the voices that articulate the play's dramatic apparatus. *The Fall* also features a prologue spoken by "Mr. Peter Buckstail" and an epilogue by "Mr. Freeman."[20] These symbolic characters represent uniquely American iterations of the patriot persona, voices for independence that play off the English caricature of colonials as crude, impetuous, and somewhat uncivilized—the young Belcour of Cumberland's *The West Indian* without the refining influence of landed wealth. By deploying an exaggerated version of the rustic stereotype in these voices, Leacock converts the stereotype into a powerful propaganda tool.

This double identity allows the bourgeois reading public of Philadelphia and New England, as well as the young gentlemen of Harvard (like their forerunners in Philadelphia dressed as James Thomson's sailors and singing "Rule, Britannia"), to express their status as revolutionaries by participating in the generation through performance of this "American" identity, in spite of their lingering cultural ties to Great Britain. In a similar vein, attorneys and merchants had participated in the Stamp Act riots in Boston during 1765 wearing workmen's trousers. The staged performance of these self-consciously colonial (or American) and lower-class "Yankee" personae offers their audience a similar means of political participation in the development of a sense of post-British nationality, something akin to Strand's performative understanding of the acts of reading and playgoing. These actions both assert the political and cultural distinctness of Great Britain and the North American colonies and disguise the geographical, socioeconomic, and political differences between the rebellious colonies themselves with the broad brushstrokes of a national "type," an early glimpse of the post-Revolutionary character that would eventually come to be known as the "stage Yankee" or "Yankee Jonathan."[21]

The play's embedded performances also contain didactic elements common to Revolutionary-era theatricals, including calls for the audience to join the fight: "The Tragedy's begun, beat, beat the drum," demands Peter Buckstail, "Let's all advance equipt like volunteers, / Oppose the foe, and banish all our fears. / We will be free—or bravely we will die."[22] Likewise, the play's prefatory material contains a speech by "The GODDESS OF LIBERTY," a character reminiscent of the sentimental sacrificial victim and the nubile "Liberty" figure of the Stamp Act protests. "Liberty" blesses the audience, hoping that "martyr'd patriots whisper in your ear, / To tread the paths of virtue without fear" and imploring, in the tradition of Whig sentimentalism, "Hail! My last hope, the cries, inspired by me, / Wish, write, talk, fight, and die—for LIBERTY."[23] Leacock's iterations of the patriot and the sacrificial victim not only present "American" manifestations of these personae but also deliver patriotic exhortations of immediate relevance to their intended audience. Leacock attempts to efface the ambiguities created by the political, economic, and cultural interconnections of Britain and the colonies with homespun versions of the transatlantic symbols of liberty and patriotic sacrifice. Such performances simultaneously mock the British taste for theatrical representation and assert a specifically American desire for a "new" dramaturgy to meet the aesthetic needs of the Revolution.

One of the key aspects of this new dramaturgy in *The Fall of British Tyranny* is an allegorical feature common to both revolutionary propaganda and English political tragedies such as *Tamerlane* or the dramas of the "opposition" tradition: Leacock employs semi-fictionalized versions of public figures in Great Britain and North America, sketching them as tyrants, patriots, and, occasionally, sacrificial victims.[24] The play's supreme villain, for instance, is an aspiring minister named Lord Paramount, a thinly disguised version of George III's quondam royal favorite, the Earl of Bute. Paramount's very existence as a character in the script gives credence to the spurious assertion made by some Wilkites in Britain and patriots in the colonies that Bute continued to command the British government as late as 1776, thus resurrecting a tyrannical bogeyman from a decade earlier. Paramount is a classic stage tyrant, wildly ambitious and prone to histrionic outbursts and bouts of self-revelation to the audience in the vein of Richard III and Rowe's Bajazet. "Oh! Ambition, thou darling of my soul!" he soliloquizes in the play's opening scene, "stop not 'till I rise superior to all superlative, 'till I mount triumphantly the pinnacle of glory."[25]

The play's entire first act consists of an elaborate series of meetings aimed at restoring a Stuart, and thus, by the revolutionaries' definition, tyrannical, king to the throne of Great Britain, conducted by Paramount/Bute with his minions in the British ministry. This motley crew includes Lord Catspaw (Lord North, the sitting prime minister, symbolically reduced to a mere functionary of Bute) and Brazen, a turncoat Whig meant to symbolize Solicitor General Alexander Wedderburn, a vociferous opponent of colonial independence and a former elocutionary student of the theater impresario Thomas Sheridan and the actor James Quin.[26] The first act, however, establishes Paramount as the play's undisputed chief tyrant. He is an open advocate of absolute rule and derides as procedural obstacles legislative government and the rule of law—the very British political "inheritance" upon which the American revolutionaries claimed to be attempting to build. Thus his character touches upon contemporary colonial complaints against the British while also resurrecting the political struggles of the seventeenth century and the threat of Jacobitism associated with Bute in the 1760s. Paramount declares (again in soliloquy, the classic form for tyrannical self-revelation), "Charters, magna Chartas, bill of rights, acts of assembly, resolves of congresses, trials by juries (and acts of parliament too) when they make against us, must all be annihilated; a suspending power I approve of, and of royal proclamations."[27]

Paramount's signature fault, his ambition, is underscored not only by his advocacy of tyrannical government but also by his jealous vanity and his awareness of theatrical form in politics. He refers to his mission to restore Britain and America to slavery as "a task that would have . . . stagger'd even Julius Caesar" and resents the public's adoration of London's lord mayor, John Wilkes (tellingly renamed "Lord Patriot" in the play). Paramount's envy of Lord Patriot ironically echoes, as Philbrick notes, the jealousy of the tribunes for Caesar's popular appeal in *Julius Caesar* 1.2.[28] Paramount's Caesarian vanity and aspirations, as well as his metatheatricality, make him a particularly adept reader of performances, quick to detect the public's desire for the staged leadership of the tyrant's fatal opposite, the patriot. The appetite of the populace for displays of political humility, according to Paramount, shapes Wilkes/Lord Patriot's desire for applause and his talent for "bowing to the gaping multitude, and every upstart he sees at a window."[29]

Leacock, through Paramount's speeches, seems to suggest that patriotic self-presentation such as that practiced by Wilkes/Lord Patriot is a performance as studied as the histrionics attributed to the tyrant figure, albeit in the service of justice rather than arbitrary power. This acknowledgment of performance as an essential component of political representation and its subjection to conflicting interpretations is perhaps nowhere more evident than in Paramount's final soliloquy in 1.5, where the aspiring tyrant's meditations include a paraphrase of the opening scene of Addison's *Cato*. Paramount adapts Portius's annunciation of Caesar's approach toward Utica, welcoming the arrival of "[t]he great, th' important day, / Big with the fate of Britain and America," and proving that in the theater the devil can cite scripture for his own purpose.[30]

The play's second act consists of two long dialogues among British public figures seen (sometimes inaccurately) as pro-American by the patriot movement. The first scene's cast consists of Lord Wisdom (Chatham), Lord Religion (the Bishop of St. Asaph, an opponent of the Intolerable Acts), and Lord Justice (the Earl of Camden, a patron of Wilkes); the second scene features Lord Patriot (Wilkes), Bold Irishman (Burke), and Colonel (Isaac Barré). Although each character defends the Americans and pledges his willingness to sacrifice for liberty, the most compelling of these characters is Lord Wisdom. While Pitt himself violently opposed American independence (his last speech in Parliament advocated crushing the rebellion), his symbolic representative in Leacock's play is passionate and eloquent in defense of the American cause, no doubt due to lingering colonial admiration for Pitt's amenable dealings with the American colonies in the past.[31]

Lord Wisdom uses both the sentimental (and at times salacious) imagery of threatened feminine virtue used by the play's "Goddess of Liberty" prologue and the Catonic rhetoric of self-sacrificing patriotism popular among American revolutionaries. "View the constitution, is she not disrob'd and dismantled?" demands Lord Wisdom, "Is she not like a virgin deflower'd? . . . View Britain herself as a sheep without a shepherd! And lastly view America, for her virtue bleeding and for her liberty weltering in her blood!"[32] Lord Wisdom, moreover, follows a rhetorical logic both opposed to and akin to the one employed by Paramount. Paramount's plans to destroy the liberties of America generate sacrificial political victims that galvanize his patriotic opposition. Lord Wisdom, in a speech echoing both the trademark lamentation of Addison's Cato and Thomas Hopkinson's 1766 depiction of Pitt as pleading "The cause of sinking Liberty" during the Stamp Act Crisis, asserts the need for a blood sacrifice to maintain the liberty that he cherishes. He offers up either one of Paramount's tools or himself (through his Catonic lamentations) as candidates for this sacrifice: "Liberty flourishes in the wilds of America . . . whilst I have a tongue to speak I will support her wherever found . . . and with the voice of an arch-angel will demand for a sacrifice to the nation those miscreants who have wickedly and wantonly been the ruin of their country. Oh, Liberty! Oh, my country!"[33] Curiously, the professions of devotion to American liberty made by Lord Wisdom and the other British "patriot" characters, like Lord Wisdom's recognizable allusion to the commanding words of Addison's tragic hero, temper the play's assertion of a revolutionary political identity with an acknowledgment of the cultural ties between Britain and the colonies. The British patriots in Leacock's play, at least, still see themselves as the countrymen of the Americans, even though the American characters seem to be moving steadily toward an independent national identity.

The language of sacrificial violence employed by Lord Wisdom, however, remains a vocabulary common to the British and American patriots in the play, binding together political factions and social classes across the Atlantic. The first two scenes of the third act present rousing pro-war dialogues between a citizen of Boston, a selectman elected to the Continental Congress, and a sympathetic minister. The citizen declares, "To arms! My dear friends, to arms! And death or freedom be our motto," echoing a catchphrase from Addison's *Cato* as stirring and recognizable as the one employed by Lord Wisdom.[34] Yet despite the lingering cultural ties between Britain and the colonies, as Michael K. Warner notes, "the Revolution demanded not only the reinterpretation of existing British cultural texts, but also the fashioning of new histories and mythologies: National culture began with a moment of sweeping amnesia about colonialism. Americans learned to think of themselves as living in an immemorial nation."[35] An example of one such new mythology dominates the third act of *The Fall of British Tyranny*. The progress of the plot in the third act from the revolutionary outbursts of the anonymous citizen in 3.2 through the "historical" scenes 3.4, 3.5, and 3.7, which chronicle the outbreak and aftermath of the battle of Bunker Hill with a nod to historical verisimilitude, is interrupted in 3.6 by an allegorical pastoral scene. This discussion between the shepherds Roger and Dick features an element of popular folk celebrations with strong ties to the patriot movement and its changing sense of national identity in the Revolutionary era: a song celebrating St. Tammany's Day.[36]

Tammany (Tamanend), a seventeenth-century leader of the Lenape nation about whom little is actually known, evolved into a myth among the colonials for maintaining cordial relations with European settlers. Colonials gave him the honorific of a "saint," and by the time of the Revolution "Tammany" had become an icon in the May Day celebrations of urban fraternal societies in North America, particularly the Society of the Sons of St. Tammany in Philadelphia. As Philip J. Deloria observes, during the Stamp Act Crisis these societies "turned their May Day songs and revels into overtly politicized demonstrations of patriotic Americanness."[37] The St. Tammany song in Leacock's play is no exception. By including this fusion of Tammany's legend with Revolutionary politics in the text, Leacock constructs an alternative genealogy for the American revolutionaries. Like the "Indian" disguise of the Boston Tea Party protesters, this ad hoc identity is rooted not in the familiar narrative of transatlantic settlement but in the "immemorial" presence of the American Indians upon the continent.

These Indian personae construct a state of primitive, pre-statist freedom combining liberal natural rights theory and the tradition of the noble savage.[38] The Tammany song and other reinscriptions of British American colonials as the sons of American Indians resemble the autochthonous axis of Joseph Roach's concept of a "performance of origin," the reenactment of a founding mythology through either diasporic or autochthonous means. Much as British nationalism developed both the diasporic myth of the Trojan/Roman founding and the racialist theory of Germanic autochthony, its American offshoot, which commonly extended the route of the Trojan/Roman diaspora across the Atlantic to the colonies, developed its own autochthonous founding myth by appropriating the identity of the indigenous peoples of North America, thereby neutralizing the ineradicable traces of British identity left by the diasporic settlement narrative.[39]

The St. Tammany's Day song "naturalizes" the patriot construction of America as the aboriginal home of freedom. In particular, it deploys Locke's theory of natural rights with a vengeance, explaining during the course of its twenty-one verses that

In freedom's bright cause, Tamm'ny pled with applause,
And reason'd most justly from nature;
For this, this was his song, all, all the day long,
Liberty's the right of each creature, brave boys,

before lauding the freedom of Tammany's subjects, for whom

No duties, nor stamps, their blest liberty cramps,
A king, tho' no tyrant, was he;
He did oft 'times declare, nay sometimes wou'd swear,
The least of his subjects were free, my brave boys.[40]

The song also recreates the traditional end of the Tammany myth, in which the aged king, having outlived his usefulness, sets fire to his lodge and sacrifices himself as a sort of burnt offering, a gesture of civic renewal combining regicide, suicide, and the sacrificial rhetoric of the Revolution.

Tammany thus serves as both the patriot king of his people and as a Girardian sacrificial victim, a position that Gordon Sayre notes is commonly associated with the Indian chief in early American literature.[41] Tammany is both a model of "natural" patriotic leadership and a marginalized figure obliging enough to step out of the way of the advancing white men through ritual suicide. The spectacles of urban northerners dressing up like "Indians" for street theater rituals, and of Virginia militia members and burgesses wearing tomahawks at their sides—an affectation that gained currency in 1775—follow the logic of surrogation evident in Leacock's text.[42] The "chief" becomes yet another in a long line of patriot effigies, and the space that he creates allows anyone to become, at least for the purposes of masquerade, a patriotic "Indian." One need only be white, male, and willing to risk death for this immemorial America.

Leacock's text focuses on not only the (sometimes false) cultural memories of liberty and tyranny that should inspire his audience to sacrifice for the Revolution but also the process of commemoration that will incorporate those who fall into the chain of heroism. As Sarah Purcell notes, the sense that death in battle constituted martyrdom "was important because in order for death to become the ultimate patriotic duty Americans had to be reassured that their sacrifices would be remembered."[43] Leacock takes great pains to provide these assurances in his third act. In one notable instance, Leacock assumes the cultural authority of a clergyman. The Bostonian minister in 3.2, responding to the citizen who has declared his willingness to volunteer for battle against the British, promises his parishioner, "Posterity will crown the urn of the patriot who consecrates his talents to virtue and freedom."⁴⁴ In addition, the third act combines a narrative of exemplary sacrifice with sympathetic appeals similar to Leacock's use of endangered female characters in the prefatory material. While the "goddess of Liberty" acts as a threatened potential sacrificial victim meant to stir her male audience to action, the third act also assures audience members that their manly self-sacrifice will be remembered by the women they leave behind.⁴⁵

The third act's closing scene features just such a sequence, starring a woman named Clarissa, whose husband, son, and brother are killed at Bunker's (Breed's) Hill, along with General Joseph Warren. Upon being informed of this terrible news, Clarissa both acts the role of a female patriot, bearing up under her load of grief for these "martyrs to liberty," and promises to weep for them unceasingly, "meditating on [their] virtues and dear memories."⁴⁶ Clarissa concludes the scene with three couplets that downplay the horror of a battlefield death by stressing the glory of patriotic service:

Eager the patriot meets his desperate foe
With full intent to give the fatal blow;
The cause he fights for animates him high,
His wife, his children, and his liberty:
For these he conquers, or more bravely dies,
And yields himself a willing sacrifice.

Left alone in the world, Leacock's Clarissa offers a memorial that in its devotion to the patriot cause can best be compared with the figure of Addison's Cato kneeling over the body of the slain Marcus. The slain American patriot will live on, commemorated in a more solemn fashion than the self-sacrificing outsider Tammany, whose comic and festive musical memorial immediately precedes the sufferings of Clarissa.

The play's third act, in transferring the action from London council chambers to the American colonies, attempts to refashion both the patriot and the martyr image through the construction of new American forms of patriot identity and commemoration for martyrdom. The play's fourth act reasserts the dependence of the Revolutionary imagination on the tyrant figure, although in a manner hardly flattering to the American patriot cause. The fourth act, although it contains one scene related to the British evacuation of Boston, centers on the activities of Lord Kidnapper, an allegorical representation of Lord Dunmore, the former governor of Virginia. Dunmore, facing the opposition of the Virginia legislature, relocated to a warship off the coast of Virginia in June 1775 and carried out a campaign against the Virginia mainland using an "Ethiopian Regiment" of runaway slaves who joined Dunmore after he issued a proclamation emancipating Virginia slaves willing to fight for the British.⁴⁷ Before eventually being forced to retreat to New York in defeat, Dunmore had attacked the town of Hampton and set fire to Norfolk on New Year's Day 1776. His largely African American troops had also defeated a superior force of Queen Anne's County militia at Kemp's Landing outside Norfolk in November 1775. (During this battle the patriot commander, Joseph Hutchings, was captured by two of his own slaves.) Owing to the combination of British "tyranny" and the widespread colonial fear of slave insurrection, which threatened to turn upside-down the worldview upon which patriots based their own free status, Dunmore and the slave regiment that he raised became symbols of British tyranny.

Dunmore evolved in the public imagination into a tyrant figure capable of uniting disparate colonial factions. His emancipation proclamation converted some conservative Virginians, including Robert Carter and William Byrd III of the Governor's Council, into patriots.⁴⁸ On 22 July 1776, after the reading of the Declaration of Independence at Huntington, Long Island, a patriot crowd conducted a mock execution and ritual burning of an effigy of George III, the face of which had been blackened to symbolize "Dunmore's regiment," thus marking George III as both tyrannical and, due to his blackface, a wholly different "race" from the newly freed American patriots, who saw themselves as formerly "enslaved" by the British monarchy.⁴⁹

The six "Kidnapper" scenes of *The Fall of British Tyranny*, written by the Philadelphian Leacock for widespread colonial distribution, chronicle the recruitment by Kidnapper of a group of slaves led by Cudjo, a slave who speaks a cretinized, mock-ebonic dialect that later became a stock comic device of the nineteenth-century American stage.⁵⁰ The cynical Kidnapper recruits his slave legion while explicitly planning to sell them back into slavery. He also recruits a harem of runaway slave women, replacing the stage tyrant's traditional association with rape by alluding instead to miscegenation. Dunmore had long been accused of excessive libidinality and after his emancipation proclamation in 1775, the jokes in Virginia about his philandering began to associate him with slave women for the first time.⁵¹ (Apparently, these crude jests must have reached Philadelphia.) The alliance, both political and sexual, of the tyrant Kidnapper with the runaway slaves, like the blackface on the effigy of George III, demonstrates the unfortunate ease with which the libertarian rhetoric used by American patriot activists allowed them to shrug off their own complicity in other forms of tyranny in pursuit of a clearly defined sense of national identity. Only some "slaves" would be allowed to break their shackles.

In the fifth and final act of *The Fall of British Tyranny*, Leacock's attention returns to the figures of the sacrificial victim and the patriot. In particular, scenes 5.1 and 5.2 depict the aftermath of the failed (and ill-advised) assault on Montreal made by Colonel Ethan Allen and his men on 25 September 1775, after which Allen was taken prisoner. Allen, facing his captors, adopts the exemplary (and implicitly metatheatrical) rhetoric of the Catonic effigy. He offers himself as a sacrificial surrogate for all of his men, faced as they are with torture and possible execution: "I am the only guilty person (if guilt there be), let me alone suffer for them all."[52] Even more tellingly, Allen, professing his complete self-identification with the fate of the patriot cause, proffers himself as a voluntary sacrifice, an edifying spectacle for his British captors, the reader holding Leacock's pamphlet, and the actor and audience of any potential theatrical production: "Come, see me suffer—mark my eye, and scorn me, if my expiring soul confesses fear—Come, see and be taught virtue, and to die as a patriot for the wrongs of my country."[53] The play's glorification of Allen's character, it should be noted, is one of Leacock's more significant propagandistic revisions of history, converting the flaws of American partisans into virtues. Allen was condemned by both General Richard Montgomery, the officer in charge of American operations against Canada, and George Washington for the emulousness and rashness of his attempt on Montreal.[54]

Although he is not actually executed, Leacock's Allen achieves emblematic status through patriotic histrionics. Both Allen's example and that of his commander General Montgomery, who was killed in the American assault on Quebec, provide sacrificial examples to the memory of which the patriot commanders of the Continental Army rededicate themselves. By invoking these figures, George Washington, Charles Lee, and Israel Putnam find examples of contemporary courage that lead them to rededicate themselves (and, by extension, the literary and theatrical audience) to national service in the closing scenes of the fifth act, as news of the assault on Canada trickles into their camp during scenes 5.3 and 5.4. The play concludes with the generals, led by Washington, renewing their pledges to defend the American cause in rhetoric that reflects the particular logic of the transmission of the effigies adored in the transatlantic republic of letters. General Lee declares that in the aftermath of the death of Montgomery and his men, "I doubt not, out of their ashes will arise new heroes," inspired by the example of their fallen predecessors.[55] Putnam, echoing the familiar Catonic liberty-or-death motto, declares, "Let each American be determined to conquer or die in a righteous cause."

The climactic moment is reserved for Washington, however, who declares that since he has unsheathed his sword, "never will I sheathe it, till America is free, or I'm no more," joining, like Allen in 5.1 and a long line of patriot figures before him, his own fate to that of the emerging nation and declaring a preference for suicidal martyrdom over defeat.[56]

Lee and Putnam join Washington by drawing their own swords, generating a powerful closing tableau. Not only a powerful theatrical moment, the revolutionary drawing of the swords, with America's new patriot leader Washington initiating the gesture, echoes the rhetoric of American radicals throughout the mid-1770s. In one of a series of essays published by the *Boston Gazette* in February 1775, John Adams quoted the martyred English republican Algernon Sidney, reminding his readers, "He that draws his sword against the prince, say the French, ought to throw away the scabbard; for though the design [of a revolution] be never so just, yet the authors are sure to be ruined if it miscarry."[57]

A year earlier Adams's fellow Harvard man, Josiah Quincy Jr., who like Adams had been influenced by the study of oratory and drama during his collegiate years, had written:

SPIRITS AND GENII . . . rose in Rome—and have since adorned Britain: such also will one day make glorious this more Western world. AMERICA hath in store her BRUTI and CASSII—her Hampdens and Sydneys—Patriots and Heroes, who will form a BAND OF BROTHERS: —men who will have memories and feelings—courage and swords:—COURAGE, that shall enflame their ardent bosoms, till their hands cleave to their swords, and their SWORDS to their Enemies hearts.[58]

Washington, Lee, and Putnam form their own band of brothers, Revolutionary-era Horatii bound to the American republic by their oath. (Indeed, one can scarcely read this scene without having proleptic visions of the French Revolution and David's painting of the *Oath of the Horatii*, with Washington doubling as both brother and father.) Leacock uses the rhetoric of American patriot activists to create a play that illustrates not only an awareness of the physical and oral poetry of the stage but also a sense of its own value, as a performance text, for disseminating the principles of the patriot movement in the early stages of the Revolution.[59]

Brackenridge and Bunker Hill

While *The Fall of British Tyranny* incorporates the major tropes of both political and performance culture into one massive piece of revolutionary propaganda, the play's relationship to the writings of patriot activists such as Adams and Quincy is nonetheless a vexed one. Although Leacock's text may use tropes (the drawing of the sword, the aspiring minister) that also prevail in patriot pamphlets and periodical essays, the play strikes with the immediacy attributed to the democratic stage by de Tocqueville, displaying little of the concern for historical precedent—the political genealogy of patriotic virtue—displayed by the Harvard men and other intellectual activists. Leacock's depiction of current events, which largely disregards historical precedents for the Revolution, suggests a high/low dichotomy in Revolutionary literature of a sort more commonly associated with nineteenth-century American culture. This dichotomy pits a self-consciously transatlantic "high" culture, primarily associated with print, against an aggressively nativist, egalitarian stage.

Not every pamphlet playwright was as eager as Leacock to embrace historical contingency without reference to the past, however. The pamphlet plays of Hugh Henry Brackenridge close this potential rift in Revolutionary literary and theater culture by both seeking out new, American exemplary figures willing to accept martyrdom for the cause of liberty and incorporating these figures within genealogical catalogues of past heroes. Brackenridge's career led him from a childhood in Scotland and the Pennsylvania frontier country to the College of New Jersey, brief Revolutionary service, and the literary scene of Philadelphia before he returned to the frontier to become a well-known journalist, lawyer, and judge in Pittsburgh. He also composed two of the best among the Revolutionary pamphlet plays: *The Battle of Bunkers-Hill* and *The Death of General Montgomery*.[60] A former student of oratory under John Witherspoon at the College of New Jersey, Brackenridge successfully manipulates current events, Roman and British history, and contemporary dramaturgy toward a goal shared with both Leacock and his former teacher John Witherspoon: stirring patriotic feelings among his audience.

Brackenridge, unlike Witherspoon, seems to have endorsed the staged performance of theatrical texts for the inculcation of patriotism. Brackenridge wrote *Bunkers-Hill* as a script to be performed by his students during his tenure as a schoolmaster at the Somerset Academy in Maryland, which began after his 1771 graduation from the College of New Jersey. In his dedication to the play, Brackenridge expresses his hope that this "short Performance in Honour of some brave Men, who have fallen in the cause of Liberty" will be reproduced "in other American seminaries."[61] And although Brackenridge disavows in his preface to *The Death of General Montgomery*— which may have been written during his service as a chaplain in Washington's army—that the piece was "intended for performance on the stage," this note may well have been meant only to comply with the congressional ban on theatrical performances. It may also indicate, however, that while Brackenridge shared Witherspoon's disdain for the professional theatre, he felt differently about the potential moral benefits of other forms of theatrical performance. Brackenridge explains that his second play was intended "for the private entertainment of a few Gentlemen of taste, and martial enterprise."[62] This phrase is broad enough to allow for the beneficial effects of possible private (and especially scholastic, as in the case of Harvard) productions of the play, as well as merely reading the text. In any case, Brackenridge clearly understood the representational immediacy and power of the dramatic form and of theatrical performance, which Witherspoon referred to as "the grace of elocution and the power of action."[63] Such faculties were, after all, the tools of the actor, the minister, and the statesman alike in the eighteenth century.

Unlike his fellow propagandist Leacock, Brackenridge mingles an admiration for Roman republicans and British rebels with his glorification of contemporary American heroes, no doubt reflecting the education in republican principles that he received at the College of New Jersey.[64] Like his fellow young rebel Quincy, Brackenridge impresses into the patriot movement the Roman Bruti (the undoers of Tarquin and Julius Caesar respectively) and also the figures of John Hampden and Algernon Sidney, men whose examples were particularly apt for imbuing the American rebellion with a sense of British, as well as American, patriotism. (The political "resurrection" of seventeenth-century heroes for eighteenth-century purposes was also common among Wilkite sympathizers.)[65]

Sidney's life and afterlife offer a microcosm of the political history of England in the long eighteenth century: a wounded veteran of the battle of Marston Moor, he spent time in exile as an opponent both of Cromwell's dictatorship and the revenant Stuarts, wrote political treatises popular in both Britain and North America, and after conspiring against James II was executed in connection with the Rye House Plot. Sidney, who according to popular legend staged *Julius Caesar* in 1656 as a gesture critical of Cromwell and played the role of Brutus himself, was especially valuable for propagandistic purposes in the eighteenth century because of his status as an executed opponent of Stuart prerogative.[66] As Alan Craig Houston observes, while Sidney's political writings were subject to varying interpretations, "by his martyrdom, [Sidney] graphically demonstrated the evils of unchecked power." Thus, "[t]he single most important fact about Sidney's life [to the colonists] was the manner of his death."[67]

With the onset of the Revolution, the example of Sidney the citizen-soldier became especially useful for patriot propagandists, as did the example of John Hampden, an MP famous both for his opposition to Charles I's ship money levy and for his wartime service against the Royalists, which led to his death from wounds suffered at the battle of Chalgrove Field in 1643.[68] Comparisons between American radicals and Hampden as figures of political resistance became popular even with Edmund Burke, who in his "Speech on American Taxation" noted, "The feelings of the colonies were formerly the feelings of Great Britain. Theirs were formerly the feelings of Mr. Hampden, when called upon for the payment of twenty shillings [the amount of the ship money levy]."[69] As the Americans began to accrue their own canon of heroes slain in battle, however, Hampden's military service and death, like Sidney's, took on greater significance in patriot propaganda than his parliamentary exploits.[70]

Brackenridge put the legacies of Hampden and Sidney to good use while composing *The Battle of Bunkers-Hill*, in which the character who serves as both the patriot leader and the principal martyr is Joseph Warren, a former president of the Massachusetts Assembly and officer of the Continental Army who died in battle during the British assault on the American fortifications around Boston on 17 June 1775. (The British eventually took the hill, though at the cost of heavy casualties.) Fittingly, Warren himself had gained widespread recognition for his own skills as a performer. Warren delivered the anniversary addresses commemorating the Boston Massacre in both 1772 and 1775. As Sandra Gustafson notes, the Massacre orations created a new form of ceremony in Boston, a spectacle in which the individual speaker held a spellbinding power over the socially heterogeneous crowd. While the connection between such ceremonial speakers and ministers in the pulpit is obvious, the similarity between the Massacre orators' influence on crowds to a theatrical star's grip on an audience is also striking.[71]

Warren also capitalized on the symbolic power associated with the republican orator through costuming. He delivered his 1775 address while wearing a toga, a choice that asserted a historical and philosophical continuity between republican Rome and the New England colonies.[72] Warren also delivered this address in full view of a number of armed British soldiers. Gustafson observes that the figure of the republican orator had emerged in Revolutionary culture as an incarnation of "the eternal nation," while "the wounded victim [such as those hurt or killed at the Boston Massacre] of martial violence experience[d] the particularity of individual suffering occasioned by the wars that protect and enhance the state." Warren, by clothing himself in a toga and delivering his commemoration of the slain and wounded in full view of the armed "enemy," drew both figures together into the "orator-victim," a figure of the national body that combines the role of patriot leader and sacrificial victim.[73] In choosing to commemorate Warren's actual battlefield death, during which his dual roles as patriot and martyr merged literally rather than (as in the oration) figuratively, Brackenridge wrote a heroic tragedy for a man who had already carefully scripted his own life to fit the role.

In elevating Warren to the lofty symbolic heights achieved by his play, Brackenridge participated in a political canonization also carried out in Warren's hometown of Boston by the attorney Perez Morton. Warren had been buried without ceremony in an unmarked grave by the British, and this dishonor had caused an uproar among patriot sympathizers.[74] At the re-interment of Warren's corpse in 1776, Morton delivered a commemorative oration in King's Chapel that placed a heavy emphasis on ritual bloodshed and immortality, a pattern that would be repeated in Brackenridge's play. Morton began his address with a thundering apostrophe to Warren's remains, "*Illustrious Relics!*" and later in the speech declares Warren to be a greater military champion than the slain General Wolfe, the hero of Quebec, "For while he died contending for a single country, you fell in the cause of virtue and mankind." Morton's Warren is a composite hero equally adept at philosophy, oratory, and warfare: "like [Interregnum republican philosopher James] Harrington he wrote, like Cicero he spoke, like Hampden he lived, and like Wolfe he died!"[75] Warren, then, serves as both a singularly American patriot martyr and as the most recent embodiment of a political genealogy spreading from Rome to England to North America.

While Warren's canonization is the central aim of Brackenridge's play, the symbolism of sacrificial violence manifests itself throughout the text in many forms. Precious little killing actually takes place on the stage in Brackenridge's script, however. The first three acts consist largely of historical exposition in the form of dialogues between the patriot commanders (Warren, Putnam, Gardiner) and their British counterparts (Thomas Gage, John Burgoyne, Lord Howe), and rousing pre-battle speeches to the troops, in which the audience serves as both British regulars or American rebels. The last two acts of *Bunkers-Hill*, with the exception of Warren's spectacular dying speech in the fourth act, dramatize the failure of the initial British assault, their subsequent defeat of the Americans, and the commemoration of the dead following the battle more through the discussion of violence than through the actual display of violence and its effects.

The rhetoric of sacrificial bloodshed nonetheless dominates the dialogue on both sides of the political argument. Putnam, a veteran of the Seven Years' War, declares in the play's opening scene, a conference of the American commanders, his willingness to die not for "liberty" but for peace: "could I with my life redeem the times, / The richest blood that circles round my heart, / Should hastily be shed."[76] In a more bellicose fashion, Colonel Thomas Gardiner, preparing his American troops for the British assault, encourages them to emulate "those three hundred at Thermopylae, / And give our Country, credit in our deaths."[77]

The British commanders' similar fondness for sacrificial rhetoric also illustrates Brackenridge's adoration of classical metaphors. In an exhortation to his troops, General Howe encourages them to slaughter the Americans, demanding that they "offer up this band, a hecatomb, / To Britain's glory, and the cause of kings," thus equating a rout of the rebel army with the Greek tradition of the hecatomb, a sacrificial offering en masse of slaughtered livestock to the gods. Howe's metaphor not only dehumanizes the Americans but also subtly implies an element of divine prerogative in "the cause of kings."[78] Brackenridge uses sacrificial imagery as a common point of cultural reference between his American and

British characters, and also as a point of moral discrimination between the Catonic, self-sacrificing American officers and Howe, the high priest of carnage. Even the Americans, however, are susceptible to the desire for symbolic retribution. After Warren's death, Gardiner (who also died in the battle) commands his counterattacking troops to "offer up, a reg'ment of the foe, / Achilles-like, upon the Heroe's tomb," a figure that mirrors the slaughter encouraged by Howe, although Gardiner acknowledges the humanity of the enemy and, rather than defining his soldiers as servants of the king, places them in the transcendent role of Achilles.[79]

The play's central exemplum of patriotic sacrifice, the literal embodiment of Brackenridge's dulce et decorum est spirit, is the death of General Warren, the discussion of which has been delayed for the purpose of establishing the centrality of sacrificial rhetoric to Brackenridge's dramaturgy. Warren's death scene begins with the heroic commander entering "[m]ortally wounded, falling on his right knee, covering his breast with his right hand, and supporting himself with his firelock in his left."[80] Warren had, in fact, died after being shot in the face at close range, making such a dying soliloquy quite unlikely, to say the least, but Brackenridge offers the gifted orator a chance to give the speech he was denied in real life.[81] The bloody but unbowed Warren distinguishes himself as a patriot martyr in his concern for the transmission of the disembodied ideal of liberty and his lack of concern for himself in this situation, declaring: "Oh my Countrymen, let not the cause, / The sacred cause of liberty, with me / Faint or expire."[82]

In Warren's dying speech Brackenridge also has the general place himself within a familiar pantheon of classical republicans and British opponents of the House of Stuart. Warren, in his threnody, proclaims:

[N]ow I go to mingle with the dead,
Great Brutus, Hampden, Sidney, and the rest,
Of old or modern memory, who liv'd,
A mound to tyrants, and strong hedge to kings,
Bounding the inundation of their rage,
Against the happiness and peace of man.[83]

Warren's speech closes with the assertion that these heroes "beckon [him] along" to glory, much as Brackenridge's representation of Warren—through both the heroic representation of Warren's death and the idealized political genealogy that Brackenridge, like Perez Morton, constructs for Warren himself—beckons the reader. *Bunkers-Hill* also follows the argument made in Brackenridge and Freneau's *The Rising Glory of America* that the creole settlements of North America had supplanted the decadent political cultures of Europe and would revitalize their civic traditions, which American propagandists claimed as their own through the use of ad hoc political genealogies.

Constructing a genealogy of his own for the rebels, Brackenridge's General Howe contrasts the spirited American volunteers with his own vitiated troops, who under "Royal tyranny" have lost the ancestral "energy of soul, which fill'd, / Their Henry's [*sic*], Edwards, thunder-bolts of war; / Their Hampdens, Marlboroughs, and the immortal Wolfe."[84] Even after achieving a victory over the rebels, Howe declares that the Americans

In feats of prowess shew their ancestry,
And speak their birth legitimate;
The sons of Britons, with the genuine flame,
Of British heat, and valour in their veins.[85]

At the close of the play, Howe orders that Warren be buried with full military honors, a gesture that revises the history of the battle and suggests that, despite the political differences separating the two countries, their common cultural texts remain equally legible. Warren's burial with honors amounts to Howe's recognition of the legitimacy of Warren's claim to a place among the heroes revealed in his dying vision, a claim to honorable "birth" for the entire project of the Revolution.

Ghost Stories: General Wolfe and General Montgomery

Brackenridge's *Bunkers-Hill* retains a measure of goodwill between its British and American characters. Brackenridge himself, before the Battle of Brandywine in 1777, delivered a sermon to Washington's troops in which he declared, "Even though hostile, I feel myself interested in [Britain's] fate . . . I could wish that, bounded in her empire, she were immortal in her date," and expressed lingering admiration for the shared figures of transatlantic British culture: Shakespeare, Locke, and an extensive catalogue of opposition leaders and political martyrs, "[Britain's] statesmen and patriots of every name—her Thomas Mores—her William Temples—her Hampdens—her Sidneys—her Raleighs—her Harringtons—her Russells, and all the illustrious throng that adorns her chronology in every age."[86] Brackenridge's second play, *The Death of General Montgomery*, leaves little room for such cultural understanding between opposing armies of patriots. By the end of the play, which depicts the defeat of the Americans at Quebec and the capture of General Richard Montgomery's surviving troops on New Year's Day 1776, the British officers will offer American prisoners to their Indian allies for a cannibal feast, the British commander of Quebec (in an episode fabricated by Brackenridge) will hang Montgomery's corpse from the walls of the city, and a captured American officer will envision the descent of all Englishmen to hell during the Last Judgment.[87]

The Death of General Montgomery does, however, allow for the lingering connection between Britain and American through a distinctly American interpretation of the genealogy of British military heroism involving "repetition with revision." Brackenridge elevates the fallen Montgomery to the status of a sacrificial effigy through comparisons to the general's heroic "predecessors," including not only Hampden and Sidney but also General Wolfe, whose greatest victory and death both took place before the walls of Quebec in 1759. Although Wolfe, who wrote during the British campaign against Louisbourg in 1758 that "[t]he Americans are in general the dirtiest, the most contemptible, cowardly dogs that you can imagine," would surely have been surprised by his idealization among American revolutionaries, his death nonetheless offered a powerful sacrificial "ancestor" for the American drive for independence.[88] As early as 1774, for instance, the patriot writer Charles Lee had heaped praise upon Wolfe as "not only the first of soldiers" but also as a patriot "passionately attached to the liberties of his country, and of mankind," and as a potential opponent of stationing redcoats in the colonies, since "he was particularly an enemy to large standing armies in time of peace."[89]

The prominence of General Wolfe's example in the construction of Montgomery's martyrdom represents an important change in rhetorical strategy for Brackenridge after *Bunkers-Hill*. Although Brackenridge's fascination with the Greek hecatomb persists in *The Death of General Montgomery*, the characters shy away from classical examples in their paeans to liberty in lieu of the example of Wolfe, not a martyr to classical republican patriotism but a casualty in a British conflict fought on North American soil. Montgomery's troops were, in fact, seeking to wrest from British control on 1 January 1776 the same battlefield that Americans had helped Wolfe to claim in 1759 as part of a combined force of British regulars and colonial militia. The legend that sprang up around Wolfe after the battle, which would no doubt have suited the general's burning desire for a heroic death and his maudlin attachment to Thomas Gray's "Elegy Written in a Country Churchyard," seems particularly ironic in light of actual events. Wolfe's health had suffered a total breakdown during the Quebec campaign, and he was practically bedridden before the battle, which itself could easily have been a disaster, as Fred Anderson has noted. The fame of the British victory at Quebec and Wolfe's enshrinement within the pantheon of British military heroes, indeed, seem in retrospect to be truth effects of Wolfe's dying while conquering a North American battlefield, a sacrifice especially appealing to colonials flush with war profits and "the self-consciously sentimental members of the English ruling and middle classes."[90]

For American revolutionaries like Brackenridge, however, Wolfe's battlefield death developed an almost typological resonance as a foreshadowing of hoped-for American victories in the war's early campaign against

Canada. Comparisons with Wolfe were especially significant in the case of Montgomery, an Irish-born veteran of the Seven Years' War who saw colonial service in New York, the Caribbean, and Pontiac's Rebellion. After returning to Britain in 1767, Montgomery had become close with a number of opposition politicians, including Burke and Isaac Barré, before emigrating in 1772 to New York, where he purchased a small estate north of New York City and married into the prominent Livingston family, eventually joining his in-laws in the patriot movement.[91] Montgomery's service in the American cause, like the lingering attachment of colonials to the myth of Wolfe's heroism, attests to the complicated nature of the Anglo-American relationship during the Revolutionary period—an ambivalence on full display even in Brackenridge's virulently anti-British play.

Even before the 1777 publication of Brackenridge's play, Montgomery and Wolfe had become a matched pair in the public imagination. In 1776 William Smith had delivered a highly controversial eulogy for the British-born General Montgomery that had incorporated the figure of Wolfe, and Thomas Paine had used both Wolfe and Montgomery as figures in a pair of dramatic dialogues, as Ginger Strand explains, "to inspire the living by the example of the dead."[92] Congress commissioned Smith to deliver a funeral oration on 19 February 1776, and although the results of the funeral only gave ammunition to Smith's enemies (who considered his loyalty deeply suspect), his oration was widely reprinted.[93] Smith's oration, delivered months before the Declaration of Independence, expresses hope for an eventual reconciliation with Britain, but describes Montgomery as a "proto-martyr to our Rights."[94] Smith also compares Montgomery to Hampden and Sidney, and in his climactic description of the death of Montgomery, he pairs Montgomery with Wolfe on the Plains of Abraham outside Quebec: "Having approached those plains which the blood of Wolfe hath consecrated to deathless fame, our hero seemed emulous of glory, and animated with a kindred spirit" (36–37).[95]

Although Paine and Smith had starkly opposed opinions on revolution and independence in the early phases of the war, the two men shared a common canon of heroes with Brackenridge. As in the cases of Smith and Brackenridge, Paine uses Wolfe and Montgomery to drive home his point. In *A Dialogue between General Wolfe and General Gage in a Wood near Boston*, first published in the *Pennsylvania Journal* in January 1775, Wolfe's Ghost appears in order to plead with General Gage, supreme commander of all British regulars in the colonies, not to enforce the Intolerable Acts in the name of "an illustrious band of British heroes to whom the glory of Old England is still dear," thereby offering Gage the opportunity to abandon the role of the tyrant in favor of the role of the patriot.[96] Paine's second effort, *A Dialogue between the Ghost of General Montgomery just arrived from the Elysian Fields; and an American Delegate, in a Wood near*

Philadelphia, was printed in Philadelphia as a pamphlet during the Continental Congress's debates over declaring independence.

The *Dialogue* pamphlet, both in its text and in this telling detail of its publication history, can be read as a script for pro-independence activists during these debates. The American delegate raises a variety of common objections to declaring independence (the great military power of Britain, the fear of unrestricted republicanism), only to be refuted by the Ghost of Montgomery. Montgomery serves not only as a mouthpiece for Paine's pro-independence, republican arguments but also as an uncanny inspiration, allowing Paine to appropriate Montgomery's authority as a martyr, along with that of his subordinates Jacob Cheesman and John Macpherson—fellow casualties at Quebec—and an additional litany of heroes stretching from the usual seventeenth-century suspects (Hampden, Sidney, Sidney's co-conspirator Lord William Russell) to the fallen commanders at Bunker Hill and beyond: "The day in which the colonies declare their independence will be a jubilee to Hampden—Sidney—Russell—Warren—Gardiner—Macpherson—Cheesman, and all the other heroes who have offered themselves as sacrifices upon the altar of liberty."[97] Among these heroes, Paine's Montgomery also includes Wolfe, of whom he was at first "jealous" when he fell at Quebec without achieving victory, although he has since made peace with having fallen merely in the attempt "to obtain permanent freedom" for America.

Brackenridge, casting Montgomery and Wolfe (in another supernatural cameo appearance) together in *The Death of General Montgomery*, also deploys (as he had in *Bunkers-Hill*) a genealogy of patriotic performance, which serves as an alternative to the bloodline of kings, for the political purposes that he and Paine (though not, at least initially, Smith) shared. Brackenridge begins the play with his characteristically cosmopolitan vision of patriotism, an easy commerce between Roman, British, and American identities. General Montgomery, speaking to his subordinate Benedict Arnold in the small hours of the night preceding the assault on Quebec, even suggests that his troops have overtaken their Roman (not to mention British) predecessors:

O gallant souls! A sacrifice more rich,
If such should fall, was never offer'd up,
On hill or mountain, to the sacred cause
Of Liberty; not even when Cato died
At Utica, or many a Roman brave,
With noble Brutus, on Pharsalia's plain.[98]

Rather than envisioning the walls of Quebec as a second Utica or Pharsalia, Montgomery's speech meditates instead, as he expresses to his aide-de-camp Macpherson in 1.2, on the place of Quebec's Plains of Abraham in a romanticized chivalric history of the British presence in North America:

> It seems to me, Macpherson, that we tread,
> The ground of some romantic fairy land,
> Where Knights in armour, and high combatants,
> Have met in war. This is the plain where Wolfe,
> Victorious Wolfe, fought with the brave Montcalm. (15)

Brackenridge, through Montgomery, converts Wolfe's taking of Quebec into an episode of chivalrous single combat.

The immortality conferred upon such champions as Brackenridge's Wolfe by exemplary narratives, as Ginger Strand notes, represents "compensation for death," in this case a chance to claim a place in the canon of patriot martyrs.[99] As a result of such genealogies of martyrdom, which disregard temporal disjunctions and the shifting tides of national identity, Montgomery the revolutionary pictures Wolfe and Montcalm as reunited friends in Elysium and envisions both of these servants of colonialist monarchies bedecking him with laurels in the afterlife. Meanwhile Macpherson, playing Portius to Montgomery's Cato, expresses his willingness to die in a decidedly "American" fashion, declaring that when he enlisted:

> I . . . counted it but gain,
> If fighting bravely, in my country's cause,
> I tasted death, and met an equal fame
> With those at Lexington, and Bunker Hill.[100]

The difference between the thoughts on mortality expressed by Montgomery and Macpherson in 2.2 represents a crucial problem for Brackenridge in this play, as it was for Smith and Paine. How does one "Americanize" Wolfe, thereby resolving the contradictions inherent in the analogy between the sieges of Quebec in 1759 and 1776, binding fast the fate of a British general dead for over fifteen years and the American casualties of the ongoing Revolution? Brackenridge's first solution to the problem is to evade the question of British and American identity. He initially upholds Wolfe's example not for his political allegiances but simply for the "courageous" manner of his death and his subsequent fame—a self-supporting manner of effigy fashioning in which the exemplary original serves as a neutral role open to revision and reinterpretation. Brackenridge's vision of Wolfe, not unlike Nathan Hale and much like many a tragic actor throughout history, is celebrated for two (largely interrelated) reasons: his ability to die convincingly, and, somewhat reflexively, his widespread fame. Although Macpherson is at first inclined to use analogies with Bunker Hill in describing the campaign against Quebec, as the American attack approaches he echoes Montgomery's admiration for Wolfe: "For my ambition, is to die like Wolfe, / Wept by his country, and by many a bard, / Of silver-tongue, high storied in his urn," a sentiment echoed by the other junior officers throughout the play (19).

Depicting Wolfe the patriot and Wolfe the sacrificial victim as ideologically neutral "roles" that exist merely for the playing, however, represents at best an incomplete solution to Brackenridge's problem as a propagandist. Celebrity alone does not fill the enlistment rolls. Paine, faced with a similar dilemma, attempts an ideological recuperation of Wolfe in his "Dialogue" by emphasizing French tyranny and, ironically, the glories of the British system of constitutional government. Paine's ghostly General Wolfe explains to General Gage, "I rejoiced less in the hour of my death, in the honor of my victory, than in the glory of having communicated to an inslaved people the glorious privileges of an English constitution."[101]

Brackenridge follows a similar line in the crucial scene of *The Death of General Montgomery*'s third act, a lengthy speech made by Montgomery as he recalls his earlier service under Wolfe during the siege of 1759, in which Wolfe's character is, as in Paine's dialogue, revised according to a familiar pattern in Revolutionary propaganda. He is transformed from His Majesty George II's loyal servant to a patriot martyr and friend of America, a champion of the quicksilver abstraction "Liberty" around the globe:

If Wolfe had liv'd, would he have drawn his sword,
In Britain's cause—in her unrighteous cause,
To chain the American, and bind him down?
O no, his soul, by Nature elegant,
With liberal sentiment and knowledge, stor'd,
Would not have suffered it; I rather think,
Nay, well I know it, that himself had led,
Perhaps, once more, an army to Quebec,
To drive the tyrants out. He had obey'd,
Rather, the dictates of an upright soul,
Than the commandments of a tyrant King.[102]

Montgomery's recasting of Wolfe as a posthumous American sympathizer gains an air of authority from his own transition from Hanoverian soldier to republican insurrectionist, from Irish-born Briton to American. Brackenridge denies Montgomery—who was killed suddenly by grapeshot, along with Macpherson and Cheesman, while charging a fortified house in Quebec's Lower Town—a death speech, however, apparently for reasons of verisimilitude.

This decision robs Montgomery of his chance to tie himself explicitly to Wolfe as he dies, as Brackenridge's version of Joseph Warren does with Hampden and Sidney and Perez Morton's funeral oration for Warren does with Wolfe.[103] Only in the heat of the offstage battle, after Captain Burr, Montgomery's lieutenant, stumbles upon the corpses of Montgomery, Macpherson, and Cheesman, does the full power of such repetitions with revision, especially comparisons with Wolfe, become readily apparent onstage. As Burr concludes a eulogy for Montgomery in which he vows to display his uniform, soaked with Montgomery's blood, to the remaining American forces in order to urge them to victory, the Ghost of General Wolfe enters the stage, like Hamlet's father with all his sins upon his head, to bring Montgomery into the fold of martyrdom and curse the tyranny of Great Britain.

This deus ex machina resolves the apparent political contradictions of associating Wolfe and the patriot cause by capturing them both in the ephemeral flesh of an actor. Wolfe's ghost curses the "False council'd King and venal Parliament" of Britain, lamenting:

Have I then fought, and was my life blood shed,
To raise your power to this ambitious height,
Disdainful height, of framing laws to bind,
In cases whatsoever, free-born men,
Of the same lineage, name and quality?[104]

Moreover Wolfe, whom comparison with Montgomery has helped to convert into an American patriot *avant la lettre*, closes the circuit by certifying Montgomery's apotheosis to patriot martyrdom, assuring the audience that from Montgomery's "death shall amply vegetate, / The grand idea of an empire new."[105] While Brackenridge devotes the play's extensive fifth act to the failure of the assault on Quebec and the capture of Benedict Arnold and the remaining Americans by the British, Wolfe's speech is the play's climax. This stage moment, like the historical incident that it recounts, apparently retained its hold upon the imagination of American drama enthusiasts throughout the war until its own physical culmination in the 1781 staging at Harvard reported by Abbé Robin, a revival of the school's theatrical tradition that serendipitously occurred during the year when the Revolution swung irrevocably in favor of the Americans and their French allies.

Summing up his analysis of the propaganda plays of the American Revolution, Jared Brown declares that "it is not difficult to find fault" with these texts as works of literary and dramatic art. "Nevertheless," Brown argues, the plays "represent the first important stirrings of American drama, and an opportunity for American writers to confront American issues, develop American concerns, and explore American values in their own voices."[106] While the propaganda plays of the American Revolution may represent the stirrings of a longing for an "American" drama, the fabric of these texts is also shot through with evidence of the interdependent relationship between Great Britain and the colonies. The foundational myths of British patriotism, the history of the imperial brush wars of the eighteenth century, and the commercial and cultural economy of the circum-Atlantic trade route all make themselves felt in the struggles of American partisans to invent a dramatic identity that both preserves and defies British traditions. That these plays should have been staged, thereby bringing early American print culture into contact yet again with theatrical performance, seems only fitting. The republic that Brackenridge and his fellow revolutionaries fought—on battlefields literal and fictional—to establish was, like the theater itself, haunted. These new "American" playwrights, like their theatrical forebears practicing the socially engaged art form of the drama, faced during the Revolutionary era one of the fundamental questions in the construction of fictions both theatrical and national: when confronted by an ancestral ghost, do you exorcise it, or worship it?

Epilogue
Post-Revolutionary Patriotism and the American Theater

Although the Continental Congress effectively reduced theater in the United States during the Revolution to an amateur affair carried out by soldiers, college students, and pamphleteers, the Revolution neither dissolved the American Company nor sated the American public's appetite for professional theater. The American Company prospered in Jamaica during the war, and although David Douglass retired from the stage in 1777, the company continued, first under the management of the actor John Henry, and beginning in 1779, under Lewis Hallam Jr.[1] As the Revolution drew toward a close in North America, meanwhile, Thomas Wall, formerly of the American Company, formed a new troupe, the Maryland Company, in Baltimore in 1781. This company acted regularly in Baltimore and Annapolis throughout 1782–85, first under the management of Wall and, later, of Dennis Ryan.[2] The Maryland Company's repertoire during 1782–83 revived a number of popular patriotic plays, indicating a lingering appetite among American audiences for representations of tyranny and patriotism. The revival of these plays also, however, underscored the difficulty for both citizens and theater managers of joining the insurgent spirit of the Revolution with patriotic allegiance to a postrevolutionary state.

The roughly one hundred documented performance nights of the Maryland Company in Baltimore and Annapolis during 1782–83 feature several familiar plays popular with pre-Revolutionary audiences for political as well as aesthetic reasons: *Richard III* (five performances), *Tamerlane* (two), *Cato* (two), *The Recruiting Officer* (two), and *Hamlet* (two).[3] The Maryland Company also produced several other plays featuring the familiar theatrical combination of tyrants, patriots, and sacrificial victims. Some of these plays had been performed on the colonial stage, but some of them were new to the North American theater. In the case of both revivals and new plays, significant tailoring of the productions was often required to suit local political conditions.

Revivals could be particularly challenging to re-frame for a republican audience. For instance, on five occasions between 1782 and 1783 the

Maryland Company performed Thomas Otway's *Venice Preserved* (1682), a Tory tragedy about a failed plot to overthrow the Republic of Venice, the senate of which Otway depicts as a council of greedy, lecherous old men crippled by partisan infighting and cowardice. Douglass had eliminated *Venice Preserved*, which had been somewhat successful in the colonies during the early 1760s, from the American Company's repertoire after 1767, although it later became a favorite among British military actors during the Revolution.[4] Wall attempted to neutralize the play's anti-republican aspects in an occasional prologue condemning the conspiracy ("We . . . detest the plan") and encouraging the citizens of the revolutionary republic to emulate their patriotic predecessors from the Roman, rather than the Venetian, republic: "You've fought like Romans, now like Romans feel."[5] Whether due to Wall's efforts or not, the play remained in production in the United States (as it did in Britain) into the nineteenth century.

Less successful were some of the Maryland Company's efforts to introduce new plays, such as Henry Brooke's 1739 heroic play, *Gustavus Vasa, The Deliverer of His Country*, which they performed twice in 1782.[6] Brooke was associated with Bolingbroke, and *Gustavus Vasa* (which was banned under the Licensing Act for criticizing George II and Robert Walpole) revolves around a Swedish general, exiled after the Danish conquest of his country, who returns to overthrow the Danish tyrant Cristiern and his Swedish vice-regent Trollio, claiming the throne for himself as a patriot king.[7] Wall's Maryland Company ostensibly produced this play at the urging of "Cato," who in a letter to the *Maryland Journal* argued that the play "is replete with the most exalted ideals of true heroism, and should be adopted by us to show that we can sympathize in the desires, and applaud the courage of, a people who prefer death to the imperious will of a tyrant; nor can it fail of success on the stage, when every bosom present at the representation, will see the patriot flames rekindled for the service of his country."[8]

The announcement of *Gustavus Vasa*'s premiere participated in not only the "rekindling" of the patriot flame in Baltimore but the conversion of George Washington into America's answer to the patriot king. The printer Robert Bell had issued this play in Philadelphia in 1778, dedicating his edition to Washington, and Wall likewise advertised the play as "Inscrib'd to General Washington."[9] These two performances did poorly at the box office, but the play remained popular. In June 1782, a writer in Boston's *Continental Journal* found inspiration for the new era of American freedom in the "noble sentiments spoken in the character of Gustavus Vasa, in the excellent dramatic performance of that name."[10] Much of the play's success, however, came from Bell's tying of the play to Washington, an association that would hold until Washington's death. Indeed, on one occasion in 1784 the students of Washington College in Maryland, under the direction of William Smith (late of the College of Philadelphia), performed the play before Washington himself, reciting an epilogue praising Washington as "the Champion of his Country's Cause, / The Friend of Mankind, Liberty, and Laws."[11] The inexactness of the analogy constructed by the pairing of a republican American general and Brooke's Gustavus, who restores the integrity of his country's monarchy, never seems to have troubled the reading or theatrical public, even though the play was not an instant hit in the playhouse.[12]

The problematic parallels between Washington and Gustavus Vasa illustrate only one of the major difficulties in the relationship between the United States and its resurgent theater during the 1780s. Lewis Hallam and John Henry each returned to the United States from the Caribbean in 1784 at the head of his own acting company (the two eventually joined forces under the banner of the "Old American Company"), but the players faced strong opposition to the revival of the theater in some of their main venues, including New York and Philadelphia, in the latter of which a playhouse would not be officially licensed until 1789.[13] The resistance of some Americans to the resumption of theatrical activity, which for the Old American Company took place in New York in 1785, centered on familiar financial and moral arguments, but some champions of civic duty also accepted the return of the theater. The Old American Company's debut in New York was facilitated by David Douglass's acquiescence to the will of Congress in departing North America in 1775, a gesture that established the company's "American" bona fides.[14]

The greatest challenge for professional acting companies in the 1780s was reintegrating themselves into the urban cultural life of the United States, overcoming not only such familiar obstacles as local opposition to theatrical performances but also problems of potential cultural incongruity caused by the continued dominance of British plays on the stages of the independent United States. The Maryland Company's dedication of *Gustavus Vasa* to General Washington, after all, may have seemed politically savvy to Thomas Wall, but their two performances had ultimately failed to fill the Baltimore theater with spectators eager to have their patriotic flames rekindled by Brooke's play.

This process of reintegrating the professional theater into society, which reflects the struggles of Americans in the early national period to define the nature of their political and cultural relationships with Great Britain, has often been tied to the growth of cultural nationalism in late eighteenth-century America. This nationalist narrative in theater history commonly focuses on the 1787 premiere of the first new play by an American author produced professionally after the Revolution: Royall Tyler's *The Contrast*. Tyler, a young Massachusetts attorney, had been dispatched to New York early in 1787 to pursue fugitive insurgents from Shays' Rebellion. During this period he appears to have become acquainted with the professional theater and to have turned his own attention to playwriting.[15] As the ensuing analysis will show, this nationalist model is not without its flaws, but Tyler's attempt to preserve some elements of Revolutionary-era culture in a play written amid the rapid social changes of the 1780s, as well as his effort to use romantic comedy (rather than political tragedy) as a vehicle for patriotic sentiment, are without question important achievements in the history of the American theater.

The Contrast, Tyler's first known play, focuses on the romantic fortunes of a number of young New Yorkers. Sentimental, bookish Maria Van Rough, daughter of a wealthy merchant, has lost interest in her fiancé, an Anglophile fop named Billy Dimple. Dimple, meanwhile, carries on romantic dalliances with Maria's friends Letitia and Charlotte. When Charlotte's brother, the Revolutionary War veteran Colonel Henry Manly, arrives from Massachusetts to lobby for the addition of some of his former soldiers to the national pension list, he and Maria quickly fall in love. They are prevented from pursuing their romance by Maria's engagement, but Maria's father soon discovers that Dimple is bankrupt and determines to break up the match. Meanwhile, Dimple attempts to force himself sexually upon Charlotte, who is rescued by her brother Manly; this transgression costs Dimple the affections of all concerned and makes way for Manly's engagement to Maria. Enriching the romantic main plot is a second "low" plot that follows the misadventures in the city of Manly's servant Jonathan, a bumptious New England farm boy and the progenitor of a new theatrical line of business on the American stage—the stage Yankee.[16]

The Contrast premiered during the Old American Company's 1787 season in New York, playing on four occasions. These performances were followed by a performance in Baltimore in August 1787, a staged reading in Philadelphia in December 1787, and revivals in Baltimore and New York during August 1788 and June 1789 respectively.[17] Thomas Wignell, the actor who originated the role of Jonathan, published the play in 1790, and by 1804 a total of thirty-eight recorded performances had taken place in locations ranging from Boston to Charleston.[18]

The Contrast has been used as evidence of both the striking originality of the literature of the early republic and of its derivativeness. Its patriotic intentions can scarcely be in doubt. Jean-Christophe Agnew maintains that only the "newly awakened nationalism" displayed in *The Contrast*, a play "aimed at a British target . . . juxtaposing the homespun honesty of its American characters against the calculating hypocrisy and theatricality of their British counterparts," liberated the American theater from Puritanism and British cultural domination.[19] (There are, in fact, no British characters in the play.) Agnew and other critics have weighed *The Contrast*'s obvious debts to such British texts as Chesterfield's *Letters to His Son* and Sheridan's *The School for Scandal* against its patriotic rhetoric and introduction of the "Yankee Jonathan," arguing over the degrees to which the play is merely derivative of its British influences and to which it partakes of a one-dimensional, anti-British literary nationalism.[20] Meanwhile, other recent interpretations have downplayed Tyler's debts to British literature and instead examined its treatment of Shays' Rebellion and New York's reputation for political recalcitrance under the Articles of Confederation.[21]

The Contrast sustains such widely varied readings in part because of the postcolonial condition of early republican literature; cultural independence was slow to follow from political independence.[22] Perhaps nowhere was the continuing British literary dominance of the United States more obvious than in the theater, where British plays made up the vast majority of the repertoire until well into the nineteenth century. Tyler's comedy both resists this British hegemony over the early national stage and embraces it. His play, while it may be derivative in following the model of Sheridan's *The School for Scandal*, includes in its dialogue such important symbols of Revolutionary culture as patriot street theater and representations of Native Americans—material decidedly new and specifically tied to the American patriot movement. Moreover, Sheridan, Tyler's obvious model in composing the comedy, had excellent pro-American credentials as a Member of Parliament.[23]

Even in choosing to mimic a British comedy, then, Tyler chose one by a pro-American playwright. In addition, Tyler's introduction of a rape attempt into the play's climactic scene echoes not British comedy but the patriot tragedies so popular with colonial and Revolutionary audiences. Dimple's financial and sexual luxuriance suggest a de-fanged tyrant figure, one who does not possess power but threatens corruption and decline from within the republic. Charlotte, facing ravishment by Dimple, is in danger of becoming a sacrificial victim. Manly, playing the role of the patriot, not only rescues his sister from the "tyrant" Dimple but also attempts to play the role of the patriot orator outlined by Sandra Gustafson in his efforts to draw the attention of Congress to the sacrifices of his wounded former comrades from the war.[24] Although Tyler's play is a comedy, the cast of characters contains familiar elements of the tyrant, sacrificial victim, and patriot. *The Contrast* owes considerable debts not only to Sheridan but also to the patriotic plays of Addison and Rowe; yet Tyler fashions these "British" models into a play that also incorporates many vestiges of American patriot political culture into its dialogue.

Despite the play's lofty patriotic aims, Tyler's characters all plainly show the influence of British culture, and especially British literature.

The foppish Dimple and his social-climbing manservant, Jessamy, regularly consult Chesterfield, the great prophet of polite hypocrisy, on the rules of proper social behavior.[25] (It is worth noting here that George Washington, the embodiment of the Revolution, was also familiar with Chesterfield's advice book.)[26] The aspiring coquette Charlotte, meanwhile, displays a familiarity with *The Spectator*.[27] Even the nativist Manly, who, far from being a cosmopolitan, praises the "laudable partiality which ignorant, untravelled men entertain for everything that belongs to their country" as the ore from which the "the noble principle of patriotism" may be refined (79), is well versed enough in British political philosophy to have read Edward Montagu's *Reflections on the Rise and Fall of Ancient Republics* and Bernard Mandeville's *The Fable of the Bees* (63). The bookish Maria, meanwhile, is Tyler's champion reader of British texts, having consumed, according to Letitia, a good deal of sentimental literature, including the poetry of Shenstone and the novels of Sterne and Richardson: "Why, she read Sir Charles Grandison, Clarissa Harlow, Shenstone, and the Sentimental Journey" (5). Maria's taste in literature, moreover, highlights the play's concern with the reintegration of patriotic heroism into post-Revolutionary society, a theme that emerges in the play's second scene, during which Maria is discovered reading.

Seated in her library, Maria sings a poem by the British poet Anne Home Hunter that has been set to music, titled "Alknomook, The Death Song of the Cherokee Indian" (11). The song, written from the perspective of a Cherokee warrior being tortured by his captors, is a fine example of the genre of the *chanson de mort*, or death song, a genre of Native American literature that captured the European imagination in the eighteenth century. As Julie K. Ellison observes, this genre offers a familiar blend of pathos and stoicism in a new, North American setting:

The sun sets in the night, and the stars shun the day;
But glory remains when their lights fade away!
Begin, ye tormentors! Your threats are in vain,
For the son of Alknomook shall never complain.[28]

The Indian death song echoes the widespread appropriation of native identity by the patriot movement throughout the course of the Revolution, from the rituals of the Sons of Saint Tammany to the use of "war paint" by the rioters of the Boston Tea Party. Maria's song "naturalizes" both this important genre of Native American performance and the ideal of the patriotic Indian warrior, incorporating them into the play's vision of post-Revolutionary civic life.[29] The fusion of stoic fortitude and Indian imagery in the song—so redolent of Revolutionary culture—that Maria discerns in the song "ever calls forth [her] affections."[30]

Maria's sentimental reaction to the song prefigures Manly's appearance as the play's hero. Having finished the song, Maria declares: "The manly virtue of courage, that fortitude which steels the heart against the keenest misfortunes, which interweaves the laurel of glory amidst the instruments of torture and death, displays something so noble, so exalted, that in despite of the prejudices of education I cannot but admire it, even in a savage" (11–12). The Cherokee in this song is an enemy, not a North American Juba, but in spite of the bitter history of race relations in North America, Maria feels the same romantic temptations as Addison's Marcia. Fortunately, at least from the perspective of Maria's merchant father, the close association of this song with the culture of the American Revolution renders the dying Cherokee only a surrogate for the sort of man who can truly open Maria's heart: a veteran of the Continental Army.

Concluding her meditations on the attractions of stoic heroism, Maria declares her passion for both the accoutrements of the Continental Army's uniform, "A cockade, a lapell'd coat, and a feather," and also the "safe asylum" available to women "in the arms of a man of honour"—arms raised, she notes, "for our protection, . . . nerv'd by virtue and directed by honour" (12–13). Maria desires a man who has learned stoicism and self-identification with the public good in the service of the republic, and who wears the marks of his service. Like the members of the Old American Company's audience, her imagination demands a new type of the Anglo-American stage patriot. As the anti-type of the effeminate beaux of New York society, Manly serves as the metaphorical equivalent of Maria's Alknomook, alien and outmoded in postwar society yet also carrying within himself the "American" traits idealized by the patriot movement.

Manly possesses all the trappings and personal qualities needed to embody this complex new iteration of the patriot. A member of the Society of the Cincinnati, a politically influential veterans' group, he carries a sword presented to him by the Marquis de Lafayette and proudly wears his old regimental coat, which Charlotte insists has fallen quite out of fashion.[31] He also displays the stage patriot's rhetorical self-identification with the state, a trait that Tyler also attributes to Washington, to whom one of the first copies of the play was sent upon its publication.[32] When Charlotte encourages Manly to cashier his commission notes, debts owed to him by the government for his service, Manly refuses to redeem the notes until the government can more readily afford to repay its creditors. "If that is not in my day," Manly announces, "[The notes] shall be transmitted as an honourable certificate to posterity, that I have humbly imitated our illustrious WASHINGTON, in having exposed my health and life in the service of my country, without reaping any other reward than the glory of conquering in so arduous a contest."[33] Given Manly's predilection for such ostentatious displays of republican virtue, it is no wonder the nonplused Charlotte suggests that the belles of New York society will think her brother is "a player run mad, with [his] head filled with old scraps of tragedy."[34]

Charlotte's withering remark about her brother's patriotic rhetoric signals an ambivalence toward Manly's histrionics that runs throughout Tyler's play, an awareness that the cultural forms of the Revolutionary era were at risk of degenerating into anachronism by the late 1780s. Although Manly's devotion to Washington and membership in the Society of the Cincinnati suggest that he has Federalist sympathies, his republican patriotic rhetoric was commonly used by both Federalists and Anti-Federalists. Like Addison's Cato, Manly is politically ambiguous, and both Federalists and Anti-Federalists in the audience might find reason to claim him.[35] As he would later do in *The Bay Boy*, moreover, Tyler used Addison's play to color his own depiction of the Revolution and its aftermath. In Manly's second scene, for instance, Tyler pens a soliloquy decrying the dangers of "Luxury" that, through allusions to *Cato*, offers both instruction for the audience and a gently ironic critique of Manly himself.

In this scene Manly is discovered alone on a city street, in a parody of Cato's fifth-act soliloquy, and opens his moralizing monologue, "It must be so, Montague," an echo of Cato's line, "It must be so—Plato thou reason'st well!"[36] Manly then delivers an extended disquisition on the virtues of the confederated Greek states, who when they practiced abstemious republican virtue proved "the scourge of tyrants, and the safe asylum of freedom" before falling victim to luxury and indolence. Manly concludes his speech by lamenting, "Oh! That America! Oh! That my country, would, in this her day, learn the things which belong to her peace," possibly an echo of Cato's aggrieved outcry, "O liberty! O virtue! O my country!"[37] In Manly's soliloquy, Tyler follows the well-worn convention of constructing a genealogy of libertarian patriotism for a revolutionary hero from classical history and British plays, but Manly's taste for high tragedy seems out of place in the bustling streets of postwar New York. Charlotte's observation that her brother speaks like a player run mad, an alien escapee from the realms of popular literature, is at least partially correct.[38] Manly's allusions to *Cato* also mirror the lingering onstage presence of Addison's tragedy, which, although performed less often after 1782 than in its colonial heyday, remained in production with some regularity until 1795, when it appears to have vanished from the repertoire.[39]

Whether or not the critic recognized Tyler's allusions to *Cato*, a review of *The Contrast* in the *New York Daily Advertiser* for 18 April 1787 singled out Manly's soliloquy as quite beyond belief: "A man can never be supposed in conversation with himself, to point out examples of imitation to his countrymen."[40] As Daniel F. Havens points out, however, Manly's moralizing soliloquy and his patriotic rhetoric remains "in accord with the taste of his age for heroic drama."[41] Indeed, Hallam and Henry revived a number of patriotic plays from the pre-war American Company repertoire in their first two seasons in New York, from November 1785 to August 1786 and from February to June 1787. The 1785–86 season, which ran seventy-two shows in all, featured revivals of *Venice Preserved*, *Macbeth*, *Tamerlane*, and *Richard III*, the last of which was performed three times.

These seasons also illustrate that patriotic entertainment was developing a comic face in the post-Revolutionary theater to match its tragic and heroic aspects. In 1785 Hallam and Henry introduced John O'Keefe's musical farce *The Poor Soldier* (1783), which chronicles the romantic misadventures of a brave Irish soldier, Pat, who has been wounded in the American Revolution, and his cowardly civilian friend Darby. The farce was a smash hit, and the Old American Company performed it an astonishing fifteen times during the 1785–86 season. During the thirty-six-night 1787 season in which *The Contrast* premiered and was acted four times, Hallam and Henry also staged *Cato*, *The Recruiting Officer*, *Richard III*, and *Macbeth*, and played *The Poor Soldier* four times, adding to this total two performances of O'Keefe's *Love in a Camp* (1786), a sequel to *The Poor Soldier* that finds both Pat and Darby in the service of the Prussian Army.[42] Whatever dispute the *Daily Advertiser*'s theater critic may have had with Tyler's mock-Addisonian soliloquy, American audiences continued to display an appetite for British plays with patriotic and martial themes, as well as for new texts authored by Americans and influenced both by the British theatrical tradition and American politics.

O'Keefe's farces, which contrast Pat's simple heroism with Darby's aversion to battle, provide populist comic relief for the lofty sentiments of the patriotic tragedies and heroic plays being revived in the postwar American repertoire. In *The Poor Soldier*, for instance, when Pat returns to his native village in Ireland, he encounters Darby and sings him a song praising military life, each verse ending with a repetition of the phrase "row-de-dow."[43] Darby is enchanted by the idea of service, but when the uniformed Pat places his hat on Darby's head, he reveals a scar from "a wound I got in battle endeavouring to save my captain's life—I was left for dead in the field of battle, bleeding in my country's cause—there was glory for you" (10–11). Darby promptly returns Pat's hat and exits on the double, declaring, "The devil row-de-dow me if you get me to be a soldier" (11). Only after Pat is promoted for his battlefield bravery in the final scene does Darby, inspired by his friend, sell his farm for an officer's commission and enlist. Darby's romance with military life does not extend to *Love in a Camp*, however, in which Darby is frequently threatened with punishment for dereliction of duty, only to be rescued by Pat. On one such occasion, he laments, "Oh that I ever sold my farm."[44] Pining for the tranquility of a home that he has sold, Darby represents a burlesque

Cincinnatus: he serves as a comic counterpoint to both Pat's selfless volunteerism and the high-flown patriotism displayed on the postwar American stage by characters such as Colonel Manly and his predecessors in the British dramatic canon.

Given the prominence of O'Keefe's farces in the Old American Company's repertoire, it is perhaps no surprise that Tyler uses Manly's servant Jonathan to offer a comic, democratic parallel to Manly's patriotic character—especially since the same actor, the popular comedian Thomas Wignell, played both Darby and Jonathan.[45] From this coincidence of casting, moreover, emerges perhaps the play's best-known scene: Jonathan's account of his trip to the theater, where he accidentally takes in a double bill of *The School for Scandal* and *The Poor Soldier*. Although Jonathan holds the stereotypical New England view of the theater—that it is "the shop where the devil hangs out the vanities of the world upon the tenterhooks of temptation"—once he has mistakenly entered the theater, which he believes to be merely a house with a missing wall, he quickly settles in to observe the business of his new neighbors.[46]

Jonathan's tastes are decidedly patriotic: he is drawn to the heroic Pat, for instance, "a soldier fellow, who talked about his row de dow, dow" (56). And although, in a delightful metatheatrical joke, Jonathan declares that his favorite character was Wignell in one of his other theatrical personae, "Darby;– that was his baptizing name . . . Darby Wag-all," he does not wholly approve of Darby's character, since "he was afraid of some of them 'ere shooting irons, such as your troopers wear on training days" (56–57). Jonathan, by contrast, declares himself to be "a true born Yankee American son of liberty" who was "never afraid of a gun yet in all my life" (57). Wignell, through the lines of Tyler and O'Keefe, embodies both the simple patriotic prejudices of the American common man praised by Colonel Manly and their burlesque opposite, Darby's preference for discretion over valor when confronted with Pat's life-threatening experience in the American war. The theatrical power of this Janus-faced depiction of patriotism in the form of Wignell's person is intensified by the audience's knowledge that Jonathan's martial spirit may be pure play-acting, like Darby's (and Wignell's). Jonathan did not participate in the pitched battles of the Revolution, having been left behind on the family farm by his father and six brothers "to take care of mother" (37).

In addition to introducing his naïve patriot Jonathan to the pageantry of the post-Revolutionary professional theater, Tyler decorates Jonathan's understanding of the world around him with scraps of colonial and Revolutionary performances—echoes of the recent past that have left lingering marks on the cultural, and in some cases, physical, landscape of the new United States. In Jonathan's first scene, for instance, after meeting his opposite number Jessamy on the street, Jonathan confesses to sympathizing with Daniel Shays and his fellow insurgents. When Jessamy asks him why he did not join the ranks of the rebels, Jonathan paraphrases Colonel Manly's response to the Rebellion, declaring, "It was a burning shame for the true blue Bunker Hill sons of liberty, who had fought Governor Hutchinson, Lord North, and the Devil, to have any hand in kicking up a cursed dust against a government which we had, every mother's son of us, a hand in making."

Jonathan's imagination blends decades of political grievances against unpopular colonial officials (Hutchinson) and crown policies (Lord North served as George III's chief minister during the Revolution) in a pageant that echoes the pre-Revolutionary street theater of patriotism and tyranny, particularly the urban folk parades of New England and New York. In Jonathan's imagination, Governor Hutchinson and Lord North ride like straw effigies through the streets of America alongside the devil in a Pope Day cart. This image of both popular unity and popular unrest, clownish and clumsy as Jonathan's imagination may be, nonetheless draws a sharp distinction between the American Revolution and all future civil broils.

Jonathan's imagined Pope Day is not the only element of patriot street theater, with its pitched battles between effigies of the patriot and the tyrant, which Tyler introduces to the postwar stage, however. Asked by Jessamy what sights he has seen in New York, Jonathan relates that he "went to see two marble-stone men and a leaden horse that stands out doors in all weathers," only to discover that "one [of the men] had got no head, and t'other weren't there" (37–38). Jonathan clearly refers here to two statues erected on the Bowling Green in 1770—one of Pitt the Elder in a toga, striking an oratorical pose and holding the Magna Carta in his right hand, and the other of George III poised upon a warhorse.[47] The statue of George III was, as most of Tyler's New York audience must surely have known, toppled by an angry mob on 9 July 1776 after the first reading of the Declaration of Independence in New York. Although Jonathan speculates that "the leaden man was a damn'd tory, and . . . took wit in his anger and rode off in the time of the troubles," the statue was in fact beheaded by the crowd in an act of symbolic regicide; the statue's body was sent to Litchfield, Connecticut, where it was melted, like the toy soldiers of Benjamin Martin's dead son Thomas in *The Patriot*, into ammunition for the Continental Army.[48] After the British captured New York in September 1776, a group of British officers decapitated the Pitt statue on St. Andrew's Night (30 November), possibly as a retaliatory gesture against one of the political patron saints of the rebellious colonists.[49] Like Jonathan's patchwork understanding of history, the cultural and physical landscapes of Tyler's United States (and our own) are palimpsests of colonial and revolutionary history, scored with the markings of past performances.

If Jonathan is a repository of American patriotic mythology, however, Tyler nonetheless acknowledges, as he does in his depiction of Colonel Manly's Catonic ruminations, the need to adapt these cultural forms to the commercial society of the post-Revolutionary world. Called upon by a New York servant girl, Jenny, whom he is courting, to sing her a song, Jonathan admits that, except for meeting-house hymns, he can sing only one hundred and ninety verses of "Yankee Doodle." The four verses that he sings for Jenny include a description of a cannon that "made a noise—like father's gun, / Only a nation louder." Jonathan's New England slang, "a nation louder" translates as "a great deal louder," but the description of the cannon could also serve as a punning description of the patriot effigy's magnification of the actions of individual citizens into exemplary performances that lay the groundwork for myths of national origin.[50] Nonetheless, Jonathan's verses are decidedly unsuited to romantic comedy, and Jenny rebuffs the attentions of her "true blue Bunker Hill son of liberty" admirer, who will perhaps, given the chance, prove a fighter not a lover.

Although Thomas Wignell dedicated the print edition of *The Contrast* to that chief emblem of Revolutionary and postwar patriotism, George Washington, and Tyler, through Manly's effusions, praises Washington's exemplary patriotism, there are no records to prove that the early national period's most prominent playgoer ever saw the piece in performance. The play was revived, however, as part of the Old American Company's New York season of 1789, which lasted from April to December, except for two weeks' hiatus owing to Washington's inauguration, and also included performances of *Richard III*, *Gustavus Vasa*, *The Poor Soldier*, and *Love in a Camp*.[51] (That *Cato* was not performed during this season, given its association with Washington, is surprising.) The coincident revivals of Tyler's play and O'Keefe's farces are especially interesting, since Washington seems to have had several theatrical encounters with Jonathan's alter ego, Darby. The Old American Company had played in Philadelphia for six weeks during the Constitutional Convention in 1788, at which time Washington saw, along with Dryden's *Tempest*, a performance of *Love in a Camp*.[52] During the company's 1789 season in New York, moreover, Washington attended a number of performances, two of which brought him into contact again with Wignell's performance of O'Keefe's anti-patriot everyman.

On 6 May 1789, Washington, as Jonathan does in *The Contrast*, attended a double bill of *The School for Scandal* and *The Poor Soldier*, an uncanny moment of life imitating art.[53] And on 24 November 1789, Washington attended the theater for Thomas Wignell's benefit night, a performance of Sheridan's *The Critic*, followed by O'Keefe's *The Toy* and a new farce by a young playwright named William Dunlap, *Darby's Return*. "On the appearance of THE PRESIDENT," reports the *Gazette of the United States,* "the audience rose and received him with the warmest acclamations—the genuine effusions of the hearts of FREEMEN."[54] The "patriot king" had entered the theater, where the monarch is both seen and unseen, and as much a part of the show as the actors.

The effusions of the "FREEMEN" in the audience were followed by a tribute to Washington in Dunlap's closing piece. In this farce Darby returns to his village and recounts not only the events of *The Poor Soldier* and *Love In A Camp,* but also the details of a recent visit that he made to the United States. While there he witnesses, among many other spectacles, the ratification of the Constitution and the inauguration of the first president:

A man who'd fought to free the land from woe,
Like me had left his farm a soldiering to go;
But having gain'd his point, he had like me,
Return'd his own potatoe ground to see.[55]

Although Dunlap, in his *History,* reports that Washington "looked grave" as Wignell sang his praises in a thick brogue, the playwright reports with considerable pride that the president's foreboding expression eventually gave way to "a hearty laugh."[56]

At this moment the post-Revolutionary American theater, an artistic sphere occupied by Royall Tyler, William Dunlap, and Thomas Wignell, brought into contact two new "American" manifestations of the political and theatrical cultures of the British Atlantic. A self-consciously theatrical head of a new state, the commander in chief and surrogate "patriot king" of a revolutionary republic, received a tribute in the form of a comparison between himself and his comic mirror image, a lowborn Irish farmer and cowardly former soldier who originated on the London stage. Like a modern moviegoer watching Mel Gibson's fantasia on the colonial rebellion, Washington, from his box in the John Street Theatre, witnessed Thomas Wignell engaging in one of the most basic practices of performance in an Atlantic society. Wignell's theatrical interaction with the president at that moment constitutes a performance of origins, defining the public face of the American experiment, whether that of George Washington, Darby, or Benjamin Martin, by enacting both what the audience thought it was, and what it thought it was not.

Notes

Prologue

1. *The Patriot*, prod. Dean Devlin and dir. Roland Emmerich, Sony Pictures Entertainment, 2000, videotape.
2. For lives of Marion and Morgan, see Robert D. Bass, *Swamp Fox: The Life and Campaigns of General Francis Marion* (Orangeburg, S.C.: Sandlapper Publishing Co., 1974); and Don Higginbotham, *Daniel Morgan, Revolutionary Rifleman* (Chapel Hill: University of North Carolina Press, 1961).
3. A number of excellent works on the importance of depictions of Native Americans to early American culture have emerged in recent years. For the connection between British conquest and the mourning and commemoration of a valorized enemy, see Sandra M. Gustafson, *Eloquence Is Power: Oratory and Performance in Early America* (Chapel Hill: University of North Carolina Press, 2000), 75–139; and Gordon Sayre, *The Indian Chief as Tragic Hero* (Chapel Hill: University of North Carolina Press, 2005). For the connection between the climate of the Americas and the supposed degeneration of both native people and British colonials, see Richard Godbeer, *Sexual Revolution in Early America* (Baltimore: Johns Hopkins University Press, 2002), 152; and Kathleen Wilson, *The Island Race: Englishness, Empire, and Gender in the Eighteenth Century* (London: Routledge, 2003), 13. For the importance of the assumed "Indian" identity to colonials, see Philip J. Deloria, *Playing Indian* (New Haven, Conn.: Yale University Press, 1998). For the revision of the colonials' self-image from colonizer to colonized, see Michael K. Warner, "What's Colonial About Colonial America?" in *Possible Pasts: Becoming Colonial in Early America*, ed. Robert Blair St. George (Ithaca, N.Y.: Cornell University Press, 2000), 62. For a meditation on "vanishing" Indians unrelated to my present argument, see Laura M. Stevens, *The Poor Indians: British Missionaries, Native Americans, and Colonial Sensibility* (Philadelphia: University of Pennsylvania Press, 2004).
4. For a thorough examination of the relationship between these two wars, see Fred Anderson, *Crucible of War: The Seven Years' War and the Fate of Empire in British North America, 1754–1766* (New York: Alfred A. Knopf, 2000).
5. While observing the funeral procession of Crispus Attucks, according to Byles's friend Nathaniel Emmons, Byles said, "'They call me a brainless Tory; but tell me, my young friend, which is better—to be ruled by one tyrant three thousand miles away, or by three thousand tyrants one mile away?'" Quoted in Arthur W. H. Eaton, *The Famous Mather Byles* (1914; Boston: Gregg Press, 1972), 146.

6. See Jay Fliegelman, *Prodigals and Pilgrims: The American Revolution against Patriarchal Authority* (Cambridge: Cambridge University Press, 1982.)

7. For a life of Tarleton, see Robert D. Bass, *The Green Dragoon: The Lives of Banastre Tarleton and Mary Robinson* (New York: Henry Holt and Co., 1957).

8. In the case of the church burning, the film is particularly unfair to Tarleton's memory. At least one church burning did occur during Cornwallis's campaign in the South, when British troops burned a Presbyterian church at Indian Town, North Carolina. The church, however, was empty, and the culprit was not Tarleton but Major James Wemyss, whose use of terror tactics against civilians became notorious. See John Buchanan, *The Road to Guilford Courthouse: The American Revolution in the Carolinas* (New York: Wiley, 1997), 185.

9. Eola Willis, *The Charleston Stage in the XVIII Century* (Columbia, S.C.: The State Company, 1924), 59–77.

10. Garry Wills, *Cincinnatus: Washington and the Enlightenment* (New York: Doubleday, 1984), 136–37.

11. See, for instance, Gustafson. See also Bruce McConachie, "American Theatre in Context, from the Beginnings to 1870," in *The Cambridge History of American Theatre*, ed. Don B. Wilmeth and Christopher Bigsby, vol. 1 of 3 (Cambridge: Cambridge University Press, 1998), 111–81; Christopher Grasso, *A Speaking Aristocracy: Transforming Public Discourse in Eighteenth-Century Connecticut* (Chapel Hill: University of North Carolina Press, 1999); William Pencak et al., eds., *Riot and Revelry in Early America* (University Park: Pennsylvania State University Press, 2002).

12. See Gillian Russell, *Theatres of War: Performance, Politics, and Society, 1793–1815* (Oxford: Clarendon Press, 1995). For a good account of Morgan's tactics at the Cowpens, see Lawrence E. Babitz, *A Devil of a Whipping: The Battle of Cowpens* (Chapel Hill: University of North Carolina, 1998), 61–99.

13. Benedict Anderson, *Imagined Communities* (London: Verso, 1983), 58.

14. For the influence of the "Country party" opposition on colonial politics, see Bernard Bailyn, *The Origins of American Politics* (New York: Alfred. A. Knopf, 1970), 35–37.

Chapter 1

1. For two recent samples of such work being done by a variety of scholars in different but interrelated fields ranging from the colonial era to the late twentieth century, see Wilmeth and Bigsby; and Jeffrey D. Mason and J. Ellen Gainor, eds., *Performing America* (Ann Arbor: University of Michigan Press, 1999).

2. For work centering on the nineteenth-century American theater, see Lawrence W. Levine, *Highbrow/Lowbrow: The Emergence of Cultural Hierarchy in America* (Cambridge, Mass.: Harvard University Press, 1988); Rosemarie K. Bank, *Theatre Culture in America, 1825–1860* (Cambridge: Cambridge University Press, 1997); and Alan L. Ackerman Jr., *The Portable Theatre: American Literature and the Nineteenth Century Stage* (Baltimore: Johns Hopkins University Press, 1999). For early republican and colonial works, see S. E. Wilmer, *Theatre, Society, and the Nation: Staging American Identities* (Cambridge: Cambridge University Press, 2002), 1–79; Heather S. Nathans, *Early American Theatre from the Revolution to Thomas Jefferson: Into the Hands of the People* (Cambridge: Cambridge University Press, 2003); Jeffrey H. Richards, *Drama, Theatre, and Identity in the American New Republic* (Cambridge: Cambridge University Press, 2005); and Odai Johnson, *Absence and Memory in Colonial American Theatre: Fiorelli's Plaster* (New York: Palgrave Macmillan, 2006).

Unfortunately, I was not able to consult Odai Johnson's book in the preparation of this manuscript. I have, however, consulted a number of his recent articles: "'God Prevent It Ever Being Established': The Campaign against Theatre in Colonial Boston Newspapers," *New England Theatre Journal* 10 (1999): 13–25; "Thomas Jefferson and the Colonial American Stage," *Virginia Magazine of History and Biography* 108.2 (2004): 139–54; "New Evidence of Early Actors in New York," *Theatre Notebook* 58 (2004): 3–6; and "Working up from Postholes: (Im)material Witnesses, Evidence, and Narrativity in the Colonial American Theatre," *Theatre Survey* 46.2 (November 2005): 183–98. For a useful account of theater censorship with a great deal of primary source documentation, see George B. Bryan, *American Theatrical Regulation, 1607–1900* (Metuchen, N.J.: Scarecrow Press, 1993). Also of enormous importance to anyone working on the performing arts in colonial culture is the CD-ROM database *The Performing Arts in Colonial American Newspapers, 1690–1783*, comp. Mary Jane Corry, Kate Van Winkle Keller, and Robert M. Keller (New York: University Music Editions, 1997). The access that this tool provides to a wide range of colonial newspapers had a transformative effect on my research for this project.

3. Jeffrey H. Richards, *Theater Enough: American Culture and the Metaphor of the World Stage, 1607–1789* (Durham, N.C.: Duke University Press, 1991), 244.

4. Jean-Christophe Agnew, *Worlds Apart: The Market and the Theater in Anglo-American Thought, 1550–1750* (Cambridge: Cambridge University Press, 1986), 150, 151.

5. Wilson, *Island Race*, 163. For further considerations of the theater's connections to colonial trade with Britain, see Peter A. Davis, "Puritan Mercantilism and the Politics of Anti-Theatrical Legislation in Colonial America," in *The American Stage: Social and Economic Issues from the Colonial Period to the Present*, ed. Ron Engle and Tice L. Miller (Cambridge: Cambridge University Press, 1993), 18–29; and Davis, "Plays and Playwrights to 1800," in Wilmeth and Bigsby, 219–22.

6. Joseph Roach, *Cities of the Dead: Circum-Atlantic Performance* (New York: Columbia University Press, 1996), 5.

7. For the relative ease with which West Indians repatriated themselves to Britain, see Andrew Jackson O'Shaughnessy, *An Empire Divided: The American Revolution and the British Caribbean* (Philadelphia: University of Pennsylvania Press, 2000), 3–33. For the history of the "three judges," Whalley, Dixwell, and Goffe, in New Haven, see Ezra Stiles, *A History, of Three of the Judges of King Charles the First* (Hartford: Elisha Babcock, 1794). For a further meditation on the nature of early American identity and the theater, see Richards, *Drama*, 17–33.

8. See Roach, *Cities*, 2, 4–5.

9. For an example of recent work that refutes these amnesiac tendencies, see Woody Holton, *Forced Founders: Indians, Debtors, Slaves, and the Making of the American Revolution in Virginia* (Chapel Hill: University of North Carolina Press, 1999).

10. Jay Fliegelman, *Declaring Independence: Jefferson, Natural Language, and the Culture of Performance* (Stanford, Calif.: Stanford University Press, 1993), 2, 105. For other important works on oral performance in early American culture, see Christopher Looby, *Voicing America: Language, Literary Form, and the Origins of the United States* (Chicago: University of Chicago Press, 1996); and Gustafson, especially 140–99. Also useful is Karen Halttunen, *Confidence Men and Painted Women: A Study of Middle-Class Culture in America, 1830–70* (New Haven, Conn.: Yale University Press, 1982), which discusses the importance of charisma in the nineteenth-century public sphere.

11. David Waldstreicher, *In The Midst of Perpetual Fetes: The Making of American*

Nationalism, 1776–1820 (Chapel Hill: University of North Carolina Press, 1997), 17. See also Simon P. Newman, *Parades and the Politics of the Street: Festive Culture in the Early American Republic* (Philadelphia: University of Pennsylvania Press, 1997); and Peter Shaw, *American Patriots and the Rituals of Revolution* (Cambridge, Mass.: Harvard University Press, 1989).

12. Michael Warner, *The Letters of the Republic: Publication and the Public Sphere in Eighteenth-Century America* (Cambridge, Mass.: Harvard University Press, 1990), 3. Warner also acknowledges the racial, gender, and class limitations of colonial print culture (14–18).

13. See, for instance, John Loftis, *Comedy and Society from Congreve to Fielding* (Stanford, Calif.: Stanford University Press, 1959) and Loftis, *The Politics of Drama in Augustan England* (Oxford: Clarendon Press, 1963).

14. William Dunlap, *A History of the American Theatre and Anecdotes of the Principle Actors* (1833; New York: Burt Franklin, 1963), 55. Dunlap's history is very useful for studies of the theater after the American Revolution; as a professional manager and playwright, he experienced much of this history firsthand. For the pre-Revolutionary theater, however, Dunlap's research is often spotty and at times completely unreliable. Also, note that the volume cited is a reproduction of Dunlap's improved second edition. This quotation is not found in the 1832 first edition.

15. See Walter J. Meserve, *An Emerging Entertainment: The Drama of the American People to 1828* (Bloomington: Indiana University Press, 1977); and Gary A. Richardson, *American Drama from the Colonial Period through World War I: A Critical History* (New York: Twayne, 1993).

16. Johnson, "Working up from Postholes," 186.

17. Ibid.

18. Meserve and Richardson do briefly treat the tradition of collegiate performance, and their studies of the propaganda plays of the Revolutionary era as early "American" dramas are useful in understanding the role of theater in the growth of the patriot movement in America. These studies focus on the growth of American drama in the early republic and the nineteenth century, however, and necessarily curtail their treatment of the colonial and Revolutionary theater.

19. A small number of studies following this multimedia method have been undertaken. Fredric M. Litto's seminal article "Addison's *Cato* in the Colonies" explores the origins of Addison's play in British politics and its pervasive presence in early American print and performance culture. Jared Brown's *The Theater in America during the Revolution* examines propaganda plays from the American Revolution alongside wartime productions by military amateurs and professional actors. Julie K. Ellison's *Cato's Tears and the Making of Anglo-American Emotion* explores the development of early modern British codes of masculine public behavior through readings of a variety of transatlantic political, poetic, and dramatic texts. See Fredric M. Litto, "Addison's *Cato* in the Colonies," *William and Mary Quarterly*, 3rd ser., 23.3 (July 1966): 431–49; Jared Brown, *The Theater in America during the Revolution* (Cambridge: Cambridge University Press, 1995); Julie K. Ellison, *Cato's Tears and the Making of Anglo-American Emotion* (Chicago: University of Chicago Press, 1999).

20. Richards, *Theater*, 237.

21. Julie Stone Peters, *Theatre of the Book, 1488–1800: Print, Text, and Performance in Europe* (Oxford: Oxford University Press, 2000), 8, 61, 252.

22. Carl and Jessica Bridenbaugh, *Rebels and Gentlemen: Philadelphia in the Age of Franklin*, 2nd ed. (New York: Oxford University Press, 1942), 80.

23. For the widespread presence of foreign affairs correspondence in colonial newspapers, see Warner, *Letters*, 17–18. My argument here owes a debt to Kathleen Wilson's argument that global news in British newspapers contributed to a sense of national ownership of the colonies among readers in Great Britain. See Wilson, *The Sense of the People: Politics, Culture, and Imperialism in England, 1715–1815* (Cambridge: Cambridge University Press, 1998), 39–40.

24. Warner, *Letters*, 40. In creating this characterization of Warner's image of the print public sphere, I have drawn heavily on ibid., 39–49.

25. Wilson, *Sense of the People*, 123.

26. Annabel Patterson, *Early Modern Liberalism* (Cambridge: Cambridge University Press, 1997), 3.

27. Dunlap, *History*, 85–86. Emphasis in original. Lucy Rinehart notes a critical controversy over whether or not Dunlap was a Federalist sympathizer. See Rinehart, "'Manly Exercises': Post-Revolutionary Performances of Authority in the Theatrical Career of William Dunlap," *Early American Literature* 36.2 (2001): 289n. For more on Dunlap's belief in the republican potential of a national theater, see Nathans, 1.

28. Alexis de Tocqueville, *Democracy in America*, trans. George Lawrence and ed. J. P. Meyer (New York: Harper Perennial, 1988), 492.

29. Dunlap, *History*, 67.

30. De Tocqueville, 489.

31. See Isaac Kramnick, "The 'Great National Discussion': The Discourse of Politics in 1787," *William and Mary Quarterly*, 3rd ser., 45.1 (January 1998): 4–5.

32. Patterson, *Early Modern Liberalism*, 279–305; Joyce Appleby, *Liberalism and Republicanism in the Historical Imagination* (Cambridge, Mass.: Harvard University Press, 1992), 164, 184–85; Kramnick, "Great National Discussion," 4.

33. Ann Fairfax Withington, *Toward a More Perfect Union: Virtue and the Formation of American Republics* (New York: Oxford University Press, 1991), 20.

34. Jeremy Collier, *A Short View of the Immorality, and Profaneness of the English Stage, together with the Sense of Antiquity on this Argument* (London: S. Keble, 1698), 1, quoted in Jonas Barish, *The Antitheatrical Prejudice* (Berkeley: University of California Press, 1981), 222–23. For Barish's studies of puritan anti-theatricality, see 80–131 and 155–90.

35. George Farquhar, *The Works of the Late Ingenious Mr. George Farquhar* (London: J. Knapton, R. Smith, G. Strahan, and B. Lintott, 1713), 73.

36. *The Tatler*, ed. Donald F. Bond, 3 vols. (Oxford: Clarendon Press, 1987), 2:423.

37. *New York Gazette*, 7 December 1761, quoted in David D. Mays, "The Achievements of the Douglass Company in North America: 1758–1774," *Theatre Survey* 23.2 (November 1982): 143; *New York Journal*, 28 January 1768, quoted in Davis, "Puritan Mercantilism," 25.

38. Kramnick, "Great National Discussion," 16–21.

39. *Maryland Gazette* (Annapolis), 4 October 1770.

40. Thomas Jefferson, *The Papers of Thomas Jefferson*, ed. Julian P. Boyd, 29 vols. (Princeton, N.J.: Princeton University Press, 1955–2002), 12:356.

41. Kramnick makes a similar point about the difficulty of stopping a revolution before it eats its children. See Kramick, "Great National Discussion," 23, 31. J. G. A. Pocock in his seminal study of classical republicanism notes the importance of receding liberty to Country party ideology: "What may be termed the ideology of the country was founded on a presumption of real property and an ethos of civic life, in which the ego knew and loved itself in its relation to a *patria*,

respublica, or common good, organized as a polity, but was perpetually threatened by corruption operating through private appetites and false consciousness" (Pocock, *The Machiavellian Moment: Florentine Political Thought and the Atlantic Republican Tradition* [Princeton, N.J.: Princeton University Press, 1975], 486).

42. Rene Girard, *Violence and the Sacred*, trans. Patrick Gregory (1972; Baltimore: Johns Hopkins University Press, 1977), 255.

43. Roach, *Cities*, 36.

44. Witness, for instance, the swaggering bully-boy Herod of the medieval York Cycle, or Bottom's sublime bit of theatrical taxonomy in *A Midsummer Night's Dream*: "What is Pyramus, a lover, or a tyrant?" (1.2.17).

45. John Barrell, *Imagining the King's Death: Figures of Treason, Fantasies of Regicide, 1793–1796* (Oxford: Oxford University Press, 2000), 81.

46. Girard, 149.

47. Soame Jenyns, *The Objections to the Taxation of Our American Colonies, by the Legislature of Great Britain, Briefly Consider'd* (London: J. Wilkie, 1765), 9.

48. Rebecca Bushnell, *Tragedies of Tyrants: Political Thought and Theater in the English Renaissance* (Ithaca, N.Y.: Cornell University Press, 1990), 38. Bushnell's description of this type of tyrant illustrates the problem of untangling republican and liberal ideas. Property is central to Locke's individualist conception of rights, but the tyrant's typical deprivation of not just one of his subjects, but "his people," of property suggests the collective public of classical republicanism.

49. The equation of the person of the tyrant with the state itself in this argument, whereby the elimination of the tyrant liberates the entire society, has strong symbolic associations with the doctrine of the "King's two bodies." See Ernst Kantorowicz, *The King's Two Bodies: A Study in Mediaeval Political Theory* (Princeton, N.J.: Princeton University Press, 1957).

50. Bushnell, 4. See also Michel Foucault, *Discipline and Punish: The Birth of the Prison*, trans. Alan Sheridan (1975; New York: Vintage, 1995), 29.

51. Patterson, *Early Modern Liberalism*, 152. Emphasis mine.

52. Alan Craig Houston, *Algernon Sidney and the Republican Heritage in England and America* (Princeton, N.J.: Princeton University Press, 1991), 224. See also Patterson, *Early Modern Liberalism*, 152n.

53. Roach, *Cities*, 122.

54. Ruth Bloch, *Gender and Morality in Anglo-American Culture* (Berkeley: University of California Press, 2003), 140–42; Appleby, 29. For an intriguing account of how this discourse extended to the person of the "stage virgin" Anne Oldfield on the London stage, see James Peck, "'Albion's Chaste Lucrece': Chastity, Resistance, and the Glorious Revolution in the Career of Anne Bracegirdle," *Theatre Survey* 45.1 (May 2004): 89–113.

55. For a detailed exploration of the implications of these paternal analogies, see Fliegelman, *Prodigals*.

56. Shaw, 52.

57. Timothy Hampton, *Writing from History: The Rhetoric of Exemplarity in Renaissance Literature* (Ithaca, N.Y.: Cornell University Press, 1990), 222. Jonathan Goldberg also usefully points out the importance of theatricality to political charismatics such as tyrants and patriots, a point exemplified by Shakespeare's Julius Caesar in his public rejection of a crown: "Between his infirm body and the crown he desires, Caesar constructs a performance in which his body can be owned or disowned, in which his deeds are countenanced or discountenanced, in which he is present and absent in his actions and words . . . The language of state, we know, is not a cover. The show that Caesar puts on manifests power"

(Goldberg, *James I and the Politics of Literature: Jonson, Shakespeare, Donne, and Their Contemporaries* [Baltimore: Johns Hopkins University Press, 1983], 174).

58. Gustafson, 135.

59. Ibid., 145.

60. Adams, *Diary and Autobiography of John Adams*, ed. L. H. Butterfield, 3 vols. (Cambridge, Mass.: Belknap Press, 1967), 1:200–201. See also Shaw, 58. The reversibility of the patriot and the tyrant was not always salutary for liberty. On 13 August 1776, just weeks after the publication of the Declaration of Independence, Thomas Jefferson wrote in a letter to Edmund Pendelton, "Remember how universally the people ran into the idea of recalling Charles II after living many years under a Republican government?" (Jefferson, 1:492).

61. Newman, 37.

62. As Pocock observes, the Atlantic tradition of classical republicanism chose Brutus as its hero in recognition of "the fact of the republic's mortality." See Pocock, 53.

63. Cathy N. Davidson, *The Revolution and the Word: The Rise of the Novel in America* (New York: Oxford University Press, 1986), 39.

64. The first study of Washington's relationship to the theater is Paul Leicester Ford, *Washington and the Theatre* (New York: Dunlap Society, 1899). The best recent work on the subject is Paul K. Longmore's insightful *The Invention of George Washington* (Berkeley: University of California Press, 1988).

65. Ford, 5–7.

66. Goldberg, 57; Wilson, *Island Race*, 35. Goldberg argues, "The King observes, and is observed; as much as the masquers themselves, he is onstage."

67. Longmore, 80.

68. Gustafson, 223–27. For Washington's embodiment of the post-Revolutionary republic, see Gustafson's chapter "Forms of State" (200–232), with which my own analysis shares a number of key points.

69. Ezra Stiles, *The Literary Diary of Ezra Stiles*, ed. Franklin Bowditch Dexter, 3 vols. (New York: Charles Scribner's Sons, 1901), 1:485. See also Longmore, 139; and Gustafson, 215.

70. *The Crisis*, 9 March 1776; 6 April 1776. The paper's 25 February 1775 issue also features an extended parody comparing Lord North to Richard III. See also Jonathan Bate, *Shakespearean Constitutions: Politics, Theatre, Criticism, 1730–1830* (Oxford: Clarendon Press, 1989), 110–11.

71. Newman, 37. See also Gustafson, 215.

72. Benjamin Rush to Thomas Ruston, 29 October 1775, in Rush, *Letters of Benjamin Rush*, ed. Lyman H. Butterfield, 2 vols. (Princeton, N.J.: Princeton University Press, 1951), 1:92. See also Longmore, 182.

73. See John H. Hazelton, *The Declaration of Independence: Its History* (1906; reprint, New York: Da Capo Press, 1970), 251–80. See also A. J. Wall, "The Statues of King George and the Honourable William Pitt Erected in New York City, 1770," *New York Historical Society Quarterly* 4 (1920): 36–57; and Winthrop D. Jordan, "Familial Politics: Thomas Paine and the Killing of the King, 1776," *Journal of American History* 60.2 (September 1973): 294–308.

74. Newman, 37; Fliegelman, *Prodigals*, 200; Longmore, 192, 200–201. See also *Kentucky Gazette*, 5 July 1788; *Virginia Gazette*, 19 February 1779, 26 February 1779; and Friederike Charlotte Luise Riedesel, *Letters and Journals Relating to the War of the American Revolution, And the Capture of the German Troops at Saratoga*, trans. William L. Stone (Albany: J. Munsell, 1867), 165. Fliegelman also notes that during 1778, the same year that Washington received the designation of "Father of his

Country," a Boston printer produced an edition of Daniel Defoe's satire on the amalgamated English racial identity, "The True-Born Englishman" (*Prodigals*, 78). For more on the colonial appropriation of ceremonies dedicated to the monarchy, see Waldstreicher, 43–44.

75. Girard, 12, 107.

Chapter 2

1. James Staunton Babcock, *Memoir of Captain Nathan Hale* (New Haven, Conn.: S. Babcock, 1844), 12. While the account of Hale's death is incomplete, several biographies documenting the life of the young soldier do exist, of which Babcock's is the first, and possibly the best. Also indispensable is George Dudley Seymour's *Documentary Life of Nathan Hale* (New Haven, Conn.: private printing, 1941), which reprints the known documents related to Hale's life, thereby providing a means for verifying Babcock's account and a useful corrective to the enthusiasm of Hale biographers. As a genre Hale biographies, mainly published in New Haven, follow Babcock's lead by tending toward fulsome sentimentality and incorporating paeans to the undying glory of Yale University into their historical narratives. For typical examples of such Hale hagiography, see Henry Phelps Johnson, *Nathan Hale, 1776* (New Haven, Conn.: Yale University Press, 1914) and Artemus Jean Haynes, *The Story of Nathan Hale* (New Haven, Conn.: n.p., 1907).

2. William Hull, *Revolutionary Services And Civil Life of General William Hull; Prepared From his Manuscripts, by his Daughter, Mrs. Maria Campbell: Together with the History of the Campaign of 1812, And Surrender of the Post of Detroit, by his Grandson, James Freeman Clarke* (New York: D. Appleton and Co., 1848), 35. Hull's is the principal account of Hale's execution, at the time of which he, like Hale, held the rank of captain. Part, though not all, of his account is also reprinted in Seymour, 307–10.

3. Hull, 38. See also Seymour, 310. Another British witness to Hale's execution, Lieutenant Frederick Mackenzie, also praises Hale's "great composure and resolution" before the gallows (Seymour, 292).

4. Hull, 38. Seymour does not reproduce the passage related to the destruction of Hale's letters. Hull's account claims that one letter was intended for Hale's mother, but she predeceased her son, and evidence from the diary of Hale's brother Enoch, as related to him by another captive American officer and schoolmate of the Hale brothers, Jack Wyllys [*sic*], confirms that the letter was intended for Enoch. See Seymour, 298, 452–53.

5. Hull, 38; Seymour, 310.

6. See Foucault, 3–72. See also Agnew, 145.

7. Seymour, 27–28. The lines quoted are 4.4.181–82. See Joseph Addison, *Cato* (London: Jacob Tonson, 1713), 1:335–420. All quotations from Addison's play are taken from this edition.

8. Sarah J. Purcell, *Sealed with Blood: War, Sacrifice, and Memory in Revolutionary America* (Philadelphia: University of Pennsylvania Press, 2002), 21.

9. *Kentish Gazette* (Canterbury), 6–9 November 1776, reprinted in Seymour, 302.

10. These works are also referenced in my earlier discussion of what scholars of early American theater history should attempt to accomplish as the field evolves.

11. Meserve, 25. See also Litto, 435.

12. *Catalogue of Books in the Linonian and Brothers' Libraries* (New Haven, Conn.: Oliver Steele, 1808); Thomas Clap, *A Catalogue of Yale College in New Haven* (New London, Conn.: T. Green, 1743). The Linonian collection included Addison's collected *Works* and also the collected works of Shakespeare and Wycherley. The more extensive college library, while it contained only *Cato* instead of Addison's *Works*, included not only Shakespeare and Wycherley but also the plays of Steele, Thomas Otway, and Nicholas Rowe. While it did not possess Addison as early as the library at Yale, Harvard's library possessed copies of Shakespeare's works as early as 1723. See *Catalogues Librorum Bibliothechae Collegii Harvardini Quod est Cantabrigiae in Nova Anglia* (Boston: B. Green, 1723), A95; and Meserve, 25.

13. Gordon S. Wood, *The Radicalism of the American Revolution* (New York: Alfred A. Knopf, 1992), 101. For the connections between Roman republican dramas in Britain and the advent of Whig politics, see Ellison, 23–73.

14. Lisa A. Freeman, "What's Love Got to Do with Addison's *Cato?*" *Studies in English Literature* 39 (1999): 464; Cheryl Z. Oreovicz, "Heroic Drama for an Uncertain Age: The Plays of Mercy Warren," in *Early Literature and American Culture: Essays Honoring Harrison T. Meserole*, ed. Kathryn Zabelle Derounian-Stodola (Newark: University of Delaware Press, 1992), 197.

15. Linda Colley, *Britons: Forging the Nation, 1707–1837* (New Haven, Conn.: Yale University Press, 1992), 5.

16. Loftis, 59. For Pope's prologue, see Pope, "Prologue to Mr. Addison's *Cato*," in *The Poems of Alexander Pope*, vol. 6, *Minor Poems*, ed. Norman Ault and John Butt (New Haven, Conn.: Yale University Press, 1954), 96–98.

17. Samuel Johnson, *The Lives of the Most Eminent English Poets*, 4 vols. (London: C. Bathurst et al., 1783), 2:348. See also Litto, 435.

18. Bailyn, *The Ideological Origins of the American Revolution* (Cambridge, Mass.: Belknap Press, 1967), 21. Bailyn notes that John Adams would declaim Cicero's orations "aloud, alone at night in his room," a clear instance of a crossover between New England's culture of the book and its oral culture.

19. [Anon.], *English Advice to the Freeholders &c. of the Province of Massachusetts Bay* (Boston: James Franklin, 1722), 3–4; Warner, *Letters*, 64, 76.

20. *New York Weekly Journal*, 28 January 1733. The passage echoes this comment from Trenchard and Gordon: "A Tory under Oppression, or out of Place, is a Whig; a Whig with Power to oppress, is a Tory." See Trenchard and Gordon, *Cato's Letters*, ed. Ronald Hamowy, 4 vols. in 2 (Indianapolis: Liberty Fund, 1995), 2:687. For the lines in Addison, see *Cato*, 1.3.44–45. The *Journal* issue was actually published in 1734. For Cosby's connections with Walpole, see Nathans, 29.

21. Ellison, 17.

22. Bailyn, *Ideological Origins*, 44.

23. Wood, 15. The increasing exertions of royal prerogative that marked George III's relationship with the North American colonies, of course, came to mar this idealized image.

24. *The London Magazine* January 1749, 37, quoted in Albert Furtwangler, "Cato at Valley Forge," in Furtwangler, *American Silhouettes: Rhetorical Identities of the Founding Fathers* (New Haven, Conn.: Yale University Press, 1987), 40. Furtwangler's essay also appears, though without the quotation from *The London Magazine*, in *Modern Language Quarterly* 41 (1980): 38–53. *The London Magazine* reproduces the entire extended prologue and epilogue, which are in fact small comic scenes that involve not only young George but also his siblings. *The London Magazine* reprints not only George's entire prologue but also an extended epilogue between two of his sisters and a long address from Cato to Portius added to the play.

25. *The London Magazine*, February 1749, 93.
26. Addison, *Cato*, 1.1.4–6.
27. Given Addison's status as one of the first great critical interpreters of Milton, it is worth considering the similarities between the empty rhetoric employed by Sempronius in this scene and the nihilism of Moloch in the Council of Demons section of *Paradise Lost* (2.51–105).
28. Ellison, 52.
29. Quoted in Moses Coit Tyler, *The Literary History of the American Revolution*, 2 vols. (New York: G. P. Putnam's Sons, 1897), 2:185.
30. Seymour, recognizing Hale's dying allusion to *Cato*, suggests that Hale's participation in the Linonian Society's debates might have helped to develop the self-control that he needed on the scaffold, although sadly he does not mention Hale's experience as an actor in the society's theatricals.
31. Ellison, 69.
32. Purcell, 21.
33. Babcock, 14. Babcock also connects Hale with a group of such martyrs that is, to say the least, diverse, including the Roman Horatii, Joan of Arc, William Wallace, and the English republicans Hampden, Sidney, and Russell.
34. The statue at Yale University is located on the Old Campus, near Connecticut Hall, the only surviving building from Hale's years in New Haven. The statue is also located very close the Department of English, a coincidence that provided considerable food for thought during the planning stages of this book. Based on my own empirical observations, Hale's statue is the only sculpture on campus that visitors can readily identify without first reading the inscription. The statue was installed in 1914 as a gift from the alumni of the university.
35. My thanks to Sandra Rux, formerly of the Hale Homestead in Coventry, for clarifying the history of the Federal Triangle statue of Hale.
36. George D. Vaill, "Only One Life, But Three Hangings," *American Heritage Magazine* 24.5 (August 1973); available at www.americanheritage.com.
37. I am here using Roach's definition of performance as "repetition with revision," a careful balance of preservation and improvisation. See Roach, *Cities*, 28–30.
38. *Boston Gazette*, 14 September 1760, quoted in David Shields, *Oracles of Empire: Poetry, Politics, and Commerce in British America, 1690–1750* (Chicago: University of Chicago Press, 1990), 104–5.
39. Robert E. Moody, "Boston's First Play," *Proceedings of the Massachusetts Historical Society* 92 (1980): 117–39. See also Shields, *Oracles*, 104–9.
40. *New York Gazette*, 2 November 1730, quoted in Shields, *Oracles*, 105. Shields observes that the poem achieved considerably notoriety: it was copied into commonplace books and widely parodied.
41. The play's epilogue displays a similar concern with the status of New England as a stronghold for the defense of retreating liberty, closing with the lines "since we crost the vast Atlantick Sea, / With all [Belcher's] art we will not baffled be, / But Roman like preserve our Libertie" (Robert Moody, 139).
42. Johnson and Burling, 109–21. See also Rankin, 24–7; Odell, 20; *Virginia Gazette*, 10 September 1736; Willis, 29–30, 36; and Litto, 435–36.
43. See *New York Weekly Journal*, 25 February 1733, 4 and 11 March 1733, and 12 November 1734. For the stage history of this performance, see Nathans, 29–30; and Johnson and Burling, 108. For more on the Zenger case, see Warner, *Letters*, 49–56.
44. Kenneth A. Lockridge notes that Gooch was popular in Virginia at least in

part because he was generally content to let the colonials handle the business of governance. See Lockridge, *The Diary, and Life, of William Byrd II of Virginia, 1674–1744* (Chapel Hill: University of North Carolina Press, 1987), 125–26.

45. *South Carolina Gazette*, 1 February 1735, quoted in Rankin, 26. See also Willis, 14; and Johnson and Burling, 114.

46. *South Carolina Gazette*, 5 September 1743, quoted in Willis, 29–30.

47. For the Harvard performances and Ames's comment on Newport, see Albert Matthews, "Early Plays at Harvard," *The Nation* 98 (19 March 1914): 295. The Harvard performances took place between 1758 and 1760. For the 1750 Boston performance, see Johnson and Burling, 134–36; and Johnson, "God Prevent," 20. For the Providence season, see Johnson and Burling, 227–29.

48. Adams, *Diary and Autobiography*, 3:262–63.

49. Adams, *The Life and Works of John Adams, Second President of the United States*, ed. Charles Francis Adams, 10 vols. (Boston: Charles C. Little and James Brown, 1851), 3:457–58.

50. Patterson, *Early Modern Liberalism*, 283.

51. Adams, *Works*, 3:456.

52. Addison, *Cato*, 4.4.34–35.

53. Adams, *Works*, 3:461–62.

54. Pauline Maier, *From Resistance to Revolution: Colonial Radicals and the Development of American Opposition to Britain, 1765–1776* (New York: Alfred A. Knopf, 1972), 88–91. See also James S. and Helen M. Morgan, *The Stamp Act Crisis: Prologue to Revolution* (Chapel Hill: University of North Carolina Press, 1953), 157.

55. *New Hampshire Gazette* (Portsmouth), 30 August 1775, 31 October 1765. The lines from Addison are 1.1.3–4. The *Gazette* dates its excerpt from Trenchard and Gordon as 21 April 1722.

56. Morgan, 225.

57. *Boston Gazette, and Country Journal*, 30 December 1765. See also William R. Nester, *The First Global War: Britain, France, and the Fate of North America, 1756–1775* (Westport, Conn: Praeger, 2000), 248.

58. This text is also partially reproduced in Silverman, 81.

59. Newman, 25; Withington, 154.

60. For more on the relationship between inanimate and performed effigies, see Roach, *Cities*, 36–39. The most thorough available account of the mock funeral protests against the Stamp Act is Withington, 144–85. My own account draws heavily on these pages. For the protests in St. Kitt's and St. Nevis, see O'Shaughnessy, 89.

61. Withington, 167, 104–6; *Boston Gazette*, 11 November 1765. Withington observes that New England funerals, already designed as communal performances, became a way of performing patriotism under the austerity rules: "It was impossible to avoid making a public statement. Frugal funerals offered proof of political purity, and each frugal funeral increased the membership of the politically pure" (104). For the evolution and specifics of these regulations on funerals, see Withington, 95–99.

62. Withington, 145–49; Shaw, 179–82; Morgan, 201.

63. Addison, *Cato*, 1.1.3–4.

64. *Boston Gazette, and Country Journal*, 11 November 1765; *Newport Mercury*, 4 November 1765. This text is partially reprinted in Silverman, 79.

65. *Newport Mercury, Supplement*, 28 October 1765, quoted in Maier, 70.

66. *Massachusetts Spy* (Worcester), 13 December 1770. The *Boston Gazette* ran a parody of Pope's prologue in 1756 in praise of the mechanical microcosm being displayed by one Mr. Bridges. See *Boston Gazette, and Country Journal*, 26 April 1756.

67. Chester Noyes Greenough, "New England Almanacs, 1766–75, and the American Revolution," *Proceedings of the American Antiquarian Society* 45 (1935): 307, quoted in Litto, 443.

68. Silverman, 211. Silverman quotes an anonymous poem read aloud at the first anniversary commemoration of the Massacre in 1771. Gustafson suggests that the Boston Massacre orations established the political hegemony of radical orators in New England (186).

69. Richards, *Theater*, 215.

70. Litto, 446; *Cato*, 3.5.79–81.

71. Warren, *The Adulateur* (Boston: "Printed and sold at the new Printing Office, near Concert Hall," 1773), 1; *Cato*, 2.3.34–38.

72. *Adams Family Correspondence*, ed. L. H. Butterfield and Marc Friedlander, 4 vols. (Cambridge, Mass.: Belknap Press, 1973), 1:88, quoted in Richards, *Theater*, 239.

73. *Pennsylvania Evening Post* (Philadelphia), 14 September 1775. The *Post* labels the poem as a "PROLOGUE spoken by a Great personage before the tragedy of Cato, in the year 1749, when he performed the part of Portius." See also Johnson and Burling, 129. Johnson and Burling, the only other scholars to note this printing, suggest that perhaps the prologue originates with the 1749 performance of *Cato* in Philadelphia by Murray and Kean's troupe. A comparison with the *London Magazine* version of Prince George's prologue shows that the texts are identical, however.

74. *Georgia Gazette*, 6 December 1775. The letter quotes Addison, *Cato*, 3.5.74–81.

75. Gustafson, 158. For the evolution of popular oratory in Virginia, see Gustafson, 14, 159–61. For other considerations of the oral/dramatic model of Virginia culture, see Rhys Isaac, *The Transformation of Virginia, 1740–1790* (Chapel Hill: University of North Carolina Press, 1982), 242–60, 323–57.

76. William Wirt, *Sketches of The Life and Character of Patrick Henry* (Philadelphia: DeSilver and Thomas, 1836), 141–42.

77. Gustafson, 164. Randolph also compares Henry's charismatic oratory to that of the elder Pitt. See Gustafson, 163.

78. Wirt, 149. See also Litto, 444–45. Gustafson argues that this speech had a transformative effect on Revolutionary politics, creating a "mimetic dynamic to produce an expansive national identity figured as voice" (165).

79. Addison, *Cato*, 2.4.79–80.

80. Ibid., 2.1.23–25.

81. Ellison, 69. Litto observes both Henry's indebtedness to *Cato* and the duality of the allusion, although he offers little in the way of commentary on the significance of the allusion. See Litto, 444–45. Lloyd J. Matthews offers an alternative source text for Henry's declaration in *Julius Caesar*, 1.2.13–17, which Shaw tentatively endorses. See Lloyd J. Matthews, "Patrick Henry's 'Liberty or Death' Speech and Cassius's Speech in Shakespeare's *Julius Caesar*," *Virginia Magazine of History and Biography* 86 (1978): 299–305; and Shaw, 57.

82. Fliegelman, *Declaring Independence*, 28–34, 123.

83. Addison, *Cato*, 1.4.42.

84. Adams, *Diary and Autobiography*, 1:222. For other considerations of the unease generated by this new popular oratory, especially as it relates to the figure of Henry himself, see Gustafson, 145–49, 158–63.

85. Adams, *Papers of John Adams*, ed. Robert J. Taylor et al., 10 vols. (Cambridge, Mass.: Belknap Press, 1977–89), 2:59.

86. Trenchard and Gordon, 2:687. See also H. Trevor Colbourn, *The Lamp of*

Experience: Whig History and the Intellectual Origins of the American Revolution (Chapel Hill: University of North Carolina Press, 1965), 49.

87. Gustafson, 145.

88. *Maryland Gazette*, 17 September 1772; *Henry VI, Part 2*, 4.7.11–13.

89. Jonathan Boucher, *A View of the Causes and Consequences of the American Revolution* (1797; reprint, New York: Russell and Russell, 1967), 321. Emphasis mine. In an undelivered 1773 speech called "On American Education," Boucher argues that teaching the study or oratory is dangerous in a monarchy, since "along with their rules and modes of speaking, we sometimes adopt the sentiments and principles of our great masters in the art, who were republicans, that orators are in general adverse to government. If I am not much mistaken, I have not infrequently heard speeches replete with sedition, whilst yet the speaker had no serious ill-will nor mischievous intention against government, nor any other aim than the credit of making a popular harangue" (198).

90. Arthur M. Schlesinger, *Prelude to Independence: The Newspaper War on Britain, 1764–76* (Boston: Northeastern University Press, 1980), 142, quoted in Fliegelman, *Declaring Independence*, 123.

91. Rankin, 178–79; [Myles Cooper], *The Patriots of North America* (New York: J. Rivington, 1775), 3; James Thomas Flexner, *The Young Alexander Hamilton* (Boston: Little, Brown, and Company, 1978), 78–80. David W. Robson disputes the claim that Cooper wrote *The Patriots*, or any other loyalist pamphlet. See Robson, *Educating Republicans: The College in the Era of the American Revolution, 1750–1800* (Westport, Conn: Greenwood Press, 1985), 40.

92. Addison, *Cato*, 2.1.81.

93. Wirt, 83. Emphasis in original.

94. Addison, *Cato*, 2.1.30–31.

95. Quoted in Gustafson, 168–69.

96. Gustafson, 169. See also Fliegelman, *Declaring Independence*, 104.

97. Newman, 37.

98. Longmore, 11.

99. See Gustafson, 223–28. Gustafson maintains that "his self-effacing persona allowed him to resolve the contradictions of republican authority, at least temporarily" (225).

100. To Governor Jonathan Trumbull, 18 July 1775, in *Papers of George Washington, Revolutionary Series*, ed. Philander D. Chase, 12 vols. (Charlottesville: University of Virginia Press, 1985–2001), 1:131, 132, quoted in Longmore, 188. Lines quoted are *Cato*, 4.4.141–42.

101. *The Papers of George Washington, Revolutionary Series*, 1:458, 2:493–94. See Addison, *Cato*, 1.3.44–45. Wills cites two lines as particular favorites of Washington's, "And shows thee in the fairest point of light" (1.2.34) and "In the calm light of mild philosophy" (1.1.14). See Wills, 133–34. Ford concurs with Longmore in naming these passages as personal favorites of Washington's. See Ford, 1–2. Litto also notes Washington's citation of these passages in personal letters but does not provide their epistolary particulars. See Litto, 442.

102. Brown, 45–56. See also Winthrop D. Sargent, *The Life and Career of Major John Andre* (Boston: Ticknor and Fields, 1861), 152–81; and Randall Fuller, "Theatres of the American Revolution," *Early American Literature* 34 (1999): 137–42.

103. Quoted in Richards, *Theater*, 251–52.

104. Gustafson, 215.

105. Brown, 58–59. A number of other sources discuss the Valley Forge *Cato*.

See Ford, 25–26; Litto, 147; and Fuller, 128–37. The only full-length article exclusively devoted to this performance is Furtwangler.

106. Quoted in Ford, 25–26.

107. Addison, *Cato*, 3.5.25–27.

108. Ibid., 1.4.54–58.

109. While Valley Forge certainly did not fall at the beginning of the war or qualify as a training camp, the potential staging of *The Recruiting Officer* reminds me of an observation made by Paul Fussell: "Modern mass wars require in their early stages a definitive work of popular literature demonstrating how much wholesome fun is to be had at the training camp" (Fussell, *The Great War and Modern Memory* [London: Oxford University Press, 1975], 28).

110. Addison, *Cato*, 5.4.55–59.

111. Gillian Russell, *The Theatres of War: Performance, Politics, and Society, 1793–1815* (Oxford: Clarendon Press, 1995), 28–29. For an account of the evacuation of Philadelphia featuring excerpts from the orders issued to Sir Henry Clinton, see Sargent, 182–86.

112. Litto, 447.

113. Jonathan M. Sewall, "Epilogue to Cato," in *Occasional Addresses*, ed. Laurence Hutton and William Carey (New York: Dunlap Society, 1890), 4–6. See also Brown, 65–66; and Purcell, 35–36.

114. For the newspaper reprintings, see *New Hampshire Gazette*, 31 March 1778; *Connecticut Courant*, 14 April 1778; *Massachusetts Spy* (Worcester), 16 April 1778; and *Continental Journal* (Boston): 30 April 1778. Fliegelman observes that the epilogue was reproduced in "four of the five" editions printed in the United States between 1778 and the turn of the century but does not specify which editions included the epilogue. See Fliegelman, *Prodigals*, 153. Curiously, the epilogue was not reproduced in an edition of *Cato* printed in Philadelphia in 1786.

115. Emphasis mine.

116. Johnson and Burling, 276.

117. See James Thomson, *Coriolanus* (London: Andrew Millar, 1749). Thomson had finished the play by 1747, but it was not staged until 1749 due to a casting dispute between Thomson and David Garrick. Also, it should be noted that on 2 June 1775 an essay by "Coriolanus" that denounced British soldiers as ravishing brutes ran in the *Providence Gazette*. See Kim C. Sturgess, *Shakespeare and the American Nation* (Cambridge: Cambridge University Press, 2004), 27. For evidence that the character of Coriolanus also seemed to have a decidedly loyalist image in the public imagination during the Revolution, see *Continental Journal* (Boston), 19 September 1776.

118. Jonathan Mitchell Sewall, *Miscellaneous Poems* (Portsmouth, N.H.: William Treadwell, 1801), 123. See also Brown, 66.

Chapter 3

1. *Virginia Gazette*, 22 September 1752, quoted in Arthur Hornblow, *A History of the Theatre in America from Its Beginnings to the Present Time*, 2 vols. (Philadelphia: J. B. Lippincott, 1919), 1:85–86. See also Odell, 53–54. Hornblow and Odell reprint the prologue in its entirety. Rankin reproduces only part of the text, while Dunlap and Seilhamer each reproduce an incorrect prologue.

2. See Wilson, *Island Race*, 166.

3. Barish sees this change taking place in Britain as a rhetorical shift among

anti-theatrical partisans during the long eighteenth century away from the concerns of Britain's "antimonarchical lunatic fringe" and toward those of "the conservative, royalist wing of the clergy" in the tradition of Collier's *Short View*, a shift, in other words, from an ontological to a civic criticism of theater and theatricality (222).

4. *A Sure Guide to Hell, by Belzebub* (London: "printed for Peter Imp," 1750), 33, 62. The pamphlet was first printed in the American colonies in a 1751 edition in Boston and remained a strong seller in New York as late as 1767. See Rankin, 119.

5. Mays, 146.

6. *Universal Spectator, and Weekly Journal*, 10 April 1731. See also Loftis, *Politics*, 82. The lines from Dryden are *Absalom and Achitophel*, 55–56. The passage also echoes Hobbes's critique of classical learning as a source of rebellion in *Leviathan*, 2.29. Hobbes argues that monarchs would do well to regulate the reading of Greek and Roman histories and books of political theory, since after encountering these books sometimes "they that live under a Monarch conceive an opinion, that subjects in a popular Commonwealth enjoy Liberty; but that in a Monarchy they are all Slaves." Hobbes then infers that the influence of such "democratic" writers, by inducing the citizenry to demand greater governmental accountability and more freedom from legal restraints on their behavior, reduces the social order to such a state of chaos that, ironically, "[the Commonwealth] wanteth nothing more than a strong monarch." See Hobbes, *Leviathan*, ed. Edwin Curley (Indianapolis: Hackett Publishing, 1994), 215.

7. Consider one of Davis's more sweeping claims from his earlier work, in which he maintains that by the 1770s "theatre had come to represent all that the rebellious colonists despised" ("Puritan Mercantilism," 26). In a more recent essay in *The Cambridge History of American Theatre*, Davis follows Richards and others by noting "the extent to which theatre and dramatic terminology . . . influenced the colonial mind," which prompts him to revise his earlier statements somewhat by arguing that describing even the descendants of the Puritans in New England as "inherently against theatre degrades the conflict to reductivist simplicity" and "ignores the extensive and complex reasons" for colonial hostility to the theater ("Plays and Playwrights," 220). Unfortunately, the strictures of Davis's topic, dramas composed by "native born" Americans, limit his ability to discuss the more widespread and politically influential circulation of British plays throughout colonial and Revolutionary America.

8. Johnson and Burling, 23.

9. The Murray-Kean troupe played a small, but impressive, repertoire of London favorites during their tours: *Amphitryon* (Dryden), *The Beaux Stratagem* (Farquhar), *The Beggar's Opera* (Gay), *A Bold Stroke for a Wife* (Centlivre), *The Busybody* (Centlivre), *Cato*, *The Constant Couple* (Farquhar), *The Distressed Mother* (Philips), *The Drummer* (Addison), *The Fair Penitent* (Rowe), *George Barnwell* (Lillo), *Love for Love* (Congreve), *The Orphan* (Otway), *The Recruiting Officer* (Farquhar), *Richard III* (Shakespeare/Cibber), and *The Spanish Fryar* (Dryden). See Seilhamer, 1:7. Also, it should be noted that they changed the troupe's name to the Annapolis Company in August of 1752 (Johnson and Burling, 151).

10. Upton and his crew's repertoire consisted of *A Bold Stroke for a Wife*, *The Fair Penitent*, *Othello* (Shakespeare), *The Provoked Husband* (Vanbrugh), *Richard III*, *Tunbridge Walks* (Baker), and *Venice Preserved* (Otway). See Johnson and Burling, 153–55; and Seilhamer, 1:16.

11. Johnson and Burling, 129–62; Rankin, 30–42; Seilhamer, 1:1–34. See also

Pollock, 6–7. Seilhamer, disregarding earlier amateur performances in New York, Virginia, and South Carolina, considers the Philadelphia *Cato* to be the genesis of the American theater, the point from which its students may begin to approach "its possible development as a permanent force in society" (2).

12. Johnson and Burling, 151–85; Rankin, 51–73; Seilhamer, 1:35–79. See also Pollock, 7–12; and Willis, 38–39. For the death of Lewis Hallam Sr., see also Errol Hill, *The Jamaican Stage, 1655–1900: Profile of a Colonial Theatre* (Amherst: University of Massachusetts Press, 1992), 23–24. I have compiled the following list of full-length plays performed by the London Company under the management of Lewis Hallam Sr. from Seilhamer, vol. 1, and Johnson and Burling: *The Albion Queens* (Banks), *The Beaux Stratagem, The Beggar's Opera, The Careless Husband* (Cibber), *Cato, The Committee* (Howard), *The Conscious Lovers* (Steele), *The Distressed Mother, The Drummer, The Earl of Essex* (Jones), *The Fair Penitent, The Gamester* (Moore), *George Barnwell, Jane Shore* (Rowe), *King Lear* (Tate/Shakespeare), *Love for Love, The Merchant of Venice* (Shakespeare), *Richard III, Romeo and Juliet* (Shakespeare), *The Suspicious Husband* (Hoadly), *Tamerlane, Tunbridge Walks, The Twin Rivals* (Farquhar), and *Woman Is a Riddle* (Bullock).

13. Johnson and Burling, 184–237; Rankin, 74–103; Seilhamer, 1:87–128. See also Pollock, 13–17; Willis, 41–46. Using Seilhamer and Johnson and Burling, I have compiled a list of the full-length plays acted by the London/American Company under Douglass's management between 1758 and 1774, a list that is remarkable in its breadth and variety: *The Albion Queens, Alexander The Great* (Lee), *All for Love* (Dryden), *All in the Wrong* (Murphy), *The Beaux Stratagem, The Beggar's Opera, A Bold Stroke for a Wife, The Busybody, Catherine and Petruchio* (Garrick/Shakespeare), *Cato, The Clandestine Marriage* (Garrick), *The Committee, The Conquest of Canada* (Cockings), *The Conscious Lovers, The Constant Couple, Coriolanus* (Thomson), *Cymbeline* (Shakespeare), *Cymon* (Garrick), *The Distressed Mother, Douglas* (Home), *The Drummer, The Earl of Essex, Edward, The Black Prince* (Shirley), *Every Man in His Humor* (Jonson), *The Fair Penitent, False Delicacy* (Kelly), *The Fashionable Lover* (Cumberland), *The Funeral* (Steele), *The Gamester, George Barnwell, Hamlet* (Shakespeare), *Henry IV* (Shakespeare), *The Inconstant* (Farquhar), *Jane Shore, The Jealous Wife* (Colman), *Julius Caesar* (Shakespeare), *King John* (Shakespeare), *King Lear, Lionel and Clarissa* (Bickerstaff), *Love a la Mode* (Dryden), *Love for Love, Love in a Village* (Bickerstaff), *Love Makes a Man* (Cibber), *Macbeth* (Davenant/Shakespeare), *The Merchant of Venice, The Merry Wives of Windsor* (Shakespeare), *The Miser* (Fielding), *The Mourning Bride* (Congreve), *The Orphan, The Orphan of China* (Murphy), *Othello, The Prince of Parthia* (Godfrey), *The Provoked Husband, The Recruiting Officer, The Revenge* (Young), *Richard III, The Roman Father* (Whitehead), *The School for Lovers* (Whitehead), *The Siege of Damascus* (Hughes), *She Stoops to Conquer* (Goldsmith), *The Shipwreck* (Cumberland), *The Spanish Fryar, The Suspicious Husband, Tamerlane, The Tempest* (Dryden/Davenant/Shakespeare), *The Tender Husband* (Steele), *Theodosius* (Lee), *Tom Thumb* (Fielding), *Tunbridge Walks, Venice Preserved, The Way to Win Him* (Murphy), *The Wonder; or, A Woman Keeps a Secret* (Centlivre), *A Word to the Wise* (Kelly), and *Zara* (Hill). I contend that this list illustrates one of the glories of pre-Revolutionary American culture, and in my opinion the general absence of American plays (with the exception of *The Prince of Parthia*) from the repertoire does not detract from the robust good health of the theater implied by such a rich and varied selection of plays.

14. Johnson and Burling, 234, 238–83; Rankin, 103–22; Seilhamer, 1:151–75. See also Pollock, 17–24; Willis, 50–56.

15. Verling's repertoire is impressive in scope, although derivative in introducing only one new play, Colley Cibber's *She Would and She Would Not*, to the American stage, reflecting his own beginnings as one of Douglass's actors. His company performed *The Beggar's Opera, The Beaux Stratagem, A Bold Stroke for a Wife, The Busybody, The Conscious Lovers, The Constant Couple, The Distressed Mother, Douglas, The Drummer, The Earl of Essex, George Barnwell, Hamlet, Henry IV, The Inconstant, The Jealous Wife, Love in a Village, The Merchant of Venice, The Miser, The Mourning Bride, The Orphan, Othello, The Provoked Husband, The Revenge, Richard III, Romeo and Juliet, She Would and She Would Not, The Suspicious Husband, Theodosius, Venice Preserved*, and *The Way to Keep Him*. See Johnson and Burling, 254–320; and Seilhamer, 1:235–40, 257–68. Johnson and Burling also record the activities of two other companies playing during the active period for Verling's company, one run by Mr. Mills and one run by Mr. Bayly, and several companies active in the early 1770s, including one in New Hampshire and several in the Caribbean (23). For the reappearance of the Virginia Company in the Caribbean, see Johnson and Burling, 322, 355.

16. Johnson and Burling, 283–342; Rankin, 123–34; Seilhamer, 1:210–68. See also Pollock, 24–25.

17. For New York, Philadelphia, and the Townshend Duties, see Peter D. G. Thomas, *The Townshend Duties Crisis* (Oxford: Clarendon Press, 1987), 122–23. Thomas notes that although Virginia and Maryland officially signed on to the second non-importation movement, the boycott was barely enforced in these colonies (150–52). For the continuing travels of the American Company, see Johnson and Burling, 320–410; Rankin, 135–68; Seilhamer, 1:269–95; and Pollock, 25–29.

18. Johnson and Burling, 414–75; Rankin, 169–88; Seilhamer, 1:316–36. See also Pollock, 29–32; Willis, 59–77. For the return of the American Company to the West Indies, see Hill, 25, 29.

19. See also my earlier discussion of these events in Chapter 2.

20. Johnson and Burling, 109; Rankin, 24; Odell, 10. For the possible political ramifications of the productions in Van Dam's warehouse, including the possibility that a professional company allied with the governor played in New York that season, see Johnson, "New Evidence," 3; Mary Henderson, *The City and the Theatre* (1973; New York: Back Stage Books, 2004), 19–21; and Nathans, 29–30. Henderson, apparently mistakenly, argues that two theaters were in operation during this period.

21. Johnson and Burling, 117; Rankin, 19; Odell, 19–20. For James Blair and politics, see Robson, 21–22. For Gooch's concerns about military readiness, see Isaac, 109–10. Rankin notes that in 1718 Governor Alexander Spotswood held a public festival, including the staging of a play, to celebrate the birthday of George I. See Rankin, 14.

22. Willis, 26, 33; Shields, *Civil Tongues*, 288–90.

23. Farquhar's sword could cut both ways, however. During their theatrical campaign to discredit Marlborough in 1710, the Tories apparently commissioned a staging of *The Recruiting Officer* at the Haymarket Theatre, into which was inserted a satirical interlude mocking Marlborough for his avarice. See Zacharias Conrad von Uffenbach, *London in 1710 from the Travels of Zacharias Conrad von Uffenbach*, ed. and trans. W. H. Quarrell and Margaret Mare (London: Faber and Faber, 1934), 138–39; and Loftis, *Politics*, 54–55.

24. See John Ross, introduction to Farquhar, *The Recruiting Officer*, ed. John Ross (London: A&C Black, 1991); and Joseph Roach, "Territorial Passages," in *Of Borders*

and Transitions: Theatre History, Practice, and Theory, ed. Michael A. Kobialka (Minneapolis: University of Minnesota Press, 1999), 110–24.

25. Farquhar, *Works*, 72. See also Roach, *Cities*, 101–4.

26. Trenchard and Gordon, 1:451.

27. The most famous impressment scene is Shakespeare's *2 Henry IV*, 3.2. The original cast of the play provides a key link to the *Henry IV* plays. While Captain Plume was originally played by the genteel Mr. Wilks, Kite was first played by Richard Estcourt, a comedian who had played Falstaff the previous season. This casting began a tradition of genteel Plumes and Falstaffian Kites that might have influenced audience interpretations of the play. See Terence M. Freeman, *Dramatic Representations of British Soldiers and Sailors on the London Stage, 1660–1800: Britons Strike Home* (Lewiston, N.Y.: Edwin Mellen, 1995), 198–200.

28. Eric Rothstein, *George Farquhar* (New York: Twayne, 1967), 138. See also Kevin J. Gardner, "George Farquhar's *The Recruiting Officer*: Warfare, Conscription, and the Disarming of Anxiety," *Eighteenth Century Life* 25 (Fall 2001): 43–61.

29. "The Recruiting Officer: or, The Merry Volunteers," in Thomas Durfey, *Wit and Mirth: or Pills to Purge Melancholy*, 6 vols. (London: J. Tonson, 1719–20), 5:319–21.

30. Farquhar, *Recruiting Officer*, 29.

31. Ellison, 56.

32. Farquhar, *Recruiting Officer*, 28. Gardner provides an informative reading of the importance of military drill to both Farquhar's play and Marlborough's army (51–53).

33. Rothstein calls Plume "the happy scapegoat for whatever moral censure the audience may care to levy against the tricks of recruiting" (139).

34. Faruqhar, *Recruiting Officer*, 108–11. See Rothstein: "The bumpkins are happy; they have been dealt with justly; they are enlisted for country and queen" (134).

35. Farquhar, *Recruiting Officer*, 119, 104.

36. Addison, *Cato*, 4.4.141–42.

37. Farquhar, *Recruiting Officer*, 70.

38. Maier, 6. White pines being indigenous to virtually the entire East Coast between New England and the Carolinas, this restriction had a widespread effect. For a more extensive account of the political and economic tensions that resulted from the White Pine Acts, see Robert Greenhalgh Albion, *Forests and Sea Power: The Timber Problem of the Royal Navy* (1926; reprint, Hamden, Conn.: Archon Books, 1965), 249–69.

39. Herbert L. Osgood, *The American Colonies in the Eighteenth Century*, 3 vols. (New York: 1924–25) 3:58–61; Maier, 6–7.

40. Dora Mae Clark, "The Impressment of Seamen in the American Colonies," in *Essays in Colonial History Presented to Charles Mclean Andrews by His Students* (New Haven, Conn.: Yale University Press, 1931), 198–224. See also Carl Bridenbaugh, *Cities in Revolt: Urban Life in America, 1743–1776* (New York: Alfred A. Knopf, 1965), 115–16. Attempting to rally public support for providing troops to the British war effort in 1747, Benjamin Franklin praised the New England volunteers for their military prowess and for proving that Americans remained Britons capable of performing great feats for the public good. See Wilson, *Island Race*, 12.

41. *Minutes of the Common Council of Philadelphia, 1704–76* (Philadelphia: Crissy and Markley, 1852), 523, quoted in Rankin, 31.

42. Consider the following passage written by an anonymous critic of the crown

in 1760: "But permit me to remind you of those notorious instances of violated property, the enlistment of your servants in the late Spanish War, who were a part of your property as firmly secured by the laws of your country as any you enjoy, as much as the ox you have paid for or the inheritance you have purchased" (*A Letter to the People of Pennsylvania* [Philadelphia: W. Dunlap, 1760)], 15).

43. Johnson and Burling, 142–62; Rankin, 6–11, 32–33, 39–40; Odell, 37, 40. Johnson and Burling (150) and Rankin (38) each record an additional performance of *The Recruiting Officer* in November 1751 in Norfolk, Virginia. Aubrey C. Land notes that during the "Golden Age" of Annapolis history the town was the racing capitol of the Chesapeake and attracted a number of theater companies during the September racing season. See Land, *Colonial Maryland, A History* (Millwood, Ky.: KTO Press, 1981), 195–97. Rhys Isaac makes a similar point about the annual races staged in Williamsburg and Fredericksburg, Virginia (Isaac, 101).

44. *New York Gazette and Weekly Post-Boy*, 24 September 1750.

45. Willis, 41. See also Johnson and Burling, 179; Rankin, 72; Odell, 32–44; and Litto, 436–37. Seilhamer does not record the 1754 Charleston season. For the 1754 military buildup, see Fred Anderson, *Crucible of War: The Seven Years' War and the Fate of Empire in British North America, 1754–1766* (New York: Alfred A. Knopf, 2000), 66–73.

46. Johnson and Burling, 142–48, 161–62; Rankin 32, 38, 42; Seilhamer, 1:6–9; Odell, 32–44.

47. Johnson and Burling, 153–54, 168; Rankin, 64; Seilhamer, 1:16–17, 53; Odell, 44–46.

48. Johnson and Burling, 176; Rankin, 70; Pollock, 8–9. For Washington's misadventure at Fort Duquesne, see Fred Anderson, *Crucible*, 50–65.

49. Milton, *Complete Poems and Major Prose*, ed. Merritt Y. Hughes (New York: Macmillan Publishing Company, 1959), 792.

50. See Cibber, *An Apology for the Life of Colley Cibber*, ed. Robert W. Lowe, 2 vols. (1889; reprint, New York: AMS Press, 1966), 1: 62–67.

51. Colley Cibber, *The Tragical History of King Richard III* (London: B. Lintott and A. Bettesworth, 1700), 5.9.21–22.

52. Ibid., 5.9.35. At least one observant colonial reader's attention was captured by this play's conflict between tyranny and patriotism. John Adams, then a student at Harvard, copied the long opening scene in which Richard kills Henry VI in the Tower of London into his daybook for 1755–56. See Adams, *Papers*, 1:10.

53. Loftis, *Politics*, 31.

54. Rowe, *Tamerlane*, ed. Landon C. Burns Jr. (Philadelphia: University of Pennsylvania Press, 1966), 2.2.81–85.

55. Ibid., 5.1.347–50. The caging of Bajazet echoes Marlowe's *Tamburlaine the Great*, although Rowe's hero and Marlowe's seem scarcely related. Also, compare Tamerlane's lines with *Macbeth*, 5.8.25–27: "We'll have thee, as our rarer monsters are, / Painted on a pole, and underwrit, / 'Here may you see the tyrant.'" Not for nothing did Rowe edit an edition of Shakespeare.

56. Richard Moody, ed., *Dramas from the American Theatre, 1762–1909* (Cleveland: World Publishing Company, 1966), 2.

57. Arthur H. Scouten, *The London Stage, 1729–1747: A Critical Introduction* (Carbondale: Southern Illinois University Press, 1968), lxxxiii; Newman, 20–21.

58. Newman, 20.

59. For an account of the history of Pope Day that includes excerpts of first-person recollections of the event, see Sherwood Collins, "Boston's Political Street

Theatre: The Eighteenth-Century Pope Day Pageants," *Educational Theatre Journal* 25 (December 1973): 401–9.

60. Wilson, *Sense of the People*, 95.

61. *Pennsylvania Gazette*, 19 March 1754. See also Johnson and Burling, 177; Rankin, 69; Seilhamer, 1:68; and Pollock, 9. For Hopkinson's epilogue, see *The Miscellaneous Essays and Occasional Writings of Francis Hopkinson*, 3 vols. (Philadelphia: T. Dobson, 1792), 3:52–53.

62. *Pennsylvania Gazette*, 19 March 1754.

63. Ibid., 25 April 1754.

64. Fred Anderson, *Crucible*, 219–31.

65. Johnson and Burling, 190–99; Rankin, 79–85; Seilhamer, 1:94–95, 102–3. See also Odell, 75–79; and Pollock, 16–17.

66. Johnson and Burling, 201–9; Seilhamer, 1:114–15, 121.

67. Johnson and Burling, 220. Kathleen Wilson leaves open the possibility of *Cato* being performed by the London Company in Jamaica during the Seven Years' War (*Island Race*, 166).

68. *New York Journal*, 7 December 1761. See also Mays, 142–43; George B. Bryan, 27–28; Johnson and Burling, 88–109; Rankin, 74–88; Seilhamer, 1:94,102–3, 114–15; and Odell, 76–79. For the postwar depression and opposition to the theaters, see Rankin, 96.

69. Ford, 18; Johnson and Burling, 186. Ellison observes that Washington's identification with Juba "elides the fact of Juba's Numidian [racial] difference" (69). Washington's affection for Sally Fairfax, wife of the wealthy and influential George Fairfax, does carry something of Juba's sense of futility. For the belief among the English that "Virginians were blacker than night," see Godbeer, 207. For the Forbes campaign of 1758–59, in which Washington also participated, see Willliam R. Nester, *The First Global War: Britain, France, and the Fate of North America, 1756–1775* (Westport, Conn.: Praeger Publishers, 2000), 125–82; and Fred Anderson, *Crucible*, 267–85.

70. Albert Matthews. See also Odell, 107–8.

71. *New York Mercury*, 8 January 1759. See also Seilhamer, 1:96–97.

72. For the political struggles that kept Maryland out of the Seven Years' War, see Land, 207–36. Ironically, Land notes, Maryland Governor Horatio Sharpe had considerable military experience (235).

73. *Maryland Gazette*, 6 March 1760. See also Rankin, 86; Seilhamer, 1:116; and Pope, "Prologue," 14, 16. For more on Maryland's sitting out of the war, see Fred Anderson, *Crucible*, 322–23.

74. Nester, 232–47; Fred Anderson, *Crucible*, 560–80, 641–51.

75. Johnson and Burling, 230–37; Rankin, 101–3; Willis, 43–46. For the local economic conditions of Virginia and South Carolina, see Fred Anderson, *Crucible*, 582–84, 598. Douglass retained plays like *Cato* and *Tamerlane* while enduring considerable criticism from colonial merchants during the early years of the economic downturn, suggesting that the relationship between the colonies and the theater was more complicated than Davis's economic model indicates.

76. Johnson and Burling, 240–41.

77. Richards, *Theater*, 202.

78. The most comprehensive account of the riots is Withington, 144–85, on which my account draws heavily.

79. Morgan, 124, 233; Shaw, 177–80; *Boston Evening Post*, 9 September 1765; Silverman, 76; Withington, 147–49.

80. O'Shaughnessy, 81, 89.

81. Withington, 164; Morgan, 124; Shaw, 177–80; *Boston Gazette*, 4 and 11 November 1765.

82. Davis, "Puritan Mercantilism," 22, 26.

83. Johnson and Burling, 244–49; Rankin, 108–10; Odell, 94–96. For more on the political and economic backdrop of the Sons of Liberty's opposition to the reopening of theater, see Nathans, 32–33; and Gary A. Richardson, "Nationalizing the American Stage: The Drama of Royall Tyler and William Dunlap as Post-Colonial Phenomena," in *Making America/Making American Literature: Franklin to Cooper*, ed. Robert A. Lee and W. M. Verhoeven (Amsterdam: Rodopi, 1996), 234–35.

84. John Montresor, *The Montresor Journals*, ed. G. D. Scull (New York: New York Historical Society, 1882), 362.

85. *New York Mercury*, 5 May 1766.

86. Montresor, 364; *New York Gazette*, 8 May 1766. See also Odell, 94.

87. Rankin, 110.

88. Johnson and Burling, 243–44; Rankin, 101, 112. See also Pollock, 17–21.

89. For the Charleston *Cato*, see Johnson and Burling, 247; Rankin, 106; and Willis, 51. For the Philadelphia *Richard III*, see Johnson and Burling, 266; and Seilhamer, 1:158–59.

90. *Pennsylvania Journal*, 12 February 1767; Pope, "Prologue," 3–4. For the performance dates, see Johnson and Burling, 257, 262; Rankin, 112, 115; Seilhamer, 1:154–55. Nathans suggests that political opposition to the theater in Pennsylvania may have extended beyond the traditional ranks of the Quakers and Presbyterians by the mid-1760s. See Nathans, 18–19.

91. *Pennsylvania Journal*, 19 February 1767; *Spectator*, 4:66. For Governor Penn's cultivation of the actors, see Silverman, 107. It is also worth noting that at least one future Revolutionary general, Anthony Wayne, attended the Southwark Theatre regularly during this period. See Meserve, 32.

92. *Theatrical Entertainments Consistent with Society, Morality, and Religion. In a Letter to the Author of 'The STAGE the High Road to Hell* (London: Baker and Leigh, 1768), 1.

93. Adams, *Works*, 3:461; *Macbeth*, 1.7.58. Adams quotes 1.7.54–59. For the 1759 *Macbeth* in Philadelphia, see Johnson and Burling, 196; Rankin, 84; Seilhamer, 1:105; and Pollock, 17. For a broader consideration of anti-Scottish sentiment in the colonies, beginning with the unpopularity of Bute, see Ian Charles Cargill Graham, *Colonists from Scotland: Emigration to North America, 1707–1783* (Ithaca, N.Y.: Cornell University Press, 1956), 128–49. See also Holton, 41. Holton notes that in some cases even the children of Scottish immigrants displayed mistrust of their parents' countrymen.

94. Bate, 71–73; Maier, 56, 71; Arthur Lee, "Oppression, A Poem" (London: C. Moran, 1764), 4; Shaw, 181–83.

95. Thomas, 33–34. For a helpful chronicle of the parliamentary debate over colonial policy toward North America before the passage of the Townshend Duties, see Thomas, 18–35.

96. Silverman, 136.

97. Johnson and Burling, 289–312; Rankin, 123–32; Seilhamer, 1:210–14; Odell, 118–37. For anti-impressment riots, see Jesse Lemisch, "Jack Tar in the Streets: Merchant Seamen in the Politics of Revolutionary America," *William and Mary Quarterly*, 3rd ser., 25.3 (July 1968): 393, 396. For the conflict between New York and Parliament, see Bernhard Knollenberg, *Growth of the American Revolution* (New York: Free Press, 1975), 38–41.

98. *New York Journal*, 21 January 1768; Seilhamer, 1:241. The best overall account I have found of non-importation during this period is Thomas, 121–79. See also Maier, 114–38.

99. For the Jamaican connections of Governor Moore, see Wilson, *Island Race*, 160. For the economic opposition to the theater, see Nathans, 32–34.

100. See T. H. Breen, "Baubles of Britain: The American and Consumer Revolutions of the Eighteenth Century," *Past and Present* 119 (May 1988): 73–104.

101. *Boston Weekly New-Letter*, 22 December 1768.

102. Maier, 124; Johnson and Burling, 294, 389. For *Cato* performance dates, see Johnson and Burling, 298, 470. For the connection between the *Liberty* riot and impressments, see Lemisch, 391–92.

103. *King John* premiered in Philadelphia on 12 December 1768. See Johnson and Burling, 318; and Seilhamer, 1:242. *Cymbeline* premiered somewhat earlier, on 15 June 1767 at the Southwark. See Johnson and Burling, 276. *The Tempest* premiered at the Southwark on 23 January 1770. See Johnson and Burling, 359. See also Pollock, 21, 28; and Odell, 120–21.

104. Johnson and Burling, 287–89, 353–57; Rankin, 140–61.

105. For Washington's attendance of *The Recruiting Officer*, see Johnson and Burling, 389; and Rankin, 159. For Jefferson's theater attendance, see Johnson, "Thomas Jefferson."

106. William Eddis, *Letters from America*, ed. Aubrey C. Land (Cambridge, Mass.: Belknap Press, 1969), 48.

107. For Boucher's authorship of this poem, see Rankin, 155. For the sermon's text and source, see Jonathan Boucher, *A View of the Causes and Consequences of the American Revolution* (1797; reprint, New York: Russell and Russell, 1967), 399; and *Richard III*, 5.3.12–13. For Boucher's battle of wits with Paca, see *Maryland Gazette*, 18 March, 25 March, and 1 April 1773. The American Company had performed *The Beggar's Opera* in Annapolis as recently as 25 February 1769 and *Lethe* as recently as 1 September 1772. See Johnson and Burling, 326, 410. Given the poor quality of the records for the Annapolis season of 1772, it is possible that *The Beggar's Opera* was performed during that season. For the political context of Boucher and Paca's argument, see Gregory A. Stiverson and Phebe R. Jacobson, *William Paca: A Biography* (Baltimore: Maryland Historical Society, 1976), 60–64. It is also noteworthy that Boucher, Eddis, and Paca were all members of the Homony social club (55–56).

108. *Maryland Gazette*, 3 September 1772. For the attribution to Eddis, see Rankin, 167.

109. Rankin, 140, 161. For the prologue, see *Virginia Gazette*, 21 May 1767.

110. William Mountfort, *The Fall of Mortimer, An Historical Play, [Dedicated to the right Honourable John Earl of Bute &c &c &c]* (London: G. Kearsley, 1763), viii. For the Oxford cartoon, see Fredric George Stephens, *Catalogue of Prints and Drawings in the British Museum*, div. I, IV, no. 4329. See also Shaw, 54–55. For the anti-Walpole agenda of Mountfort's play, see Loftis, *Politics*, 105–6. The poisoning of old Hamlet, of course, is not actually staged in *Hamlet*, although the poisoning scene in *The Murder of Gonzago* repeats it with revision.

111. *The Stage the High Road to Hell, Being an Essay on the Pernicious Nature of Theatrical Entertainments* (London: W. Nicoll, 1767), 7; *Theatrical Entertainments . . . In a Letter to the Author of "The STAGE the High Road to Hell,"* 10.

112. Josiah Quincy, *Memoir of the Life of Josiah Quincy Jun. Of Massachusetts: By His Son, Josiah Quincy* (Boston: Cummings, Hilliard, and Company, 1825), 12. Quincy has altered *Hamlet*, 2.2.553–55. Quincy attended *Hamlet*, along with several other

plays including *The Beggar's Opera*, in 1779 during a trip to England. See Withington, 23.

113. For *Hamlet*'s North American theatrical premiere, see Johnson and Burling, 194; Rankin, 83; Seilhamer, 1:105; and Pollock, 17.

114. See also Phillip Davidson, *Propaganda and the American Revolution, 1763–1783* (Chapel Hill: University of North Carolina Press, 1941), 241; and *Hamlet* 3.1.58–62. For the affiliation of these newspapers with the Sons of Liberty, see Maier, 91. Johnson and Burling, Rankin, and Seilhamer record regular performances of *Hamlet* from 1759 to 1774. Moses Coit Tyler notes that on 30 January 1766 the *Middlesex Journal* in Massachusetts published a parody of Hamlet's soliloquy sympathetic to the loyalist point of view under the title "The Pausing American Loyalist." See Moses Coit Tyler, 2:54.

115. For Cassius's lines, see *Julius Caesar*, 1.2.135–41. For the reference, see Bate, 70–73; *Political Register*, 1767. See also Shaw, 55–56.

116. *Connecticut Gazette*, 12 July 1765, quoted in Philip Davidson, 130. See *Julius Caesar*, 4.2.270–74.

117. Adams, *Papers*, 1:194; *Julius Caesar* 1.3.89.

118. *Supplement to the Boston Gazette and Country Day Journal*, 19 February 1770. For the battle of Golden Hill, which began with an attempt by British troops to cut down a liberty pole, see Knollenberg, 227–28.

119. *Maryland Gazette*, 21 October 1773.

120. Johnson and Burling, 365; Rankin, 138–39; Pollock, 28.

121. Mackrabie to Sir Philip Francis, 9 June 1770, *The Francis Letters by Sir Philip Francis et. al*, ed. Beata Francis and Eliza Keary (London: Hutchinson and Company, 1901), 117–18. See also Rankin, 139.

122. Maier, 11–15; Knollenberg, 82–84.

123. Hugh Kelly, introduction to *A Word to the Wise* (London: J. Dodsley, 1770); *Pennsylvania Chronicle*, 31 October 1772.

124. Johnson and Burling, 432; Rankin, 174; Seilhamer, 1:297–98; Pollock, 29. For the cited text, see Cockings, *The Conquest of Canada* (London: J. Cooke, 1766), 5.5.220–22. Cockings originally composed the play while working as bureaucrat in Boston. After its London publication, it was reprinted in Philadelphia and Baltimore in 1772, and in Albany in 1773. See Kent G. Gallagher, *The Foreigner in Early American Drama: A Study in Attitudes* (The Hague: Mouton and Company, 1966), 75–76.

125. *Pennsylvania Journal*, 17 February 1773. See also Johnson and Burling, 432; Rankin, 174; Seilhamer, 1:302–3; and Pollock, 29.

126. Johnson and Burling, 437–51; Rankin, 175–81; 316–25; Odell, 160–71. For Washington and Gage's attendance of *Hamlet*, see Meserve, 61–62.

127. Eddis, 71. Eddis's emphasis on disinterested patriotism echoes his earlier prologue for the American Company.

128. Eddis, 110.

129. Rankin, 182.

130. Eddis, 81.

131. *South Carolina Gazette*, 28 February 1774. See also Willis, 66. The attempt to ban the theater had occurred prior to either the reopening of the theater or the printing of the notice quoted above, which was reprinted well into the theatrical season "by particular desire."

132. *South Carolina Gazette*, 25 October 1773. See also Silverman, 250–51.

133. Johnson and Burling, 461–65; Rankin, 183–86; Seilhamer, 1:329–32; Willis, 73–74.

134. Quincy, *Memoir*, 72. According to Rebecca Starr, Quincy went to South Carolina in part to stump for the creation of a permanent intercolonial Committee of Correspondence. See Starr, *A School for Politics: Commercial Lobbying and Political Culture in Early South Carolina* (Baltimore: Johns Hopkins University Press, 1998), 64–65. Starr explains that while South Carolinian merchants hoped to avoid another non-importation boycott over the tea duty, they worked hard both at home and in Britain to secure its repeal, using their clout as a commercial lobby and a network of political connections including Richard Champion, a wealthy South Carolinian who had re-emigrated to Britain some years earlier and played an instrumental role in the election of Edmund Burke as MP for Bristol in 1774 (62–66).

135. *South Carolina Gazette*, 21 March 1774. See also Johnson and Burling, 466; Rankin, 185; and Willis, 66.

136. [John Allen], *An Oration Upon the Beauties of Liberty, Or the Essential Rights of the Americans . . . Humbly Dedicated to the Right Honourable Earl of Dartmouth* (Boston: D. Kneeland and N. Knight, 1773), xiv.

137. John Hancock, *An Oration; Delivered march 5; 1774 at the Request of the Inhabitants of the Town of Boston: To Commemorate the Bloody Tragedy of the Fifth of March 1770* (Boston: Edes and Gill, 1774), 14. Emphasis in original. Hancock's oration was reprinted by the New York printer James Rivington, usually considered to be a fiercely partisan Tory, in his almanac for 1775. See Philip Davidson, 311.

138. Hiller Zobel, *The Boston Massacre* (New York: W.W. Norton, 1970), 194–96.

139. Given the history of amateur performances of *The Recruiting Officer* in Boston and Hancock's having resided in England for a year during 1760, however, it is not impossible that Hancock knew Farquhar's play. Also, it is worth noting that a Bostonian had created a parody of the famous song "The British Grenadiers" a few weeks before the Massacre. The song promotes the superiority of British warriors to those of ancient Greece and Rome, while the American parody focuses its treatment of the *translatio imperii* theme on North America. See Silverman, 145–46.

140. Johnson and Burling, 467–69; Seilhamer, 331–32; Willis, 73–74.

141. [Myles Cooper], *A Friendly Address, to All Reasonable Americans, on the Subject of our Political Confusions: in which the Necessary Consequences of Violently Opposing the King's Troops, and of a General Non-Importation are Fairly Stated* (New York: J. Rivington, 1774), 33; Quincy, *Memoir*, 138; Quincy Jr., *Observations upon the Act of Parliament, Commonly Called the Boston Port Bill* (Boston: Edes and Gill, 1774), 55. The *Boston Weekly New-Letter* ran a letter to the editor quoting the same line from *Julius Caesar* as Cooper's pamphlet in January 1775. See Philip Davidson, 288.

142. Kathleen Wilson records opposition performances in Bristol during 1769, in Newcastle during April 1770, and in Hull during December 1770. John Wilkes's supporters also staged the play after his release from the King's Bench prison in 1770. See Wilson, *Sense of the People*, 219, 342. Annabel Patterson notes that Burke may make an allusion to *Cato* in his speech on conciliation with the American colonies. See Patterson, *Nobody's Perfect: A New Whig Interpretation of History* (New Haven, Conn.: Yale University Press, 2002), 113–14.

143. Johnson and Burling, 470; Rankin, 185; Seilhamer, 1:333–34; Willis, 70–71, 73–74.

144. *South Carolina Gazette*, 4 July 1774. Emphasis in original. See also Richards, *Theater*, 224.

145. *South Carolina Gazette*, 4 July 1774. See also *South Carolina Gazette*, 19 September 1774; and Johnson and Burling, 472–74.

146. *South Carolina Gazette*, 30 May 1774. See also Willis, 72.
147. "Extract from the Votes and Proceedings of the Continental Congress," *Boston Gazette and Country Journal*, 7 November 1774, quoted in George B. Bryan, 29.
148. *New York Journal*, 15 December 1774; Johnson and Burling, 475.
149. The West Indian colonies, which had fought their share of political battles with British colonial authorities in the preceding decade, attempted to intervene in the imperial crisis with North America during 1774–75. See O'Shaughnessy, 137–59.
150. *New York Mercury*, 6 February 1775; Johnson and Burling, 475.
151. *Jamaica Gazette* (Kingston), 1 July 1775, quoted in Richardson Wright, *Revels in Jamaica, 1682–1838* (New York: Dodd, Mead, and Company, 1937), 63–64. See also Wright, 25.

Chapter 4

1. Tyler, *The Prose of Royall Tyler*, ed. Marius B. Péladeau (Rutland, Vt.: Charles E. Tuttle Company, 1972), 142–43.
2. Ibid., 143.
3. Ibid., 143–44. The lines quoted are Addison, *Cato*, 1.1.22–25. The original subject of this inquiry is, of course, Julius Caesar.
4. See my discussion of the evolution of the colonial repertoire in Chapter 3.
5. *Tatler*, 1:167.
6. My thanks to Joseph Roach for introducing me to Richard Schechner's concept of behavioral "strips."
7. Robson, 29.
8. Johnson and Burling, 95–96.
9. Richardson, *American Drama*, 5.
10. John L. Clark, "Educational Dramatics in Nineteenth-Century Colleges," in *History of Speech Education in America*, ed. Karl R. Wallace (New York: Appleton-Century-Crofts, 1954), 521–51. Although largely concerned with college theater in the nineteenth century, Clark's essay also examines the colonial roots of college theater.
11. Meserve, 44.
12. Thomas Firth Jones, *A Pair of Lawn Sleeves: A Biography of William Smith, 1727–1803* (Philadelphia: Chilton Publishing Company, 1972), 17–19; Carl and Jessica Bridenbaugh, *Rebels and Gentlemen: Philadelphia in the Age of Franklin*, 2nd ed., (New York: Oxford University Press, 1942), 57–59. See also Meserve, 43; and Nester, 9.
13. [William Smith], *A Brief State of the Province of Pennsylvania* (London: R. Griffiths, 1755). See also Jones, 32–33.
14. Bridenbaugh, 139; Seilhamer, 1:70–72; Meserve, 43; Pollock, 10–12; Rankin, 71; Johnson and Burling, 177. While on a 1763 fundraising trip to London for the College, Smith convinced David Garrick to let him use the Drury Lane Theatre for a benefit. See Jones, 68.
15. Bridenbaugh, 103; Jones, 30–31.
16. *The American Magazine, or Monthly Chronicle for the British Colonies*, 1.3 (January 1758) and 1.4 (February 1758).
17. William Smith, *True pleasure, Cheerfulness, & Happiness, the Immediate Consequence of RELIGION Fully and concisely proved With remarks on the THEATRE,*

Addressed to a Young Lady in Philadelphia (Philadelphia: William and Thomas Bradford, 1757), 13.

18. See Gillian Russell, 131. Russell notes that these productions were also vital to "the construction of 'manliness,'" meaning in this case "the capacity to bond successfully in an institutional context." She also observes that such productions were widely carried out at many other public schools and military academies.

19. Bridenbaugh, 104–10; Stiverson and Jacobson, 33–34; Quinn, 20; Seilhamer, 1:189; Pollock, 12–13; Rankin, 118; Johnson and Burling, 271; Hopkinson, *Miscellaneous Essays and Occasional Writings*, 3:52–53.

20. *Pennsylvania Gazette*, 20 January 1757. See also John L. Clark, 528; Meserve, 44–45; Quinn, 18–20. Meserve offers no comment on the production, but Quinn offers a summary of the plot including several quotations. For confirmation of the Loudoun performance, see Smith, *The Works of William Smith, D.D.*, 2 vols. (Philadelphia: Maxwell and Fry, 1803), vol. 1, part 2, 235n. For more on Loudoun, see Richard Moody, ed., 1; and Nester, 16–18.

21. Although *The Idea of a Patriot King* was not published until 1749, Bolingbroke began composing the essay in 1738, shortly after returning to Britain from a temporary exile. See Isaac Kramnick, *Bolingbroke and His Circle: The Politics of Nostalgia in the Age of Walpole* (Cambridge, Mass.: Harvard University Press, 1968), 32–35.

22. *The Craftsman*, 6 September 1735, quoted in James Sambrook, *James Thomson (1700–1748): A Life* (Oxford: Clarendon Press, 1991), 139.

23. Sambrook 171, 200–205.

24. For George II's resistance to troop deployments in North America, see Nester, 206.

25. Thomson and Mallet, *Alfred: A Masque* (London: Andrew Millar, 1751).

26. *Pennsylvania Gazette*, 20 January 1757; *New Hampshire Gazette*, 18 March 1757 and 25 March 1757. See also Johnson and Burling, 184. The articles in the *New Hampshire Gazette* appear under the name "J. Duché," but it seems unlikely, given the emphasis of these essays on the educational advantages of theater and their authoritative tone, which speaks of the growth of drama at the college from the perspective of one who directed that development, that the student Duché would have written them.

27. *Pennsylvania Gazette*, 20 January 1757.

28. Ibid.

29. Ibid., 10 February 1757.

30. Ibid., 3 February 1757.

31. Ibid., 10 February 1757. The ambiguous designation "our gallant Chief" could apply to either the king or to Loudoun.

32. John L. Clark, 523; Moody, 2; Pollock, 9; Johnson and Burling, 178.

33. Albert Matthews. Among the other plays performed, William Whitehead's *The Roman Father* was performed on 22 June 1758. Joseph Addison's *The Drummer* was staged on 20 April 1759, and Thomas Otway's *The Orphan* was staged on 21 April 1759. On 6 July and 23 November 1759, Edward Young's *The Revenge* was staged.

34. For the Harvard production, see Albert Matthews; and John L. Clark, 523–24. For the Yale tavern productions, see Arthur W. Bloom, "A History of the Theatre in New Haven, Connecticut before 1860" (Ph.D. dissertation, Yale University, 1966), 8, 26. For enlistment in New England, see Fred Anderson, *Crucible*, 227.

35. *Boston Post-Boy*, 27 March 1760. The text of the prologue was appended to a letter to the editor protesting the suppression of the performance. An excerpt

of the letter and prologue was also printed in the *Maryland Gazette* on 27 March 1760.

36. For more on the Knowles riots, see Maier, 5; Lemisch, 391; and Carl Bridenbaugh, *Cities in Revolt: Urban Life in America, 1743–1776* (New York: Alfred A. Knopf, 1965), 115–16.

37. Albert Matthews.

38. See Sambrook, 240. See also John Loftis, "Thomson's *Tancred and Sigismunda* and the Demise of the Drama of Political Opposition," in *The Stage and the Page: London's "Whole Show" in the Eighteenth Century Theatre*, ed. George Winchester Stone (Berkeley: University of California Press, 1981), 34–54.

39. Loftis finds ambiguous moments in the plot that suggest a Jacobite as well as a Whig reading of the play, ambiguities that Sambrook rejects as coincidental. See Loftis, "Tancred," 37–42, and Sambrook, 240.

40. James Thomson, *Tancred and Sigismunda* (London: Andrew Millar, 1745), 2.4.3–6.

41. The Sons of Liberty are generally believed to have taken their name from the text of a speech against the Stamp Act given by Isaac Barré, a veteran of the French and Indian War and an opposition MP. See Morgan, 67–68. It is possible, however, that Barré was familiar with the play and consciously or unconsciously alluded to this drama with historical ties to opposition politics.

42. Sambrook, 241. *Tancred and Sigismunda* made at least one appearance in the pamphlet wars of the North American colonies as well. During the Parsons' Cause controversy of 1764, a dispute between the clergy of the Church of England and the citizens of the colony of Virginia, Richard Bland, an opponent of the clergy, sarcastically compared his clerical counterpart, the Reverend John Camm, to "old Siffredi in the play" for his supposed devotion to the British constitution. Bland's analogy would surely have reminded readers familiar with the play of the disastrous results of Siffredi's good intentions. See Richard Bland, *The Colonel Dismounted* (Williamsburg: Joseph Royle, 1764), 20. Bland also quotes one of Siffredi's speeches on his devotion to the state, 5.1.24–27, for further effect.

43. For a full list of commencement exercises published prior to the Revolution, see John L. Clark, 529; and Meserve, 44–45. See also Richard Moody, 2.

44. Francis Hopkinson [and William Smith], *An Exercise, Containing a Dialogue and Ode, Sacred to the Memory of his Late Gracious Majesty George II. Performed at the Public Commencement in the College of Philadelphia* (Philadelphia: W. Dunlap, 1761), 3, 4–5.

45. Ibid., 5.

46. Henry St. John, Viscount Bolingbroke, *The Works of Lord Bolingbroke*, 4 vols. (1844; reprint London: Frank Cass and Company, 1967), 2:388, 429.

47. Hopkinson, *Dialogue . . . George II*, 8.

48. Francis Hopkinson [and Jacob Duché], *An Exercise Containing a Dialogue and Ode On the Accession of His present gracious Majesty George III, Performed at the public Commencement in the College of Philadelphia* (Philadelphia: W. Dunlap, 1762), 4–5.

49. Hopkinson, *Dialogue . . . George III*, 5; Bolingbroke, 2:407.

50. *The Military Glory of Great Britain: an Entertainment, given by the late candidates for the bachelor's degree, at the close of the anniversary commencement, held in Nassau Hall New Jersey September 29th, 1762* (Philadelphia: William Bradford, 1762), 15.

51. Nathaniel Evans, *An Exercise, Containing a Dialogue and Ode on Occasion of the Peace, Performed at the Public Commencement in the College of Philadelphia, May 17, 1763* (Philadelphia: Andrew Steuart, 1763), 6. Excerpts from this dialogue also appear in the *Pennsylvania Gazette*, 26 May 1763.

52. It is worth noting here that although Reverend Smith's political allegiances

were considered suspect in Pennsylvania, he strongly opposed the Stamp Act and other measures that angered the colonial radical community. See Jones, 106.

53. *Pennsylvania Gazette*, 5 June 1766.

54. Quincy, *Memoir*, 7–8.

55. For more on the respective curricula of the New England colleges during the colonial period, see Thomas Muller, introduction to *The Collected Writings of John Witherspoon*, ed. Thomas Muller (Carbondale: Southern Illinois University Press, 1990), 19. See also Fliegelman, *Declaring Independence*, 26–28, 34–35.

56. [Thomas Hopkinson], *An Exercise, Containing a Dialogue and Ode, Performed in the College of Philadelphia* (Philadelphia: W. Dunlap, 1766), 6. The exercise was also excerpted in the *Pennsylvania Gazette* for 5 June 1766.

57. The figurative rivalry created between George III and Pitt by their respective depictions in the dialogue is a particularly apt one, given the uncomfortable relationship between the two men throughout the 1760s. See Nester, 212–13; and Stanley Ayling, *The Elder Pitt, Earl of Chatham* (New York: D. McKay, 1976), 236–37, 289–90. For more on Pitt's speech, see Fred Anderson, *Crucible*, 698–701.

58. [Hopkinson], *An Exercise, Containing A Dialogue and Ode*, 6–7.

59. Thomas Coombe, *An Exercise Containing a Dialogue and Two Odes, Performed at the Public Commencement in the College of Philadelphia, November 17, 1767* (Philadelphia: William Goddard, 1767). Portions of this exercise were excerpted in the *Pennsylvania Gazette*, 26 November 1767.

60. See my discussion of Adams and the *Dissertation* in Chapter 2.

61. Coombe, 4.

62. William Smith, *An Exercise, Containing a Dialogue and Two Odes, Performed at the Commencement in the College of Philadelphia, June 5, 1770* (Philadelphia: Joseph Cruikshank, 1770), 3, 7–8.

63. William Smith, *An Exercise, Containing a Dialogue and Two Odes Set to Music, for the Public Commencement, in the College of Philadelphia, May 17, 1775* (Philadelphia: Joseph Cruikshank, 1775), 29, 120–38, 57–63. The last passage quoted is, ironically, from the 1770 dialogue written after the Boston Massacre, which in 1775 is suddenly replayed in the form of Lexington and Concord.

64. Silverman, 443–44. Smith engaged in a heated exchange of letters with Thomas Paine over the question of American independence in the *Pennsylvania Gazette*, *Pennsylvania Journal*, and *Norwich Packet* during April and May of 1776. While Paine signed himself "The Forester," Smith adopted the moniker of "Cato." See Philip Davidson, 244–45.

65. Bloom, 8, 44–48; *Records of the Linonian Society*, vol. 1, 15 December 1768 to 8 July 1790. The title of the play enacted by Linonia on 15 February 1770 is not given in the records, nor are those of the plays enacted in 1755–56. The minutes for the Linonian Society's early meetings in this volume are vague and summary; the quality of documentation improves after 1771, when the meticulous Nathan Hale was elected as the Linonian Society's scribe. For supplemental information on early theatrical performance at Yale, see Ota Thomas, "Student Dramatic Activities at Yale College during the Eighteenth Century," *Theatre Annual* (1944): 47–60; and John L. Clark, 526–27.

66. Witherspoon, *Collected Works*, 43. See also John L. Clark, 523–24.

67. Witherspoon, *Collected Works*, 256.

68. Ibid., 263.

69. In sharp contrast to Witherspoon's endorsement of this passage, Milton in *Eikionoklastes* compared it disparagingly with the posthumous recuperation of Charles I's reputation. See Milton, *Prose and Poetry*, 784a.

70. Madison to William Bradford, 9 November 1772, in Madison, *Writings*, ed. Jack N. Rakove (New York: Library of America, 1999), 4.

71. "George the Third's Soliloquy" originally appeared in the May 1779 edition of *The United States Magazine*, while the "Dialogue" appeared in the December 1779 issue. For the texts of both poems, see Freneau, *The Poems of Philip Freneau*, ed. Fred Lewis Pattee, 2 vols. (1902; reprint, New York: Russell and Russell, 1963), 2:3–6, 9–17.

72. Richardson, *Drama*, 5.

73. Philip Freneau and Hugh Henry Brackenridge, *A Poem, On The Rising Glory of America; Being an Exercise Delivered at the Public Commencement at Nassau-Hall, September 25, 1771* (Philadelphia: Joseph Cruikshank, 1772), 4. For a good recent analysis of this dialogue that considers the text in more detail, see Susan Castillo, "Imperial Pasts and Dark Futurities: Freneau and Brackenridge's 'The Rising Glory of America,'" *Symbiosis: A Journal of Anglo-American Literary Relations* 6.1 (April 2002), 27–43.

74. Freneau and Brackenridge, 23. Freneau revised this poem considerably in his later years, omitting large portions of text presumably by Brackenridge, among which are this passage and the ensuing quotations. See Freneau, *Poems*, 1:49–83.

75. Ibid., 27.

76. *Records of the Linonian Society*. The other texts performed by the Linonians during this period were the popular farces *The Toy Shop* (performed 8 June 1771) and *Neck or Nothing* (12 April 1774), and a popular full-length play, Centlivre's *The Wonder; or, A Woman Keeps a Secret* (12 April 1774). No record exists for a celebration in 1772, but no explanation for the absence of a celebration exists in the Linonian records, either, unlike the cancellation of the festivities for 1775, leaving open the possibility that an unrecorded performance took place in 1772. See also John L. Clark, 526–27. Loftis associates *The Toy Shop*, a moralistic, allegorical piece, with the sentiments of the Country party of the late 1730s (*Politics*, 116–17).

77. *Spectator*, 1:10.

78. Quoted in Colley, 71–72. Newton asserts that this patriotic courage stems trade's contributions to an equitable division of property, providing each individual citizen with a stake worth defending.

79. Trenchard and Gordon, 1:442. See also Ellison, 188–89.

80. Trenchard and Gordon, 1: 445–46.

81. Ibid., 1:444–45.

82. Starr, 53. See also Paul Langford, *The First Rockingham Administration, 1765–1766* (Oxford: Oxford University Press, 1973).

83. *Boston Gazette and Country Journal*, 11 November 1765. See also my discussion of Stamp Act protest literature in Chapter 2.

84. Benedict Anderson, 58–59.

85. Edmund Burke, *The Writings and Speeches of Edmund Burke*, ed. P. J. Marshall, 9 vols. (Oxford: Oxford University Press, 1980–2000), 2:120, 126.

86. See Kramnick, *Bolingbroke and His Circle*, 39–75, especially the chapter titled "The Plight of the Gentry," 56–63.

87. Sir Richard Steele, *The Conscious Lovers* (London: J. Tonson, 1722). All subsequent quotations will be taken from this edition.

88. Seilhamer, 1:46, 298; Johnson and Burling, 165, 428.

89. Wright, 46.

90. See Steele, *Conscious Lovers*, 8–11. As Peter Shaw notes, "Whenever Americans employed the family analogy, whether in their political writings or in the symbolism of crowds, they made themselves into children" (195). The familial analogies of paternal king and mother country remained a persistent part of the

ongoing dialogue surrounding colonial resistance, even when such neat resolutions had come to verge on the fantastic. For instance, one of the finest Tory writers in the colonies, Daniel Leonard of Massachusetts, described the relationship between Britain and the colonies in the wake of colonial "insults" to Britain using just such sentimental language in January 1775. In an essay published in the *Boston Gazette*, Leonard opined: "We have a gracious King upon the throne; he felt the resentments of a man, softened by the relentings of a parent . . . The bowels of our mother country yearned towards her refractory, obstinate child" (John Adams and Daniel Leonard, *Novanglus and Massachusettensis; or, Political Essays, Published in the Years 1774 and 1775, on the Principal Points of Controversy, Between Great Britain and Her Colonies* [Boston: Hews and Cross, 1819], 164).

91. Steele, *Conscious Lovers*, 67.
92. Ibid., 59–60, 61.
93. Loftis, *Comedy*, 83–85.
94. Steele, *Conscious Lovers*, 63.
95. Cumberland, *The West Indian* (London: W. Griffin, 1771), 4. Cumberland had himself turned down two colonial administrative posts, crown agent for Nova Scotia and provost marshal of South Carolina, while serving as a secretary to Lord Halifax during 1761–62. See Richard J. Dircks, *Richard Cumberland* (New York: Twayne Publishers, 1976), 14. Dircks also notes that as a young student at Bury St. Edmunds, Cumberland was punished for acting the role of Juba in a student production of *Cato*, an uncanny echo of colonial identity and racial difference in his own character (22).
96. For France's ceding of Senegambia, see Fred Anderson, *Crucible*, 306–7, 505. See also Maaja A. Stewart, "Inexhaustible Generosity: The Fictions of Eighteenth-Century British Imperialism in Richard Cumberland's *The West Indian*," *The Eighteenth Century* 37.1 (Spring 1996): 52.
97. Burke, 2:126.
98. Cumberland, 6.
99. Ibid.
100. Stewart, 45.
101. Cumberland, 42. Belcour, as a West Indian and a creole, represents a clearly defined stock "Other" in the eighteenth-century drama, although Cumberland's characterization of Belcour as a sentimental hero departs from the stereotype by making Belcour the romantic lead while still embracing the usual traits of the type: "fitful spells of passion or energy, generosity bordering on imprudence, sentimentality combined with a streak of haughtiness and cruelty to subordinates, and a certain exotic grace." See Wylie Sypher, "The West Indian as a 'Character' in the Eighteenth Century," *Studies in Philology* 36 (1939): 503–20. See also O'Shaugnessy, 109–34. O'Shaugnessy notes the many political battles fought by West Indians, especially Jamaicans, with Parliament over their chartered rights during the 1760s and 1770s.
102. Seilhamer, 1:282, 297, 317, 326, 331; Rankin, 164, 166, 168, 173, 182–83. See also Willis, 70–74; Pollock, 29–30; and Johnson and Burling, 395–96, 468–69. The play underwent its first American printing, generally a sure sign of widespread popularity, in 1772.
103. *Records of the Linonian Society*. Hale's epilogue has been lost.
104. Washington saw *The West Indian* on 8 October 1772, during a trip to Annapolis. See Washington, *Diaries of George Washington*, ed. John C. Fitzpatrick, 4 vols. (Boston: Houghton Mifflin, 1925), 2:82–83; Rankin, 183; and Johnson and Burling, 413–14.

105. *South Carolina Gazette*, 4 July 1774. See also my discussion of the 1774 Charleston theater season in Chapter 3.

106. Harold G. Rugg, "The Dartmouth Plays, 1769–1782," *Theatre Annual* (1942), 55–69. See also Richard Moody, 3; and John L. Clark, 530. The manuscripts of the "Dartmouth dialogues" are in possession of the Dartmouth Library. Both dialogues are reprinted in Richard Moody, 7–10. For the changing mission of Dartmouth, see Stevens, "The Christian Origins of the Vanishing Indian," in *Mortal Remains: Death in Early America*, ed. Nancy Isenberg and Andrew Burstein (Philadelphia: University of Pennsylvania Press, 2003), 24. For the details of the Dartmouth *Cato*, see Jared Sparks, *The Life of John Ledyard, the American Traveller*, 2nd ed. (Boston: Little, Brown, 1847), 14; and John L. Clark, 528.

107. "Dialogue on the Success of Our Arms and the Rising Glory of America," in *Two Dialogues on Different Subjects: Being Exercises Delivered on a Quarter-Day, in the Chapel of Yale College, New Haven, March 28, 1776* (Hartford: E. Watson, 1776), 22, quoted in Purcell, 22. The Scipios are referred to as the "twin thunderbolts of war" in *Aeneid*, 6.1121–22.

108. Stiles, *Literary Diary*, 2:325. The British took New Haven in July 1779.

109. *Records of the Linonian Society*, vol. 1, entry for 18 November 1779; Ota Thomas, 51.

110. V. Lansing Collins, "Princeton Dramatics in the Eighteenth Century," *Princeton Alumni Weekly* 37.3 (March 1922): 227; Moody, 3; Thomas Jefferson Wertenbaker, *Princeton, 1746–1896* (Princeton, N.J.: Princeton University Press, 1946), 197. The other two plays staged were Home's *Alonzo* and Nathaniel Lee's *The Rival Queens*. For Witherspoon's part in the *Douglas* controversy, see my discussion of his personal history earlier in this chapter.

111. For the staging of the debate, see Wertenbaker, 65. For Trenchard and Gordon's take on the assassination of Julius Caesar, see Trenchard and Gordon, 1:367–88. For Princeton's ownership of *Cato's Letters*, see Robson, 73.

112. The libretto of this piece, originally known as "America Independent," was first published in the *Freeman's Journal* of Philadelphia on 19 December 1781, from which the quotation of the text is taken. It subsequently appeared in a variety of newspapers throughout the Northeastern colonies. For the four individual performances and the piece's publication history, see Gillian B. Anderson, "'Samuel the Priest Gave Up the Ghost' and *The Temple of Minerva*: Two Broadsides," *Music Library Association Notes* 31 (1975): 493–516.

113. *Freeman's Journal*, 19 December 1781.

114. Ibid., 9 January 1782.

115. Ibid.

116. *Records of the Linonian Society*, vol. 1. See also John L. Clark, 526–27.

117. See Rolin G. Osterweis, *The New Haven Green and the American Bicentennial* (Hamden, Conn.: Archon Books, 1976), 48–50. Osterweis notes that according to local legend the British did not burn Yale because of the intercession of New Haven loyalists. It is more likely, however, that the British were more concerned with leaving the city before being attacked by American forces massing outside the city than they were with destroying the campus.

Chapter 5

1. Claude C. Robin, *New Travels through North America: In a Series of Letters* (Boston: E. E. Powers and N. Willis, 1784), 17. See also Brown, 79; and Norman

Philbrick, ed., *Trumpets Sounding: Propaganda Plays of the American Revolution* (New York: Benjamin Blom, 1972), 16.

2. De Tocqueville, 490. See also my discussion of de Tocqueville's view of the American theater in Chapter 1.

3. *Journals of the Continental Congress* 12, 1001–2. See also George B. Bryan, 31–32.

4. For Massachusetts' first explicit ban on stage plays, see George B. Bryan, 20; and Clapp, 3. The pamphlet play tradition of the Revolution has roots in the English civil war of the 1640s. See S. J. Wiseman, "Pamphlet Plays in the Civil War News Market: Genre, Politics, and 'Context,'" in *News, Newspapers, and Society in Early Modern Britain*, ed. Joad Raymond (London: Frank Cass, 1999), 66–83. Julie Stone Peters notes that print and theatrical audiences could be either opposed to each other, or "likened" by eighteenth-century playwrights (242).

5. Brown and Philbrick both conclude that Robin's account confirms the performance of the plays mentioned. See Brown, 79; and Philbrick, 16.

6. John Trumbull's *The Double Conspiracy*, which follows a plot to undermine the Revolution, may be the play on "the treason of Arnold" mentioned by Robin, although Arnold is not a character in Trumbull's play. See Trumbull, *The Double Conspiracy, or Treason discovered but not punished. A matter of fact, delineated after the life, in the form of a play* (Hartford, Conn.: Hudson and Godwin, 1783).

7. Philbrick, 3.

8. Philbrick's fine introductory essays to the propaganda plays reprinted in *Trumpets Sounding* downplay the scripts themselves in favor of general historical background, and while both Meserve and Richardson record these plays in their histories of early American drama, the broad historical scope of their projects precludes detailed textual analysis. Only Arthur Hobson Quinn's dated *History of the American Drama*, among the major studies of early American dramatic literature, quotes from the plays themselves with any regularity.

9. The most comprehensive recent work on Warren is Jeffrey Richards, *Mercy Otis Warren* (New York: Twayne, 1995). Also of particular relevance to this study is Oreovicz.

10. Jared Brown gestures in this direction in *The Theater in America during the Revolution*, but his analysis is both chronologically and generically (due to his particular focus on wartime military theatricals) limited in the scope of his explorations to brief readings of some pamphlet plays.

11. Philbrick, 5; Richardson, *Drama*, 32.

12. Richardson, *Drama*, 32.

13. The plays definitely attributed to Mercy Otis Warren are *The Adulateur, The Defeat*, in *Boston Gazette* 24 May and 19 July 1773; and *The Group* (Boston: Edes and Gill, 1775). I side with Jeffrey H. Richards, however, in disputing Warren's authorship of *The Blockheads* (Richards, *Mercy Otis Warren*, 103–6). The anonymous farces *The Battle of Brooklyn* (New York: J. Rivington, 1776) and *The Blockheads* (Boston: John Gill, 1776) are both reprinted in Philbrick. Philbrick also reprints the Tory *A Dialogue, Between a Southern Delegate, and His Spouse, on his return from the Grand Continental Congress* (New York: J. Rivington, 1774) and the patriot farce *The Motley Assembly* (Boston: Nathaniel Coverly, 1779), as well as two plays discussed below, John Leacock's *The Fall of British Tyranny* (Philadelphia: Styner and Cist, 1776) and Brackenridge's *The Death of General Montgomery* (Philadelphia: Robert Bell, 1777). Other important propaganda plays include Jonathan Sewall, *The Americans Roused, in a Cure for the Spleen* (New York: J. Rivington, 1775), a Tory dialogue; *The Blockheads; or, The Fortunate Contractor* (London: G. Kearsley,

1782), a Tory ballad opera; and Brackenridge's *The Battle of Bunkers-Hill* (Philadelphia: Robert Bell, 1776). Thomas Paine also wrote two dramatic dialogues, *A Dialogue between General Wolfe and General Gage in a Wood near Boston* (1775) and *A Dialogue between the Ghost of General Montgomery just arrived from the Elysian Fields; and an American Delegate, in a Wood, near Philadelphia* (1776). For the best available texts of these dialogues, see Paine, *The Complete Writings of Thomas Paine*, ed. Philip S. Foner, 2 vols. (New York: Citadel Press, 1969), 1:46–49, 1:88–93.

14. Ginger Strand, "The Many Deaths of General Montgomery: Audiences and Pamphlet Plays of the Revolution," *American Literary History* 9 (1997): 1–20.

15. Philbrick, 133. Two later editions were published in 1776, one in Boston and the other in Providence. All references to the play will be taken from the Philadelphia edition. Some controversy surrounds not only Leacock's first name but also his exact identity; contemporary records list several men named J. Leacock living in Philadelphia during the Revolution. For more extensive consideration of this controversy, see Philbrick, 41–42; and Francis James Dallett Jr., "John Leacock and the Fall of British Tyranny," *Pennsylvania Magazine of History and Biography* 78 (1954): 456–75. Carla Mulford Micklus, however, appears to prove Leacock's identity definitely. See Micklus, "John Leacock's *A New Song, on the Repeal of the Stamp Act*," *Early American Literature* 15.2 (Fall 1980): 188–93. Philbrick's summary introduction to the play in *Trumpets Sounding* remains the best existing assessment of the play. See Philbrick, 41–55. For summary accounts of the play, see Meserve, 79–81; Brown, 75–78; and Richardson, *Drama*, 37–40. Jeffrey Richards also considers the play as an example of metatheatrical discourse in early American literature. See Richards, *Theater*, 249–51.

16. Richards, *Theater*, 249.

17. Richardson, *Drama*, 38.

18. Leacock, ii; Brown, 22–29. Brown lists the three known performances by Burgoyne's troops: Aaron Hill's tragedy *Zara*, Rowe's *Tamerlane*, and Susannah Centlivre's sentimental comedy *The Busybody*, the last of which was reputedly followed by a farce of Burgoyne's own composition, titled *The Blockade of Boston*. Popular accounts, as Brown chronicles, state that the performance of the farce was interrupted by an announcement of a rebel attack, which was originally believed to be part of the play. Francis, Lord Rawdon, a young captain under Burgoyne's command, wrote home to his father in 1775, "We are to have plays this winter . . . I am enrolled as an actor . . . General Burgoyne is our Garrick," a fascinating metaphorical fusion of military command and theatrical direction. See George F. Scheer and Hugh Rankin, *Rebels and Redcoats* (New York: World, 1957), 97; and Richards, *Theater*, 226.

19. A shot of three hundred yards, even with modern ballistics and optics, is no mean feat. Dick Rifle may have a bit of the *miles gloriosus* about him.

20. "Buckstail" is a slang term for buckskin, the stereotypical garment of frontier settlers. As with "Dick Rifle," whose name connotes the particular accuracy with which Pennsylvania frontiersmen shot their preferred weapons, Leacock, presumably a Philadelphian, seems to have used the settlers of western and central Pennsylvania, the frontiersmen with whom he would have been most likely to have contact, as his source for these character names. Philbrick associates the "Buckstail" name with the trousers of the Continental army (133n.), but since Leacock was a Philadelphian, the rifle and buckskin garments would likely have been familiar to him as "props" characteristic of the inhabitants of the Pennsylvania frontier before the outbreak of the Revolution. Leacock seems to have transferred these identifying markers to the national emblem of the citizen-soldier.

21. For the participation of costumed "gentlemen" in the Stamp Act riots, see Deloria, 33–34. Deloria attributes similar characteristics of double consciousness to the "war paint" worn by participants in the Boston Tea Party.
22. Leacock, vi. Note the Catonic "liberty or death" rhetoric exhibited in the words of Dick Rifle.
23. Ibid., v. Gillian Russell observes that General Burgoyne's prologue for *Zara*, a play produced by the British at Boston, uses a female figure, "Freedom," to exhort the audience (160–61). Gender politics, it seems, transcended the differences between the redcoats and the rebels.
24. The British and a group of Bostonian sympathizers appear to have enacted *Tamerlane* in Boston during 1776. See *Boston News Letter*, 29 February 1776; and Brown, 24.
25. Leacock, 1.
26. Philbrick, 44. For Weddburn's association with Sheridan and Quin, see William Benzie, *The Dublin Orator: Thomas Sheridan's Influence on Eighteenth-Century Rhetoric and Belles Lettres* (Menston, U.K.: Scholar Press Limited, 1972), 27. Wedderburn was also well known for delivering an extended harangue against Benjamin Franklin during a public debate in which Wedderburn cast aspersions on Franklin's good faith as a colonial agent while quoting from Edward Young's tragedy *The Revenge*. See Warner, *Letters*, 91–93.
27. Leacock, 7. The ambiguity of Paramount's "us" should be carefully noted, as it could signify either the ministerial junto, Paramount's use of the corporate first person (usually known as "the royal we"), or both.
28. Philbrick, 70n. For the widespread popularity of Wilkes in the colonies, especially among street protesters, see Shaw, 67–73.
29. Leacock, 8. Such mastery of the forms of popular appeal is, of course, a source of the hatred displayed by the tribunes, as well as the conspirators, for Shakespeare's Caesar.
30. Leacock, 14; Addison, *Cato*, 1.1.3–4. Paramount's allusion to Addison was apparently too much for the play's readers in New England; the lines were expunged from the Boston and Providence editions, suggesting that, sadly, these lines might not have been spoken during the performance at Harvard, where *Cato* had been acted repeatedly during the preceding decades.
31. Philbrick, 47. For Pitt's condemnation of the revolt of the colonies, see Francis Thackeray, *A History of the Right Honorable William Pitt, Earl of Chatham*, 2 vols. (London: C. and J. Rivington, 1827), 2:378.
32. Leacock, 15. Lord Wisdom's emphatic, emotive speeches, with their emphasis on the powers of imagination, eerily prefigure the Burke of *Reflections on the Revolution in France*. Indeed, Pitt sounds much more like the late Burke than the figure of Burke himself, Bold Irishman. For the imagination and politics in Burke, see Barrell, 8–20.
33. Leacock, 18–19. See Addison, *Cato*, 4.4.95, "O liberty! O virtue! O my country!"
34. Leacock, 24; Addison, *Cato*, 2.4.80.
35. Warner, "What's Colonial," 63.
36. For a consideration of Tammany's importance in Pennsylvania politics, see Roger D. Abrahams, "White Indians in Penn's City: The Loyal Sons of Saint Tammany," in *Riot and Revelry in Early America*, 179–204.
37. Deloria, 13–14.
38. For additional considerations of the importance of American Indian imagery

to the Revolutionary period, see Fliegelman, *Declaring Independence*, 97–99; and Ellison, 87–96, 136–47.

39. See Roach, *Cities*, 42–47.

40. Leacock, 35–36.

41. Sayre, 7–8. See also Gustafson, 5–8. Gustafson notes the false equations commonly established by European humanism between Native Americans and the orators of classical antiquity.

42. For the Virginia episodes, see Holton, 104. See also Sayre, 4–5.

43. Purcell, 19.

44. Leacock, 24.

45. On the importance of female mourners to Revolutionary martyrdom, see Purcell, 37.

46. Leacock, 42. It hardly seems like an accident that Leacock gives this sympathetic figure the name of Samuel Richardson's sentimental heroine. See Leonard Tennenhouse, "The Americanization of Clarissa," *Yale Journal of Criticism* 11.1 (Spring 1998): 177–96.

47. My account of Dunmore and his slave regiment draws heavily on Holton, 133–63.

48. Holton, 159.

49. *New York Journal*, 8 August 1776. For the ambiguities of the Declaration's text relating to race, see Fliegelman, *Declaring Independence*, 141–42. The reader will remember, perhaps, that Nathan Hale was captured at or near Huntingdon.

50. For other useful comments on representations of African Americans in early American drama, see Richards, *Drama*, 24–25; and Purcell, 24. The most extensive discussion of Act 4 is Mark Evans Bryan, "The Rhetoric of Race and Slavery in an American Patriot Drama: John Leacock's *The Fall of British Tyranny*," *Journal of American Drama and Theatre* 12.3 (Fall 2000): 41–54.

51. Holton, 152.

52. Leacock, 57. Allen is alone onstage, suggesting that the audience may be intended to fill in as supernumaries portraying his captured troops in this scene.

53. The dashes with which Leacock punctuates Allen's speech typically mark scenes calling for great emotion in eighteenth-century play scripts. They are also used to punctuate mad scenes.

54. Hal T. Shelton, *General Richard Montgomery and the American Revolution: From Redcoat to Rebel* (New York: New York University Press, 1994), 103–4.

55. Leacock, 64.

56. Ibid.

57. Adams and Leonard, *Novanglus*, 63; Algernon Sidney, *Discourses Concerning Government* (1699; London: Andrew Millar, 1763), 173. The passage Adams quotes is from a chapter devoted to proving that "[p]opular governments are less subject to civil disorders than monarchies."

58. Quincy Jr., *Observations*, 80.

59. These same political genealogies employed by the patriots, the imagery of bands of brothers modeled on the Horatii and the devoted opponents of King Charles I, also provided ammunition for American Tories firing propaganda missives from their own perches. One loyalist poem compares Washington to the Roman conspirator Catiline and Oliver Cromwell: "Wilt thou for once permit a private man / To parlee with thee, and thy conduct scan? / At Reason's bar has Catiline been heard: / At Reason's bar e'en Cromwell has appear'd." See "The American Times, Part First," in *The Loyalist Poetry of the American Revolution*, ed. Winthrop D. Sargent (Philadelphia: Collins, 1857), 10.

60. The best biographical work on Brackenridge remains Claude Milton Newlin, *The Life and Works of Hugh Henry Brackenridge* (Princeton, N.J.: Princeton University Press, 1932).

61. Brackenridge, *Bunkers-Hill*, 1. See also Newlin, 34. For other discussions of the plot of *Bunkers-Hill*, see Meserve, 81–82; Brown, 80–81; and Richardson, *Drama*, 36.

62. Brackenridge, *Montgomery*, 5; Newlin, 37. Brown accepts Brackenridge's statement that the play was never intended for the theater. See Brown, 83. For other discussions of the plot of *The Death of General Montgomery*, see Philbrick, 213–19; Meserve, 82–83; Brown, 81–83; and Richardson, *Drama*, 37.

63. Witherspoon, 256. See also my discussion of Witherspoon's views on theater and rhetorical performance in Chapter 4.

64. For more on radicalism at the College of New Jersey, see Robson, 43–46, 58–70.

65. Wilson, *Sense of the People*, 214.

66. Houston, 31. See also Peter Karsten, *Patriot Heroes in England and America: Political Symbolism and Changing Values over Three Centuries* (Madison: University of Wisconsin Press, 1978), 18.

67. Houston, 224.

68. Karsten, 15, 46–49.

69. Burke, *Works*, 2:17.

70. Karsten, 50–51.

71. Gustafson, 189.

72. *New York Gazette*, 16 March 1775.

73. Gustafson, 195.

74. Ibid., 197; Purcell, 11, 33.

75. Perez Morton, *An Oration, Delivered at the King's Chapel in Boston, April 8, 1776, on the Re-interment of the Remains of the Most Worshipful Grand-Master, Joseph Warren, Esquire* (Boston: J. Gill, 1776), 5, 11. Gustafson also quotes the "Illustrious Relics!" passage (197).

76. Brackenridge, *Bunkers-Hill*, 6. Putnam's speech seems to echo Portius's lines from *Cato*, in which Portius observes that Cato's death at the hands of Caesar "Would fill up all the guilt of civil war, / And close the Scene of blood" (1.1.5–6).

77. Brackenridge, *Bunkers-Hill*, 16.

78. Ibid., 20.

79. Ironically, this metaphor places General Warren in the role of Patroclus, hardly known for his prowess in battle, illustrating Brackenridge's willingness to sacrifice figurative accuracy for political purposes. Dennis D. Hughes notes that some dispute exists as to whether Achilles' slaying of the Trojans is part of the funeral hecatomb for Patroclus or a distinct revenge killing. See Hughes, *Human Sacrifice in Ancient Greece* (London: Routledge, 1991), 49–56.

80. Leacock, 28.

81. Purcell, 11.

82. Leacock, 28. These lines suggest a possible echo of Cato's injunction, in Addison's play, to his allies after sentencing the Roman mutineers to death. See Addison, *Cato*, 3.5.73–78.

83. Leacock, 29.

84. Leacock, 14. Note Howe's use of the term "thunder-bolts of war," tying the tradition of British military heroism to that of the Roman republic. See my discussion in Chapter 4 of the use of this phrase in a dialogue performed at Yale.

85. Ibid., 35.

86. Quoted in Newlin, 38. Brackenridge manages to include opponents of English kings ranging from Henry VIII (More) to James I (Raleigh) to Charles II and James II (Russell and Temple, allies of Sidney) in a grouping that has a decidedly genealogical construction.

87. Brackenridge wrote that he actively sought out the accounts of veterans of the campaign against Quebec to get the source material for his second play: "I have conversed with those who saw the scalps warm from the heads of our countrymen. I have had the relation from their mouth who beheld the fires lighted up, and heard, with a soul painting sympathy, the horrid shrieks and gloomy howlings of the savage tribes in the execution of the poor captives." Quoted in Newlin, 35–36. For the reticence of the commander of the British garrison, Carleton, to use his Indian allies against the Americans, see Robert McConnell Hatch, *Thrust for Canada: The American Attempt on Quebec in 1775–1776* (Boston: Houghton Mifflin, 1979), 39–41. For Carleton's magnanimity as a jailer, see Hatch, 179–80. As for Montgomery's burial, Carleton had him buried in a coffin with a small ceremony, also burying Montgomery's subordinates John Macpherson and Jacob Cheesman, who were killed alongside their commander, in Montgomery's plot, although they were interred without coffins. See Shelton, 153.

88. Quoted in Alan Rogers, *Empire and Liberty: American Resistance to British Authority, 1755–1763* (Berkeley: University of California Press, 1974), 63.

89. Charles Lee, *Strictures on a Pamphlet, Entitled "A Friendly Address to All Reasonable Americans, on the Subjects of our Political Confusions." Addressed to the People of America* (Philadelphia: William and Thomas Bradford, 1774), 7.

90. Fred Anderson, *Crucible*, 377. My account of Wolfe's character and the battle are drawn from Anderson's debunking of the mythology that surrounds the Battle of Quebec (Fred Anderson, *Crucible*, 344–72).

91. Shelton, 26–51.

92. Strand, 16.

93. Purcell, 29–31.

94. Smith, *Works*, 2:20. For the passages that so agitated Smith's opponents, see 2:28–29.

95. Smith also commemorated lower-ranking officers, such as his former student Captain Jacob Cheesman of New York, in his oration, which may also have given offense to some members of his audience. See Smith, *Works*, 2:38; and Purcell, 30. As an instructor at a military academy, I can only say that for Smith the prospect of eulogizing a former student, as he did with Cheesman, must have seemed a very bleak one.

96. Paine, *Works*, 1:48.

97. Ibid., 1:93.

98. Brackenridge, *Montgomery*, 13. For the recurrence of the hecatomb imagery, see Brackenridge's prologue and the extensive discussion between Montgomery and Arnold in the opening scene of an ox roast held at a meeting of the British and their Indian allies (8, 10–13). The move away from classical examples in Brackenridge's propaganda play suggests an early manifestation of a much broader pattern observed by Paul A. Rahe in the political culture of the United States during the post-Revolutionary period, when Americans abandoned the glorification of antiquity in favor of praising modern liberal society. See Rahe, "Antiquity Surpassed: The Repudiation of Classical Republicanism," in *Republicanism, Liberty, and Commercial Society, 1649–1776*, ed. David Wootton (Stanford, Calif.: Stanford University Press, 1994), 233–69.

99. Strand, 15.

100. Brackenridge, *Montgomery*, 16.
101. Paine, *Works*, 1:49.
102. Brackenridge, *Montgomery*, 27. Compare the historical revisionism of this speech to the depiction of Chatham as Lord Wisdom in Leacock.
103. For Montgomery's death, see Shelton, 149; and Purcell, 24.
104. Brackenridge, *Montgomery*, 37–38.
105. Ibid., 38. This imagery of renewal in this passage echoes the prophetic closing sequence of Brackenridge's and Freneau's *The Rising Glory of America*. Brackenridge is generally credited with the final third of this poem, including its prophecies of future American greatness. See Newlin, 23.
106. Brown, 84.

Epilogue

1. Hill, 78.
2. Brown, 147–61; Seilhamer, 2:51–95. See also David Ritchey, *A Guide to the Baltimore Stage in the Eighteenth Century* (Westport, Conn.: Greenwood Press, 1982), 4–11.
3. Brown, 181–86.
4. Thomas Otway, *Venice Preserv'd; Or, A Plot Dicover'd* (London: Joseph Hindmarsh, 1682). For the play's disappearance from the colonial theater and its popularity with British troops, see Seilhamer, 1:197, and Brown, 173–87. For the political ambiguity of *Venice Preserved*, see Aline Mackenzie Taylor, *Next to Shakespeare: Otway's "Venice Preserv'd" and "The Orphan" and Their History on the London Stage* (Durham, N.C.: Duke University Press, 1950), 163–64. Barrell notes that in 1794 John Thelwall and other English radicals attempted to appropriate the play for their own cause by loudly applauding the anti-government speeches of the conspirators during a production at Covent Garden. See Barrell, 567. See also Richards, *Drama*, 128. Richards notes the importance of *Venice Preserved* to both the colonial and post-Revolutionary theater.
5. *Maryland Journal*, 26 March 1782.
6. Henry Brooke, *Gustavus Vasa, The Deliverer of His Country* (London: J. Buck, 1739). This play should not be confused with the play supposedly written by Benjamin Colman, which I mentioned in Chapter 4.
7. For the ban on *Gustavus Vasa*, see Loftis, *Politics*, 150.
8. *Maryland Journal*, 28 May 1782.
9. *New Jersey Gazette* (Trenton), 15 July 1778; *Maryland Journal*, 4 June 1782.
10. *Continental Journal*, 27 June 1782.
11. William Smith, *An Account of Washington College* (Philadelphia: J. Crukshank, 1784), 39–40.
12. Brown, 153–54; Jones, 150. Smith also records a 1783 production of the play at the College of Philadelphia, after his ouster from office. See Jones, 136. Brown records that each of the Maryland Company's productions took in roughly £46, among the smallest houses of the company's run in Baltimore (183).
13. Odell, 232–36; Pollock, 41–42, 46–48.
14. In the 15 September 1785 *New York Packet*, a letter to the editor argues that if the city must tolerate the return of the theater, then the populace should recognize not the Maryland Company but "an old company of players, who I learn to the southward, are lately arrived from the West-Indies, and who have a claim to remembrance not only for having lived long amongst us, but for conducting themselves by a compliance, perfectly consonant with the desires of the first committee

in the beginning of the revolution, perfectly consonant to the wishes of the city." See also Odell, 236.

15. G. Thomas Tanselle, *Royall Tyler* (Cambridge, Mass.: Harvard University Press, 1967), 21. For a recent consideration of Tyler's dramatic career after *The Contrast*, see Richards, *Drama*, 296–315.

16. For more on the stage Yankee and other stereotypically "American" theatrical performances, see Joseph Roach, "The Emergence of the American Actor," in Wilmeth and Bigsby, 1:338–72.

17. Tanselle, 52. See also Odell, 255–57; Pollock, 45; and Ritchey, 15–20.

18. Royall Tyler, *The Contrast*, ed. Thomas J. McKee (1887; reprint, New York: Burt Franklin, 1970); Meserve, 97.

19. Agnew, 150.

20. See Meserve, 95–102; Richardson, 47–52; Roberta Borkat, "Lord Chesterfield and Yankee Doodle: Royall Tyler's *The Contrast*," *Midwest Quarterly Review* 17 (1976): 436–39; Lucy Rinehart, "A Nation's Noble Spectacle," *American Drama* 3.2 (Spring 1994): 29–52; and Donald Siebert, "Royall Tyler's 'Bold Example': *The Contrast* and the English Comedy of Manners," *Early American Literature* 13 (1978): 3–11.

21. John Evelev, "*The Contrast*: The Problem of Theatricality and Political and Social Crisis in Post-Revolutionary America," *Early American Literature* 31.1 (Spring 1996): 74–97; Trish Loughran, "The First American Contrasts: Region and Nation under the Articles of Confederation," *Explorations in Early American Culture* 5 (2001): 230–59; Richard S. Pressman, "Class Positioning and Shays' Rebellion: Resolving the Contradictions of *The Contrast*," *Early American Literature* 21.2 (Fall 1986): 87–102. See also Pressman's later editorial corrections to the essay in a letter to the editor, *Early American Literature* 22.2 (Fall 1987): 230.

22. See Richardson, "Nationalizing," 221–22.

23. Patterson, *Nobody's Perfect*, 185–86.

24. Gustafson, 195.

25. See, for instance, Tyler, *Contrast*, 46–50.

26. Gustafson, 225.

27. Tyler, *Contrast*, 2.

28. Tyler, *Contrast*, 11; Ellison, 98. See also Tanselle, 58–59. Ellison and Tanselle note that the poem dates from 1782, making it a document of the end of the Revolutionary period. Tanselle observes that this song has at times been attributed to both Tyler and Philip Freneau, a good indicator of the continuing appeal of American Indian symbolism to poets of the early national period and scholars of American literature.

29. Sayre, 14.

30. Tyler, *Contrast*, 11.

31. As a child of the Reagan era, I can never read the passage of dialogue about Manly's coat without thinking of Oliver North testifying before Congress in his Marine uniform.

32. Odell, 255–57.

33. Tyler, *Contrast*, 27. For further consideration of the importance of Manly's notes, and other financial aspects of the play, see Jennifer J. Baker, *Securing the Commonwealth: Debt, Speculation, and Writing in the Making of Early America* (Baltimore: Johns Hopkins University Press, 2005), 96–112.

34. Tyler, *Contrast*, 27.

35. See Kramnick, "Great National Discussion," 8–11. Manly's specific criticism of Mandeville, as voiced in his soliloquy, however, was a common rhetorical tactic among Anti-Federalists. See ibid., 11. Manly's own ambiguity seems to reflect the

ambiguity of republican rhetoric more generally in American culture. As Joyce Appleby notes, the liberal influence on American political philosophy saved the republican tradition from its own inherent class biases and produced a republicanism closely associated with the upwardly mobile lower orders. See Appleby, 182–83.

36. Tyler, *Contrast*, 63; Addison, *Cato*, 5.1.1.

37. Tyler, *Contrast*, 65; Addison, *Cato*, 4.4.95. For a similar outcry related to the legalization of theater, see *Freeman's Journal* (Philadelphia), 25 February 1784: "Oh the theatres! Oh my country."

38. Tyler openly makes fun of Manly's propensity to speechify in at least one other scene. After Van Rough announces his intention to break Maria's engagement to Dimple and marry her to Manly, Manly begins to reply but is quickly cut off by Van Rough, who admonishes him, "Come, come, no fine speeches; mind the main chance, young man, and you and I shall always agree" (105).

39. Seilhamer notes several post-Revolutionary performances of *Cato*, though rarely more than one per season: 3 December 1782 (Baltimore), 24 August 1785 (Savannah), 12 March 1787 (New York), 20 March 1789 (Philadelphia), 10 August 1793 (Philadelphia), 24 February 1794 (New York), and 25 March 1795 (Boston). See Seilhamer, 1:71, 202, 214, 259; and 2: 75, 80, 245.

40. *New York Daily Advertiser*, 18 April 1787. See also Odell, 256.

41. Daniel F. Havens, *The Columbian Muse of Comedy: The Development of an American Tradition in Early American Social Comedy, 1787–1845* (Carbondale: Southern Illinois University Press, 1973), 11.

42. Odell, 242–44, 250–63; Seilhamer, 2:177–90, 212–24. For further analysis of *The Poor Soldier* and its importance to the early American theater, see Richards, *Drama*, 60–84.

43. John O'Keefe, *The Poor Soldier* (Dublin: "Printed for the Booksellers," 1784), 10. Odell notes that during 1786–87 Hallam and Henry pared down the role of a cowardly French character, Bagatelle, in performance to avoid arousing the ire of Francophile audience members (253–54).

44. John O'Keefe, *Love in a Camp* (London: A. Strahan, 1800), 38, 41.

45. Seilhamer, 2:335–36. Wignell also arranged for the play's first publication in 1790.

46. Tyler, *Contrast*, 52–53.

47. Wall, 44. Jonathan's description is inaccurate, as only the Pitt statue was made of marble.

48. Tyler, *Contrast*, 38; Wall, 50–52; Silverman, 324. Wall reports that the statue's head was rescued when the British took New York and sent to England, where it came into the possession of Charles Townshend (52–53). Silverman also notes that in 1776 a marble statue of Lord Botetourt, a former royal governor of Virginia, was pulled down and smashed in Williamsburg (324).

49. Wall, 54.

50. Tyler, *Contrast*, 60.

51. Odell, 272–82. *The Contrast* was revived on 10 June (274). For the 1789 season, see also Seilhamer, 2:265–72.

52. Silverman, 571; Ford, 33.

53. Odell, 272.

54. *Gazette of the United States* (New York), 28 November 1789. See also Odell, 279.

55. William Dunlap, *Darby's Return* (Philadelphia: Berry and Rogers, 1789), 9.

56. Dunlap, *History*, 85.

Index

Adams, Abigail, 53
Adams, John, 20, 26; *A Dissertation on the Canon and Feudal Law*, 46–48, 89, 121; "Governor Winthrop to Governor Bradford," 95; interest in theater, 10, 46, 89, 197 n.52; mistrust of oratory, 55–56; mistrust of republicanism, 16–17; quotes Algernon Sidney, 152
Addison, Joseph, 19, 20, 32–33, 48, 68, 83, 89, 106, 170. See also *Cato*
African Americans, 2, 51; representations of during Revolution, 149–50
Agnew, Jean-Christophe, 11, 169
Alexander, William, 61
Allen, Ethan, 151
American Company of Comedians (Douglass), 21, 71; avoids politicized productions, 91; in Annapolis, 93; in Charleston, 4, 18, 85, 87, 99–102; in Jamaica, 104, 166; in New York, 57, 85, 89, 91, 97–98; in Philadelphia, 88–89, 91, 96–97, 98, 109, 110; repertoire under David Douglass, 194 n.13; touring history, 70–72; touring schedule aborted by congressional ban on theater, 103–4, 138; on tour in Virginia and Maryland, 85, 91; in Williamsburg, 132. See also London Company of Comedians; Old American Company
American Revolution, 1, 26, 27, 29, 59, 107; in the Carolinas, 3; in Pennsylvania, 59–60; popular depictions of, 1, 9, 178; study of, 1; transfer of social energies in, 27–29. See also names of individual leaders and battles

American Whig Society (College of New Jersey), 124–25
Ames, Nathaniel, 45; *Almanack*, 52–53
Amherst, Sir Jeffrey, 119
Anderson, Benedict, 6, 128
Anderson, Fred, 159
Annapolis, 56, 92; David Douglass promotes theater in, 20; political protests in, 86; racing season, 78, 197 n.43; theatrical performances in, 70, 72, 78, 79, 82, 97, 166, 200 n.107
Annapolis Company, 193 n.9. See also Murray-Kean Company
Anti-Federalists, 173
anti-theatricality: British, 18–19, 67; colonial, 19, 33, 67–69, 71, 82–83, 84–88, 90–91, 99, 105–6, 108, 123–24, 138–39; patristic, 81; republican, 18, 103–4, 138–39
Appleby, Joyce, 18, 25
Army, Continental, 2, 3, 61, 62, 142
Arnold, Benedict, 59, 138, 161
Attucks, Crispus, 179 n.5

Babcock, James Staunton, 40
Bailyn, Bernard, 34
Baltimore, 50, 166, 168, 169
Barbados, 27, 71
Barré, Isaac, 145, 160, 205 n.41
Barrell, John, 22
Battle of Brooklyn, The, 141
Beaumarchais, Pierre-Augustin Caron de (*Eugenie*), 135
Belcher, Jonathan, 42
Belcher Apostate, 42–44

220 Index

Bell, Robert, 134, 167
Bennett, William J. (*Our Sacred Honor*), 40
Betterton, Thomas, 19
Blair, James, 73
Bloch, Ruth, 25
Blockheads, The, 141
Board of Trade, 22
Bolingbroke, Henry St. John, Viscount, 25, 34, 117; *Craftsman*, 110; *Idea of a Patriot King*, 25, 118–19
Boston, 21, 42, 142, 149; blockade of, 5, 101–2; British occupation of, 142; hostility to theater in, 45, 105–6; Massacre, 52–53, 95, 122; political protests in, 50, 86–87, 143; Tea Party, 53, 72, 99, 147, 155–56; theatrical performances in, 45, 142, 169. *See also* Harvard College
Boston Gazette, 46, 48, 94, 95, 152
Boston Weekly News-Letter, 91, 92, 202 n.141
Boucher, Jonathan, 56, 92–93
de Bourbon, Armand, 81
Bow Street Theatre (Portsmouth, N.H.), 62
Bradford, William, 59–60
Brackenridge, Hugh Henry, 9, 124–25, 141, 153–54, 158; attitude toward theatrical performance, 153; *Battle of Bunkers-Hill, The*, 9, 140, 141, 153, 155–58; *Death of General Montgomery, The*, 9, 140, 141, 153, 158–65; plays written by performed, 9, 138–40. *See also Rising Glory of America, The*; *United States Magazine*
Brandywine, Battle of, 158
Braveheart, 1
Brooklyn, Battle of, 30
Brown, Jared, 164
Brunswick (N.J.), 86
Bunker (Breed's) Hill, Battle of, 138, 147, 155
Burgoyne, John, 138, 142
Burke, Edmund, 122, 129, 145, 154, 160, 202 n.134
Bushnell, Rebecca, 23
Bute, John Stuart, Earl of, 89–90, 93–94, 95, 144, 145
Byles, Mather, 3,
Byrd, William, III, 150

Camden, Charles Pratt, Earl of, 121, 145
Carter, Robert, 150

Cato (Addison), 4, 8, 30–65, 76, 103; allusions to, 31, 40, 42, 46, 48, 52, 53, 54, 59, 83–84, 86, 105–6, 145, 146, 173, 202 n.142; associated with radical politics, 34–35, 50–51, 68, 71, 86, 91, 93; dropped from repertoire, 71, 91, 173; editions of, 63, 93; occasional epilogue to, 62–64; parodies of, 48–49, 52, 105–6, 189 n.66; performances of, 4, 36, 43–45, 52, 59–65, 70, 72–73, 78, 82–83, 88–89, 90, 93, 101, 102, 106, 114, 133, 166, 174, 202 n.142; political ambiguity of, 33–34, 102; popularity of, 32, 33, 42, 45, 68, 102, 173; premiere of, 33–34, 73; pseudonymous use of "Cato," 48, 167, 206 n.64; similarity to Revolutionary propaganda plays, 141; suppressed staging, 114–15; theatrical vehicle for civic virtue, advertised as, 78
Cato's Letters (Trenchard and Gordon), 8, 34–35, 44, 48, 56, 74, 127–28, 135
Centlivre, Susanna: *A Bold Stroke for a Wife*, 137; *The Busybody*, 211 n.18; *The Wonder; or, A Woman Keeps a Secret*, 207 n.76
Chapel Street Theatre (New York), destruction of, 69, 87–88, 104
Charles I (king), 11, 22, 47, 57, 58, 79, 206 n.69
Charles II (king), 17, 44
Charleston, S.C., 2–3, 21; burning of, 138; hostility to theater in, 88, 99; play staged to raise relief money for Boston in, 102; political protests in, 50, 86; theatrical performances in, 4–5, 18, 44, 69, 70, 73, 77, 78, 85, 88, 99–102, 132, 169
Chatham, Earl of. *See* Pitt, William (the elder)
Cheesman, Jacob, 161, 163
Cherokee War. *See* Seven Years' War
Chesterfield, Philip Dormer Stanhope, Earl of (*Letters to his Son*), 170, 171
children, representations of, 24–25, 76
CIA (Central Intelligence Agency), 41
Cibber, Colley, 18, 79; *Love Makes a Man*, 136; *Ximena*, 136. *See also Richard III*
Cincinnatus, 5, 175; Society of the Cincinnati, 172, 173
circum-Atlantic culture, 7, 11–12, 24; and commerce, 126–27, 131; relationship to transatlantic culture, 12
Clark, John L., 107

Index   221

Clinton, Henry, 62
Cockings, George (*The Conquest of Canada*), 72, 97
Colden, Cadwallader, 87
College of New Jersey, 153; curriculum teaches oratory, 107, 123–24; performance of *Douglas*, 134; performance of *Tamerlane*, 80, 106, 113; recitation of *The Military Glory of Great Britain* (commencement dialogue), 119; Washington attends 1783 commencement, 134–35
College of Philadelphia, 9, 108; curriculum teaches oratory, 107, 109; performance of *Masque of Alfred* at, 109–13, 143. See also commencement dialogues, College of Philadelphia
colleges, colonial, social role of, 106–8
Colley, Linda, 34
Collier, Jeremy, 18–19, 124
Colman, Benjamin (*Gustavus Vasa*), 107
commemoration, 31, 39; and American Revolution, 40, 148–49, 162; and Boston Massacre, 52–53, 100, 125–26, 154, 155; of Richard Montgomery, 160–61; of James Warren, 155–56
commencement dialogues, College of Philadelphia: 1761 dialogue, 117–18; 1762 dialogue, 118–19; 1763 dialogue, 119; 1766 dialogue, 119–21; 1767 dialogue, 121–22; 1770 dialogue, 122; 1775 dialogue, 122–23
Commonwealth philosophical tradition, 16, 18
Concord (Mass.). *See* Lexington and Concord
Congreve, William (*Love for Love*), 78
Constitution: British, 16; United States, 9, 178
Continental Congress, Second, 2–3, 28, 103–4, 138–39; New England delegation, 59
Continental Journal (Boston), 167, 192 n.117
Contrast, The (Tyler), 9, 105; performances of, 157–77
Cooper, Chris, 2
Cooper, Myles, 57, 101
Coriolanus (Shakespeare), 64
Cornwallis, Lord, 3, 6, 138
Cosby, William, 35, 44, 72
Country party, British, 16, 130; influence on American Revolution, 7

Cowpens, Battle of the, 1, 6
Crisis, The, 28
Cromwell, Oliver, 57, 213 n.59
Cumberland, Richard, 208 n.95; *West Indian, The*, 131–33, 143
Cymbeline (Shakespeare), 91–92, 100

Daggett, Napthali, 48
Dale, Thomas, 73
Dartmouth, H.M.S., 53
Dartmouth College, 134; theatrical performances at, 133–34
David, Jacques-Louis (*The Oath of the Horatii*), 152
Davidson, Cathy N., 27
"Death Song of the Cherokee Indian" (Hunter), 171–72
Declaration of Independence, 81, 110, 124, 150, 160, 176
DeLancey family (New York), 87
Deloria, Philip J., 147
Dickinson, John, 52–53; *Letters from a Farmer in Pennsylvania*, 52–53
Douglass, David, 4, 11, 21, 91, 96, 129, 132, 168; assumes control of London Company, 82; heads partial company, 71, 87; proponent of theater, 20, 83–84, 85, 89–90, 106; recruits actors in London, 71, 103; repertoire of London/American Company under, 194 n.13; retires, 166
Douglass, Mrs., performing as Mrs. Hallam, 81
Dryden, John, 18, 68; *Absalom and Achitophel*, 68; *Tempest*, 71, 91, 96, 97, 100, 177
Duché, Jacob, 109, 112, 119; putative author of essays on *Alfred*, 204 n.26
Dumfries (Va.), 86, 92
Dunlap, William, 13, 17–18, 178; *Darby's Return*, 177–78
Dunmore, John Murray, Earl of, 149–50

Eddis, William, 92, 93, 98
Eden, Robert, 92
Edes, Benjamin, 46, 47
effigy: Catonic, 8, 34–35, 51, 84, 146, 151, 177; defined, 22; "free-born Englishman" as, 132; Nathan Hale as, 31, 39–41; interconnection of tyrant, sacrificial victim, and patriot, 21–23,

31–32, 69; Native American as, 147–48, 171–72; orations fuse patriot and martyr, 155, 157, 160; patriot, 5, 25–26, 28, 58, 60, 106, 108, 128–29, 150, 157, 172, 177; resurrection, 51, 151–52, 154, 164; sacrificial victim, 5, 24–25, 39, 49, 58, 106, 108, 126, 148, 150, 157; similarities of tyrant and patriot, 22–23, 38, 55, 56, 58, 98, 145; in street theater, 6, 86–87, 150; tyrant, 5, 22–24, 28, 58, 106, 108, 145, 149, 150; tyrant, sacrificial victim, and patriot reinvented and redeployed in plays by American authors, 142, 143, 170; tyrant, sacrificial victim, and patriot revived in post-Revolutionary American theater, 166
Ellis, Joseph, 9
Ellison, Julie K., 32, 39, 55, 75, 171
English Advice to the Freeholders, &c of the Province of Massachusetts Bay, 35
environment, North American, effects on residents, 2
Eusden, Laurence, 52
expansionism, colonial, 63–65

Fairfax, Sally, 83
Faneuil Hall (Boston), 142
Farquhar, George: "Essay on Comedy," 19; *The Twin Rivals*, 88. See also *Recruiting Officer, The*
Federalists, 173
Fliegelman, Jay, 12
Foucault, Michel, 23, 24
France, 51, 60, 135
Franklin, Benjamin, 35, 108
Franklin, James, 35
Frederick Louis, Prince of Wales, 36, 110–11
Frederick (Md.), 86
Freemasons: Charleston, 4–5; David Douglass and, 101
French Revolution, 22
Freneau, Philip, 124–25, 136. See also *Rising Glory of America, The*; *United States Magazine*

Gage, Thomas, 72, 97, 156, 160
Gardiner, Thomas, 156, 157, 161
Garrick, David, 142, 192 n.117; *Lethe*, 93; *Lying Valet, The*, 136
Gaspee, H.M.S., burned in Rhode Island, 96

Gay, John, 18; *Beggar's Opera*, 92
Gazette of the United States (New York), 178
George II (king), 42, 81, 110–11, 167; commemorated, 117–18; compared to Cato, 114; as patriot king, 111, 112
George III (king), 25, 26, 31, 35, 57, 58, 65, 89, 144; accession celebrated, 117–18; effigy of executed, 150; familiarity with *Cato*, 8, 32, 35–36, 54; parodied, 125; as patriot king, 118–19, 120–21; statue of, beheaded, 28
George Barnwell (Lillo), 33
Georgia Gazette, 50, 54, 94
Gibson, Mel, 1, 3, 178
Gill, James, 46, 47
Girard, Rene, 21, 22, 26, 29, 148
Godfrey, Thomas (*Prince of Parthia, The*), 109–10
Goldberg, Jonathan, 27
Gooch, William, 44, 73
Gordon, Thomas. See *Cato's Letters*
Grafton, Augustus Fitzroy, Duke of, 121
Gray, Thomas ("Elegy Written in a Country Churchyard"), 159
Grenville, George, 47, 85, 87
Gustafson, Sandra, 26, 27, 60, 155, 170
Gustavus Vasa (Henry Brooke), 167–68
Guy Fawkes Day, 6, 50, 80–81, 86. See also Pope Day

Hale, Nathan, 26, 58, 65, 162; as effigy, 31, 39–41; execution of, 30–31, 59; familiarity with *Cato*, 8, 31, 40; and George III, 31, 36; and Linonian Society, 123; statues of, 40–41; theatrical experience, 40, 133; and George Washington, 31, 40, 60
Hallam, Lewis, Jr., 166, 174
Hallam, Lewis, Sr., 66, 83, 106
Hallam, Mrs. *See* Douglass, Mrs.
Hallam, Nancy, 92
Hallam Company. *See* London Company of Comedians
Hamilton, Alexander, 57
Hamlet (Shakespeare), 66, 93–96, 98, 166
Hampden, John, 13, 152, 154, 157, 158, 160, 161, 188 n.33
Hampton (Va.), 150
Hancock, John, 100–101
Harrington, James, 156, 158
Harvard College, 105, 120; theatrical

performances at, 45, 52, 106, 107, 113–17, 133, 138–40, 143
Havens, Daniel F., 173–74
Heady, Thomas, 72–73
Henry, John, 166, 174
Henry, Patrick, 8, 54–58, 60; Catonic performance of, 54–55, 57–58; Stamp Act speech, 57–58; St. John's Day speech, 54
Henry VI, Part 2 (Shakespeare), 56
Hill, Aaron (*Zara*), 211, n.18
History Channel, 9
Hobbes, Thomas (*Leviathan*), 68
Hollis, Thomas, 46, 47
Home, John: *Alonzo*, 209 n.110; *Douglas*, 85, 109, 123, 134
Hopkinson, Francis, 81, 110, 117, 119; *Temple of Minerva, The*, 135–36
Hopkinson, Thomas, 146
Houston, Alan Craig, 154
Howe, William, 59, 62, 256
Hull, William, 30
Hume, David, 109
Huntington (N.Y.), 30, 150
Huske, John, 87
Hutchings, Joseph, 150
Hutchinson, Thomas, 46, 176

impressment: Act for Raising Recruits and, 73; colonial resistance to, 77–78, 90; in the drama, 75–76, 196 n.27; Knowles Riots caused by, 77, 115
Ingersoll, Jared, 48
Interregnum, 11, 13, 17
Intolerable Acts, 72, 101
Isaacs, Jason, 3

Jamaica, 69, 129–30, 132
James I (king), 27
James II (king), 154
Jefferson, Thomas: attends theater, 92; on bloodshed and revolution, 20–21, 27, 29
John (king), 47
John Street Theatre (New York), 71, 90
Johnson, Odai, 14
Jones, John Paul, 129–30
Julius Caesar (Shakespeare), 24, 26, 72, 93–96, 124, 145; performances of, 96, 101, 154, 202 n.141

Kean, Thomas. *See* Murray-Kean Company
Kelly, Hugh, *A Word to the Wise*, 97

King George's War, 77, 78
King John (Shakespeare), 71, 91–92, 97
Kramnick, Isaac, 18, 19,

Lafayette, Gilbert du Motier, Marquis de, 172
Leacock, John, 141, 142; *Fall of British Tyranny, The*, 9, 140–52; play written by performed, 9, 138–40
Lebanon (Conn.), 86
Ledger, Heath, 3
Lee, Arthur, 151–52; "Oppression," 90
Lee, Nathaniel (*The Rival Queens*), 209 n.110
Leeward Islands, 71
Lexington (Mass.). *See* Lexington and Concord
Lexington and Concord, battles of, 2, 54
liberalism, 18, 19
liberty: British (political ideal), 7, 8, 23, 52, 69, 98, 102, 121; bachelorhood as, 76; difficulty of defining, 23, 33, 86; personifications of, 49, 50, 51, 143–44, 146, 149; as universal ideal, 163
liberty funeral. *See* street theater
Linonian Society (Yale), 33, 134; amateur theatricals staged by, 123, 126–33, 136–37
Litto, Fredric M., 32
Locke, John, 17, 147, 158
London Chronicle, 46
London Company of Comedians, 57, 80, 129; in Annapolis, 82; in Charleston, 78; in New England, 45, 82; in New York, 82–83; in Philadelphia, 79, 81–82, 108; renamed, 71, 88; repertoire under Hallam, Sr., 194 n.12; touring history, 70; in the West Indies, 82, 86, 90; in Williamsburg, 66. *See also* American Company of Comedians
London Magazine, 36
Longmore, Paul K., 27
Loudoun, Robert Campbell, Earl of, 110, 112
Louis XIV (king), 80, 114
Louis XV (king), 80, 81
Louis XVI (king), 22
loyalists, 97
Luzerne, Anne-César, chevalier de la, 135–36
Lyttelton, George, 110–11, 115, 116

Macbeth (Davenant), 5, 28, 71, 89; performances of, 89–90, 101, 174
Macbeth (Shakespeare), 25, 89
Mackrabie, Alexander, 96
Macpherson, John, 161, 162–63
Madison, James, 124–25
Magna Carta, 47, 52
Maier, Pauline, 47
Mallett, David (*Masque of Alfred*), 110–13, 116. *See also* Thomson, James
Mandeville, Bernard, 171
Marion, Francis, 1
Marlborough, John Churchill, Duke of, 73, 74–75, 158; victory at Blenheim, 73
Maryland Company, 166–68
Maryland Gazette, 56, 98; letter relating to Tobacco Fee controversy in, 95–96
Maryland Journal, 167
Massachusetts Spy (Worcester), 52, 53, 94
Mays, David D., 67
Merchant of Venice (Shakespeare), 66
merchants, depictions of, 127–29
Milton, John, 13, 17; *Eikonoklastes*, 79, 206 n.69
monarchy, influence on American politics, 28–29
Monkton, Robert (general), 119
Montagu, Edward, 171
Montgomery, Richard, 138, 151, 159–64
Montreal, 151
Montresor, John, 30, 87–88
Moore, Henry, 90
Morgan, Daniel, 1, 6
Morris, Lewis, 35, 44, 72–73
Morton, Perez, 155–56, 157, 164
Moseley, Benjamin, 104
Murray-Kean Company, 69, 70, 77, 78, 82; repertoire of, 193 n.9
Murray, Walter. *See* Murray-Kean Company

national identity: American, acknowledgment of ties to Britain during and after the Revolution, 146, 154, 158–59, 164–65; American, difficulty of matching to theatrical texts after the Revolution, 166, 169–70, 172; American, evolution of, 3, 6, 9, 10, 63, 65, 85, 102–3, 121, 139–40, 142–43, 146–47, 163, 174; British, colonial, connected to theater, 7, 10, 11–12, 14–15, 66–69, 83–84, 92–93, 97–98, 113; British, metropolitan, 14, 34, 66; *Contrast, The,* and, 168–78; performance of origins and, 147; propaganda plays help to create a new American, 138–65
Native Americans: depictions of, 2, 133–34, 147–48, 171–72; European American appropriations of identity of, 147–48; interactions with Europeans, 4
New American Company, 71, 92; repertoire of, 195 n.15
New England Courant, 35
New England Weekly Journal, 33
New Hampshire Gazette, 48, 111
New Haven, (Conn.),11, 137. *See also* Yale College
New Jersey, 29
New London (Conn.), 86
Newman, Simon, 12, 26, 28, 50, 59
Newport Mercury, 50
Newport (R.I.), 45, 50–51, 70
newspapers, importance to colonial culture, 47–50
Newton, Benjamin, 127
Newton, Isaac, 17
New York (city): Battle of Golden Hill, 95; *Contrast, The*, premieres in, 169; hostility to theater in, 19, 71, 82–83, 90–91, 103–4, 168; political protests in, 50, 86–87; post-Revolutionary society of, 171–72; statue of George III beheaded in, 28, 176; statue of William Pitt the Elder vandalized in, 176; theatrical performances in, 44, 57, 69, 70–73, 78, 79, 82, 90–91, 132, 174, 177–78
New York (colony), 90
New York Daily Advertiser, 173–74
New York Gazette, 43, 88
New York Journal, 103
New York Mercury, 83
New York Weekly Journal, 35, 44
Norfolk (Va.), 70, 150
North, Frederick (second Earl of Guilford), 144, 176
Norwich (Conn.), 86

O'Keefe, John: *Love in a Camp*, 174–75, 177; *The Poor Soldier*, 174–75, 177; *The Toy*, 177
Old American Company, 168; in Baltimore, 169; in New York, 169, 174; in Philadelphia, 169

Oldfield, Anne, 184 n.54
oratory, 3, 5, 6, 154; and education of patriotic citizens, 9, 105–37; "elocutionary revolution" in, 55; Great Awakening invigorates, 54; parody of colonial radicals' fondness for, 56; potential for misuse of, 55–56; and radicalism, 56–57, 96; and republicanism, 12, 54–58, 96, 191 n.89; Virginian culture of, 54
Oresteia, The (Sophocles), 139
origins: American desire for, 5; performance of, 147
Orphan, The (Otway), 44, 45
Otis, James, 26, 56
Oxford, Robert Harley, Earl of, 34

Paca, William, 92–93, 109
Paine, Thomas, 160–61, 162, 163, 206 n.64
Patriot, The, 1–7, 21, 176
patriotism: and comedy, 170, 174; difficulty in defining, 16, 18, 33–34; ideological dominance of early American theater, 18; and merchants, 126–29; parodied, 174–75; and sacrificial violence, 4, 5, 26, 60; tensions between individualism and collectivism in, 4; and Tyler's *The Contrast*, 171, 175–76
Patterson, Annabel, 16, 24
Penn, Thomas, 89, 108, 122
Pennsylvania Evening Post, 54
Pennsylvania Gazette, 111
Pennsylvania Journal, 89, 161
performance: oral, 12, 15–16; print as, 13, 15–16
Peters, Julie Stone, 14
Philadelphia, 16, 28; anti-Catholicism in, 81; hostility to theater in, 78, 81–82, 108, 142, 168; liberation by Continental Army, 62; occupation of, 60–61; political protests in, 50; theatrical performances in, 69, 70, 71, 72, 78, 79, 81–82, 88–89, 90–91, 93, 96–97, 98, 109–10, 169, 177
Philbrick, Norman, 140, 145
Pitt, William (the elder), 47, 82, 110–11, 115, 116, 121, 145–46
Plato (*Phaedo*), 48, 105
plays: circulation of in North America, 15; popularity of among colonial readers, 5, 33
Pope, Alexander, "Prologue to *Cato*," 34, 84, 89, 114–15

Pope Day, 6, 50, 81, 86, 87, 176. *See also* Guy Fawkes Day
Portsmouth (N.H.), 45, 50, 62, 70, 82
Pratt, Bela Lyon, 40
Presbyterians, opposed to theater, 108, 109, 123–24
print culture, 7; and American patriot movement, 14–15; and connection to theater culture, 8, 12–13, 14, 140–44
Providence (R.I.), 45, 70, 82
Purcell, Sarah J., 31, 148
Putnam, Israel, 77, 151–52, 156
Pym, John, 13

Quakers, opposed to theater, 108
Quartering Act, 85
Quebec, 84, 97; American assault on, 159
Quin, James, 144
Quincy, Josiah, Jr., 94, 100, 120, 152

Randolph, Edmund, 54
Recruiting Officer, The (Farquhar), 5, 19, 73–77, 103; dropped from repertoire, 91; performances of, 5, 45, 70, 72–73, 78, 82, 90, 91, 92, 97, 100, 106, 114, 115, 166, 174; planned performance, 61, 62; popularity of, 73, 91
republicanism, 2, 12; difficulty of defining, 16–17, 18; hostility to theater, 18; interconnection with theater culture, 17, 172–73
Richard III (Cibber), 5, 28, 79–80, 93; dropped from repertoire, 91; performances of, 5, 70, 79, 82, 88, 90, 97, 100, 166, 174, 177
Richard III (Shakespeare), 25, 79
Richards, Jeffrey, 10, 142
Richardson, Gary, 107, 125, 140, 141, 142
Richardson, Samuel, 171
Rising Glory of America, The (Freneau and Brackenridge), 125–26, 136, 157
ritual, similarity to theater, 21, 139–40
Roach, Joseph, 11, 22, 24, 147
Robin, Claude, 138–39, 140, 164
Rockingham, Charles Watson-Wentworth, Marquess of, 121
Rome, 18, 62; Britain compared unfavorably to, 63–65; British and American surrogate identities drawn from, 33, 34, 40, 60, 84, 95–96; diaspora myth of, and British and American identities,

226 Index

147, 152; Joseph Warren compares New England to, by wearing toga, 155
Romeo and Juliet (Shakespeare), 104
Rothstein, Eric, 74, 76
Rowe, Nicholas, 18, 89, 170; *Jane Shore*, 85. See also *Tamerlane*
Royal Grenadiers, 75, 76, 100
Royal Proclamation of 1763, 63, 85
Rush, Benjamin, 28
Russell, Gillian, 6
Russell, William, 158, 161, 188 n.33
Ryan, Dennis. *See* Maryland Company

sacrifice: and communal identity, 5, 21, 96, 125–26; of enemies in propaganda plays, 156–57, 158; importance of commemoration to, 31, 148–49, 159; revolution and, 20–21, 24, 26, 40, 52–53, 60, 148–49; symbolic connections to patriotism and tyranny, 22–28; theater and, 21, 24, 84; tragedy and, 25, 139, 155–65; tragic Indian chief and, 148
Sambrook, David, 117
Savannah (Ga.), 86
Sayre, Gordon, 148
Scots: colonial mistrust of, 199 n.93; Jacobite uprising of 1715, 81, 87; theater controversy among, 109
Senegambia, 131
Seven Years' War, 2, 70, 77, 85, 107, 119, 156; Cherokee War campaign, 2; and origins of American Revolution, 2; Maryland government deadlocked over funding of, 84; Pennsylvania assembly fights troop levies for, 115; produces patriotic unity between Britain and colonies, 51, 84; George Washington's participation in, 2
Sewall, Jonathan Mitchell, 62–65
Shaw, Peter, 12
Shays' Rebellion, 20, 169, 175–76
Shelburne, William Petty, Earl of, 121
Shenstone, William, 171
Sheridan, Richard Brinsley: *The Critic*, 177; *The School for Scandal*, 170, 175, 177
Sheridan, Thomas, 144
Sidney, Algernon, 24, 26, 152, 154, 157, 158, 160, 161, 188 n.33
Silverman, Kenneth, 53
Smith, Gregory, 3
Smith, John (Dartmouth professor), 133–34

Smith, William, 9, 108; advocate of theater, 108, 109, 111; ally of the Penn family, 108, 113, 122; *American Magazine*, 109, 123; eulogy for Richard Montgomery, 160, 162; founds Washington College in Maryland, 123; removed as provost of College of Philadelphia, 123; stages *Gustavus Vasa*, 167–68; stages *Masque of Alfred*, 110–13; teaches drama and oratory while provost of College of Philadelphia, 109–10; writes commencement dialogues, 117, 122–23
Smith, William Stephens, 20
Smollett, Tobias (*The Reprisal*), 101
Sons of Liberty: in Boston, 47, 100; and *Cato*, 91; communications between colonies, 47–48, 49, 100; in Massachusetts, 95, 120; in New York, 87–88; opposed to Stamp Act, 48–49, 87–88; opposed to theater, 71, 87–88; origin of name, 205 n.41
South Carolina Gazette, 94
South Sea Bubble, 34
Southwark Theatre (Philadelphia), 71, 88, 89, 90, 109, 110
Sparta, 43, 156
Spectator, 19, 89, 127, 171
Stamp Act: John Adams opposes, 46–48; College of Philadelphia celebrates repeal of, 119; Congress, 48; Crisis, 23, 49, 51–52, 71, 85, 87, 121, 128; protests against, 49–50, 84–88, 90, 143; provokes anti-theatricality, 71, 87–88; Resolves, 48; Sons of Liberty and, 48–49, 87–88, 120; theatrical performances commemorate repeal of, 88–89
St. Asaph, Jonathan Shipley, bishop of, 145
Steele, Sir Richard, 19, 20, 73, 106–7; *The Conscious Lovers*, 126–31
Sterne, Lawrence, 171
Steuart, Andrew, 15
Stevens, Laura M., 134
Stewart, Maaja A., 132
Stiles, Ezra, 134
St. Kitt's and St. Nevis, 50, 87
Strand, Ginger, 141, 143, 160, 162
street theater, 5, 69, 176; liberty funeral, 8, 50–51, 86; Native American disguises and, 147; parades, 12–13, 84–88; Society of the Sons of Saint Tammany

Index 227

(Philadelphia) and, 147. *See also* Guy Fawkes Day; Pope Day
Sugar Act, 85
suicide, symbolic power of, 24, 26, 36
Sure Guide to Hell, by Belzebub, 67

Tamerlane (Rowe), 5, 8, 28, 80, 103, 144; dropped from repertoire, 71, 91; occasional epilogue for, 81; performances of, 70, 79, 81, 82, 88, 89, 97, 101, 113, 137, 166, 174, 211 n.18, 212 n.24; staged on William III's birthday, 80; Thomson and Mallett's *Alfred* indebted to, 111
Tammany, 147, 171
Tarleton, Banastre, 3
Tatler, 19
Tea Act, 97, 128
Thacher, Peter, 60
theater: as a didactic tool for teachers, 106–7, 109; ease of reproduction, 21; history of as academic discipline, 5–6, 12–13, 168–69; lines of business, 5, 143; power as an ideological medium, 69, 88, 138–40; similarity to war, 6, 39, 75, 142; tensions between individuality and collectivity in audience, 15–16
theater, British: championed as a school for civic virtue, 19, 20, 66, 73; and national identity, 11, 13, 14, 66, 74
theater, collegiate. *See names of individual schools*
theater, colonial and Revolutionary American: amateur, 8, 9, 12, 44–46, 72–73, 93, 102, 105–37; charity performances, 57, 102, 108; and commercial enterprise, 11, 13; commissioned performances, 4–5, 100; congressional ban on, 72, 103–4, 138, 166; evolution of repertoire, 8, 70–72, 82, 88–92, 96–99, 102–3; importance to colonial sense of Britishness, 7, 10, 13–20, 21, 66–69, 96–99, 113; importance to independent American identity, 7, 10, 13, 21–22; parody of amateur performances, 105–6; and print culture, 8, 12–13; professional, earliest, 69; promotion of as school for public virtue, 20, 83–84, 89, 92, 99; propaganda plays performed at Harvard College, 138–39; similarities to contemporary cinema, 4, 5; supplemental congressional restrictions on, 138–39. *See also names of specifics cities, plays, and venues*
theater, military: American, 59–65, 83, 138; British, 5, 97, 142, 211 n.18
theatrum mundi, 10, 39
Thomson, James: *Coriolanus*, 64; *Masque of Alfred*, 110–13, 116, 143; "Rule, Britannia," 101, 112, 143; *Tancred and Sigismunda*, 115–17, 205 n.42. *See also* Mallett, David
de Tocqueville, Alexis, 17–18, 19, 138
Tomlinson, Mr., 71, 87
Tomlinson, Mrs., 87
Tories (political party), 34, 56
Townshend Duties, 46, 90–91, 93, 96, 128
Toy Shop, The (Dodsley), 207 n.76
Trenchard, James. See *Cato's Letters*
Troy, 147
Tucker, St. George, 55
Tyler, Royall, 9, 105, 168–70; *The Bay Boy*, 105–6, 113. See also *Contrast, The*
tyranny, 21–23,

United States Magazine, 125
Upper Marlborough (Md.), 70, 82
Upton, Robert, 69; repertoire of company, 193 n.10; theater company run by, 70, 79

Valley Forge. *See* Washington, George
Van Dam, Rip, 35, 44, 72–73
Vane, Sir Henry, 13
Venice Preserved (Otway), 166–67, 174
Virginia Company. *See* New American Company

Waldstreicher, David, 12
Wall, Thomas. *See* Maryland Company
Wallace, William, 1, 188 n.33
Walpole, Robert, 95, 110, 167
war crimes: British, alleged by American propaganda, 215 nn. 87, 98; in fictional works, 2, 4
Warner, Michael K., 13, 15, 146–47
War of Jenkins' Ear, 77
War of the Spanish Succession, 8, 34, 73
Warren, Joseph, 149, 155–58, 161
Warren, Mercy Otis, 53, 140; *Adulateur, The*, 53, 141; *Defeat, The*, 141; *Group, The*, 141
Washington, George, 7; as American "patriot king," 27–29, 59–60, 135–36,

177; attends performances with the French ambassador, 135–36; attends 1783 commencement of the College of New Jersey, 134–35; celebrated in theatrical performance, 135–36; compared to Cato, 60, 61–63; compared to Coriolanus, 64; compared to Gustavus Vasa, 167–68; compared to Moses and Jesus Christ, 60; depictions in loyalist propaganda, 27; as field commander during Revolution, 30; fondness for *Cato*, 8, 32, 59, 83; and Nathan Hale, 31, 40; imagines self as Juba, 83; inauguration of, 177; interest in theater, 7, 10, 27, 83, 92, 97, 133, 177–78; participation in Seven Years' War, 2, 77, 78, 83; praised in *The Contrast*, 172–73, 177; as public performer, 27; represented in *The Fall of British Tyranny*, 151–52; Valley Forge encampment, 59–65
Washington, Martha, 60–61
Washington College, 123, 168
Wayne, Anthony, 199 n.91
Wedderburn, Alexander, 144
Whigs (political party), 34, 56, 80–82, 130
White Pine Acts of 1722 and 1729, 77
Wignell, Thomas, 169, 175, 177–78
Wilkes, John, 145; republishes *The Fall of Mortimer*, 94; and St. George's Field massacre, 97; supporters of, 144
William III (king), 54, 79, 80, 113–14
William and Mary, College of, 44, 73, 106, 107

Williamsburg, 16, 92; theatrical performances in, 44, 66, 69, 70, 72–73, 79, 93, 97
Wills, Garry, 32
Wilmington (N.C.), 50, 86
Wilson, Kathleen, 11, 16, 81
Windham (Conn.), 86
Wirt, William, 57
Witherspoon, John, 153–54; "Lectures on Eloquence," 124; opposition to theater, 123–24
Withington, Ann Fairfax, 18, 50
Wolfe, James, 84, 97, 114, 119, 156, 158, 159–60, 162–64
women, representations of, 24–25, 49–52, 127, 143–44, 146, 149, 170; excised from *Masque of Alfred*, 111, 149
Wood, Gordon S., 35
Wycherley, George, 187 n.12

Yale College, 30, 33, 40, 41; dialogues recited at, 134; theatrical performances at, 114, 123, 126–33. *See also* Linonian Society
Yankee: stage, 143, 169, 170; Tyler's Jonathan as, 175–77
"Yankee Doodle," 177
Yorktown, Battle of, 138
Young, Edward: *Busiris, King of Egypt*, 102, 133; *The Revenge*, 114, 212 n.26

Zenger, John Peter, 35, 44

Acknowledgments

Portions of Chapters 2, 3, and 4 appeared in earlier versions as "'Great Cato's Descendants': A Genealogy of Colonial Performance" in *Theatre Survey* (© 2003 Cambridge University Press) and are reprinted here by permission of the copyright holder.

Portions of Chapter 5 appeared in an earlier version as "Making 'an Excellent Die': Death, Mourning, and Patriotism in the Propaganda Plays of the American Revolution" in *Early American Literature* (© 2006 University of North Carolina Press) and are reprinted here by permission of the copyright holder.

I would like to acknowledge the following people and institutions for their assistance in the completion of this project. Thanks first of all to Joseph Roach for his insight, guidance, and commitment to the development of his students. He has been a model as well as a friend and mentor.

A number of other readers have provided me with helpful advice. For their contributions, I wish to thank Annabel Patterson, Elizabeth Dillon, Wai Chee Dimock, Jennifer Baker, Jeffrey Richards, and Fredrika Teute. Special thanks go to Heather Nathans and Sandra Gustafson, who as readers for the University of Pennsylvania Press isolated and offered detailed solutions for a number of problems that had bedeviled the manuscript since the first draft.

Thanks also go to Bob Lockhart, Dan Richter, and Erica Ginsburg at the Press, for their careful reading and advice.

For access to its resources, I thank the library system of Yale University, especially the Beinecke Rare Books and Manuscripts Library and the Manuscripts and Archives Division of Sterling Memorial Library. In particular, thanks to the Beinecke staff for removing the Linonian Society's record book from a public display so I could transcribe Nathan Hale's notes.

Thanks also to the Library of Congress, the New York Public Library, the Nimitz Library of the United States Naval Academy, and the Bailey Library of Slippery Rock University.

For a scholar working on the production of patriotic sentiment through performance, teaching at a military academy provides unique benefits. I thank my students at the United States Naval Academy for challenging and surprising me on a daily basis. Thanks in particular to the many fine performers I have met in the USNA Masqueraders and to the students in my Honors Seminar in Atlantic Performance, who must surely know as much about *Cato* as their professor by now.

While at Yale I received funding through both a University Fellowship and a Leylan Fellowship in the Humanities. I also received, at a critical stage in the research for this book, an Elizabethan Club Summer Research Fellowship from the Elizabethan Club of Yale and the Beinecke Library. During the revision and completion of the manuscript, I received funding from the Naval Academy Research Council. I am profoundly grateful to all these institutions for their support.

Friends too numerous to count, both within and without academia, have provided comfort and support along the way. George Shuffelton and Sloan MacRae, however, stand out for helping me to maintain a sense of perspective and a sense of humor. Thanks for support also go to my colleagues in the USNA English Department, particularly to Michelle Allen, John Beckman, Temple Cone, Mark McWilliams, and Christy Stanlake. Thanks especially to John for his steady encouragement and to Christy for her inspirational work as director of the USNA Masqueraders.

My parents, Tom and Linda Shaffer, have been with me every step of the way, ever since the phone call home from Washington and Lee when I announced that I wanted to go to graduate school. Thanks especially go to my mother for her assistance in preparing the manuscript. My sister and brother-in-law, Britt and Jerry Guilbert, have likewise provided encouragement and hospitality. My grandparents, Minnie and Ray Cook, did not live to see the publication of this book; I still feel their loss keenly. I give my heartfelt thanks to all of them.

Lastly, thanks to Brooke Conti for her love and support as well as her insights, which appear on virtually every page of this book.

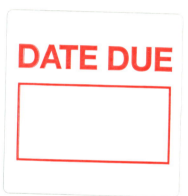